OXFORD WORLD'S CLASSICS

THE KILL

ÉMILE ZOLA was born in Paris in 1840, the son of a Venetian engineer and his French wife. He grew up in Aix-en-Provence where he made friends with Paul Cézanne. After an undistinguished school career and a brief period of dire poverty in Paris, Zola joined the newly founded publishing firm of Hachette which he left in 1866 to live by his pen. He had already published a novel and his first collection of short stories. Other novels and stories followed until in 1871 Zola published the first volume of his Rougon-Macquart series with the subtitle *Histoire naturelle et sociale d'une famille sous le Second Empire*, in which he sets out to illustrate the influence of heredity and environment on a wide range of characters and milieux. However, it was not until 1877 that his novel *L'Assommoir*, a study of alcoholism in the working classes, brought him wealth and fame. The last of the Rougon-Macquart series appeared in 1893 and his subsequent writing was far less successful, although he achieved fame of a different sort in his vigorous and influential intervention in the Dreyfus case. His marriage in 1870 had remained childless but his extremely happy liaison in later life with Jeanne Rozerot, initially one of his domestic servants, gave him a son and a daughter. He died in 1902.

BRIAN NELSON is Professor of French Studies at Monash University, Melbourne, and editor of the *Australian Journal of French Studies*. His publications include *Zola and the Bourgeoisie* and, as editor, *Naturalism in the European Novel: New Critical Perspectives* and *Forms of Commitment: Intellectuals in Contemporary France*. He has translated and edited Zola's *Pot Luck* (*Pot-Bouille*) and *The Ladies' Paradise* (*Au Bonheur des Dames*) for Oxford World's Classics. His current projects include *The Cambridge Companion to Émile Zola*.

OXFORD WORLD'S CLASSICS

*For over 100 years Oxford World's Classics have brought readers
closer to the world's great literature. Now with over 700
titles—from the 4,000-year-old myths of Mesopotamia to the
twentieth century's greatest novels—the series makes available
lesser-known as well as celebrated writing.*

*The pocket-sized hardbacks of the early years contained
introductions by Virginia Woolf, T. S. Eliot, Graham Greene,
and other literary figures which enriched the experience of reading.
Today the series is recognized for its fine scholarship and
reliability in texts that span world literature, drama and poetry,
religion, philosophy and politics. Each edition includes perceptive
commentary and essential background information to meet the
changing needs of readers.*

OXFORD WORLD'S CLASSICS

ÉMILE ZOLA

The Kill

(La Curée)

Translated with an Introduction and Notes by
BRIAN NELSON

OXFORD
UNIVERSITY PRESS

OXFORD
UNIVERSITY PRESS

Great Clarendon Street, Oxford OX2 6DP

Oxford University Press is a department of the University of Oxford.
It furthers the University's objective of excellence in research, scholarship,
and education by publishing worldwide in

Oxford New York

Auckland Bangkok Buenos Aires Cape Town Chennai
Dar es Salaam Delhi Hong Kong Istanbul Karachi Kolkata
Kuala Lumpur Madrid Melbourne Mexico City Mumbai Nairobi
São Paulo Shanghai Taipei Tokyo Toronto

Oxford is a registered trade mark of Oxford University Press
in the UK and in certain other countries

Published in the United States
By Oxford University Press Inc., New York

Editorial material © Brian Nelson 2004

The moral rights of the author have been asserted

Database right Oxford University Press (maker)

First published as an Oxford World's Classics paperback 2004

British Library Cataloguing in Publication Data

Data available

ISBN 0-19-280464-2

1

Typeset in Ehrhardt
by RefineCatch Limited, Bungay, Suffolk
Printed in Great Britain by
Clays Ltd., St. Ives plc.

CONTENTS

INTRODUCTION

The Kill (*La Carée*), published in 1872, is the second volume in Zola's great cycle of twenty novels, *Les Rougon-Macquart*, and the first to establish Paris as the centre of Zola's narrative world. Zola began work on the cycle in 1868 at the age of 28, and devoted himself to the project for the next quarter of a century. It is the chief embodiment of naturalism—Zola's brand of realism, and a logical continuation of the realism of Balzac and Flaubert.

As a writer, Zola was in many respects a typical product of his age. This is most evident in his faith in science and his acceptance of scientific determinism, which was the prevailing philosophy of the latter part of the nineteenth century in France. Zola placed particular emphasis on the 'scientific' nature of his project; his naturalist theories were quite explicit in their analogies between literature and science, the writer and the doctor. He was influenced by the philosopher Hippolyte Taine's views on heredity and environment, and by Prosper Lucas, a forgotten nineteenth-century scientist, the author of a treatise on heredity. Zola himself claimed to have based his method largely on the physiologist Claude Bernard's *Introduction to the Study of Experimental Medicine* (*Introduction à l'étude de la médecine expérimentale*), which he had read soon after its appearance in 1865. Zola espoused the Darwinian view of man as an animal whose actions were determined by his heredity and environment; and the 'truth' for which he aimed could only be achieved, he argued, from a meticulous notation of verifiable facts, a methodical documentation of the realities of nature, and, most importantly, systematic demonstrations of deterministic natural laws in the unfolding of his plots. The art of the novelist, Zola argued, represented a form of practical sociology, and complemented the work of the scientist, whose hope was to change the world not by judging it but by understanding it.

The subtitle of the Rougon-Macquart cycle, 'A Natural and Social History of a Family under the Second Empire', suggests Zola's two interconnected aims: to embody in fiction 'scientific' notions about the ways in which human behaviour is determined by heredity and environment; and to use the symbolic possibilities of a family whose heredity is warped to represent critically certain aspects of a diseased society—the decadent and corrupt, yet dynamic and vital, France of the Second Empire (1852–70). At one level, the Rougon-Macquart cycle is an account of French life from the coup d'état that placed Napoleon III on the throne to the French defeat at the hands of the Prussians at the Battle of Sedan (1 September 1870), which brought about the Empire's collapse. Through the fortunes of a single family, Zola examined the political, moral, and sexual landscape of the late nineteenth century in a way that scandalized bourgeois society. He was the first novelist to write a series of books portraying the lives of members of one family, though his example has frequently been followed since. The Rougon-Macquart family is descended from the three children, one legitimate and two illegitimate, of an insane woman, Tante Dide, who dies in the last volume of the series, *Doctor Pascal*. There are thus three main branches of the family. The first of these, the Rougons, prospers, its members spreading upwards in society to occupy commanding positions in the worlds of government and finance. *His Excellency Eugène Rougon* describes the corrupt political system of Napoleon III, while *The Kill* and *Money*, linked by the same protagonist, Saccard, evoke the frenetic contemporary speculation in real estate and stocks. The second branch of the family is the Mourets, some of whom are successful bourgeois adventurers. Octave Mouret is an ambitious philanderer in *Pot Luck*, a savagely comic picture of the hypocrisies and adulteries behind the façade of a new bourgeois apartment building. In *The Ladies' Paradise*, the effective sequel to *Pot Luck*, he is shown making his fortune from women as he creates one of the first big Parisian department stores. The Macquarts are the working-class members of the family, unbalanced and descended from the alcoholic Antoine Macquart. Members of this branch figure prominently in all of Zola's most powerful novels: *The Belly of Paris*, which uses the central food markets, Les Halles, as a gigantic figuration of the appetites and greed of the bourgeoisie; *L'Assommoir*, a poignant evocation of the lives of the working class in a Paris slum area; *Nana*, the novel of a celebrated prostitute whose sexual power ferments destruction among the Imperial Court; *Germinal*, perhaps Zola's most famous novel, which focuses on a miners' strike in the coalfields of north-eastern France; *The Masterpiece*, the story of a half-mad painter of genius, containing portrayals of a number of literary and artistic celebrities of the period; *Earth*, in which Zola brings an epic sweep to his portrayal of peasant life; *La Bête humaine*, which opposes the technical progress represented by the railways to the homicidal mania of a train driver, Jacques Lantier; and *La Débâcle*, which describes the Franco-Prussian War and is the first important war novel in French literature.

Zola's naturalism is not as naive and uncritical as is sometimes assumed. His formulation of the naturalist aesthetic, while it advocates a respect for truth that makes no concessions to self-indulgence, shows his clear awareness that 'observation' is not a totally unproblematic process. He recognizes the importance of the observer in the act of observation, and this recognition is repeated in his later, celebrated formula (used in his polemical essay 'The Experimental Novel', 1880) in which he describes the work of art as 'a corner of nature seen through a temperament'. He fully acknowledged the importance, indeed the artistic necessity, of the selecting, structuring role of the individual artist and of the aesthetic he adopts. It is thus not surprising to find him, in a series of newspaper articles in 1866, leaping to the defence of Manet and the Impressionists—defending Manet as an artist with the courage to be individual, to express his own temperament in defiance of current conventions. As far as Zola's own work is concerned, it is his powerful mythopoeic imagination that makes his narratives memorable; the influences of heredity and environment pursue his characters as relentlessly as the forces of Fate in an ancient tragedy. What makes Zola one of the great figures of the European novel is the poetic richness of his work. He uses major features of contemporary life—the market, the machine, the department store, the stock exchange, the theatre, the city itself—as giant symbols of the society of the day. Out of his fictional (rather than theoretical) naturalism emerges a sort of sur-naturalism. The originality of *The Kill* lies in its remarkable symbolizing vision, expressed in its dense metaphoric language.

Zola began to make his mark in the literary world as a journalist in the late 1860s, particularly with his uncompromising attacks on the Second Empire (1852–70), which he saw as reactionary and corrupt. Zola conceived *The Kill* from the beginning as a representation of the uncontrollable 'appetites' unleashed by the Second Empire. In republican circles in the 1850s and 1860s denunciation of the political and financial corruption that accompanied the Haussmannization of

Paris, and of the moral corruption of Imperial high society, was a common theme. Zola's originality was to combine into a single, powerful vision, through style and narrative, the themes of 'gold' (Saccard's lust for money) and 'flesh' (Renée's lust for pleasure); hysterical desire becomes the governing trope of the novel.

In *The Kill*, the ambitious Aristide Rougon (who later changes his name to Saccard) comes to Paris from the provincial town of Plassans. When he arrives, he walks excitedly through the streets, as if taking possession of the city. In an early scene in the novel, he looks down over the city from a restaurant window on the Buttes Montmartre and sees Paris as a world to be conquered and plundered. Having had the opportunity, by virtue of his employment at the Hôtel de Ville, to discover the plans for the rebuilding of the city by Baron Haussmann, he realizes that he can use this knowledge to make his fortune. Stretching out his hand, open and sharp like a sabre, he sketches in the air the projected transformations of the city: 'There lay his fortune, in the cuts that his hand had made in the heart of Paris, and he had resolved to keep his plans to himself, knowing very well that when the spoils were divided there would be enough crows hovering over the disembowelled city' (p. 70).

The novel's title gives the work its dominant image. A hunting term, *la curée* denotes, literally, the part of an animal fed to the hounds that have run it to ground. Figuratively, the title evokes the scramble for political spoils and financial gain that characterized the Second Empire. The wedding between Maxime and Louise is arranged at a time when 'the rush for spoils filled a corner of the forest with the yelping of hounds, the cracking of whips, the flaring of torches' (p. 112), thus suggesting that Renée is the quarry, hunted and caught in Saccard's speculative schemes. The daughter of an old bourgeois family, she is made pregnant by a rape. In return for saving her honour by marrying her, Saccard receives a large sum of money, together with Renée's dowry in the form of prize real estate. With this capital he launches his speculative ventures. He buys up properties designated for purchase by the state, which he 'sells' to fictitious purchasers, driving up the price with each 'sale' so as to obtain high compensation prices from the authorities. Saccard and his young wife soon start to lead separate lives, and little by little Renée and her stepson Maxime become lovers. When Saccard discovers their affair, he seizes the opportunity to despoil Renée of her real estate and to precipitate Maxime's marriage to the aristocratic Louise de Mareuil. Renée knows she is trapped, and realizes that Saccard has directed the hunt from the beginning, setting his snares 'with the subtlety of a hunter who prides himself on the skill with which he catches his prey' (p. 188).

The serialization of *The Kill* in the newspaper *La Cloche* was stopped by the government—ostensibly for immorality, but almost certainly for political reasons. In a letter dated 6 November 1871 to Louis Ulbach, editor of *La Cloche*, Zola wrote:

I must point out, since I have been misunderstood and prevented from making myself clear, that *The Kill* is an unwholesome plant that sprouted out of the dungheap of the Empire, an incest that grew on the compost pile of millions. My aim, in this new *Phaedra*, was to show the terrible social breakdown that occurs when all moral standards are lost and family ties no longer exist. My Renée is the 'Parisienne' driven crazy and into crime by luxury and a life of excess; my Maxime is the product of an effete society, a man-woman, passive flesh that accepts the vilest deeds; my Aristide is the speculator born out of the upheavals of Paris, the brazen self-made man who plays the stock market using whatever comes to hand—women, children, honour, bricks, conscience. I have tried, with these three social monstrosities, to give some idea of the dreadful quagmire into which France was sinking.

Referring to his novel as 'a combative book', Zola asked Ulbach: 'Should I give the names and tear off the masks in order to prove that I am a historian, not a scandalmonger? It would surely be futile. The names are still on everyone's lips.'

Haussmann's Paris

In December 1848 Louis-Napoleon Bonaparte, the nephew of Napoleon Bonaparte, was elected President of the Second Republic. On 2 December 1851 he staged a coup d'état that gave him dictatorial powers. A year later he established himself as Napoleon III, Emperor of the Second Empire. The familiar pattern of nineteenth-century French history was thus repeated: a liberal revolution gave way to a conservative political reaction. Louis-Napoleon seized power through a violent coup, his only claim to the throne being the fact that he was descended from Napoleon I. To establish his authority, and acquire a kind of legitimacy, he pursued a policy of modernization and 'progress'. He determined to make Paris clean and salubrious, and above all 'modern'. He thus initiated what has remained the largest urban renewal project in the history of the world. For this grand scheme he selected a talented and ambitious civil servant, Georges Eugène Haussmann, whom he appointed Prefect of the Seine, and therefore—since there was no elected mayor at the time—chief administrator of Paris.

The Haussmannization of Paris was, at one level, official state planning on a monumental and highly symbolic scale, glorifying the Napoleonic Empire as if it were a new Augustan Rome, and attempting to turn Paris into the capital of Europe. The nineteenth-century bourgeoisie was to find its apotheosis, argues Walter Benjamin, in the construction of the boulevards under the auspices of Haussmann; before their completion the boulevards were covered over with tarpaulins, to be unveiled like monuments.[1] Another view of the spectacular modernization of the city is to see it as intimately linked to rationalization and to forms of social and political control. For Benjamin, 'the real aim of Haussmann's works was the securing of the city against civil war. He wished to make the erection of barricades in Paris impossible for all time.'[2] In the revolutions of 1789, 1830, and 1848 the barricade had been a potent weapon of resistance in the dense, rabbit-warren streets of the working-class slums. Haussmann's straight boulevards and avenues linked the new barracks in each *arrondissement*, thus allowing the rapid deployment of troops in case of insurrection. Many of the new streets were designed to cut through the densest and politically most hostile districts of Paris. Haussmann admitted quite candidly that one of his aims was to control the unruly and ungovernable poor. He was a great respecter of authority, and saw the keeping of order as one of his main duties. For him there was little difference between this kind of control and the improvement of the city's sanitation; it was simply another form of hygiene.

The first project entrusted to Haussmann was the creation of a vast new central market. A twenty-one-acre site was cleared to create the market complex known as Les Halles, which functioned as the

---

[1] Walter Benjamin, 'Paris, the Capital of the Nineteenth Century', in id., *The Arcades Project*, trans. Howard Eiland and Kevin McLaughlin (Cambridge, Mass., and London: The Belknap Press, 1999), 11–12.

[2] *The Arcades Project*, 12.

so-called 'belly of Paris' until 1968, when it was pulled down. Another of his tasks was to extend the Rue de Rivoli from the Bastille to the Place de la Concorde, thus allowing Louis-Napoléon to fulfil his uncle's plan to create an effective east–west crossing of the city. This ruthlessly straight street, over 3 kilometres long, set a precedent for the transformation of Paris. Although the official cost had trebled to 11 million francs by its completion in 1855, it achieved Napoleon I's goal, and also allowed for the rapid deployment of troops from the barracks near the Tuileries Palace to the industrial east of the city, a traditional centre of political unrest. Haussmann's next major enterprise was the creation of a new central boulevard on the north–south axis, crossing the Rue de Rivoli by the Tour Saint-Jacques and reaching down to the river at the Place du Châtelet. Work began in 1855, with huge disruption as hundreds of buildings were demolished to create the space needed for this great new artery.

Haussmann had taken full advantage of a new law of expropriation, permitting compulsory purchase of private property by the government, to buy up whole blocks of land on either side of the projected route of the boulevard in order to resell it to property speculators at great profit and thus offset the cost of the project. With the completion of the Boulevard du Centre, now called Boulevard Sébastopol, the centre of the capital was connected directly to the Gare de l'Est and other mainline stations to the north and east of France. The new boulevard was opened by the Emperor with great fanfare, celebrating the achievement as one of national importance. On either side, the newly built apartment blocks erected by property speculators began to give the city an architectural uniformity. As soon as work on this north–south crossing had begun, plans were made to continue it across the Île de la Cité to the Left Bank, to join the cutting of a huge southern extension, another 2 kilometres long, the Boulevard Saint Michel.

Throughout the 1850s and 1860s a great number of buildings were torn down. Hundreds of thousands of people were evicted. Working-class people in particular were forced into cheaper outlying areas. On Haussmann's own estimate, the new boulevards and open spaces displaced 350,000 people; 12,000 of them were uprooted by the building of the Rue de Rivoli and Les Halles alone. In compensation, the work itself provided profitable new employment, attracting many more people into Paris from the provinces. New and better housing of all categories was erected under strict building regulations by private developers, who then demanded higher rents.[3] Property speculation became all the rage. The building work was unremitting, in some places proceeding by night as well as by day, using the new technology of electric arc lights. At the height of the fever of reconstruction, one in five Parisian workers was employed in the building trade. The devastation of old Paris was deeply controversial, but Haussmann pursued it with a ruthless logic. By 1870 over 1,200 kilometres of new streets had been built, nearly double what had existed before. Well over half of these streets had sewers running underneath them, and most were well lit with gas.[4] There were policemen, night patrols, and bus shelters. Men were even provided with ways to relieve themselves (more or less) in public. Eighty thousand new apartment blocks had been built, many receiving fresh running water. The city had twice as many trees as in 1850, most of them transplanted full grown, and had almost doubled in size and population. The Bois de Boulogne and the Bois de Vincennes were made into public parks, and in a new spacious context, such urban buildings as the Louvre, the Hôtel de Ville, the Palais Royal, the Bibliothèque Nationale, Notre Dame, and the Opéra became monuments. Paris became the centre of Europe, with six new railway lines converging on the capital. In 1867 the Second Empire was at the height of its power, and, as Walter Benjamin wrote, the phantasmagoria of capitalist culture attained its most radiant unfolding in the World Exhibition held in Paris that year. Paris was acknowledged as the capital of luxury and fashion—the capital, indeed, of the nineteenth century.[5]

Haussmann's project was fantastically expensive: in fact the debt incurred to finance the transformation of Paris was not retired until 1929. Louis-Napoleon, when he appointed Haussmann Prefect of the Seine, and gave him as his major task the transformation of Paris, told him that he could not raise taxes to finance the project. Haussmann was thus forced into using a series of clever expedients—a mixture of direct grant, public loans, and 'creative accounting'—in

---

[3] By Haussmann's own estimate, rents in the centre of the city doubled between 1851 and 1857.

[4] Haussmann's proudest moments included breaking the monopoly of the cab company—the Compagnie des Petites Voitures—in 1866, and promoting that of the makers of streetlamps—the Compagnie Parisienne d'Éclairage—in 1856.

[5] *The Arcades Project*, 8.

order to realize his plans. The first thing he did was go into deficit spending on a very large scale. The Pereire brothers became his major financiers, and the traditional banks were shut out. He then set about attracting private capital by giving land to developers, who were obliged to pay upfront for their various construction projects. They loaned him money at virtually no interest, in exchange for bonds, which were then floated on the stock market. Furthermore, he compelled the developers (private investors) to follow his regula- tions of height, roof lines, and facing materials—all of which gave the city a new face. These materials—cut stone rather than cheaper brick, for example—were dictated partly by the planned uniformity of the buildings and partly because every piece of stone that came into Paris was charged an excise tax, which Haussmann then ploughed into his projects. Another scheme he used for a while was to confiscate much more land than he needed, develop it, and sell it back at the improved rates. Haussmann considered such 'creative' methods justified in economic terms, because in the end they increased state and city revenues and allowed the balancing of pri- vate and public investment. However, he encountered growing criti- cism, not only because of the escalating cost of his works, but also because of the perceived irregularities of his financial practices. In a celebrated pamphlet, *The Fantastic Accounts of Haussmann* (*Les Comptes fantastiques d'Haussmann*), published in 1868, Jules Ferry played on the title of Offenbach's recent operetta *The Tales of Hoffmann* (*Les Contes d'Hoffmann*) to denounce the financial manipu- lations of Haussmannization. Haussmann was finally forced out of office at the same time that Napoleon III became embroiled in the war with Prussia that led to the humiliating siege of Paris and the collapse of the Empire.

Character and Milieu

The Kill begins with a description of an urban spectacle, a traffic jam in the Bois de Boulogne. The motifs of the description are typical of the novel and define Second Empire society as represented by Zola—a society of flamboyant materialism and of new social spaces, in which people are seen as the products of their social environment. Theatricality and the play of light on glittering surfaces are the keynotes of the scene; conventional boundaries—between nature and society, public and private, interior and exterior—are blurred (as we shall see later in relation to the liminal space of the new boulevards), and social norms transgressed at many levels.[6]

The barouche in which Renée and Maxime are seated reflects patches of the surrounding landscape in such a way that it almost becomes part of the natural world, while the characters are disconnected from nature, concerned with social rather than natural phenomena. Renée, as if leaning from an opera box, uses her eyeglass to examine Laure d'Aurigny and to establish that 'Tout Paris was there' (p. 6). 'Silent glances were exchanged from window to window; no one spoke, the silence broken only by the creaking of a harness or the impatient pawing of a horse's hoof' (p. 6). The occupants of the carriages, as if waiting for a show to begin, do not interact in any way other than by seeing and being seen. Although outdoors, Zola's characters behave as if indoors; the categories of public and private appear interchangeable. Though part of an urban spectacle, they also become part of nature: the women are decorated in such a way that they seem almost like botanical specimens. Renée wears a bonnet adorned with a little bunch of Bengal roses, while rich costumes spill out through the carriage doors like foliage. The park itself is strikingly artificial—a contrived, carefully planned 'scrap of nature' (p. 8). It is as if nature is subject to interior decoration. The lake is a mirror, in which the black foliage of the theatrically grouped trees is 'like the fringe of curtains carefully draped along the edge of the horizon'. Light conspires with this 'newly painted piece of scenery' to create 'an air of entrancing artificiality' (p. 8). Tree-trunks become colonnades, lawns become carpets; the park gates form a lace curtain shielding this outsize drawing room from the exterior, creating a semi-transparent boundary which becomes further blurred as the sun goes down. It is at dusk, as the light disappears, that the boundary between nature and the world becomes completely blurred; the prospect of the transformation of the park into 'a sacred grove' where 'the gods of antiquity hid their Titanic loves, their adulteries, their divine incests' (p. 11), creates in Renée 'a strange feeling of illicit desire',

---

[6] For an extended analysis of the novel's opening chapter, see Larry Duffy, 'Preserves of Nature: Traffic Jams and Garden Furniture in Zola's *La Curée*', in *Les Lieux Interdits: Transgression and French Literature*, ed. with an introduction by Larry Duffy and Adrian Tudor (Hull: University of Hull Press, 1998), 205–16.

thus setting the scene for the drama of forbidden desire played out in the novel.

In the second half of the opening chapter, the description of Saccard's opulent mansion near the Parc Monceau reflects the same indifferentiation, the same confusion of interior and exterior, social and natural, public and private. Luxury and decoration characterize the buttercup drawing room, with its extravagantly foliated furniture and its lawn-like carpet. The mansion itself is described as 'a miniature version of the new Louvre, one of the most typical examples of the Napoleon III style, that opulent bastard of so many styles' (p. 17). The comparison identifies it with the regime, while its eclectic architectural style[7] implies both a blurring of boundaries and the illegitimacy associated with the regime. The extravagance and excess that characterize the mansion are the hallmarks of the Second Empire itself, to which it is a monument.

On summer evenings, when the rays of the setting sun lit up the gilt of the railings against its white façade, the strollers in the gardens would stop to look at the crimson silk curtains behind the ground-floor windows; and through the sheets of plate glass so wide and clear that they seemed like the window-fronts of a big modern department store, arranged so as to display to the outside world the wealth within, the petty bourgeoisie could catch glimpses of the corners of tables and chairs, of portions of hangings, of patches of ornate ceilings, the sight of which would root them to the spot, in the middle of the pathways, with envy and admiration. (p. 17)

The voracious desires of Zola's three 'social monstrosities' are seen as an inevitable product of Second Empire Paris, and Zola constantly correlates narrative developments with their social settings. Lengthy descriptions of houses, interiors, social gatherings, and the like emphasize the connections between individuals and their milieu. Indeed, as Claude Duchet has remarked, *The Kill* is 'less a study of characters placed in a particular milieu than a study

---

[7] 'The Second Empire is the classical period of eclecticism—a period without a style of its own in architecture and the industrial arts, and with no stylistic unity in its painting. New theatres, hotels, tenement-houses, barracks, department stores, market-halls, come into being, whole rows and rings of streets arise, Paris is almost rebuilt by Haussmann, but apart from the principle of spaciousness and the beginnings of iron construction, all this takes place without a single original architectural idea': Arnold Hauser, *The Social History of Art*, 4: *Naturalism, Impressionism, The Film Age* (London: Routledge & Kegan Paul, 1962 (1951)), 58.

of a milieu placed in particular characters'.[8] Despite Zola's theoretical commitment to documentary accuracy, it would be profoundly mistaken to equate his naturalism with inventory-like descriptions. His descriptions provide not merely the framework or tonality of his world but express its very meaning.

The new city under construction becomes a vast symbol of the corruption of Second Empire society. The description of the visit of Renée and Maxime to the Café Riche is a striking example of Zola's use of imagery to suggest the complicity of the city.[9] Descriptions of the boulevard seem to stimulate Renée's erotic feelings: 'The wide pavement, swept by the prostitutes' skirts and ringing with peculiar familiarity under the men's boots, and over whose grey asphalt it seemed to her that the cavalcade of pleasure and brief encounters was passing, awoke her slumbering desires' (p. 123). Renée is as if intoxicated by the urban scene. The boulevard seen from an open window—the pleasure-seeking crowds, the café tables, the chance encounters, the solitary prostitute—acts as a symbolic correlative to her mounting excitement; indeed, it is as if she is seduced less by Maxime than by the boulevard itself. Afterwards,

[w]hat lingered on the surface of the deserted road of the noise and vice of the evening made excuses for her. She thought she could feel the heat of the footsteps of all those men and women rising up from the pavement that was now growing cold. The shamefulness that had lingered there— momentary lust, whispered offers, prepaid nights of pleasure—was evaporating, floating in a heavy mist dissipated by the breath of morning. Leaning out into the darkness, she inhaled the quivering darkness, the alcove-like fragrance, as an encouragement from below, as an assurance of shame shared and accepted by a complicitous city. (p. 133)

The 'complicitous city' is a very active agent in Renée's progressive degradation. The public spaces of the city become the lovers' personal preserve: 'The lovers adored the new Paris. They often drove through the city, going out of their way in order to pass along certain boulevards' (p. 168). Every boulevard 'became a corridor of their house' (p. 169). The Saccard apartment becomes an extension of the Rue de Rivoli: 'The street invaded the apartment with its rumbling

---

[8] Claude Duchet, Introduction to the Garnier-Flammarion edition of *La Curée* (Paris, 1970), 17–31 (p. 21).

[9] This episode is analysed with great finesse by Christopher Prendergast in his *Paris and the Nineteenth Century* (Oxford: Blackwell, 1992), 40–5.

carriages, jostling strangers, and permissive language' (p. 104). Renée's mental instability alarms Maxime, who associates her illness with the disorder of the street: 'Maxime began to be frightened by these fits of seeming madness, in which he thought he could hear, at night, on the pillow, all the din of a city obsessed with the pursuit of pleasure' (p. 179). The promiscuity of Haussmann's Paris is all-pervading, and finally it takes possession of Renée's mind.

Money, Movement, Madness

The links between Haussmannization and a burgeoning capitalism were profound. The shaping force of capitalism was reflected in the physical, visual changes made in the city.

Capitalism was assuredly visible from time to time, in a street of new factories or the theatricals of the Bourse; but it was only in the form of the city that it appeared as what it was, a shaping spirit, a force remaking things with ineluctable logic—the argument of freight statistics and double-entry bookkeeping. The city was the *sign* of capital: it was there one saw the capital take on flesh—take up and eviscerate the varieties of social practice, and give them back with ventriloqual precision.[10]

In purely economic terms, capitalism took a firm grip on French society during Napoleon III's reign. Public works were the motor of capitalism—they were the avant-garde of the economy to come, laying the groundwork for the 'consumer society'. Vast amounts of money were invested in the expansion of the railways and in the coal and iron industries. A modern banking system, based on credit and investment, was developed, and was greatly stimulated by the wild speculation in real estate and public works engendered by Haussmann's reconstruction of the city. In this context, money became a liquid asset. It flows metaphorically through Zola's text in all directions. Saccard's growing mastery as a speculator is evoked in typically phantasmagoric terms, by an image of an ever-expanding sea of gold coins in which he swims:

Saccard was insatiable, he felt his greed grow at the sight of the flood of gold that glided through his fingers. It seemed to him as if a sea of twenty-franc pieces stretched out around him, swelling from a lake to an ocean,

[10] T. J. Clark, *The Painting of Modern Life: Paris in the Art of Manet and His Followers* (London: Thames & Hudson, 1985), 69.

filling the vast horizon with a strange sound of waves, a metallic music that tickled his heart; and he grew bolder, plunging deeper every day, diving and coming up again, now on his back, now on his belly, swimming through this vast expanse in fair weather and foul, and relying on his strength and skill to prevent him from ever sinking to the bottom. (p. 94)

The money flowing from his safe seems inexhaustible. Zola stresses the ways in which, in this new context, wealth was founded solely on financial conventions. Saccard's fortune is a paper fortune, and has no firm foundations: 'In truth, no one knew whether he had any clear, solid capital assets. ... the flow from his cash-box continued, though the sources of that stream of gold had not yet been discovered' (p. 113). Images of subsidence and collapse abound: 'companies crumbled beneath his feet, new and deeper holes yawned before him, over which he had to leap, unable to fill them up. ... Moving from one adventure to the next, he now possessed only the gilded façade of missing capital' (pp. 137–8). Here lies the significance, as Priscilla Ferguson has noted, of the speculative fever that dominates the novel: 'Investment in real estate, once the most conservative of investments, becomes extraordinarily volatile and immensely profitable for those able to manipulate the system.'[11]

The affinities between Zola's descriptive style and Impressionist painting of urban scenes lie in the fact that in both everything is placed under the sign of volatility. All is flux and change, ephemerality and fragmentation. Impressionist representation becomes a blur, in which the general impression eclipses particular detail. Recurring water imagery, suggesting fluidity and impermanence, combines with the play of light, which dissolves surfaces and objects. Even inanimate things in Zola seem to be set in motion, to vibrate with a dynamic inner life. The themes of money and pleasure are linked by the motifs of mobility and excess. Saccard's speculations and Renée's social behaviour are characterized by their sheer extravagance: 'Saccard left the Hôtel de Ville and, being in command of considerable funds to work with, launched furiously into speculation, while Renée filled Paris with the clatter of her equipages, the sparkle of her diamonds, the vertigo of her riotous existence' (p. 78). Saccard's schemes seem to expand exponentially. Movement and excess

[11] Priscilla Parkhurst Ferguson, *Paris as Revolution: Writing the 19th-Century City* (Berkeley: University of California Press, 1994), 127.

correspond to a kind of manic delirium in the characters. The lexical character of *The Kill* reflects a sense of madness and instability: ' "It will be sheer madness, an orgy of spending, Paris will be drunk and overwhelmed!" '(p. 69), 'violent fever, ... stone-and-pickaxe madness' (p. 96), '[i]t was pure folly, a frenzy of money, handfuls of louis flung out of the windows' (p. 113). Saccard's very name evokes both money ('sac d'écus'—money bags) and upheaval ('saccager'—to sack). His dynamism finds expression in the gutting of entire buildings and the destruction of whole neighbourhoods.

The extravagance of Saccard's schemes corresponds to the buildings he inhabits and to his social mobility as he progresses from one dwelling to another. He leaves his cramped lodgings in the Rue Saint-Jacques for an elegant rented apartment in the Marais; then, on his marriage, he moves into an imposing apartment in a new house in the Rue de Rivoli; and finally he inhabits his most spectacular residence, the mansion in the Parc Monceau. The life of buildings is defined by their permeability to all the influences, all the noisy activity of the street. The apartment in the Rue de Rivoli, for example, is described thus: 'There was a slamming of doors all day long; the servants talked in loud voices; its new and dazzling luxury was continually traversed by a flood of vast, floating skirts, by processions of tradespeople, by the noise of Renée's friends, Maxime's schoolfellows, and Saccard's callers.' Every day Saccard receives an endless stream of profiteers of the most varied kinds, 'all the scum that the streets of Paris hurled at his door every morning' (p. 93). The apartment becomes a public thoroughfare, a centre of promiscuous activity, engulfing all who enter. The stress on accelerated movement and animation points towards the disappearance of all constraints, of all fixity and permanence. The 'whirlwind of contemporary life', which had made the doors on the first floor in the Rue de Rivoli constantly slam, becomes, in the mansion in the Parc Monceau, 'an absolute hurricane which threatened to blow away the partitions' (p. 114). The mansion, like the apartment in the Rue de Rivoli, becomes a theatre of excess, in which the Saccards engage in a kind of brazen, Babylonian exhibitionism:

It was a disorderly house of pleasure, the brash pleasure that enlarges the windows so that the passers-by can share the secrets of the alcoves. The husband and wife lived there freely, under their servants' eyes. They divided the house into two, camping there, as if they had been dropped, at the end of a tumultuous journey, into some palatial hotel where they had simply unpacked their trunks before rushing out to taste the delights of the new city. (p. 114)

Henry James was quick to note Zola's ability to render experience in concrete, pictorial terms, in the form of 'immediate vision and contact'.[12] Metaphor crowds upon metaphor, reflecting a general sense of Bacchanalian frenzy:

the Saccards' fortune seemed to be at its height. It blazed in the heart of Paris like a huge bonfire. This was the time when the rush for spoils filled a corner of the forest with the yelping of hounds, the cracking of whips, the flaring of torches. The appetites let loose were satisfied at last, shamelessly, amid the sound of crumbling neighbourhoods and fortunes made in six months. The city had become an orgy of gold and women. Vice, coming from on high, flowed through the gutters, spread out over the ornamental waters, shot up in the fountains of the public gardens, and fell on the roofs as fine rain. At night, when people crossed the bridges, it seemed as if the Seine drew along with it, through the sleeping city, all the refuse of the streets, crumbs fallen from tables, bows of lace left on the couches, false hair forgotten in cabs, banknotes that had slipped out of bodices, everything thrown out of the window by the brutality of desire and the immediate satisfaction of appetites. Then, amid the troubled sleep of Paris, and even more clearly than during its feverish quest in broad daylight, one felt a growing sense of madness, the voluptuous nightmare of a city obsessed with gold and flesh. The violins played until midnight; then the windows became dark and shadows descended over the city. It was like a giant alcove in which the last candle had been blown out, the last remnant of shame extinguished. There was nothing left in the darkness except a great rattle of furious and wearied lovemaking; while the Tuileries, by the riverside, stretched out its arms, as if for a huge embrace. (p. 112)

The themes of gold and flesh, speculation and dissipation, interact in this paradigmatic evocation of the frenzied social pursuits of the Second Empire. The interlinked motifs of the passage are the city, animality, appetites, fire, water, disorder, and madness. The principal syntactic characteristic of the extract is the eclipse of human subjects by abstract nouns and things: 'fortune', 'the rush for spoils', 'appetites', 'the city', and 'vice', suggesting the absence of any controlling human agency. Imagery of the hunt emphasizes the reduction of

---

[12] *The House of Fiction*, ed. Leon Edel (London: Hart-Davis, 1959), 180–92.

men to animal level and the unbridled indulgence of brute instincts. The imagery of fire and water indicates Zola's moral reprobation. The comparison with 'a giant alcove', reinforced by the references to orgiastic excess, underline the wild promiscuity of the age. 'There was nothing left', in the final sentence, and the coupling of 'furious and wearied', suggest a dying fall, enervation and exhaustion; the sound of orgasm is equated with a death-rattle.

Perversion, Promiscuity, Parody

It has often been observed that the debate over the modernity of the city, which has led to postmodern theories and practices of urban space, began with Haussmannization. The significance of Haussmann's transformation of Paris is that it not only reshaped the city physically but also broke down or blurred boundaries of every kind—cultural, perceptual, social, and sexual. ' "Just imagine!" ', exclaims Monsieur Hupel de la Noue, at the reception described in the opening chapter, ' "I've lived in Paris all my life, and I don't know the city any more. I got lost yesterday on my way from the Hôtel de Ville to the Luxembourg. It's amazing, quite amazing!" ' (p. 26). This sense of disorientation is indicative of a more general confusion, a general crisis of identification. Hupel de la Noue expresses with unwitting eloquence what many people felt— that they had lost Paris and were living in someone else's city. Social life became marked by a new anomie. 'Modernity' itself is to be understood in terms of an overwhelming sense of fragmentation, ephemerality, and chaotic change. Marshall Berman describes the experience of modernity as follows:

There is a mode of vital experience—experience of space and time, of the self and others, of life's possibilities and perils—that is shared by men and women all over the world today. I will call this body of experience 'modernity'. To be modern is to find ourselves in an environment that promises adventure, power, joy, growth, transformation of ourselves and the world—and, at the same time, that threatens to destroy everything we have, everything we know, everything we are. Modern environments and experiences cut across all boundaries of geography and ethnicity, of class and nationality, of religion and ideology; in this sense, modernity can be said to unite all mankind. But it is a paradoxical unity, a unity of disunity; it pours us all into a maelstrom of perpetual disintegration and renewal, of struggle and contradiction, of ambiguity and anguish. To be modern is to be part of a universe in which, as Marx said, 'all that is solid melts into air'.[13]

The entire economy of *The Kill* is placed under the sign of a generalized promiscuity. Sexual promiscuity pervades the novel, dramatizing the 'life of excess' that characterizes the regime. Moreover, all forms of family hierarchy and domestic order are erased; the architecture of family life collapses, like the buildings demolished by Haussmann's workmen. Saccard's assumption of a false name upon his arrival in Paris not only typifies his role as a swindler, but also represents his abdication of any parental responsibility. His continual absence means that Renée 'could hardly be said to be married at all' (p. 98), while for Maxime, 'his father did not seem to exist' (p. 106). The father, the stepmother, and the stepson lead quite separate lives. Family ties are converted into purely commercial ones: 'The idea of a family was replaced for them by the notion of a sort of investment company where the profits are shared equally' (p. 104). This phrase recalls the famous formulation in *The Communist Manifesto*: 'The bourgeoisie has torn away from the family its sentimental veil, and has reduced the family relation to a mere money relation.'[14] Father and son calculate the use they can make of each other. Saccard 'could not be near a thing or a person for long without wanting to sell it or derive some profit from it. His son was not yet twenty when he began to think about how to use him' (p. 110). Saccard and Maxime even share prostitutes, just as they will come to share Renée. As for Renée's father, he has shut himself away on the Île Saint-Louis, effectively removing himself from a position of influence over his daughter.[15]

It is in the absence of the father that Renée and Maxime play out the novel's drama of perversion. Renée's desire is directed towards the narcissistic, androgynous Maxime—the 'man-woman' announced in Zola's preface to the novel. Roddey Read comments:

[13] Marshall Berman, *All That is Solid Melts into Air: The Experience of Modernity* (London: Verso, 1983), 15.

[14] Karl Marx and Friedrich Engels, *The Communist Manifesto*, ed. with an Introduction and Notes by David McLellan (Oxford World's Classics, 1992), 5.

[15] For excellent interdisciplinary studies of the novelistic production of familial discourse in France, see the book by Nicholas White listed in the Select Bibliography. Roddey Reid's book, *Families in Jeopardy: Regulating the Social Body in France, 1750–1910* (Stanford: Stanford University Press, 1993), to which I am indebted for some of the points made in this section, contains a detailed reading of *The Kill*.

'In effect, Renée's transgression turns out to be a double one: incest with her stepson, and incest with one who is not even a properly gendered man.'[16] The figure of the feminized, unproductive male, so prominent in the rhetoric of Decadence, signals an emphasis on pure consumption, a generalized sense of exhaustion, and a defiant celebration of the deviant. Maxime's sexual ambivalence compounds Renée's hysterical confusion. She cross-dresses and accompanies Maxime to cafés not normally frequented by women of polite society. Maxime, the text tells us, is caught off guard, because he thought he was playing with a boy: 'He had taken her for a boy and romped with her, and it was not his fault that the game had become serious. He would not have laid a finger on her if she had shown even a tiny bit of her shoulders. He would have remembered that she was his father's wife' (p. 134). The lovers' trysts in the hothouse confirm that Renée desires the woman in Maxime as much as he desires the man in her:

Renée was the man, the ardent, active partner. Maxime remained submissive. Smooth-limbed, slim, and graceful as a Roman stripling, fair-haired and pretty, stricken in his virility since childhood, this epicene creature became a girl in Renée's arms. He seemed born and bred for perverted sensual pleasure. Renée enjoyed her domination, bending to her will this creature of indeterminate sex. (p. 158)

Sexual pathology and deviant desire, figured in the 'incestuous'[17] affair of Renée and Maxime, signals a diseased social body, a society that has become profoundly warped. If the characters of *The Kill* put on a kind of freak show, the society they represent embodies a generalized system of pathology in which the themes of gold and flesh become interchangeable.

The deterritorialization of desire and identity—their drift from normative boundaries and teleologies—matches the flow of exchange value in Saccard's real-estate speculations.

In this fashion the drama of 'perversion' and the conversion of familial bonds into commercial ones mutually signify each other; the drama of the Second Empire is one of the flattening of all hierarchies and differences (sexual, gender, familial, and social) into what Marx called the relations of

---

[16] Reid, *Families in Jeopardy*, 265.

[17] The inverted commas are appropriate because their affair, though portrayed as incestuous, is not actually so, since Renée is not Maxime's mother. In *The Kill* even incest is, ironically, inauthentic.

general equivalence imposed by exchange value as embodied in the commodity form, to which Zola adds the twist of sexual 'pathology'.[18]

Saccard uses Renée to promote his business schemes, while the conditions of her dowry have turned her into a kind of real-estate investment for him. But Renée realizes this, and the supreme power of money, too late. As Reid points out, at the very moment when she assumes the consciously rebellious position of a depraved, incestuous stepmother ('I have my crime'), the incest taboo proves to be nonexistent, or rather is displaced by another law, the law of the marketplace.[19] This occurs, very appropriately, in the episode of the costume ball[20] held at Saccard's mansion in the Parc Monceau for the purpose, unbeknown to Renée, of announcing Maxime's engagement to Louise. That evening Saccard discovers his wife's affair with his son, and the 'recognition' scene in Renée's bedroom brings together the novel's twin themes of 'gold' and 'flesh'. Renée, rendered hysterical by Maxime's attempts to end their relationship, plans to kidnap her stepson. To do so she needs money, and hits on the idea of signing over to Saccard, for ready cash, the prize real estate (part of her dowry), which he badly needs to carry out yet another real-estate speculation. Saccard suddenly appears at the door, surprising the two lovers. A terrible hush falls over the room.

Saccard, no doubt hoping to find a weapon, glanced round the room. On the corner of the dressing table, among the combs and nail-brushes, he caught sight of the deed of transfer, whose stamped yellow paper stood out on the white marble. He looked at the deed, then at the guilty pair. Leaning forward, he saw that the deed was signed... .

'You did well to sign, my dear,' he said quietly to his wife. (pp. 237–8)

---

[18] Reid, *Families in Jeopardy*, 245. For a systematic application to *The Kill* of Marxist analysis of commodification, see David F. Bell, *Models of Power: Politics and Economics in Zola's 'Rougon-Macquart'* (Lincoln, Nebr., and London: University of Nebraska Press, 1988) ('Deeds and Incest: *La Curée*', 57–95).

[19] Reid, *Families in Jeopardy*, 272.

[20] 'Costume ball' is the term I have used in my translation. The term Zola uses (*bal travesti*) requires some comment. It connotes disguise, concealment, dissimulation, masquerade, and, in the context of *The Kill*, deception, parody, and perversion. It did not, in the late-nineteenth century, denote transgression of gender codes in the form of cross-dressing (drag); it was not until the 1950s that this sense of *travesti* developed (see *Dictionnaire historique de la langue française* (Paris: Robert, 1993), 2160–1). 'Transvestite ball' would therefore be incorrect, while A. Teixeira de Mattos's 'fancy-dress ball' is not appropriate in its connotations and for the social context.

The weapon Saccard uses to defend himself, and to compensate damagingly for the worst possible familial insult, is an economic weapon par excellence—the signed deed of transfer. To the amazement of Renée and Maxime, instead of exploding in anger and reasserting his legal possession of his wife, he calmly takes the deed to the Parisian property that constituted Renée's dowry and had been intended for her children. Renée stands speechless as father and son walk off, arm in arm, to rejoin the party and announce Maxime's engagement to Louise: 'Her crime, the kisses on the great grey-and-pink bed, the wild nights in the hothouse, the forbidden love that had consumed her for months, had culminated in this cheap, banal ending. Her husband knew everything and did not even strike her' (p. 238). In the degraded world of the Second Empire, even incest can be used to facilitate a new business venture. The only law is that of the marketplace.

The final, traumatic encounter with Saccard causes a shock of recognition. 'She saw herself in the high wardrobe mirror. She moved closer, surprised at her own image, forgetting her husband, forgetting Maxime, quite taken up with the strange woman she saw before her' (p. 238). Her self-disgust is intensely associated with the decoration and the profusion of artefacts and discarded clothes in her dressing room. Throughout the novel, detailed descriptions of the luxurious physical decor of bourgeois existence express a vision of a society which, organized under the aegis of the commodity, turns people into objects. The significance of Renée's contemplation of herself in the mirror lies in her realization that, in the eyes of society, she is valued not as a person but in commercial terms, as a marketable commodity: 'Saccard had used her like a stake, like an investment, and ... Maxime had happened to be there to pick up the louis fallen from the gambler's pocket. She was an asset in her husband's portfolio' (p. 241).

The degradation of that society is conveyed parodically, through the metaphor of the theatre. In Chapter 5, when Renée and Maxime attend a performance of Racine's *Phèdre*, Renée's imaginary identification with the tragic destiny of the female protagonist, destroyed by her passion for her stepson, lasts for only a brief moment: when the curtain falls, she is left alone with her sordid drama: 'How mean and shameful her tragedy was compared with the grand epic of antiquity!' (p. 180). Racine's play is transformed, in a hallucinatory metamorphosis, into one of Offenbach's most popular operettas, itself a semi-parodic appropriation of the classics for modern times:[21] 'Everything was becoming distorted in her mind. La Ristori was now a big puppet, pulling up her tunic and sticking out her tongue at the audience like Blanche Muller in the third act of *La Belle Hélène*; Théramène was dancing a cancan, and Hippolyte was eating bread and jam and stuffing his fingers up his nose' (pp. 180–1). In the larger drama played out in the novel, 'a lascivious Hippolytus, an ignoble Theseus and an eager Phaedra stage a farce whose conclusion is a real estate transaction'.[22] As Marx said of the 1848 revolution, tragedy cannot be re-enacted by the bourgeoisie without being transformed into a farce.[23]

Closing the Accounts

Renée returns, at the end of the novel, to her old family home. She partakes simultaneously of two different worlds: the traditional bourgeois world embodied by her father, Monsieur Béraud du Châtel, and the corrupt *nouveau riche* society of the Second Empire. Contrasting images of old and new, cold and heat, silence and noise, total immobility and dynamic movement, characterize the symbolic juxtaposition of the austere Hôtel Béraud on the Île Saint-Louis and Saccard's ostentatious new mansion in the Parc Monceau. The Hôtel Béraud conveys a stark vision of the past. Renée and Saccard find it a 'lifeless house' (p. 80), 'a thousand miles away from the new Paris, ablaze with every form of passionate enjoyment and resounding with the sound of gold' (p. 79). The new Paris is associated with vice and promiscuity, but Zola's imagery repeatedly associates the city also with light, the sun, flames, heat, and colour—with all the noise and activity of modern life.

Zola was fascinated by change, and specifically by the emergence of a modern society. Saccard, a hyperbolic projection of Haussmannization in its most ruthless and spectacular forms, personifies the energy, the life-force of Zola's vision of modern life. He embodies,

---

[21] Zola detested Offenbach, who, as Walter Benjamin remarked, 'set the rhythm' of Parisian life during the Second Empire (*The Arcades Project*, 8).

[22] Sandy Petrey, 'Stylistics and Society in *La Curée*', *Modern Language Notes*, 89 (1974), 626–40 (p. 635).

[23] See Mark Cowling and Martin James (eds.), *Marx's 'Eighteenth Brumaire': (Post)-modern Interpretations* (London: Pluto Press, 2002).

like Haussmann, what David Harvey has called the 'creative destruction' that constitutes an essential condition of modernity and of 'progress'.[24] Zola's indictment of Second Empire society is unrelenting; but at the same time he cannot help admiring his protagonist for his phenomenal dynamism, which places him on the side of modernity and, for Zola, on the side of life and of the future. One of the most abiding images in this novel full of arresting images is that of Saccard leaping over obstacles, 'rolling in the mud, not bothering to wipe himself down, so that he could reach his goal more quickly, not even stopping to enjoy himself on the way, chewing on his twenty-franc pieces as he ran' (p. 240).

[24] David Harvey, 'Modernity and Modernism', in *The Condition of Postmodernity* (Oxford: Blackwell, 1989), 10–38.

TRANSLATOR'S NOTE

Literary translation is anything but a mechanical task. It is, to begin with, an act of interpretation. The choices made by the translator are the result of careful analysis, informed by varying degrees of intuitive understanding, of the work being translated. Specifically, literary translation may be regarded as both a form of close reading (applied literary criticism) and a form of writing (a craft as well as an art). As Susan Sontag has argued ('The World as India', *Times Literary Supplement*, 13 June 2003), literary translation is a branch of literature. The translator should strive, as St Jerome himself wrote in AD395, to reproduce the general style and emphases of the translated text—thus making the translator a kind of co-author (what a pleasure and privilege, and also what a challenge). Literary translation is both creative and imitative; indeed, it is a form of creative imitation. 'Imitation' is the term used by Robert Lowell (*Imitations*, 1971) to indicate homage, appropriation, and the recognition of an affinity between translator and author. I have endeavoured, in my translation of *La Curée*, to capture the structures and rhythms, the tone and texture, and the lexical choices—in sum, the particular idiom—of Zola's novel, as well as to preserve the 'feel' of the social context out of which the novel emerged and which it represents.

I am very happy to have produced the first translation of *La Curée* into English since A. Teixeira de Mattos's translation of 1895 (which was preceded by Henry Vizetelly's version, *The Rush for the Spoil*, in 1886). The translation is based on the text of *La Curée* edited by Henri Mitterand and published in volume 1 of his Bibliothèque de la Pléiade edition of *Les Rougon-Macquart* (Paris: Gallimard, 1960) and as a separate volume (Gallimard, Folio, 1981). I hasten to note that the absence of a twentieth-century translation does not betoken a lack of popularity. *La Curée*, sometimes regarded as the best of the novels that preceded *L'Assommoir*, occupies a middle-ranking position in the league table of paperback (Livre de Poche) sales in France. Since the 1960s critical interest in the novel has been high, especially since 1987, when Zola was finally allowed out of purgatory in terms of the canonization embodied in the French *agrégation* examination syllabus, with *La Curée* chosen to induct its author into that particular Hall of Fame.

I am grateful to Marie-Rose Auguste, Patrick Durel, David Garrioch, Susan Harrow, Gérard Kahn, Robert Lethbridge, Judith Luna, Valerie Minogue, Jeff New, and Rita Wilson, who all helped in various ways. I would like to thank the British Centre for Literary Translation at the University of East Anglia, and its then Director, Peter Bush, for a grant that enabled me to spend a month there as translator in residence and to participate in the Centre's summer school. I am also grateful to the French Ministry of Culture for a grant that enabled me to spend some time at the Centre International des Traducteurs Littéraires in Arles, where Claude Bleton and Christine Janssens maintain such a wonderfully hospitable and relaxed working environment. Thanks, finally, to Francis Clarke and Geoff Woollen for permission to use the map of Paris originally produced for Susan Harrow's monograph on *La Curée*.

SELECT BIBLIOGRAPHY

The Kill (*La Curée*) was serialized in *La Cloche* from 29 September to 5 November 1871, when publication was stopped on advice from the censorship authorities. The novel was published as a volume by the Librairie Charpentier in January 1872. It is included in volume 1 of Henri Mitterand's superb scholarly edition of *Les Rougon-Macquart* in the 'Bibliothèque de la Pléiade' (Paris: Gallimard, 1960). Paperback editions exist in the following popular collections: GF Flammarion, introduction by Claude Duchet (Paris, 1970); Folio, ed. Henri Mitterand, introduction by Jean Borie (Paris, 1981); Classiques de Poche, commentary by Philippe Bonnefis, preface by Henri Mitterand (Paris, 1996); L'École des Lettres, Seuil, ed. François-Marie Mourad (Paris, 1997); La Bibliothèque Gallimard, ed. Catherine Dessi-Woelflinger (Paris, 1999); Pocket, ed. Marie-Thérèse Ligot (Paris, 1999 [1990]). There is also a luxury edition of the novel, ed. Jacques Noiray (Paris: Imprimerie Nationale, 1986).

Biographies of Zola in English

Brown, Frederick, *Zola: A Life* (New York: Farrar, Straus & Giroux, 1995; London: Macmillan, 1996).

Hemmings, F. W. J., *The Life and Times of Émile Zola* (London: Elek, 1977).

Schom, Alan, *Émile Zola: A Bourgeois Rebel* (New York: Henry Holt, 1987; London: Queen Anne Press, 1987).

Walker, Philip, *Zola* (London: Routledge & Kegan Paul, 1985).

Studies of Zola and Naturalism in English

Baguley, David, *Naturalist Fiction: The Entropic Vision* (Cambridge: Cambridge University Press, 1990).

—— (ed.), *Critical Essays on Émile Zola* (Boston: G. K. Hall, 1986).

Bell, David F., 'Deeds and Incest: *La Curée*', in *Models of Power: Politics and Economics in Zola's 'Rougon-Macquart'* (Lincoln, Nebr., and London: University of Nebraska Press, 1988), 57–95.

Hemmings, F. W. J., *Émile Zola*, 2nd edn. (Oxford: Clarendon Press, 1966).

Lethbridge, R., and Keefe, T. (eds.), *Zola and the Craft of Fiction* (Leicester: Leicester University Press, 1990).

Nelson, Brian, 'Speculation and Dissipation: *La Curée*', in *Zola and the Bourgeoisie* (London: Macmillan; Totowa, NJ: Barnes & Noble, 1983), 63–95.

—— (ed.), *Naturalism in the European Novel: New Critical Perspectives* (New York and Oxford: Berg, 1992).

Schor, Naomi, *Zola's Crowds* (Baltimore: Johns Hopkins University Press, 1978).

Wilson, Angus, *Émile Zola: An Introductory Study of his Novels* (London: Secker & Warburg, 1953; rev. edn. 1964).

Articles, Chapters, and Books in English on The Kill

Allan, John C., 'Narcissism and the Double in *La Curée*', *Stanford French Review*, 5: 3 (1981), 295–312.

Duffy, Larry, 'Preserves of Nature: Traffic Jams and Garden Furniture in Zola's *La Curée*', in *Les Lieux Interdits: Transgression and French Literature*, ed. with an introduction by Larry Duffy and Adrian Tudor (Hull: University of Hull Press, 1998), 205–16.

Ferguson, Priscilla Parkhurst, 'Haussmann's Paris and the Revolution of Representation', in *Paris as Revolution: Writing the 19th-Century City* (Berkeley: University of California Press, 1994), 115–51.

Harrow, Susan, 'Myopia and the Model: The Making and Unmaking of Renée in Zola's *La Curée*', in Anna Gural-Migdal (ed.), *L'Écriture du féminin chez Zola et dans la fiction naturaliste/Writing the Feminine in Zola and Naturalist Fiction* (Berne: Peter Lang, 2003), 251–70.

—— 'Exposing the Imperial Cultural Fabric: Critical Description in Zola's *La Curée*', *French Studies*, 54 (2000), 439–52.

—— *Zola: 'La Curée'*, Glasgow Introductory Guides to French Literature (Glasgow: University of Glasgow French & German Publications, 1998).

Lethbridge, Robert, 'Zola's *La Curée*: The Genesis of a Title', *New Zealand Journal of French Studies*, 6: 1 (1985), 23–37.

—— 'Zola: Decadence and Autobiography in the Genesis of a Fictional Character', *Nottingham French Studies*, 17 (May 1978), 39–51.

Petrey, Sandy, 'Stylistics and Society in *La Curée*', *Modern Language Notes*, 89 (1974), 626–40.

Reid, Roddey, 'Perverse Commerce: Familial Pathology and National Decline in *La Curée*', in *Families in Jeopardy: Regulating the Social Body in France, 1750–1910* (Stanford: Stanford University Press, 1993), 240–77.

White, Nicholas, *The Family in Crisis in Late Nineteenth-century French Fiction* (Cambridge: Cambridge University Press, 1998), *passim*.

Background and Context: Haussmann, the Second Empire, and Modernity

Baguley, David, *Napoleon III and His Regime: An Extravaganza* (Baton Rouge: Louisiana State University Press, 2000).

Benjamin, Walter, *The Arcades Project*, trans. Howard Eiland and Kevin McLaughlin (Cambridge, Mass., and London: The Bellknap Press, 1999).

Berman, Marshall, *All That is Solid Melts into Air: The Experience of Modernity* (New York: Simon and Schuster, 1982; London: Verso, 1983).

Buck-Morss, Susan, *The Dialectics of Seeing: Walter Benjamin and the Arcades Project* (Cambridge, Mass., and London: MIT Press, 1989).

Carmona, Michel, *Haussmann: His Life and Times and the Making of Modern Paris*, trans. Patrick Camiller (Chicago: Ivan R. Dee, 2002).

Christiansen, Rupert, *Paris Babylon: Grandeur, Decadence and Revolution 1869–75* (London: Pimlico, 2003).

Cowling, Mark, and Martin, James (eds.), *Marx's 'Eighteenth Brumaire': (Post)modern Interpretations* (London: Pluto Press, 2002).

Clark, T. J., *The Painting of Modern Life: Paris in the Art of Manet and His Followers* (Princeton: Princeton University Press, 1984; London: Thames & Hudson, 1985; rev. edn., 1999).

Harvey, David, *Paris: Capital of Modernity* (New York and London: Routledge, 2003).

—— 'Modernity and Modernism', in *The Condition of Postmodernity* (Oxford: Blackwell, 1989), 10–38.

—— *Consciousness and the Urban Experience: Studies in the History and Theory of Capitalist Urbanization* (Baltimore: Johns Hopkins University Press, 1985), 'Paris, 1850–1870', 63–220.

Herbert, Robert L., *Impressionism: Art, Leisure, and Parisian Society* (New Haven, Conn.: Yale University Press, 1988).

Jordan, David, *Transforming Paris: The Life and Labors of Baron Haussmann* (New York and London: The Free Press, 1995).

Olsen, Donald J., *The City as a Work of Art: London, Paris, Vienna* (New Haven, Conn.: Yale University Press, 1986).

Pinkney, David H., *Napoleon III and the Rebuilding of Paris* (Princeton: Princeton University Press, 1958).

Plessis, Alain, *The Rise and Fall of the Second Empire, 1852–1871* (Cambridge: Cambridge University Press, 1985).

Price, Roger, *Napoleon III and the Second Empire* (London: Routledge, 1997).

Sutcliffe, Anthony, *The Autumn of Central Paris: The Defeat of Town Planning, 1850–1970* (London: Edward Arnold, 1970).

Film Versions

La Cuccagna (Italy, 1917). Directed by Baldassare Negroni. Starring Hesperia (Renée) and Alberto Collo (Maxime).

La Curée, English title *The Game is Over* (France, 1965). Directed by Roger Vadim. Starring Jane Fonda (Renée), Michel Piccoli (Saccard), Peter McEnery (Maxime).

Theatrical Version

Renée, a drama in five acts, was based on *La Curée* and the short story 'Nantas' (written 1878, published 1884). Written by Zola in 1880, at the instigation of Sarah Bernhardt, the play was rejected by several Parisian theatres before being produced at the Théâtre du Vaudeville on 16 April 1887. It ran for thirty-eight performances. The text was published by Charpentier in May 1887, with a preface by Zola.

Further Reading in Oxford World's Classics

Zola, Émile, *L'Assommoir*, trans. Margaret Mauldon, ed. Robert Lethbridge.
—— *The Attack on the Mill*, trans. Douglas Parmée.
—— *La Bête humaine*, trans. Roger Pearson.
—— *La Débâcle*, trans. Elinor Dorday, ed. Robert Lethbridge.
—— *Germinal*, trans. Peter Collier, ed. Robert Lethbridge.
—— *The Ladies' Paradise*, trans. Brian Nelson.
—— *The Masterpiece*, trans. Thomas Walton, revised by Roger Pearson.
—— *Nana*, trans. Douglas Parmée.
—— *Pot Luck*, trans. Brian Nelson.
—— *Thérèse Raquin*, trans. Andrew Rothwell.

A CHRONOLOGY OF ÉMILE ZOLA

1840   (2 April) Born in Paris, the only child of Francesco Zola (b. 1795), an Italian engineer, and Émilie, née Aubert (b. 1819), the daughter of a glazier. The naturalist novelist was later proud that 'zolla' in Italian means 'clod of earth'

1843   Family moves to Aix-en-Provence

1847   (27 March) Death of father from pneumonia following a chill caught while supervising work on his scheme to supply Aix-en-Provence with drinking water

1852–   Becomes a boarder at the Collège Bourbon at Aix. Friendship with Baptistin Baille and Paul Cézanne. Zola, not Cézanne, wins the school prize for drawing

1858   (February) Leaves Aix to settle in Paris with his mother (who had preceded him in December). Offered a place and bursary at the Lycée Saint-Louis. (November) Falls ill with 'brain fever' (typhoid) and convalescence is slow

1859   Fails his *baccalauréat* twice

1860   (Spring) Is found employment as a copy-clerk but abandons it after two months, preferring to eke out an existence as an impecunious writer in the Latin Quarter of Paris

1861   Cézanne follows Zola to Paris, where he meets Camille Pissarro, fails the entrance examination to the École des Beaux-Arts, and returns to Aix in September

1862   (February) Taken on by Hachette, the well-known publishing house, at first in the dispatch office and subsequently as head of the publicity department. (31 October) Naturalized as a French citizen. Cézanne returns to Paris and stays with Zola

1863   (31 January) First literary article published. (1 May) Manet's *Déjeuner sur l'herbe* exhibited at the Salon des Refusés, which Zola visits with Cézanne

1864   (October) *Tales for Ninon*

1865   *Claude's Confession.* A *succès de scandale* thanks to its bedroom scenes. Meets future wife Alexandrine-Gabrielle Meley (b. 1839), the illegitimate daughter of teenage parents who soon separated, and whose mother died in September 1849

1866   Resigns his position at Hachette (salary: 200 francs a month)

and becomes a literary critic on the recently launched daily *L'Événement* (salary: 500 francs a month). Self-styled 'humble disciple' of Hippolyte Taine. Writes a series of provocative articles condemning the official Salon Selection Committee, expressing reservations about Courbet, and praising Manet and Monet. Begins to frequent the Café Guerbois in the Batignolles quarter of Paris, the meeting-place of the future Impressionists. Antoine Guillemet takes Zola to meet Manet. Summer months spent with Cézanne at Bennecourt on the Seine. (15 November) *L'Événement* suppressed by the authorities

1867   (November) *Thérèse Raquin*

1868   (April) Preface to second edition of *Thérèse Raquin*. (May) Manet's portrait of Zola exhibited at the Salon. (December) *Madeleine Férat*. Begins to plan for the Rougon-Macquart series of novels

1868–70   Working as journalist for a number of different newspapers

1870   (31 May) Marries Alexandrine in a registry office. (September) Moves temporarily to Marseilles because of the Franco-Prussian War

1871   Political reporter for *La Cloche* (in Paris) and *Le Sémaphore de Marseille*. (March) Returns to Paris. (October) Publishes *The Fortune of the Rougons*, the first of the twenty novels making up the Rougon-Macquart series

1872   *The Kill*

1873   (April) *The Belly of Paris*

1874   (May) *The Conquest of Plassans*. First independent Impressionist exhibition. (November) *Further Tales for Ninon*

1875   Begins to contribute articles to the Russian newspaper *Vestnik Evropy* (*European Herald*). (April) *The Sin of Father Mouret*

1876   (February) *His Excellency Eugène Rougon*. Second Impressionist exhibition

1877   (February) *L'Assommoir*

1878   Buys a house at Médan on the Seine, 40 kilometres west of Paris. (June) *A Page of Love*

1880   (March) *Nana*. (May) *Les Soirées de Médan* (an anthology of short stories by Zola and some of his naturalist 'disciples', including Maupassant). (8 May) Death of Flaubert. (September) First of a series of articles for *Le Figaro*. (17

October) Death of his mother. (December) *The Experimental Novel*

1882   (April) *Pot Luck* (*Pot-Bouille*). (3 September) Death of Turgenev

1883   (13 February) Death of Wagner. (March) *The Ladies' Paradise* (*Au Bonheur des Dames*). (30 April) Death of Manet

1884   (March) *La Joie de vivre*. Preface to catalogue of Manet exhibition

1885   (March) *Germinal*. (12 May) Begins writing *The Masterpiece* (*L'Œuvre*). (22 May) Death of Victor Hugo. (23 December) First instalment of *The Masterpiece* appears in *Le Gil Blas*

1886   (27 March) Final instalment of *The Masterpiece*, which is published in book form in April

1887   (18 August) Denounced as an onanistic pornographer in the *Manifesto of the Five* in *Le Figaro*. (November) *Earth*

1888   (October) *The Dream*. Jeanne Rozerot becomes his mistress

1889   (20 September) Birth of Denise, daughter of Zola and Jeanne

1890   (March) *The Beast in Man*

1891   (March) *Money*. (April) Elected President of the Société des Gens de Lettres. (25 September) Birth of Jacques, son of Zola and Jeanne

1892   (June) *La Débâcle*

1893   (July) *Doctor Pascal*, the last of the Rougon-Macquart novels. Fêted on visit to London

1894   (August) *Lourdes*, the first novel of the trilogy *Three Cities*. (22 December) Dreyfus found guilty by a court martial

1896   (May) *Rome*

1898   (13 January) 'J'accuse', his article in defence of Dreyfus, published in *L'Aurore*. (21 February) Found guilty of libelling the Minister of War and given the maximum sentence of one year's imprisonment and a fine of 3,000 francs. Appeal for retrial granted on a technicality. (March) *Paris*. (23 May) Retrial delayed. (18 July) Leaves for England instead of attending court

1899   (4 June) Returns to France. (October) *Fecundity*, the first of his *Four Gospels*

1901   (May) *Toil*, the second 'Gospel'

1902   (29 September) Dies of fumes from his bedroom fire, the chimney having been capped either by accident or anti-Dreyfusard design. Wife survives. (5 October) Public funeral

1903   (March) *Truth*, the third 'Gospel', published posthumously. *Justice* was to be the fourth

1908   (4 June) Remains transferred to the Panthéon

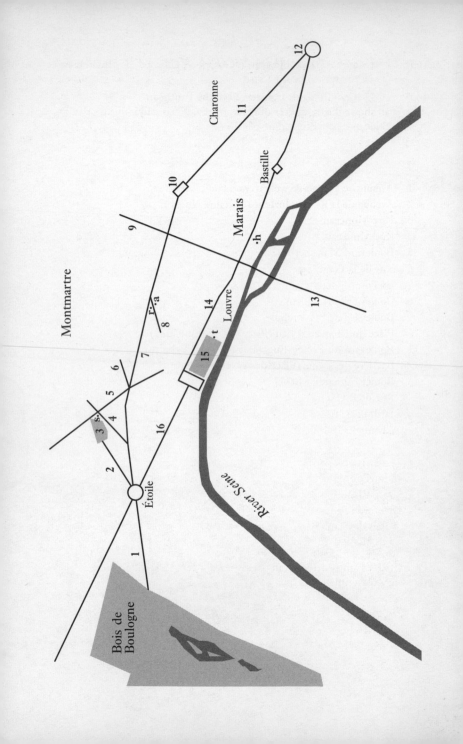

The Paris of *The Kill*

This map shows the main axes of Haussmann's Paris and indicates the principal locations mentioned in *The Kill*.

Present-day names are given in parentheses where they differ from those of Zola's time.

THE KILL

PREFACE

IN the natural and social history of a family during the Second Empire, *The Kill* is the note of gold and flesh. The artist in me refused to diminish the glamour of this life of excess that illuminated the entire reign with the suspect light of a bawdy house. A vital aspect of this history would have remained obscure.

I wanted to show the premature exhaustion of a race which has lived too quickly and ends in the man-woman of rotten societies, the furious speculation of an epoch embodied in an unscrupulous temperament, the nervous breakdown of a woman whose circle of luxury and shame increases tenfold native appetites. And, with these three social monstrosities, I have tried to write a work of art and science which should at the same time be one of the strangest chapters in our social history.

If I feel that I must explain *The Kill*, this true portrait of social collapse, it is because its literary and scientific aspects seemed to be so poorly understood in the newspaper in which the novel was being serialized that I was obliged to stop its publication and suspend the experiment.

Paris, 15 November 1871
Émile ZOLA

CHAPTER I

ON the drive home, the barouche* was reduced to a crawl by the long line of carriages returning by the side of the lake.* At one point they had to pull up completely.

The sun was setting in a grey October sky,* streaked on the horizon with thin clouds. One last ray, falling from the distant shrubbery of the waterfall, threaded along the roadway and bathed the long line of stationary carriages with pale red light. The golden glints, the bright flashes given off by the wheels, seemed to have settled along the straw-coloured edges of the barouche, while the dark-blue panels reflected patches of the surrounding landscape. Higher up, in the red light that lit them up from behind and made the brass buttons of their capes half-folded across the back of the box shine even more brightly, sat the coachman and the footman, in their dark-blue liveries, drab breeches, and black and yellow striped waistcoats, erect, solemn, and patient, like well-bred servants untroubled by an obstruction of carriages. Their hats, decorated with black cockades, looked very dignified. The horses, a pair of splendid bays, snorted impatiently.

'Look,' said Maxime, 'that's Laure d'Aurigny* over there, in that brougham.'*

Renée sat up, and blinked with the exquisite grimace caused by her short-sightedness.

'I thought she had disappeared,' said Renée. 'She has changed the colour of her hair, hasn't she?'

'Yes,' replied Maxime with a laugh. 'Her new lover hates red.'

Awakened from the melancholy dream that had kept her silent for an hour, stretched out on the back seat of the carriage as on an invalid's chaise longue, Renée leaned forward to look, resting her hand on the low door of the barouche. Over a gown consisting of a mauve silk polonaise* and tunic, trimmed with wide, plaited flounces, she wore a little coat of white cloth with mauve velvet lapels, which made her look very smart. Her strange, fawn-coloured hair, like the colour of fine butter, was barely concealed by a tiny bonnet adorned with a little bunch of Bengal roses. She continued to screw up her eyes in a way that made her look like a cheeky little boy, her smooth

forehead furrowed by a long crease, her upper lip protruding like a
sulky child's. Then, finding that she could not see, she took her
eyeglass, a man's double eyeglass with a tortoiseshell frame, and,
holding it in her hand without placing it on her nose, examined at
leisure the fat Laure d'Aurigny, with an air of complete detachment.

The carriages did not move. In the mass of dark patches made by
the line of broughams, of which so many had crowded into the
Bois that autumn afternoon, gleamed the glass of a carriage window,
the bit of a bridle, the plated socket of a lamp, the braid on the livery
of a lackey perched on his box. Here and there a piece of fabric,
part of a woman's silk or velvet dress, flashed from an open landau.
Little by little a deep silence had replaced all the activity and movement, which had subsided into stillness. The people in the carriages
could hear the conversations of those on foot. Silent glances were
exchanged from window to window; no one spoke, the silence
broken only by the creaking of a harness or the impatient pawing of
a horse's hoof. The muffled sounds of the Bois died away in the
distance.

Tout Paris was there, in spite of the lateness of the season: the
Duchesse de Sternich, in a chariot;* Madame de Lauwerens, in a
smart victoria* and pair; the Baronne de Meinhold, in an enchanting
light-brown cab; the Comtesse Vanska, with her piebald ponies;
Madame Daste, with her famous black steppers; Madame de
Guende and Madame Teissière in a brougham; little Sylvia in a
dark-blue landau. Then there was Don Carlos, in mourning, with his
solemn, old-fashioned liveries; Selim Pasha, with his fez and without
his tutor; the Duchesse de Rozan, in a miniature brougham, with her
powdered livery; the Comte de Chibray, in a dog cart; Mr Simpson,
driving his perfectly appointed drag; and the whole American colony.
Then, finally, two Academicians in a hired cab.*

The front carriages were finally able to proceed, and one by one
the whole line began to move slowly forward. It was like an awakening. A thousand shimmering lights seemed to appear, quick flashes
played on the wheels, sparks flew from the horses' harness. On the
ground, on the trees, appeared broad reflections of trotting glass.
The glitter of wheels and harness, the blaze of varnished panels
glowing with the redness of the setting sun, the bright notes of
colour cast by the dazzling liveries perched up full against the sky,
and by the rich costumes spilling out through the carriage doors,

were accompanied by a continuous, hollow rumbling sound, marked by the rhythmic trot of the horses. The procession continued, with the same effects of light and noise, unceasingly and in a single movement, as if the front carriages were dragging all the others behind them.

Renée yielded to the sudden movement of the barouche, and letting go of her eyeglass, threw herself back on the cushions. Shivering, she drew towards her a corner of the bearskin that filled the inside of the carriage as with a sheet of silky snow, and thrust her gloved hands into the long, soft, curly hair. A breeze began to blow. The warm October day, which had given the Bois a feeling of spring and brought the great ladies out in open carriages, threatened to end in a bitterly cold evening.

For a moment Renée remained huddled in the warmth of her corner, lulled by the pleasurable sound of the turning wheels of the carriages. Then, raising her head to look at Maxime, whose eyes were calmly undressing the women displayed to view in the adjacent broughams and landaus, she said:

'Tell me, do you really think that Laure d'Aurigny is attractive? You sounded very keen on her the other day, when they were discussing the sale of her diamonds! By the way, did you see the necklace and aigrette* your father bought for me at the sale?'

'Yes, he does things very well,' said Maxime without answering, laughing mischievously. 'He knows how to pay Laure's debts as well as give his wife diamonds.'

Renée shrugged slightly.

'You little devil!' she murmured with a smile.

Maxime was leaning forward, looking attentively at a lady whose green dress interested him. Renée sank back, and with half-closed eyes gazed languidly at both sides of the avenue, seeing nothing. On the right, copses and low-cut trees with russet leaves and slender branches passed slowly by; at intervals, on the track reserved for riders, slim-waisted gentlemen galloped past, their steeds raising little clouds of fine dust behind them. On the left, at the foot of the narrow lawns intersected by flower-beds and shrubs, the lake, clear as crystal, without a ripple, lay as though neatly trimmed along its edges by the gardeners' spades; and on the far side of this translucent mirror, the two islands, between them the grey bar of the connecting bridge, displayed their smiling slopes and, against the pale sky, the theatrical grouping of fir trees and evergreens, whose black foliage, like the fringe of curtains carefully draped along the edge of the horizon, was reflected in the water. This scrap of nature, like a newly painted piece of scenery, lay bathed in a faint shadow, in a pale blue haze that gave the distant scene an exquisite charm, an air of entrancing artificiality. On the other bank, the Chalet des Îles, as if freshly varnished, shone like a new toy; and the paths of yellow sand, the narrow garden walks that wind among the lawns and around the lake, edged with iron hoops in imitation of rustic woodwork, stood out more curiously, in the dying light, against the soft green of grass and water.

Renée, used to the artful charms of these sights, and yielding once more to her languor, had lowered her eyelids altogether, and looked only at her slender fingers twisting the long hairs of the bearskin. There was a sudden jolt in the even trot of the line of carriages and, looking up, she nodded to two young ladies lolling side by side in a chariot that was noisily leaving the road that skirts the lake, in order to go down one of the side avenues. The Marquise d'Espanet, whose husband, an aide-de-camp to the Emperor, had recently scandalized the discontented members of the old nobility by loudly declaring his total support for the Empire, was one of the most celebrated ladies of the court; her companion, Madame Haffner, was the wife of a well-known manufacturer from Colmar, a multi-millionaire whom the Empire was turning into a politician.* Renée, who had been at school with the two inseparables, as people had nicknamed them knowingly, called them by their first names, Adeline and Suzanne.

As she was about to sink back into her corner, after giving them a smile, a laugh from Maxime made her turn round.

'No, don't, I'm too depressed: don't laugh, I'm serious,' she said, seeing that the young man was looking at her ironically, making fun of the way she was huddled in her corner of the barouche.

Maxime put on a comic voice:

'How unhappy we are: how jealous.'

She looked surprised.

'Me!' she said. 'Jealous of what?'

Then she added, with a pout of contempt, as if remembering:

'Ah, yes, that fat Laure! I hadn't given her a thought, believe me. If, as everybody says, Aristide has paid that woman's debts and saved her a trip abroad, it only proves that he's less fond of money than I thought. This will put him back in the ladies' good graces. The dear man can do whatever he likes.'

She smiled, saying the words 'the dear man' in a tone of benign indifference. Suddenly, becoming depressed again, casting around her the despairing glance of women who do not know what form of amusement to indulge in, she murmured:

'Oh, I'd like to... But no, I'm not jealous, not in the least.'

She stopped, not sure what to say.

'You know, I'm bored,' she said at last, abruptly.

Then she sat silent, her lips tightly closed. The line of carriages was still travelling along the side of the lake, with its even trot and a noise like a distant waterfall. On the left, between the water and the roadway, rose little bushes of evergreens with thin straight stems, forming curious little clusters of pillars. On the right, the copses and low trees had come to an end; the Bois opened out into broad lawns, vast expanses of grass, with here and there a group of tall trees; the greensward ran on, with gentle undulations, to the Porte de la Muette, whose low gates, which seemed like a piece of black lace stretched along the ground, were visible in the distance; and on the slopes, in the hollows, the grass was quite blue. Renée stared blankly before her, as if this widening of the horizon, these gentle meadows, soaked in the evening air, made her feel more keenly the emptiness of her life.

After a pause, she repeated querulously:

'Oh, I'm bored, bored to death.'

'You're not much fun, you know,' said Maxime calmly. 'Your nerves are bad, obviously.'

'Yes, my nerves are bad,' she repeated dryly.

Then she became motherly:

'I'm growing old, my dear child; I'll soon be thirty. It's terrible. Nothing gives me pleasure. You're only twenty, you can't understand.'

'Did you bring me here to listen to your life story?' interrupted the young man. 'It would take an eternity.'

She greeted this impertinence with a faint smile, as if it were the outburst of a spoilt child who said anything he pleased.

'You have every right to complain,' continued Maxime. 'You spend more than a hundred thousand francs* a year on your ward robe, you live in a mansion, you have splendid horses, your every whim is satisfied, and the newspapers report every new gown of yours as an event of the highest importance; women envy you and men would give ten years of their lives to kiss your fingertips. Isn't it true?'

She nodded. Her eyes lowered, she had resumed curling the hairs of the bearskin.

'Don't be so modest,' Maxime continued. 'Admit that you're one of the pillars of the Second Empire. We needn't hide these things from each other. Wherever you go, to the Tuileries,* to the houses of ministers, to the houses of mere millionaires, high or low, you're treated like a queen. There isn't a pleasure you haven't tasted, and if I had the courage, if my respect for you did not hold me back, I'd say...'

He paused for a few seconds, laughing, then finished his sentence boldly:

'I'd say you've bitten every apple.'

She did not bat an eyelid.

'And you're bored!' resumed the young man, with comic indignation. 'It's scandalous! What is it you want? What on earth are you dreaming about?'

She shrugged, as if to imply that she did not know. Though she kept her head bowed, Maxime could see that she looked so serious and so sad that he thought it best to hold his tongue. He watched the line of carriages, which, when they reached the end of the lake, spread out, filling the whole of the intersection. They swept round majestically; the quicker trot of the horses sounded noisily on the hard ground.

The barouche, making a large circuit to join the line, rocked in a way that Maxime found vaguely pleasurable. Then, yielding to his desire to heap criticism on Renée, he said:

'You know, you deserve to ride in a cab! It would serve you right! Look at these people going back to Paris, they're all at your feet. They greet you as if you were their queen, and your dear friend, Monsieur de Mussy, can hardly prevent himself from blowing kisses at you.'

A horseman was in fact greeting Renée. Maxime had been talking in a hypocritical, mocking voice. But Renée barely turned round, and shrugged. This time Maxime made a gesture of despair.

'Really,' he said, 'has it come to this? Good God, you've got everything: what more do you want?'

Renée looked up. Her eyes glowed with the desire of unsatisfied curiosity.

'I want something different,' she replied softly.

'But since you have everything,' resumed Maxime, laughing, 'there is nothing different. What does "something different" mean?'

'What?' she repeated.

She fell silent. She had turned right round, and was watching the strange picture fading behind her. It was almost night; twilight was spreading slowly like fine ash. The lake, seen from the front, in the pale light that still hovered over the water, became rounder, like a huge tin fish; on either side, the plantations of evergreens, whose slim, straight stems seemed to rise up from its still surface, looked at this hour like purple colonnades, delineating with their even shapes the studied curves of the shore; and shrubs rose in the background, confused masses of foliage forming large black patches that closed off the horizon. Behind these patches was the glow of the dying sunset, which set fire to only a small portion of the grey immensity. Above the still lake, the low copses, the strangely flat perspective, stretched the vast sky, infinite, deepened and widened. The great slice of sky hanging over this small piece of nature caused a thrill, an indefinable sadness; and from these paling heights fell so deep an autumnal melancholy, so sweet and heart-breaking a darkness, that the Bois, wound little by little in a shadowy shroud, lost its worldly graces, and widened out, full of the powerful charm that forests have. The wheels of the carriages, whose bright colours were fading in the twilight, sounded like the distant voices of leaves and running water. Everything was slowly dying away. In the middle of the lake, in the general evanescence, the lateen sail* of the great pleasure-boat stood out strongly against the glow of the sunset. It was now impossible to distinguish anything but this sail, this triangle of yellow canvas, enormously enlarged.

Renée, satiated as she was, had a strange feeling of illicit desire at the sight of this landscape that had become unrecognizable, of this scrap of nature, so worldly and artificial, which the great pulsating darkness had transformed into a sacred grove, one of the ideal glades in whose recesses the gods of antiquity hid their Titanic loves, their adulteries, their divine incests.* As the barouche drove towards Paris, it seemed to her that the twilight was carrying off behind her, in its tremulous veil, the land of her dreams, the shameful, mythical

alcove in which her sick heart and weary flesh might at last have
found satisfaction.

When, fading into the shadows, the lake and bushes showed only
as a black bar against the sky, Renée turned round abruptly and, in
an annoyed tone, resumed her interrupted sentence:

'What? Something different, yes! I want something different.
How can I know what! If I knew... You know, I'm sick of balls, sick
of suppers, sick of pleasures of that sort. It's so boring. And men are
insufferable, absolutely insufferable.'

Maxime began to laugh. A certain excitement was discernible
beneath the aristocratic manner of the society lady. She no longer
fluttered her eyelids, and the line on her forehead stood out even
more; her lip, so much like a sulky child's, protruded as if desperately seeking the nameless pleasures she pined for. She saw that
Maxime was laughing, but was too excited to stop; lying back,
swayed by the rocking of the carriage, she continued in short, sharp
sentences:

'Absolutely, yes, you're all insufferable. I don't include you,
Maxime, you're too young. But if I told you how oppressive I found
Aristide in the early days! And the others! The men I've had as
lovers... You know, we're good friends, you and I: I can confide in
you; well, there are days when I'm so tired of living the life of a rich
woman, adored and worshipped, that I feel I'd rather be somebody
like Laure d'Aurigny, one of those ladies who live quite independent
lives.'

As Maxime began to laugh even more, she insisted:

'Yes, a Laure d'Aurigny. It must surely be less boring.'

She sat silent for a few minutes, as if imagining the life she would
lead if she were Laure. Then, with a note of discouragement in her
voice, she resumed:

'But I suppose those women must have their problems too. There's
no pleasure in life. It's deadly. As I said, there ought to be something
different, you understand; I can't imagine what, but something else,
something that would happen to nobody but oneself, something
completely new, a rare, unknown pleasure...'

She spoke slowly. She uttered these last words as if trying to
discover something, and sank into a deep reverie. The barouche went
up the avenue leading out of the Bois. It was getting darker; the
copses ran along on either side like grey walls; the yellow iron chairs

on which, on fine evenings, the bourgeois love to disport themselves in their Sunday best, were lined up along the footpaths, empty, with the desolate air of garden furniture in winter; and the dull rhythmical sound of the carriages could be heard along the avenues like a sad refrain.

Maxime undoubtedly appreciated the bad form of thinking that life could be enjoyable. Though young enough to give himself over to the occasional outburst of contented admiration, he was too selfish, too cynical and indifferent, and already too world-weary not to declare himself disgusted, sick, played out. He usually took a certain pride in making this confession.

He threw himself back in the carriage like Renée, and assumed a plaintive tone.

'Yes, you're right,' he said. 'It's deadly. Actually, I'm no better than you at finding enjoyment; I've often dreamt of something different too. There's nothing more pointless than travel. As for making money, I prefer to spend it, though even that isn't always as much fun as one imagines. Loving and being loved: we soon get sick of that, don't we?'

Renée did not respond, and he went on, wanting to shock her with a piece of gross blasphemy:

'I'd like a nun to fall in love with me. That might be fun. Have you ever dreamt of loving a man you couldn't think about without committing a crime?'

She did not react, and Maxime concluded that she was not listening. She seemed to be sleeping with her eyes open, the nape of her neck resting against the padded edge of the barouche. She lay listlessly, thinking, prey to the dreams that kept her in a sombre mood, and from time to time a slight nervous tremor passed over her lips. She was slowly overcome by the shadow of the twilight; all that this shadow contained of sadness, of discreet pleasures and secret hopes, penetrated her, enveloping her with an air of morbid languor. Doubtless, while staring at the round back of the footman on his box, she was thinking of those fleeting delights, of those entertainments that had faded so quickly, and of which she was now so weary; she pictured her past life, the instantaneous satisfaction of her appetites, the sickening luxury, the appalling monotony of the same loves and the same betrayals. Then, like a ray of hope, there came to her, with shivers of longing, the idea of that 'something different' that her conscious mind could hardly grasp. Her dreams wandered. The word she strove to find escaped into the night, became lost in the movement of the carriages. The gentle vibration of the barouche was but one more impediment to the formulation of her desire. An immense temptation rose from the empty space, from the copses asleep in the shadows on either side of the avenue, from the noise of wheels and from the gentle oscillation that made her so pleasantly drowsy. A thousand tremulous emotions passed over her body: unrealized dreams, nameless delights, confused longings, all the monstrous voluptuousness that a drive home from the Bois under a paling sky can infuse into a woman's heart. She kept both hands buried in the bearskin, she was quite warm in her white cloth coat with the mauve velvet lapels. She put out her foot, stretching, and her ankle lightly touched Maxime's warm leg; he took no notice. A jolt aroused her from her torpor. She raised her head, and her grey eyes looked curiously at the young man who sat lounging in an attitude of sheer elegance.

At this moment the barouche left the Bois. The Avenue de l'Impératrice* stretched out in the darkness, with the two green lines of its painted fences meeting on the horizon. In the side-path reserved for riders, a white horse formed a bright patch in the grey shadows. Here and there, on the other side, along the roadway, were late strollers, groups of black spots, making their way slowly back to Paris; and high up, at the end of the procession of carriages, the Arc de Triomphe, seen at an angle, stood out in its whiteness against a vast expanse of sooty sky.

As the barouche went up the avenue at an increased pace, Maxime, charmed by the English appearance of the scene, looked out at the irregular architecture of the private houses, with their lawns running down to the pavements. Renée, still dreaming, amused herself by watching the gaslamps in the Place de l'Étoile being lit, one by one, on the edge of the horizon, and as each of these bright jets splashed the dying day with its little yellow flame, she seemed to hear mysterious voices; it seemed that Paris was being lit up for her, making ready the unknown pleasure for which her senses yearned.

The barouche turned into the Avenue de la Reine-Hortense* and pulled up at the end of the Rue Monceau, a few steps from the Boulevard Malesherbes,* in front of a large mansion standing between a courtyard and a garden. The two gates, heavily ornamented with gilt decorations, which opened into the courtyard, were flanked by a pair of lamps shaped like urns, similarly covered with gilding, and in which flared broad gas jets. Between the two gates, the concierge lived in a pretty lodge vaguely suggestive of a little Greek temple.

Maxime sprang lightly to the ground as the carriage was about to enter the courtyard.

'You know,' said Renée, grasping him by the hand, 'dinner is at half-past seven. You have more than an hour to dress. Don't keep us waiting.'

And she added with a smile:

'The de Mareuils are coming... Your father wants you to pay Louise every attention.'

Maxime shrugged.

'What a bore!' he murmured peevishly. 'I don't mind marrying her, but wooing her is just silly. I would appreciate it, Renée, if you would rescue me from Louise this evening.'

He put on his comic look, the accent and grimace he borrowed from Lassouche* whenever he was about to tell one of his stock jokes.

'Will you, stepmother dear?'

Renée shook hands with him in masculine fashion, and quickly, with nervous, jesting boldness, said:

'If I hadn't married your father, I'm sure you would have wanted to court me.'

The young man seemed to find the idea very funny, for he was still laughing when he turned the corner of the Boulevard Malesherbes.

The barouche entered and drew up in front of the steps. These steps, broad and low, were sheltered by a great glass awning, with a scalloped bordering with gilded acorns. The house's two storeys rose up above the servants' quarters, whose square windows, glazed with frosted glass, appeared almost at ground level. At the top of the steps the hall door projected outwards, flanked by slender columns set into the wall, forming a slight break, marked at each storey by a bay window, and ascending to the roof, where it finished in a pediment. The storeys had five windows on either side, placed at regular intervals along the façade, and simply framed in stone. The roof was cut off square above the attic windows, with broad and almost perpendicular sides.

On the garden side the façade was far more sumptuous. A regal flight of steps led to a narrow terrace that skirted the whole length of the ground floor; the balustrade of this terrace, designed to match the railings of the Parc Monceau,* was even more heavily gilded than the awning or the lamps in the courtyard. Above this rose the mansion, having at each corner a pavilion, a sort of tower half enclosed in the body of the building, and containing rooms that were circular in shape. In the centre there bulged out slightly a third turret, more deeply contained in the building. The windows, tall and narrow in the turrets, wider apart and almost square on the flat portions of the façade, had on the ground floor stone balustrades and on the upper floors gilded wrought-iron railings. The display of decoration was profuse. The house was hidden under its sculpture. Around the windows and along the cornices ran volutes of flowers and branches; there were balconies shaped like baskets full of blossoms, and supported by tall, naked women with wide hips and jutting breasts; and here and there were fanciful escutcheons, clusters of fruit, roses, every flower it is possible for stone or marble to represent. The higher one looked, the more the building burst into blossom. Around the roof ran a balustrade on which urns, at regular intervals, stood blazing with flames of stone; and there, between the bull's-eye windows of the attics, which opened on to an incredible mass of fruit and foliage, mantled the crowning portions of this amazing spectacle, the pediments of the turrets, in the midst of which the naked women reappeared, playing with apples, adopting poses amidst sheaves of rushes. The roof, loaded with these ornaments and surmounted by a cresting of embossed lead, with two lightning conductors and four huge, symmetrical chimneystacks carved like all the rest, seemed the finishing-piece of this architectural firework display.*

On the right was an enormous hothouse,* built on to the side of the house and communicating with the ground floor through the glass door of a drawing room. The garden, separated from the Parc Monceau by a low railing concealed by a hedge, had a considerable slope. Too small for the house, so small that a lawn and a few clumps of evergreens filled it entirely, it was there simply as a mound, a green pedestal on which the house stood proudly planted in its gala dress. Seen from the gardens, across the well-trimmed grass and the glistening foliage of the shrubs, this remarkable edifice, still new and pallid, had the wan face, the purse-proud, foolish self-importance of a female parvenu, with its heavy headdress of slates, its gilded flounces, and its mass of sculpture. It was a miniature version of the new Louvre,* one of the most typical examples of the Napoleon III style, that opulent bastard of so many styles. On summer evenings, when the rays of the setting sun lit up the gilt of the railings against its white façade, the strollers in the gardens would stop to look at the crimson silk curtains behind the ground-floor windows; and through the sheets of plate glass so wide and clear that they seemed like the window-fronts of a big modern department store,* arranged so as to display to the outside world the wealth within, the petty bourgeoisie could catch glimpses of the corners of tables and chairs, of portions of hangings, of patches of ornate ceilings, the sight of which would root them to the spot, in the middle of the pathways, with envy and admiration.

But at this moment the shadows were falling from the trees, and the façade slept. On the other side, in the courtyard, the footman was respectfully helping Renée to alight. At the far end of a glass covered-way on the right, the stables, banded with red brick, opened wide their doors of polished oak. On the left, as if for balance, built into the wall of the adjacent house, there was a decorative niche, within which a sheet of water flowed continuously from a shell which two Cupids held in their outstretched arms. Renée stood for a moment at the foot of the steps, gently tapping her dress, which refused to fall properly. The courtyard, which had just been filled with the noise of the equipage, was empty again, its aristocratic silence broken only by the ceaseless murmur of the flowing water. In the black mass made by the house, where the first of the great autumn dinner-parties was presently to require the chandeliers to be lit, the bottom windows alone were illuminated, glowing brightly and casting reflections on the little cobblestones of the courtyard, neat and regular as a draughtboard.

Renée pushed open the hall door and found herself face to face with her husband's valet, who was on his way to the kitchens carrying a silver kettle. The man looked magnificent, dressed all in black, tall, broad-shouldered, pale-complexioned, with the conventional side-whiskers of an English diplomat and the solemn, dignified air of a judge.

'Baptiste,' asked Renée, 'is Monsieur home yet?'

'Yes, Madame, he's dressing,' replied the valet, with a movement of the head which a prince acknowledging a crowd might have envied.

Renée slowly climbed the staircase, pulling off her gloves.

The hall was very luxurious. There was a slight sense of suffocation on entering. The thick carpets that covered the floor and the stairs, and the wide red velvet hangings that concealed the walls and the doors, gave the hall the heavy silence and the slightly warm, fragrant atmosphere of a chapel. Draperies hung high, and the lofty ceiling was decorated with roses set on a lattice of golden beading. The staircase, whose double balustrade of white marble had a handrail covered with crimson velvet, was formed by two converging flights between which, at the back, was the door to the main drawing room. On the first landing a vast mirror filled the whole wall. Below, on marble pedestals, at the foot of the branching staircase, stood two bronze-gilt women, bare to the waist, holding great lamps set with five burners, their bright light softened by ground-glass globes. On each side was a row of wonderful majolica vases, in which rare plants were displayed.

As Renée climbed the staircase, at each step her reflection in the mirror grew bigger; she wondered, with the feeling of uncertainty common to the most popular actresses, whether she was really as delightful as people told her.

Then, when she had reached her apartment, which was on the first floor and overlooked the Parc Monceau, she rang for Céleste, her maid, and had herself dressed for dinner. This took a full hour and a quarter. When the last pin had been inserted, she opened a window, as the room was very warm, and, leaning on the sill, sat thinking. Behind her Céleste moved about discreetly, putting things away.

A sea of shadow filled the gardens below. The tall, inky masses of foliage, shaken by sudden gusts of wind, swayed heavily to and fro as with the movement of the tides, the sound of their dead leaves like the lapping of waves on a pebbly beach. Now and then this ebb and flow of darkness was pierced by the two yellow eyes of a carriage, appearing and disappearing between the shrubbery, along the road connecting the Avenue de la Reine-Hortense with the Boulevard Malesherbes. Before this melancholic autumnal scene, Renée felt her heart fill once more with sadness. She remembered herself as a child in her father's house, that silent house on the Île Saint-Louis, where for two centuries the Bérauds du Chatel, a family of judges, had lived sober, sombre lives. Then she thought of the suddenness of her marriage, of the widower who had sold himself to become her husband and bartered his name of Rougon for that of Saccard, the two dry syllables of which, when she first heard them, had reverberated in her ears like two rakes gathering up gold; he had taken her and cast her into this life of excess, in which her poor head was becoming more and more confused every day. Then she fell to dreaming, with childlike joy, of the pleasant games of battledore* she had played with her little sister Christine so many years before. And one morning she would awaken from the dream of pleasure she had lived in for the past ten years, mad, soiled by one of her husband's speculations, in which he himself would go under. It came to her as a sudden foreboding. The trees sighed more loudly. Renée, distressed by these thoughts of shame and punishment, yielded to the instincts, dormant within her, of the honest old bourgeoisie; she made a promise to the inky black night that she would change her ways, that she would spend less on clothes, seek some innocent amusement, as in her happy schooldays when the girls sang '*Nous n'irons plus au bois*' as they danced slowly under the plane trees.

At this moment Céleste, who had been downstairs, returned and murmured in her mistress's ear:

'Monsieur begs Madame to go down. There are already several people in the drawing room.'

Renée shivered. She had not noticed the keen air that had frozen her shoulders. As she walked past her mirror, she stopped and glanced at herself in a habitual movement. She smiled involuntarily and went downstairs.

Most of the guests had, in fact, arrived. She found in the drawing room her sister Christine, a young girl of twenty, very simply dressed in white muslin; her aunt Élisabeth, the widow of Aubertot the notary, an exquisitely charming little old woman of sixty, in black satin; her husband's sister, Sidonie Rougon, a lean, smooth-tongued woman of indeterminate age, with a complexion like soft wax, made to seem even more waxen by the dull hue of her dress; then the de Mareuils: the father, Monsieur de Mareuil, who was just out of mourning for his wife, a tall, handsome man, shallow and serious, bearing a striking resemblance to the valet Baptiste; and the daughter, poor little Louise as she was called, a child of seventeen, puny, slightly humpbacked, wearing with a sickly grace a white foulard dress with red spots; then a whole group of serious-looking men, with many decorations, official gentlemen with silent, sallow faces, and further on another group, young men with dissolute looks and low-cut waistcoats, standing round five or six ladies of extreme elegance, foremost among whom were the two inseparables, the little Marquise d'Espanet, in yellow, and the fair-haired Madame Haffner, in violet. Monsieur de Mussy, the horseman whose greeting Renée had not acknowledged, was there too, with the uneasy look of a lover who feels his days are numbered. And, among the long trains spread over the carpet, two contractors, two bricklayers who had made a lot of money, Mignon and Charrier, with whom Saccard was to settle a business matter the next day, moved clumsily about in their heavy boots, hands behind their backs, most uncomfortable in their dress-clothes.

Aristide Saccard, standing by the door, managed to greet each new arrival while holding forth to the group of serious-looking men with his southern twang and animated manner. He shook their hands, with a cordial word of welcome. Short and sly-looking, he bent and bowed like a puppet; and the most striking feature of his intense, cunning, swarthy little person was the red splash of his Legion of Honour ribbon, which he wore very wide.

Renée's entrance provoked a murmur of admiration. She was really divine. Above a tulle skirt, decorated at the back with a cascade of flounces, she wore a bodice of pale-green satin bordered with English lace, caught up and fastened with large bunches of violets; a single flounce adorned the front of the skirt, and bunches of violets, held together by garlands of ivy, fastened a light muslin drapery. Her head and bust appeared adorably gracious above these regal, richly elaborate petticoats. The dress was so low-cut that her nipples were almost visible, while her arms were bare and she had clusters of violets at her shoulders: she seemed to emerge quite naked from her sheath of tulle and satin, like one of those nymphs whose busts issue from sacred oaks. Her white neck and shoulders, her supple body, seemed so happy in their semi-freedom that the eye expected every moment to see the bodice and skirts slide to the floor, like the dress of a bather enraptured with her own flesh. Her fine blond hair, gathered up high, helmet-shaped, with a sprig of ivy through it, and held together by a knot of violets, accentuated her nudity by uncovering the nape of her neck, which was lightly shaded by little curls, like threads of gold. She was wearing a necklace with pendants, of perfect transparency and on her forehead an aigrette made of sprigs of silver set with diamonds. She stood for a few moments on the threshold, magnificent in her dress, her shoulders shimmering in the hot light like watered silk. She had hurried downstairs, and was a little out of breath. Her eyes, which the darkness of the Parc Monceau had filled with shadow, blinked in the sudden flood of light, giving her the hesitant look of the shortsighted, which in her was so charming.

On seeing her, the little Marquise sprang from her seat, ran up, took her by both hands, and examining her from head to foot, murmured in fluty tones:

'You beautiful, beautiful creature...'

Meanwhile there was much moving about; all the guests came and paid their respects to the beautiful Madame Saccard, as Renée was known to everyone. She touched hands with most of the men. Then she kissed Christine and asked after her father, who never came to the house in the Parc Monceau. Smiling, still bestowing greetings, her hands held languidly together, she stood before the circle of ladies, who gazed with great interest at the necklace and aigrette.

The fair-haired Madame Haffner could no longer resist the temptation. She came closer, stared at the gems, and asked, with envy in her voice:

'That's the necklace and aigrette, isn't it?'

Renée nodded. Thereupon all the women burst into praise: the jewels were magnificent, divine; then they proceeded to discuss, with admiration, Laure d'Aurigny's sale at which Saccard had bought them for his wife;* they complained that those creatures got the best of everything: soon there would be no diamonds left for respectable women. In these complaints could be discerned their longing to feel on their bare skin some of the jewellery that Tout Paris had seen on the shoulders of a celebrated courtesan, and which might perhaps whisper in their ears some of the scandals that so intrigued these great ladies. They knew about the high prices, they mentioned a gorgeous cashmere shawl and some magnificent lace. The aigrette had cost fifteen thousand francs, the necklace fifty thousand. These figures roused Madame d'Espanet to enthusiasm. She called Saccard over, exclaiming:

'Let me congratulate you! What a good husband you are!'

Aristide Saccard came up, bowed, and pretended to be modest.

But his grinning features betrayed his satisfaction; and he watched out of the corner of his eye the two contractors, the bricklayers who had made their fortunes, as they stood a few steps away, listening with obvious respect to the mention of such figures as fifteen and fifty thousand francs.

At this moment Maxime, who had just come in, charmingly pinched in his dress-clothes, leant familiarly on his father's shoulder and whispered to him as to a close friend, glancing in the direction of the bricklayers. Saccard wore the satisfied smile of an actor called before the curtain.

More guests arrived. There were at least thirty people in the drawing room. Conversation was resumed; in moments of silence the faint clatter of silver and crockery could be heard through the walls. At last Baptiste opened the folding doors and majestically uttered the sacramental phrase:

'Dinner is served, Madame.'

Then, slowly, the procession formed. Saccard gave his arm to the little Marquise; Renée took the arm of an old gentleman, a senator, Baron Gouraud, before whom everyone bowed down with great humility; as to Maxime, he was obliged to offer his arm to Louise de Mareuil; the other guests followed, in double file; and right at the end, the two contractors, swinging their arms.

The dining room was a huge, square chamber, whose panelling of varnished pear-wood rose to head height and was decorated with thin gold beading. The four large panels had obviously been pre-pared so that they might be filled with still-life paintings; but this had never been done, the landlord doubtless having recoiled before purely artistic expenditure. They had been hung simply with dark green velvet. The chairs, curtains, and door-hangings of the same material gave the room a very sober appearance, designed to focus on the table all the splendour of the light.

Indeed, at this hour the table, standing in the middle of the wide, dark Persian carpet which deadened the sound of footsteps, and under the glaring light of the chandelier, surrounded by chairs whose black backs, with fillets of gold, encircled it in a dark frame, seemed like an altar, like a chapel of rest, as the bright reflections of the crystal glass and silver plate sparkled on the dazzling whiteness of the cloth. Beyond the carved chair-backs one could just make out, in a hazy floating shadow, the wood panelling, a large low sideboard, and pieces of velvet hanging here and there. The eye was naturally drawn back to the splendour of the table. A beautiful matt silver centrepiece, glittering with its chased work, stood in the middle; it represented a group of satyrs carrying off nymphs; above the group, issuing from a large horn, an enormous bouquet of real flowers hung down in clusters. At each end of the table stood vases with more flowers, a pair of candelabra matching the centre group, each consisting of a satyr running off with a swooning woman on one arm and holding in the other a ten-branched candlestick that added the brilliancy of its candles to the lustre of the central chandelier. Between these principal ornaments the first dishes, large and small, were ranged symmetrically, flanked by shells containing the hors d'oeuvres, and separated by porcelain bowls, crystal vases, flat plates, and tall preserve-stands, filled with that portion of the dessert that was already on the table. Along the line of plates ran an army of glasses, carafes, decanters, and salt-cellars, and all this glass was as thin and light as muslin, uncut, and so transparent that it cast no shadow. The centrepiece and candelabra seemed like fountains of fire; sparks glittered in the burnished silver dishes; the forks, the spoons, and the knives with mother-of-pearl handles were like bars of flame; kaleidoscopic colours filled the glasses; and in the midst of this rain of light, of this mass of incandescence, the decanters threw red stains on the dazzling white cloth.

On entering, a discreet expression of bliss spread over the faces of the men as they smiled at the ladies on their arms. The flowers imparted a freshness to the heavy atmosphere. The aroma of cooked food mingled with the perfume of the roses. The sharp odour of prawns predominated, with the sour scent of lemons.

Then, when all the guests had found their names written on the back of the menu-card, there was a noise of chairs, a great rustling of silken dresses. The bare shoulders, studded with diamonds, and separated by black coats, which served to emphasize their pallor, added their creamy whiteness to the gleam of the table. The dinner began amidst little smiles exchanged between neighbours, in a half-silence broken only by the dull clatter of spoons. Baptiste carried out his role as head waiter with his usual statesmanlike air; under his orders were, in addition to the two footmen, four assistants whom he only engaged for great dinners. As he removed each course to the end of the room and carved it at a side-table, three of the servants moved noiselessly around the table, dish in hand, naming the contents in an undertone as they handed them to the guests. The others served the wine and saw to the bread and the carafes. The removes* and entrées thus slowly went round and disappeared; the ladies' pearly laughter grew no shriller.

The guests were too numerous for the conversation to become general. Nevertheless, with the second course, when the game and side-dishes had replaced the removes and entrées, and the great wines of Burgundy, Pomard, and Chambertin succeeded the Léoville and Château-Lafitte, the sound of voices increased, and bursts of laughter made the thin crystal ring. Renée, seated at the middle of the table, had on her right Baron Gouraud, and on her left Monsieur Toutin-Laroche,* a retired candle-manufacturer and now a municipal councillor, a director of the Crédit Viticole,* and a member of the committee of inspection of the Société Générale of the Ports of Morocco,* a lean, important person, whom Saccard, sitting opposite between Madame d'Espanet and Madame Haffner, addressed at one moment, in unctuous tones, as 'My dear colleague', and at another as 'Our great administrator'. Next came the politicians: Monsieur Hupel de la Noue, a provincial prefect who spent eight months of the year in Paris; three deputies, among whom Monsieur Haffner displayed his wide Alsatian face; then Monsieur de Saffré, a charming young man, secretary to one of the ministers; and Monsieur Michelin, the First Commissioner of Public Highways. Monsieur de Mareuil, a perpetual candidate for the Chamber of Deputies, sat square, facing the Prefect, at whom he constantly made sheep's eyes. As to Monsieur d'Espanet, he never accompanied his wife on social occasions. The ladies of the family were placed between the most prominent of these personages. Saccard had, however, kept his sister Sidonie, whom he had placed further off, for the seat between the two contractors, Charrier on her right, Mignon on her left, as being a position of trust in the process of conquest. Madame Michelin, the wife of the First Commissioner, a plump, pretty, dark-haired woman, sat next to Monsieur de Saffré, with whom she carried on an animated conversation in a low voice. At either side of the table were the young people, auditors to the Council of State,* sons of powerful fathers, budding millionaires, Monsieur de Mussy casting despairing glances at Renée, and Maxime, apparently quite charmed by Louise de Mareuil, who sat on his right. Little by little they had begun to laugh very loudly. It was their end of the table that produced the first outbursts of gaiety.

Meanwhile Monsieur Hupel de la Noue inquired courteously:

'Shall we have the pleasure of seeing His Excellency* this evening?'

'I fear not,' answered Saccard with an air of self-importance that concealed a secret annoyance. 'My brother is so busy. He has sent us his secretary, Monsieur de Saffré, with his apologies.'

The young secretary, who was being monopolized by Madame Michelin, looked up on hearing his name, and cried out at random, thinking that he had been spoken to:

'Yes, yes, there's a Council meeting this evening at nine o'clock in the office of the Keeper of the Seals.'

All this time Monsieur Toutin-Laroche, who had been interrupted, was holding forth, as if he were delivering a peroration amid the attentive silence of the City Council:*

'The results are superb. This City loan will be remembered as one of the finest financial operations of the age.* Yes, Messieurs!'

At this point his voice was drowned once more in the laughter that broke out suddenly at one end of the table. In the midst of this outburst of merriment could be heard Maxime's voice, as he concluded an anecdote: 'Wait, I haven't finished. The poor horsewoman was picked up by a road-labourer. They say she's giving him a brilliant education so that she can marry him later on. Only her husband, she says, shall boast of having seen a certain black mole she's got just above her knee.' The laughter increased; Louise laughed heartily, louder than the men. And amid this laughter, as though deaf, a footman interposed his pale, serious face between each guest, discreetly offering slices of wild duck.

Aristide was annoyed at the lack of attention paid to Monsieur Toutin-Laroche. He repeated, to show that he had been listening:

'The City loan...'

But Monsieur Toutin-Laroche was not a man to lose his train of thought.

'Ah! Messieurs,' he continued when the laughter had subsided, 'yesterday was a great consolation to us, since our administration is exposed to such base attacks. They accuse the Council of leading the City to destruction, and you see, no sooner does the City issue a loan than they all bring us their money, even those who complain.'

'You've worked wonders,' said Saccard. 'Paris has become the capital of the world.'

'Yes, it's quite amazing,' interjected Monsieur Hupel de la Noue. 'Just imagine! I've lived in Paris all my life, and I don't know the city any more. I got lost yesterday on my way from the Hôtel de Ville to the Luxembourg.* It's amazing, quite amazing!'

There was a pause. Everyone was listening now.

'The transformation of Paris', continued Monsieur Toutin-Laroche, 'will be the glory of the Empire. The nation is ungrateful; it ought to kiss the Emperor's feet. As I said this morning in the Council meeting, when we were discussing the success of the loan: "Gentlemen, let that rabble of an Opposition say what they like; to turn Paris upside-down is to make it productive." '*

Saccard smiled and closed his eyes, as if to savour the subtlety of the epigram. He leant behind Madame d'Espanet and said to Monsieur Hupel de la Noue, loud enough to be heard:

'He's wonderfully witty.'

During this discussion of the changes being made in Paris, Charrier had been craning his neck, as if to take part in the conversation. His partner Mignon was fully occupied with Madame Sidonie. Saccard had been watching the two contractors out of the corner of his eye since the beginning of dinner.

'The Government', he said, 'has had such strong support. Everyone has been keen to contribute to the great project. Without the help of the wealthy companies, the city would never have made such progress.'

He turned round, and with a sort of fawning brutality said:

'Messieurs Mignon and Charrier know something about that; they've done their share of the work and they will have their share of the glory.'

The bricklayers who had made their fortunes received this crude compliment with complacent smiles. Mignon, to whom Madame Sidonie was saying, in her mincing tones: 'Ah, Monsieur, you flatter me; no, pink would be too young for me...', left her in the middle of her sentence to reply to Saccard:

'You're too kind; we just did our job.'

But Charrier was not so clumsy. He drank his glass of Pomard and managed to deliver himself of a sentence:

'The changes in Paris', he said, 'have given the working man a living.'

'And we can add,' resumed Monsieur Toutin-Laroche, 'that they have given a tremendous boost to finance and industry.'

'Don't forget the artistic side: the new boulevards are quite majestic,' added Monsieur Hupel de la Noue, who prided himself on his taste.

'Yes, yes, it's all quite wonderful,' murmured Monsieur de Mareuil for the sake of saying something.

'As to the cost,' declared Haffner, the deputy who never opened his mouth except on great occasions, 'that will be for our children to bear, nothing could be fairer.'

As he said this, he looked at Monsieur de Saffré, who appeared to have given momentary offence to the pretty Madame Michelin, and the young secretary, to show that he had been following the conversation, repeated:

'Nothing could be fairer indeed.'

Each member of the group of serious-looking men at the middle of the table had had his say. Monsieur Michelin, the Chief Commissioner, smiled and wagged his head; this was his usual way of taking part in a conversation: he had smiles of greeting, of response, of approval, of thanks, of leave-taking, quite a collection of smiles, which saved him almost any need to open his mouth, an arrangement which he no doubt considered more polite and more conducive to his advancement.

One other personage had remained silent, Baron Gouraud, who was munching his food slowly like a drowsy ox. Until now he had appeared absorbed in the contemplation of his plate. Renée, who paid him every attention, received nothing in return but little grunts of satisfaction. So it was a great surprise to see him lift his head and observe, as he wiped his greasy lips:

'As a landlord, whenever I have an apartment done up and painted, I raise the rent.'

Monsieur Haffner's statement: 'The cost will be for our children to bear', had aroused the senator. All discreetly clapped their hands, and Monsieur de Saffré exclaimed:

'Ah, excellent, excellent, I must send that to the papers tomorrow.'

'You're quite right, Messieurs, we live in good times,' said Mignon, by way of summing up, in the midst of the smiles and approving remarks provoked by the Baron's epigram. 'I know quite a few who have done very well out of it. You see, everything seems fine when you're making money.'

These last words seemed to freeze the serious-looking men. The conversation stopped, and everyone tried to avoid his neighbour's eyes. The bricklayer's aphorism struck home, deadly as the paving-stone of La Fontaine's bear.* Michelin, who was beaming at Saccard, stopped smiling, anxious not to seem to have applied the contractor's words to the master of the house. The latter cast a glance at Madame Sidonie, who was tackling Mignon once more, saying: 'So you like pink, Monsieur?' At the same time, Saccard paid an elaborate compliment to Madame d'Espanet; his swarthy, foxy face almost touched her milky shoulders as she threw herself back and tittered.

They reached the dessert. The lackeys moved round the table at a quicker pace. There was a pause while the cloth was covered with the remainder of the fruit and sweets. At Maxime's end of the table the laughter increased; Louise's shrill little voice was heard saying: 'I assure you, Sylvia wore blue satin as Dindonnette';* and another childish voice added: 'Yes, but the dress was trimmed with white lace.' The room was becoming quite hot. The flushed faces seemed softened by a sense of inner contentment. Two lackeys went round the table serving Alicante and Tokay.

Renée had seemed distracted since the beginning of dinner. She fulfilled her duties as hostess with a mechanical smile. At every outburst of merriment from the end of the table where Maxime and Louise sat side by side, joking like close friends, she threw a sharp glance in their direction. She felt bored. The serious-looking men were too much for her. Madame d'Espanet and Madame Haffner kept looking at her in despair.

'What do you think of the elections?'* Saccard suddenly asked Monsieur Hupel de la Noue.

'They'll turn out very well,' answered the latter, smiling; 'but I haven't had any candidates appointed as yet from my department. It seems the minister hasn't made up his mind yet.'

Monsieur de Mareuil, who had thanked Saccard with a glance for broaching the subject, looked as if he had stepped on hot coals. He blushed and nodded in embarrassment when the Prefect turned to him and continued:

'I've heard a lot about you in the country, Monsieur. Your estates have won you many friends, and your devotion to the Emperor is well known. Your chances are excellent.'

'Papa, isn't it true that little Sylvia used to sell cigarettes in Marseilles in 1849?' cried Maxime at this moment from the end of the table.

Aristide Saccard pretended not to hear, and his son continued in a softer tone:

'My father knew her extremely well.'

This aroused suppressed laughter. Meanwhile, while Monsieur de Mareuil kept nodding, Monsieur Haffner resumed in sententious tones:

'Devotion to the Emperor is the only virtue, the only form of patriotism, in these days of self-interested democracy. He who loves the Emperor loves France. We would be truly delighted if Monsieur were to become our colleague.'

'Monsieur will succeed,' said Monsieur Toutin-Laroche in his turn. 'Everyone with a fortune should gather round the throne.'

Renée could bear it no longer. The Marquise was stifling a yawn in front of her, and as Saccard was about to resume, she said to him, with her pretty smile:

'Take pity on us, dear, and spare us your horrid politics.'

Then Monsieur Hupel de la Noue, with a Prefect's gallantry, exclaimed that the ladies were right, and he began to tell an indecent story of something that had happened in his town. The Marquise, Madame Haffner, and the other ladies laughed heartily at some of the details. The Prefect told his story in a very piquant style, with innuendoes, omissions, and vocal inflections that gave a very improper meaning to the most inoffensive expressions. Then they talked of the first of the Duchess's Tuesdays, of a burlesque play the night before, of the death of a poet, and of the end of the autumn racing season. Monsieur Toutin-Laroche, who had his amiable moments, drew a comparison between ladies and roses, and Monsieur de Mareuil, in the confusion in which he had been plunged by his electoral aspirations, delivered himself of some profound observations on the new fashion in bonnets. Renée continued to gaze blankly into space.

Meanwhile the guests had stopped eating. A hot breath seemed to have passed over the table, clouding the glasses, crumbling the bread, blackening the fruit-peel on the plates, and destroying the symmetry of the cloth. The flowers drooped in the great horn of chased silver, and the guests sat drowsily before the remains of the dessert, lacking the energy to rise from their seats. Leaning half forward, with one arm resting on the table, they had the blank look, the general air of exhaustion, that accompanies the cautious, circumspect inebriation of men and women of fashion getting tipsy by degrees. The laughter had subsided and the chatter had ceased. Much had been drunk and eaten, and the men with decorations* were more solemn than ever. In the heavy atmosphere of the room, the ladies could feel the beads of perspiration on their necks and temples. They awaited the signal to adjourn to the drawing room, serious, a little pale, as if their heads were gently swimming. Madame d'Espanet was very pink, while Madame Haffner's shoulders had assumed a waxen whiteness. Monsieur Hupel de la Noue was examining the handle of his knife; Monsieur Toutin-Laroche continued to toss disconnected sentences at Monsieur Haffner, who wagged his head in reply; Monsieur de Mareuil was dreaming, his eyes fixed on Monsieur de Michelin, who smiled at him archly. As for the pretty Madame Michelin, she had long since stopped talking; very red in the face, she kept one hand under the table, where it was doubtless held by Monsieur de Saffré, who leant forward awkwardly, with knitted eyebrows and the grimace of a man solving an algebraical problem. Madame Sidonie, too, had made her conquests: Mignon and Charrier, both leaning on their elbows with their faces turned towards her, seemed enraptured to receive her confidences; she confessed that she loved everything made with milk, and that she was frightened of ghosts. Aristide Saccard, his eyes half closed, sunk in the beatitude of a host who realizes that he has made his guests thoroughly drunk, had no thought of leaving the table; with respectful fondness he watched Baron Gouraud laboriously digesting his dinner, his right hand spread over the white cloth; it was the hand of a sensual old man, short, thick-set, and covered with purple blotches and short red hairs.

Renée mechanically finished the few drops of Tokay at the bottom of her glass. Her face tingled, her lips and nose were nervously contracted; she had the blank expression of a child who has drunk neat wine. The good bourgeois thoughts that had come to her as she sat looking at the shadows in the Parc Monceau were drowned in the stimulation of food and wine and light, and of the disturbing surroundings, impregnated with hot breath and merriment. She no longer exchanged discreet smiles with her sister Christine and her Aunt Élisabeth, both of them modest and retiring, barely uttering a word. With a stony glance she had made poor Monsieur de Mussy lower his eyes. Though her thoughts seemed elsewhere, and she carefully refrained from turning round, leaning back in her chair, against which the satin of her bodice rustled gently, her shoulders betrayed a slight tremor with each fresh burst of laughter from the corner where Maxime and Louise were still making merry, as loudly as ever, amid the dying buzz of conversation.

Behind her, half in shadow, his tall figure beetling over the disordered table and the torpid guests, stood Baptiste, pale and solemn, with the scornful attitude of a flunkey who has gorged his masters. He alone, in the alcohol-laden atmosphere, beneath the bright light of the chandelier which was turning to yellow, remained correct, with his silver neckchain, his cold eyes in which the sight of the women's shoulders kindled no spark, and his air of a eunuch waiting on Parisians of the decadence and retaining his dignity.

At last Renée rose, with a nervous movement. All followed her example. They adjourned to the drawing room, where coffee was served.

The drawing room was long and vast, a sort of gallery that ran from one pavilion to the other, taking up the whole of the façade on the garden side. A large French window opened on to the steps. This gallery glittered with gold. The ceiling, gently curved, had fanciful scrolls winding round great gilt medallions that shone like bucklers. Roses and dazzling garlands encircled the arch; fillets of gold, like threads of molten metal, ran round the walls, framing the panels, which were hung with red silk; festoons of roses, topped with tufts of full-blown blossoms, hung down along the sides of the mirrors. An Aubusson carpet spread its purple flowers over the polished floor. The furniture of red silk damask, the door-hangings and window-curtains of the same material, the huge ormolu clock on the mantelpiece, the porcelain vases standing on the consoles, the legs of the two long tables inlaid with Florentine mosaic, the very flower-stands placed in the window recesses, oozed and sweated with gold. In each corner of the room was a great lamp placed on a pedestal of red marble, and fastened to it by chains of bronze gilt that fell with symmetrical grace. From the ceiling hung three chandeliers with crystal pendants, streaming with drops of blue and pink light, whose hot glare made all the gold in the room shine even more brightly.

The men soon withdrew to the smoking room. Monsieur de Mussy went up to Maxime and took him familiarly by the arm; he had known him at school, though he was six years his senior. He led him out to the terrace, and after they had lighted their cigars he began to complain bitterly about Renée.

'Can you tell me what's the matter with her? I saw her yesterday and she was charming, but today she's behaving as if it was all over between us. What have I done? It would be really nice of you, my dear Maxime, if you would ask her, and tell her how much I'm suffering because of her.'

'Oh, I couldn't do that!' replied Maxime, laughing. 'Renée's nerves are very bad, and I'm not prepared to create a storm, Monsieur. You'll have to settle your differences yourselves.'

And he added, after puffing slowly on his Havana:

'You want me to do you a favour, don't you?'

Monsieur de Mussy spoke of the sincerity of his friendship, and declared that he was only waiting for an opportunity to give Maxime proof of his devotion. He was very unhappy, he was so deeply in love with Renée!

'Very well then, I will,' said Maxime at last. 'I'll speak to her, but I can't promise anything, you know: she's bound to tell me to get lost.'

They went back to the smoking room and stretched out in two great lounging-chairs. There, for at least half an hour, Monsieur de Mussy related his sorrows to Maxime; he told him for the tenth time how he had fallen in love with his stepmother, how she had condescended to notice him; and Maxime, while finishing his cigar, offered him advice, explaining Renée's personality to him and suggesting how he should behave in order to win her heart.

Saccard came and sat down within a few paces of the young men. Monsieur de Mussy remained silent, while Maxime concluded by saying:

'If I were you, I'd be very direct with her. She likes that.'

The smoking room was at the end of the long gallery, one of the round rooms formed by the turrets. It was fitted up very richly and soberly. Hung with imitation Cordovan leather, it had Algerian curtains and door-hangings, and a velvet-pile Persian carpet. The furniture, upholstered in maroon-coloured shagreen leather, consisted of ottomans, easy chairs, and a circular divan that ran round part of the room. The miniature chandelier, the ornaments on the table, and the fire irons were of pale-green Florentine bronze.

A few of the younger men remained behind with the ladies, together with some older men with pale, flabby faces, who loathed tobacco. The smoking room was filled with noise and laughter. Monsieur Hupel de la Noue amused his fellow guests by repeating the story he had told at dinner, embellished with bawdy details. This was his speciality: he had two versions of every anecdote, one for the ladies and the other for the men. When Aristide came in he was surrounded and complimented; and as he pretended not to understand, Monsieur de Saffré told him, with a warmly applauded phrase, that he had served his country well by preventing the fair Laure d'Aurigny from falling into the hands of the English.

'No, really, Messieurs, you're mistaken,' stammered Saccard, with false modesty.

'Go on, there's no need to apologize,' cried Maxime humorously. 'It was a splendid thing to do at your age.'

The young man, who had just thrown away his cigar, went back to the drawing room. A great many people had arrived. The gallery was full of dress-coats, standing up and talking in low tones, and of petticoats spread out wide along the settees. Flunkeys had begun to move about with silver salvers loaded with ices and glasses of punch.

Maxime, who wanted to speak to Renée, walked the full length of the drawing room, knowing from experience the ladies' favourite sanctum. At the opposite end to the smoking room, to which it formed a pendant, there was another circular chamber, which had been made into an adorable little drawing room. With its hangings, curtains, and *portières* of buttercup satin, it had a strangely voluptuous charm. The lights of the chandelier, a piece of very delicate workmanship, sang a symphony in pale yellow, amid the sun-coloured silks. The effect resembled a flood of softened rays, as of the sun setting over a field of ripe wheat. The light expired upon the floor on an Aubusson carpet strewn with dead leaves. An ebony piano inlaid with ivory, two cabinets whose glass doors displayed a host of knick-knacks, a Louis XVI table, and a flower bracket heaped high with blossoms furnished the room. The settees, the easy chairs, and the ottomans were covered in quilted buttercup satin, divided at intervals by wide black-satin bands embroidered with gaudy tulips.

There were also two low seats, some occasional chairs, and every variety of stool, elegant and bizarre. The woodwork of the furniture could not be seen: the satin and the quilting covered everything. The curved backs had the soft fullness of bolsters. They were like beds in whose down one could sleep and make love amid the sensual symphony in pale yellow.

Renée loved this little room, one of whose glass doors opened into the magnificent hothouse at the side of the house. It was here, in the daytime, that she spent her leisure hours. The yellow hangings, far from extinguishing her fair hair, gave it a strange golden radiance; her head stood out pink and white amid the glimmer of dawn like that of a blonde Diana* awakening in the morning light; and it was doubtless because it threw her beauty into such relief that she loved this room so much.

Now she was there with her closest friends. Her sister and aunt had just taken their leave. Only the empty-headed remained in the sanctum. Half thrown back on a settee, Renée was listening to the confidences of her friend Adeline, who was whispering in her ear with kittenish airs and sudden bursts of laughter. Suzanne Haffner was greatly sought after; she was holding her own against a group of young men who stood very close to her, displaying her Germanic languour, her provocative effrontery, cold and bare like her shoulders. In a corner Madame Sidonie was quietly instilling her precepts into the mind of a young married woman with Madonna-like lashes. Further off stood Louise, talking to a tall, shy young man, who was blushing; while Baron Gouraud dozed in his easy chair in the full light, spreading out his flabby flesh, his pale, elephantine form in the midst of the ladies' frail grace and silken daintiness. A fairy-like light fell in a golden shower over the room, on the satin skirts with folds as hard and gleaming as porcelain, on the ladies' shoulders, whose milky whiteness was spangled with diamonds. A fluty voice, a laugh like a pigeon's cooing, rang out with crystal clarity. It was very warm. Fans beat slowly like birds' wings, their regular movements spreading with each stroke into the languid air the musked perfume of the bodices.

When Maxime appeared in the doorway, Renée, who was listening distractedly to the Marquise's stories, rose hastily as if to attend to her duties as a hostess. She went into the large drawing room, where the young man followed her. She took a few steps, smiling, shaking hands with people, and then, drawing Maxime aside, whispered ironically:

'Well! The burden seems a pleasant one; you obviously don't find it too much of a bother to do your own wooing.'

'I don't understand,' replied Maxime, who had come to plead on behalf of Monsieur de Mussy.

'But it seems to me that I did well not to save you from Louise. You're not losing any time, you two.'

And she added, with a note of reproach:

'It was indecent to go on like that at dinner.'

Maxime began to laugh.

'Ah yes, we were telling each other stories. I didn't know the little minx. She's rather amusing. She's like a boy.'

As Renée continued to wear an expression of prudish annoyance, the young man, who had never known her to show such indignation, resumed with his tone of urbane familiarity:

'Do you imagine, stepmamma, that I pinched her knees under the table? Damn it, I know how to behave with my future wife!... I want to talk about something serious... Listen... Are you listening?'

He lowered his voice still more.

'It's that... Monsieur de Mussy is very unhappy. He just told me so. You know, it's not for me to bring you together, if you've had an argument. But, you see, I knew him at school, and as he really seemed in despair I promised to put in a word for him.'

He stopped. Renée was looking at him very strangely.

'You won't answer?' he continued. 'No matter, I've delivered my message, and you can sort things out as you please. But I do think you're being rather cruel. I felt sorry for the poor fellow. If I were you, I would at least send him a kind word.'

Then Renée, who had kept her glittering eyes fixed firmly on Maxime, said:

'Tell Monsieur de Mussy that I find him very boring!'

She resumed her slow walk among the guests, smiling and shaking hands with people. Maxime stood where he was, looking surprised; then he laughed silently to himself.

Since he was not eager to deliver his message to Monsieur de Mussy, he strolled round the large drawing room. The reception was drawing to a close, marvellous and commonplace, like all receptions. It was almost midnight; the guests were leaving one by one. Not

wishing to go home to bed on an unpleasant note, Maxime decided
to look for Louise. He was walking past the entrance-door when he
saw, standing in the hall, the pretty Madame Michelin, whom her
husband was wrapping up gently in a blue-and-pink cloak.

'He was charming, quite charming,' she was saying. 'We talked
about you all through dinner. He'll speak to the minister, though it's
not up to him.'

A footman, next to them, was helping Baron Gouraud on with a
great fur coat. 'That's the old boy who could see the thing through!'
she added in her husband's ear, as he tied the ribbon of her hood
under her chin. 'He can do anything he likes with the minister.
Tomorrow, at the de Mareuils', I must see what...'

Monsieur Michelin smiled. He carried his wife off carefully, as if
he had something valuable and fragile under his arm. Maxime,
after glancing round to make sure that Louise was not in the hall,
went straight to the small drawing room. She was still there,
though not quite alone, waiting for her father, who had spent the
evening in the smoking room with the politicians. The ladies, the
Marquise, and Madame Haffner had left. Only Madame Sidonie
remained, explaining to some officials' wives how fond she was of
animals.

'Ah! Here's my husband,' cried Louise. 'Sit here and tell me
where my father has fallen asleep. He must have dreamt that he was
in the Chamber.'

Maxime replied in similar vein, and the two young people began
laughing loudly again as at dinner. Sitting on a very low stool at her
feet, he ended by taking her hands and playing with her as with a
schoolfriend. In fact, in her frock of white foulard with red dots,
with her high-cut bodice, her flat chest, and her ugly, cunning little
urchin's face, she might have passed for a boy dressed as a girl. Yet
at times her puny arms, her distorted form, would assume a pose
of abandonment, and her eyes, still quite innocent, would sparkle;
but not the slightest blush was brought to her cheek by Maxime's
playfulness. They laughed again, thinking themselves alone, not seeing Renée, who stood half hidden in the middle of the hothouse,
watching them from a distance.

A moment before, as she was crossing a little pathway, the sight of
Maxime and Louise had suddenly made Renée stop behind a shrub.
Around her the hothouse, like the nave of a church with a domed

glass roof supported by slender iron columns, displayed its rich vegetation, its mass of lush greenery, its spreading rockets of foliage.

In the middle, in an oval tank level with the ground, lived, with the mysterious sea-green life of water-plants, all the aquatic flora of the tropics. Cyclanthus plants, with their streaks of variegated green, formed a monumental girdle round the fountain, which looked like the truncated capital of some cyclopean column. At each end two tall tornelias reared their strange brushwood above the water, their dry, bare stems contorted like agonized serpents, and let fall roots that seemed like a fisherman's nets hung up in the air. Near the edge a Javanese pandanus spread its cluster of green leaves streaked with white, thin as swords, prickly and fretted as Malay krises. On the surface, in the warmth of the tepid sheet of slumbering water, great water-lilies opened out their pink petals, and euryales trailed their round, leprous leaves, floating on the surface like the backs of monstrous, blistered toads.

By way of turf, a broad edging of sclaginella encircled the tank. This dwarf fern formed a thick mossy carpet of light green. Beyond the great circular path, four enormous clusters of plants shot up to the roof: palms, drooping gently in their elegance, spreading their fans, displayed their rounded crowns, hung down their leaves like oars wearied by their perpetual voyage through the blue; tall Indian bamboos rose upwards, hard, slender, dropping from on high their light shower of leaves; a ravenala, the traveller's tree, erected its foliage like enormous Chinese screens; and in a corner a banana tree, loaded with fruit, stretched out on all sides its long horizontal leaves, on which two lovers might easily recline in each other's arms. In the corners were Abyssinian euphorbias, deformed prickly cactuses covered with hideous excrescences, oozing with poison. Beneath the trees the ground was carpeted with creeping ferns, adianta and pterides, their fronds outlined daintily like fine lace. Alsophilas of a taller species tapered upwards with their rows of symmetrical branches, hexagonal, so regular that they looked like large pieces of porcelain made specially for the fruit of some gigantic dessert. The shrubs were surrounded by a border of begonias and caladiums: begonias with twisted leaves, gorgeously streaked with red and green; caladiums whose spear-headed leaves, white with green veins, looked like large butterfly wings; bizarre plants whose foliage lives strangely, with the sombre or wan splendour of poisonous flowers.

Behind the shrubbery, a second, narrower pathway ran round the hothouse. There, on little terraces, half concealing the hot-water pipes, bloomed marantas, soft as velvet to the touch, gloxinias, purple-belled, and dracoenas that looked like blades of old lacquer.

But one of the charms of this winter garden was the four alcoves of greenery at each corner, spacious arbours enclosed by thick curtains of creepers. Patches of virgin forest had here erected their leafy walls, their impenetrable mass of stems, of supple shoots that clung to the branches, shot through space in reckless flight, and fell from the domed roof like tassels of ornate drapery. A stalk of vanilla, whose ripe pods gave off a pungent perfume, trailed round a moss-grown portico; Indian berries draped the thin pillars with their round leaves; bauhinias with their red clusters, quisqualias with flowers pendant like bead necklaces glided, twined, and intertwined like adders, endlessly playing and slithering amid the darkness of the undergrowth.

Under arches placed here and there between the shrubs hung baskets suspended from wire chains, and filled with orchids, fantastic plants of the air, which pushed in every direction their crooked tendrils, bent and twisted like the limbs of cripples. There were cypripediums, whose flowers resemble a wonderful slipper with a heel adorned with a dragonfly's wings; aerides, so delicately scented; stanhopeas, with pale tiger flowers, which exhale from afar a strong and acrid breath, as from the putrid mouths of convalescent invalids.

But what most struck the eye from every point of the pathways was a great Chinese hibiscus, whose immense expanse of foliage and flowers covered the whole wall on which the hothouse was built. The huge purple flowers of this giant mallow live for just a few hours. They resembled, it might have been imagined, the eager, sensual mouths of women, the red lips, soft and moist, of some colossal Messalina,* bruised by kisses, and constantly renewed, with their hungry, bleeding smiles.

Renée, standing by the tank, shivered in the midst of this lush magnificence. Behind her, a great sphinx in black marble, crouched on a block of granite, turned its head towards the fountain with a cat's cruel and wary smile; and with its polished haunches it looked like the dark idol of this tropical setting. From globes of ground glass came a light that covered the leaves with milky stains. Statues, women's heads with bare necks, swelling with laughter, stood out

white against the shrubbery, patches of shadow distorting the mad
gaiety on their faces. Strange rays of light played on the dull, still
water of the tank, throwing up vague shapes, glaucous masses
with monstrous outlines. A flood of white light streamed over the
ravenela's glossy leaves and over the lacquered fans of the latanias,
while from the lacework of the ferns drops of light fell in a fine
shower. Above shone the reflections from the glass roof, between the
sombre tops of the tall palm trees. All around was massed in darkness; the arbours, with their curtains of creepers, were covered in
shadow, like the lairs of sleeping serpents.

Renée stood musing beneath the bright light, watching Louise
and Maxime in the distance. She no longer felt the fleeting fancies,
the twilight temptations of the chilly avenues of the Bois. Her
thoughts were no longer lulled to sleep by the trot of her horses
along the fashionable turf, among the glades in which bourgeois
families take their lunch on their Sunday excursions. This time she
was filled with a keen, specific desire.

Endless love and voluptuous appetite pervaded this stifling nave
in which seethed the ardent sap of the tropics. Renée was wrapped in
the powerful bridals of the earth that gave birth to these dark
growths, these colossal stamina; and the acrid birth-throes of this
hotbed, of this forest growth, of this mass of vegetation aglow with
the entrails that nourished it, surrounded her with disturbing
odours. At her feet was the steaming tank, its tepid water thickened
by the sap from the floating roots, enveloping her shoulders with a
mantle of heavy vapours, forming a mist that warmed her skin like
the touch of a hand moist with desire. Overhead she could smell the
palm trees, whose tall leaves shook down their aroma. And more than
the stifling heat, more than the brilliant light, more than the great
dazzling flowers, like faces laughing or grimacing between the leaves,
it was the odours that overwhelmed her. An indescribable perfume,
potent, exciting, composed of a thousand different perfumes, hung
about her; human exudation, the breath of women, the scent of hair;
and breezes sweet and swooningly faint were blended with breezes
coarse and pestilential, laden with poison. But amid this strange
music of odours, the dominant melody that constantly returned,
stifling the sweetness of the vanilla and the orchids' pungency, was
the penetrating, sensual smell of flesh, the smell of lovemaking
escaping in the early morning from the bedroom of newlyweds.

Renée sank back slowly, leaning against the granite pedestal. In her green satin dress, her head and breast covered with the liquid glitter of her diamonds, she was like a great flower, green and pink, one of the water-lilies in the tank, swooning from the heat. In this moment of insight all her new resolutions vanished, the intoxication of dinner returned, imperious, triumphant, strengthened by the flames of the hothouse. She thought no longer of the soothing freshness of the night, of the murmuring shadows of the gardens, whose voices had whispered to her of the bliss of serenity. In her were aroused the senses of a woman who desires, the caprices of a woman who is satiated. Above her head, the black marble sphinx laughed its mysterious laugh, as if it had read the longing, formulated at last, that had stirred her dead heart, the elusive longing, the 'something different' she had vainly sought in the rocking of her barouche, in the fine ash of twilight, and now suddenly revealed to her beneath the dazzling light of this blazing garden by the sight of Maxime and Louise, laughing and playing, their hands interlocked.

The sound of voices suddenly came from an adjacent arbour into which Aristide Saccard had led Mignon and Charrier.

'No, Monsieur Saccard,' said the latter's coarse voice, 'we really can't take it back for more than two hundred francs a metre.'

Saccard's shrill tones retorted:

'But in my share you valued each metre of frontage at two hundred and fifty francs.'

'Well, listen, we'll make it two hundred and twenty-five francs.'

The voices continued, sounding coarse and strange under the clumps of drooping palm trees. But they passed like an empty noise through Renée's dream, as there rose before her, with the fatal lure experienced by someone looking over a precipice, an unknown pleasure, hot with crime, more violent than all those she had already tasted, the last that remained in her cup. She felt weary no longer.

The shrub that half concealed her was a malignant plant, a Madagascan tanghin tree with wide, box-like leaves with whitish stems, whose smallest veins distilled a venomous fluid. At a moment when Louise and Maxime laughed more loudly in the reflected yellow light of the sunset in the little boudoir, Renée, her mind wandering, her mouth dry and parched, took between her lips a sprig of the tanghin tree that was level with her mouth, and sank her teeth into one of its bitter leaves.

CHAPTER II

ARISTIDE ROUGON swooped down on Paris the day after 2 December,* like a bird of prey scenting the field of battle from afar. He came from Plassans,* a sub-prefecture in the south of France, where his father, in the recent political upheaval, had at last secured a long-coveted appointment as receiver of taxes. He himself, still young, had compromised himself like a fool, gaining neither fame nor fortune, and considered himself fortunate to have emerged safe and sound from the fray.* He came in a great hurry, furious at having taken a wrong turn, cursing the provinces, talking of Paris with the ravenous hunger of a wolf, swearing 'that he would never be such a fool again'; and his bitter smile as he said these words assumed a terrible significance on his thin lips.

He arrived in the early days of 1852. He brought with him his wife Angèle, an insipid, fair-haired person, whom he installed in cramped lodgings in the Rue Saint-Jacques* like an inconvenient piece of furniture of which he was eager to rid himself. His young wife had refused to be separated from her daughter, little Clotilde, a child of four, whom Aristide would gladly have left behind in the care of his family. But he had only agreed to Angèle's wish on condition that the school in Plassans should continue to provide a roof for their son Maxime, a mischievous boy of eleven whose grandmother had promised to look after him. Aristide wanted to have his hands free: a wife and child already seemed to him a huge burden for a man determined to overcome every obstacle, not caring whether he fell flat on his face or broke his back in his attempt to succeed.

On the very evening of his arrival, while Angèle was unpacking the trunks, he felt a keen desire to explore Paris, to tread with his clodhopping country shoes the burning stones from which he hoped to extract millions. He took possession of the city. He walked for the sake of walking, marching along the pavements as if he were in some conquered country. He saw very clearly the battle that lay ahead, and was happy to compare himself to a skilful picklock who, by cunning or violence, was about to seize his share of the common wealth which so far had been cruelly denied him. Had he felt the need for an excuse, he would have invoked his desires, which for the last ten years had been stifled, his miserable provincial existence, and above all his mistakes, for which he held society at large responsible. But at this moment, filled with the excitement of the gambler who at last places his hands on the green baize, he felt only joy, a special joy in which were mingled anticipation of satisfied greed and unpunished roguery. The Paris air intoxicated him; he thought he could hear in the rumbling of the carriages the voices from *Macbeth* calling to him: 'Thou shalt be rich!' For nearly two hours he walked the streets, tasting the delights of a man who freely indulges his vices. He had not been in Paris since the happy year he had spent there as a student. Night was falling: the bright light thrown on the pavements by the shops and cafés intensified his dreams. He no longer knew where he was.

When he looked up he found he was in the Faubourg Saint-Honoré, near the middle. One of his brothers, Eugène Rougon, lived in an adjacent street, the Rue Penthièvre. When deciding to come to Paris, Aristide had reckoned particularly on Eugène who, having been one of the main participants in the coup d'état, was now a highly influential figure, a lawyer of little account about to become a politician of great importance. But with a gambler's superstition, Aristide decided not to knock at his brother's door that evening. He returned slowly to the Rue Saint-Jacques, thinking of Eugène with a dull feeling of jealousy, contemplating his shabby clothes still covered with the dust of the journey, and seeking consolation in his dream of wealth. But even this dream had turned to bitterness. Having set out in an expansive mood, exhilarated by the bustle of the Paris shops, he returned home irritated by the happiness that seemed to fill the streets, his avidity intensified, picturing to himself violent struggles in which he would take delight in beating and cheating the crowd that had jostled him on the pavement. Never had his appetite for success and pleasure been so keen.

At daybreak the next morning he was at his brother's. Eugène lived in two large, cold, barely furnished rooms that chilled Aristide to the bone. He had expected to find his brother wallowing in the lap of luxury. Eugène was working at a small black table. All he said, with a smile, in his slow voice, was:

'Ah! there you are, I was expecting you.'

Aristide was very bitter. He accused Eugène of leaving him to vegetate, of not even having the kindness to give him a word of good advice while he was floundering about in the country. He could never forgive himself for remaining a Republican until 2 December; it was an open sore with him, a source of endless embarrassment. Eugène had quietly taken up his pen. When his brother had finished, he said:

'Bah! All mistakes can be put right. You've got a promising career ahead of you.'

He uttered these words so emphatically, and with such a piercing look, that Aristide bowed his head, feeling that his brother could read his mind. The latter continued with affable bluntness:

'You've come to ask me to find you a position, haven't you? I've been thinking of you, but I haven't heard of anything yet. You know I must be careful where I put you. What you want is a position in which you can feather your nest without any risk of danger to either of us. Don't bother to argue, we're quite alone, we can say what we like...' Aristide thought it best to laugh.

'Oh, I know how clever you are,' Eugène continued, 'and that you're not likely to make a fool of yourself very easily. As soon as there's a good opportunity, I'll give you a position. In the meantime, whenever you want twenty francs or so, come and ask me.'

They talked for a while about the uprising in the south,* which had given their father his appointment as receiver of taxes. Eugène dressed while they were talking. As he was about to take leave of his brother downstairs in the street, he detained him a moment longer, and said to him softly:

'Do me the favour of not looking for work on your own account; just wait at home quietly for the appointment I promise you. I wouldn't like to see my brother hanging about in people's waiting rooms.'

Aristide had a certain respect for Eugène, whom he regarded as someone quite exceptional. He could not forgive his lack of trust, or his bluntness, which was a trifle excessive; but he went home obediently and shut himself away in the Rue Saint-Jacques. He had arrived with five hundred francs, which had been lent by his wife's father. After paying for the journey, he made the three hundred francs that remained last him a month. Angèle was a great eater; moreover she thought it necessary to trim her Sunday dress with a fresh set of mauve ribbons. That month of waiting seemed endless to Aristide. He was consumed with impatience. When he sat at the window and watched the teeming life of Paris beneath him, he was seized by an insane desire to hurl himself into the furnace in order to mould the gold like soft wax with his fevered hands. He inhaled the breath, vague as yet, that rose from the great city, the breath of the budding Empire, laden already with the odours of alcoves and financial deals, with the warm smell of sensuality. The faint traces that reached him told him that he was on the right scent, that the prey was scudding before him, that the great Imperial hunt, the hunt for adventure, women, and fortunes, was about to begin. His nostrils quivered, his instinct, the instinct of a starving animal, seized unerringly on the slightest indications of the division of the spoil of which the city was to be the arena.

Twice he called on his brother to urge him to greater effort on his behalf. Eugène received him gruffly, told him that he was not forgetting him, that he must be patient. At last he received a letter asking him to call at the Rue Penthièvre. He went, his heart pounding, as if he were on his way to an assignation. He found Eugène sitting, as ever, at his little black table in the big chilly room he used as a study. As soon as he saw him the lawyer handed him a document and said:

'Here, I got this yesterday. This is your appointment as assistant surveying-clerk at the Hôtel de Ville. Your salary will be two thousand four hundred francs.'

Aristide had remained standing. He turned pale and did not take the document, thinking that his brother was making fun of him. He had expected a salary of at least six thousand francs. Eugène, guessing what was going through his mind, turned his chair round and, folding his arms, exclaimed angrily:

'So you're a fool then, are you? You just dream like a girl. You want to live in a grand apartment, keep servants, eat well, sleep in silk sheets, and take your pleasure in the arms of the first woman who comes along in a boudoir furnished in two hours. You and your sort, if we let you, would empty the coffers before they're even full. Why on earth can't you be patient? Look how I live; if you want to pick up a fortune you might at least take the trouble to bend down.'

He spoke with profound contempt for his brother's schoolboy impatience. One could feel through his harsh words a higher ambition, a desire for limitless power; Aristide's craving for money must have seemed vulgar and puerile to him. He continued in a softer tone, with a subtle smile:

'I'm sure you have the best intentions, and I have no wish to hold you back. Men like you are valuable to us. We intend to choose our friends from among the hungriest. Don't worry, we'll keep open table, and the biggest appetites will be satisfied. After all, it's the easiest way to govern. But for heaven's sake wait until the table is laid; and if you take my advice, you'll go to the kitchen yourself and fetch your own knife and fork.'

Aristide still said nothing. His brother's colourful language failed to raise his spirits. Eugène again gave vent to his anger.

'Ah!' he exclaimed. 'I was right to begin with: you're a fool... What did you expect? What did you imagine I was going to do with you? You haven't even finished your law studies; you bury yourself for ten years in a miserable clerkship in a sub-prefecture; and you turn up on my doorstep with the odious reputation of a Republican only converted by the coup d'état. Do you think you could become a minister with a record like that? I know you're determined to suc-ceed at any cost. That's a great quality, I admit, and it's what I had in mind when I got you this position at the Hôtel de Ville.'

He stood up, thrust the nomination into Aristide's hands, and continued:

'Take it, and one day you'll thank me! I chose the position myself, and I know what you'll be able to get out of it. All you have to do is keep your ears open. If you keep your wits about you, you'll under-stand and act accordingly. Remember this: we're entering a period when anyone who wants to will be able to get rich. Make as much money as you like: you have my permission; but if you do anything stupid or create a scandal, I'll destroy you.'

This threat produced the effect that his promises had been unable to bring about. Aristide's enthusiasm was rekindled at the thought of the riches of which his brother spoke. He felt that he was at last being unleashed into the fray, authorized to cut throats, provided that he did so legally and without causing too much trouble. Eugène gave him two hundred francs to keep him going until the end of the month. Then he fell into a pensive mood:

'I'm thinking of changing my name,' he said at last. 'You should do the same. It would help us not to get in each other's way.'

'As you like,' murmured Aristide.

'There's nothing you need to do, I'll take care of the formalities. Would you like to call yourself Sicardot, your wife's name?'

Aristide raised his eyes to the ceiling and repeated the name, listening to the sound of the syllables:

'Sicardot... Aristide Sicardot... No, I wouldn't; it's clumsy and stinks of failure.'

'Think of something else then,' said Eugène.

'I'd prefer Sicard simply,' resumed Aristide after a pause. 'Aristide Sicard... that's not bad, is it? A bit frivolous, perhaps.'

He thought a moment longer and then cried triumphantly:

'I've got it... Saccard, Aristide Saccard... with two c's... Eh! there's money in that name; it sounds as if you're counting five-franc pieces.'

Eugène had a crude sense of humour. He dismissed his brother, remarking with a smile:

'Yes, it's a name that will make you either a crook or a millionaire.'

A few days later Aristide Saccard was installed at the Hôtel de Ville. It became clear that his brother had used all his influence to get him admitted without the usual examinations.

The household now settled into the monotonous life of a minor clerk. Aristide and his wife resumed their Plassans habits. Their dream of immediate wealth had evaporated, and their poverty-stricken existence seemed all the more oppressive to them because they had come to regard it as a probationary period of indeterminate length. To be poor in Paris is to be doubly poor. Angèle accepted penury with dull passivity; she spent her days in the kitchen, or lying on the floor playing with her daughter, never complaining until their money ran out. But Aristide quivered with rage at this state of poverty, at this pinched existence, in which he paced about like a caged animal. For him it was a period of unspeakable suffering; his pride was cut to the quick, his unsatisfied cravings drove him mad. His brother succeeded in getting elected to the Corps Législatif* by the *arrondissement* of Plassans, and he suffered all the more. He was too conscious of Eugène's superiority to be jealous: he accused him of not doing as much as he might have done for him. Several times he was driven by necessity to call on him to borrow money. Eugène lent him the money, but reproached him for his lack of spirit and determination. After that Aristide strengthened his resolve. He swore he would never ask anybody for a sou, and he kept his word. The last week of each month Angèle ate dry bread and sighed. This apprenticeship completed Saccard's gruesome education. His lips became even thinner; he was no longer fool enough to dream of millions aloud; his wiry body became almost emaciated, and expressed but one desire. When he trotted from the Rue Saint-Jacques to the Hôtel de Ville, his worn heels resounded on the pavement, and he buttoned himself up in his threadbare overcoat as in an asylum of hatred, while his weasel-like nose sniffed the air of the streets: an angular symbol of envy and poverty prowling the streets of Paris, dreaming of wealth and pleasure.

Early in 1853 Aristide was appointed a surveying-clerk. His salary was to be four thousand five hundred francs. This increase came just in time: Angèle's health was failing, little Clotilde had lost all her colour. He kept his poky lodgings of two small rooms, the dining room furnished in walnut and the bedroom in mahogany, and continued to lead a harsh existence, avoiding debt, not wishing to touch other people's money until he could plunge his arms into it up to his elbows. He thus denied his instincts, scorning the few extra sous he received, remaining on the lookout. Angèle was perfectly happy. She bought herself some new clothes and ate meat every day. She could no longer understand her husband's suppressed anger, nor the reason why he wore the sombre expression of a man trying to solve some huge problem.

Aristide followed Eugène's advice: he kept his ears and eyes open. When he went to thank his brother for his promotion, the latter noticed how he had changed; he complimented him on what he called his good manners. The clerk, hardened by jealousy, had acquired a supple, insinuating style. Within a few months he had transformed himself into an accomplished actor. All his southern ardour had been aroused; and he had become so adept at deception that his fellow clerks at the Hôtel de Ville regarded him as a good sort whose family connection with a deputy marked him out for some plum appointment. This connection also earned him the goodwill of his superiors. He thus enjoyed a sort of authority above his station, which enabled him to open certain doors and examine certain files without any suspicion being attached to his indiscretion. For two years he was seen wandering round the corridors, lingering in all the rooms, leaving his desk twenty times a day to go and talk to a friend, or deliver a message, or take a stroll through the offices— endless little trips that made his colleagues exclaim: 'That wretched Provençal! He can't sit still: he's got ants in his pants.' His friends

took him for an idler, and he laughed when they accused him of
having but one thought, to cheat their bosses of a few minutes. He
never made the mistake of listening at keyholes; but he had a way of
boldly opening a door and walking through a room, with a document
in his hand and a preoccupied air, and with a step so slow and
measured that he did not miss a word of the conversation. It was a
masterpiece of tactics; people stopped bothering to fall silent when
this conscientious clerk passed by, gliding through the shadows of
the offices and seeming so wrapped up in his work. He had one other
method: he was extraordinarily obliging, he offered to help his fellow
clerks whenever they fell behind with their work, and he would then
study with great care and attention the account books and documents that passed through his hands. But one of his favourite tricks
was to strike up friendships with the messengers. He went so far as to
shake hands with them. For hours at a stretch he would keep them
talking with stifled little bursts of laughter, telling them stories,
inducing them to take him into their confidence. They worshipped
him, and said of him: 'There's a man who doesn't take himself too
seriously.' He was the first to be told of any scandal. So it came about
that after two years the Hôtel de Ville was an open book to him. He
knew every member of the staff down to the most junior lamplighter,
and every official document down to the laundress's bills.

Paris at that time was a fascinating spectacle for a man like
Aristide Saccard. The Empire had just been proclaimed, after the
famous journey* in the course of which the Prince-President had
succeeded in stirring up the enthusiasm of a few Bonapartist
departments. The Chamber and the press were silent.* Society, saved
once again, congratulated itself and relaxed now that it had a strong
government to protect it and relieve it of the trouble of thinking for
itself and looking after its own affairs. The main preoccupation of
society was to know how to enjoy itself. In Eugène Rougon's happy
phrase, Paris had sat down to dinner and was wondering how to take
its pleasure after dessert. Politics terrified it, like a dangerous drug.
Men's enervated minds turned towards dissipation and speculation.
Those who had money brought it forth from its hiding-place, and
those who had none looked for forgotten treasures in every nook and
cranny. And underneath the turmoil there was a subdued quiver, a
nascent sound of five-franc pieces, of women's rippling laughter, and
the still faint clatter of plates and the sound of kisses. In the midst of

the great silence, the absolute peace of the new reign of order, there arose every kind of salacious rumour, every kind of golden and voluptuous promise. It was as if one were passing by one of those little houses whose closely drawn curtains reveal only women's shadows, and from which no sound issues but that of gold coins on the marble mantelpieces. The Empire was on the point of turning Paris into the bawdy house of Europe. The gang of fortune-seekers who had succeeded in stealing a throne required a reign of adventures, shady transactions, sold consciences, bought women, and rampant drunkenness. In the city where the blood of December* had hardly been washed away, there sprang up, timidly as yet, the mad desire for dissipation that was destined to drag the country down to the level of the most decadent and dishonoured of nations.

From the beginning Aristide Saccard could sense the rising tide of speculation, which was soon to engulf the whole of Paris. He watched its progress intently. He found himself in the midst of the hot rain of crown-pieces that fell thickly on the city's roofs. In his endless wanderings through the corridors of the Hôtel de Ville, he had got wind of the vast project for the transformation of Paris, the plan for the demolitions, the new boulevards and neighbourhoods, the huge piece of jobbery in the sale of land and property, which throughout the city was beginning to ignite the conflict of interests and the blaze of unrestrained luxury. Now his activity had a purpose. It was during this period that he developed his geniality. He even put on a little weight and stopped hurrying through the streets like a scrawny cat looking for food. At his office he was more chatty and obliging than ever. His brother, whom he visited in a more or less official manner, complimented him on putting his advice so happily into practice. Early in 1854 Saccard confided to him that he had several pieces of business in view, but that he would require a rather large advance.

'Look for it,' said Eugène.

'You're quite right, I'll look for it,' he replied good-humouredly, appearing not to notice that his brother had just refused to provide him with the initial capital.

The thought of this capital now obsessed him. His plan was formed; it matured day by day. But the first few thousand francs were not to be found. He became more and more tense; he looked at passers-by in a nervous, searching manner as if he were seeking a lender in every wayfarer. At home Angèle continued to lead her modest and contented existence. He waited for his opportunity; and his genial laughter became more bitter as this opportunity failed to present itself.

Aristide had a sister in Paris. Sidonie Rougon had married a solicitor's clerk in Plassans, and together they had set up business in the Rue Saint-Honoré as dealers in fruit from the south of France. When her brother came across her, the husband had vanished and the business had long since disappeared. She was living in the Rue du Faubourg-Poissonnière, in a little entresol consisting of three rooms. She also leased the shop on the floor beneath her apartment, a cramped and mysterious establishment in which she pretended to carry on a business in lace. In the window there were some odds and ends of point lace and Valenciennes, hung over gilt rods; but the inside looked like a waiting room, with polished wood panelling and not the least sign of goods for sale. The door and window were hung with light curtains, which protected the shop from the gaze of passers-by and heightened its discreet appearance, as of the atrium to some unknown temple. It was a rare thing for a customer to be seen calling on Madame Sidonie; usually, in fact, the handle was removed from the door. She made it known in the neighbourhood that she waited personally upon wealthy women with her lace. The convenience of the place, she used to say, was her sole reason for leasing the shop and the entresol, which were connected by a stair-case hidden in the wall. In fact the lace-dealer was never at home; she was seen hurrying in and out at least ten times a day. Moreover, she did not confine herself to the lace trade; she used her entresol to store various things picked up nobody knew where. She had water-proofs, galoshes, braces, and so on; and then, one after the other, a new oil for restoring hair, orthopaedic appliances, and a patented automatic coffee-pot, the working of which had cost her a great deal of trouble. When her brother called to see her she was selling pianos; her entresol was crammed with these instruments; there were pianos even in her bedroom, a coquettishly furnished room that clashed with the saleroom disorder of the other two. She conducted these two businesses with perfect method: the customers who came for the goods on the entresol entered and left through a carriage-entrance that led into the house from the Rue Papillon; you had to know the secret of the little staircase to be aware of the twofold nature of the lace-woman's dealings. On the entresol she called herself Madame Touche, her husband's name, while on the shop door she had put only her first name, which meant that she was generally known as Madame Sidonie.

Madame Sidonie was thirty-five; but she dressed with so little care, and had so little of the woman in her manner, that she seemed much older. In fact she appeared ageless. She always wore the same black dress, frayed at the edges, rumpled and discoloured by use, recalling a barrister's gown worn out by the wear and tear of the bar. In a black bonnet that came down over her forehead and hid her hair, and a pair of thick shoes, she trotted through the streets carrying a little basket whose handles were mended with string. This basket, from which she never parted, was a world in itself. When she lifted the lid there came from it samples of every sort, notebooks, wallets, above all handfuls of stamped bills,* the illegible handwriting on which she was peculiarly skilful at deciphering. She combined the attributes of the bailiff and the commission agent. She lived among protests,* subpoenas, and court orders; when she had sold ten francs' worth of pomade or lace, she would insinuate herself into her customer's good graces and become her business agent, attending solicitors, lawyers, and judges on her behalf. She would thus hawk about the particulars of a case for weeks at the bottom of her basket, going to endless trouble, travelling from one end of Paris to the other with an even little trot, never taking a cab. It would have been difficult to say what she gained from this sort of business; she did it to begin with out of an innate taste for shady dealings and sharp practice; but soon it began to give her a host of little advantages: dinners everywhere, one-franc pieces picked up at random. Her chief gain, however, lay in the confidences she constantly received, putting her on the scent of good business deals and useful windfalls. Living in the homes of others, she was a walking catalogue of people's wants and needs. She knew where there was a daughter who had to get married at once, a family that stood in need of three thousand francs, an old gentleman willing to lend the three thousand francs but on substantial security and at a very high rate of interest. She knew of matters more delicate than these: the sadness of a fair-haired lady who was misunderstood by her husband; the secret aspirations of a good mother who wanted to see her little girl comfortably married; the tastes of a baron keen on little supper-parties and very young girls. With a faint smile she hawked these wants and needs about; she would walk ten miles to interview people; she sent the baron to the good mother, induced the old gentleman to lend the three thousand francs to the distressed family, found consolation for the fair-haired lady, and a not too enquiring husband for the girl who had to get married. She had big affairs in hand too, affairs she could speak of quite openly and about which she told everybody who came near her: an endless lawsuit that a noble but impoverished family had employed her to look after, and a debt contracted by England to France in the days of the Stuarts, whose figures, with the compound interest added, ran up to nearly three thousand million francs. This debt was her hobby-horse: she explained the case in great detail, giving a whole history lesson, and a flush of enthusiasm would rise to her cheeks, usually flaccid and yellow as wax. Occasionally, between a visit to a bailiff and a call on a friend, she would get rid of a coffee-pot or waterproof, or sell a bit of lace, or place a piano on the hire system. These things gave her the least trouble. Then she would hurry back to her shop, where a customer had made an appointment to inspect a piece of Chantilly. The customer arrived and glided like a shadow into the discreetly veiled shop; and not infrequently a gentleman would at the same time come in by the carriage entrance in the Rue Papillon to see Madame Touche's pianos on the entresol.

If Madame Sidonie failed to make her fortune, it was because she often worked for the love of it. Adoring litigation, neglecting her own business for that of others, she allowed herself to be fleeced by the bailiffs, though this gave her the pleasure known only to the litigious. The woman in her faded away; she became a mere business-person, a commission agent bustling about Paris at all hours, carrying in her fabulous basket the most mysterious items, selling everything, dreaming of millions, and appearing in court on behalf of a favourite client in a dispute over ten francs. Short, lean, and sallow, clad in the thin black dress that looked as if it had been cut out of a barrister's gown, she had shrivelled up, and to see her creeping along the houses one would have taken her for an errand boy dressed up as a girl. Her complexion had the piteous pallor of stamped paper. Her lips smiled an invisible smile, while her eyes seemed to swim in the whirlpool of jobs and preoccupations of every kind with which she stuffed her brain. Her ways were timid and discreet, with a vague suggestion of the priest's confessional and the midwife's closet, and she had the maternal gentleness of a nun who, having renounced all worldly affections, feels pity for the sufferings of the heart. She never spoke of her husband, nor of her childhood, her family, or her personal concerns. There was only one thing she never sold, and that was herself; not that she had any scruples, but because the idea of such a bargain could not possibly occur to her. She was as dry as an invoice, as cold as a protest, and at bottom as brutal and indifferent as a bailiff's assistant.

Saccard, fresh from the country, was unable at first to fathom the depths of Madame Sidonie's numerous trades. As he had read law for a year, she spoke to him one day of the three thousand million with an air of seriousness that gave him a poor opinion of her intellect. She came and rummaged in the corners of the lodgings in the Rue Saint-Jacques, summed up Angèle with a glance, and did not return until her errands brought her to the neighbourhood and she felt a desire to discuss the question of the money. Angèle had nibbled at the story of the English debt. The agent mounted her hobby-horse, and made the gold rain down for an hour. It was the crack in this quick intelligence, the sweet mad lullaby of a life wasted in squalid dealings, the magical charm with which she captivated not only herself but the more credulous among her clients. Firm in her conviction, she ended by speaking of the three thousand million as of a personal fortune which the judges were bound sooner or later to restore to her; and this threw a wondrous halo round her poor black bonnet, which bore a few faded violets on brass wire whose metal showed through. Angèle opened her eyes wide. She often spoke with respect of her sister-in-law to her husband, saying that perhaps Madame Sidonie would make them rich one day. Saccard shrugged; he had been to the shop and entresol in the Rue du Faubourg-Poissonnière, and had felt that there was nothing there but imminent bankruptcy. He asked Eugène's opinion of their sister; but his brother became serious and simply replied that he never saw her, that he knew her to be a very intelligent woman, though somewhat dangerous perhaps. Nevertheless, as Saccard was returning to the Rue Penthièvre some time afterwards, he thought he saw Madame Sidonie's black dress leave his brother's and glide rapidly along the houses. He ran after it, but was unable to catch sight again of the black dress. The female agent had one of those slight figures that get lost in a crowd. He stood pondering, and from this moment he began to study his sister more attentively. It was not long before he grasped the scale of the work performed by this pale, nebulous little creature whose whole face seemed to melt away and become shapeless. He respected her. She was a true Rougon. He recognized the hunger for money, the longing for intrigue, which was the hallmark of the family; only in her case, thanks to the surroundings in which she had matured, thanks to Paris where each morning she had to buy her evening black bread, the common temperament had deviated from its course, producing this extraordinary hermaphrodism of a woman grown sexless, businessman and procuress in one.

When Saccard, having drawn up his schemes, set out in search of his initial capital, he naturally thought of his sister. She shook her head, sighed, and talked of her three thousand million. But the clerk would not humour her madness, he pulled her up roughly each time she got back to the Stuart debt; this myth seemed to him to do little credit to so practical an intellect. Madame Sidonie, who quietly accepted the most cutting comment without allowing her convictions to be shaken, explained to him very clearly that he would not raise a sou, as he had no security to offer. This conversation took place in front of the Bourse, where she was about to speculate with her savings. She could always be found at about three o'clock leaning against the rail, on the left, on the post-office side; it was there that she gave audience to individuals as shady and sinister as herself. As her brother was about to take leave of her, she murmured regretfully, 'Ah! If only you weren't married!' This remark, of which he did not wish to ask the precise meaning, plunged Saccard into deep thought.

Months passed. War was declared in the Crimea.* Paris, unmoved by a war so distant, devoted its energies more and more to speculation and the commerce of the flesh. Saccard stood by, gnawing his fists, in frustration at the sight of the growing mania, which he had foreseen. He felt shocks of fury and impatience from the hammers beating the gold* on the anvils of this gigantic forge. So tense were his intellect and will that he lived in a dream, like a sleepwalker stepping along the edge of a roof. He was surprised and irritated, therefore, one evening to find Angèle ill in bed. His domestic life, regular as clockwork, was upset, and this exasperated him as if it were the deliberate spitefulness of Fate. Poor Angèle complained gently; she had caught a chill. When the doctor came, he seemed very concerned; he told the husband on the landing that his wife had inflammation of the lungs and that he could not be sure that she would recover. From that moment the clerk nursed the sick woman without any feeling of anger; he stopped going to his office, he stayed by her side, watching her with an indescribable look on his face, whenever she lay asleep, flushed and panting with fever. Madame Sidonie found time, notwithstanding her huge volume of work, to call every evening and make special teas, which she claimed would work wonders. To all her other professions she added that of a natural-born sick nurse, taking an interest in suffering, in remedies, in the heartfelt conversations that take place round deathbeds. She seemed to have taken a great liking to Angèle; she had a way of loving women, bestowing upon them a thousand caresses, doubtless because of the pleasure they gave to men; she gave them all the attention that merchants bestow on their most precious wares, calling them 'Pretty one, lovely one,' cooing to them, and behaving with the transports of a lover in the presence of his mistress. Though Angèle was one of those out of whom there was nothing to be made, she cajoled her like the others, on principle. When the young wife took to her bed, Madame Sidonie's effusions became tearful; she filled the room with her devotedness. Her brother watched her moving about, tight-lipped, as if crushed with silent grief.

The illness grew worse. One evening the doctor informed them that the patient would not last the night. Madame Sidonie had come early, preoccupied, watching Aristide and Angèle with her watery eyes lit up by momentary flashes of fire. When the doctor had gone, she lowered the lamp and there was a great hush. Death entered slowly into the hot, moist room, where the uneven breathing of the dying woman sounded like the spasmodic ticking of a clock running down. Madame Sidonie had stopped dispensing her potions, letting the illness take its course. She sat down by the fireplace, next to her brother, who was poking the fire feverishly while throwing involuntary glances towards the bed. Then, as if unnerved by the closeness of the atmosphere, he withdrew to the next room. Little Clotilde, who had been shut in there, was playing with her doll very quietly on a small piece of carpet. His daughter was smiling at him when Madame Sidonie, gliding up from behind, drew him into a corner and murmured something. The door remained open. They could hear the faint rattle in Angèle's throat.

'Your poor wife,' the agent sobbed. 'I fear it will soon be over. You heard what the doctor said?'

Saccard made no answer, but sadly bowed his head.

'She was a good soul,' his sister continued, speaking as if Angèle was already dead. 'You may find many richer women, and more fashionable women; but you will never find a woman so kind.'

Seeing her pause, wipe her eyes, and wait for an excuse to change the subject, Saccard asked her simply:

'Have you got something to tell me?'

'Yes, I've been working for you in regard to the matter you know about, and I think I've found... But at the moment... Believe me, my heart is broken.'

She went on wiping her eyes. Saccard let her carry on doing this for a while, without opening his mouth. Then she came to the point.

'There's a young girl who needs to get married immediately. The sweet child has had some bad luck. She has an aunt who would be prepared to make a sacrifice...'

She spoke haltingly, still sobbing, weeping out her words as though still bewailing poor Angèle. Her aim was to make her brother lose patience and question her, so that she would not bear all the responsibility for the offer she had come to make. The clerk was indeed overcome by impatience.

'Come on, out with it!' he said. 'Why do they want the girl to get married?'

'She had just left school,' continued the agent in a mournful tone, 'when a man seduced her, in the country where she was staying with the family of one of her schoolfriends. Her father has just discovered what happened. He wanted to kill her. Her aunt, to save the dear child, became her accomplice, and they made up a story and told her father that the person responsible was a man of honour whose sole wish was to atone for his momentary lapse.'

'So in that case,' said Saccard in a tone of surprise and seeming annoyance, 'the man is going to marry the girl?'

'No, he can't, he's already married.'

They fell silent. The rattle in Angèle's throat sounded more painful in the heavy atmosphere. Little Clotilde had stopped playing; she looked up at Madame Sidonie and her father with her big, pensive eyes, as if she had understood their conversation. Saccard asked a series of brief questions:

'How old is the girl?'

'Nineteen.'

'How long has she been pregnant?'

'Three months. She's bound to have a miscarriage.'

'Is the family rich and respectable?'

'An old bourgeois family. The father used to be a judge. They're very well-to-do.'

'What would this sacrifice of the aunt's amount to?'

'A hundred thousand francs.'

They fell silent again. Madame Sidonie had stopped snivelling; she was doing business now, her voice assumed the metallic tones of a second-hand clothes-seller haggling over a bargain. Her brother gave her a sidelong glance and added, with some hesitation:

'And what do you want out of it?'

'We'll see later on,' she replied. 'You can do something for me in return.'

She waited a few seconds; and as he remained silent, she asked him straight out:

'Well, have you decided? Those poor women are at their wits' end. They want to prevent a confrontation. They've promised to give the culprit's name to the father tomorrow. If you accept, I'll send a messenger with your card.'

Saccard seemed to wake from a dream; he gave a start, and turned nervously towards the next room, where he thought he had heard a slight noise.

'But I can't,' he said in an anguished tone. 'You know very well I can't...'

Madame Sidonie stared at him, with a cold, scornful gaze. His Rougon blood, all his feelings of greed, rushed to his throat. He took a visiting-card from his wallet and gave it to his sister, who put it in an envelope after carefully scratching out the address. Then she went downstairs. It was barely nine o'clock.

Left alone, Saccard went to the window and pressed his forehead against the icy panes. He forgot himself so far as to beat a tattoo with his fingers on the glass. But the night was so black, the darkness outside hung in such strange masses, that he began to feel uneasy and returned to the room where Angèle lay dying. He had forgotten her, and received a terrible shock on finding her half raised up on her pillows; her eyes were wide open, a flush of life seemed to have returned to her cheeks and lips. Little Clotilde, still nursing her doll, was sitting on the edge of the bed; as soon as her father's back was turned, she had quickly slipped back into the room from which she had been removed and to which all her happy childish curiosity attracted her. Saccard, his head full of his sister's proposal, saw his dream dashed. A hideous thought must have shone from his eyes. Angèle, terrified, tried to throw herself back in the bed, against the wall; but death was at hand, this awakening in agony was the last flicker of the lamp. The dying woman was unable to move; she sank back, keeping her eyes fixed on her husband, as if to watch his every movement. Saccard, who had dreaded a resurrection, a devil's device of destiny to keep him in penury, was relieved to see that the wretched woman had not an hour to live. He now felt nothing but deep anxiety. Angèle's eyes told him that she had overheard his conversation with Madame Sidonie, and that she was afraid he would strangle her if she did not die quickly enough. Her eyes also betrayed the terrified amazement of a sweet and inoffensive nature that discovers at the last moment the infamy of this world, and shudders at the thought of the many years spent living with a thief. Slowly her gaze softened; she was no longer afraid, she seemed to find an excuse for the wretch, as she thought of the desperate struggle he had so long maintained against Fate. Saccard, followed by the dying woman's gaze, in which he read such deep reproachfulness, leant against the furniture for support, sought the dark corners of the room. Then, faltering, he made as if to drive away the nightmare that was tormenting him, and stepped forward into the light of the lamp. But Angèle signed to him not to speak and continued to stare at him with her look of terror-stricken anguish, to which was now added a promise of forgiveness. Then he bent down to take Clotilde in his arms and carry her into the other room. She forbade him this too, with a movement of her lips. She insisted that he should stay there. She expired gently, without taking her eyes off him, and as her sight dimmed her gaze became more and more gentle. With her last breath she forgave him. She died as she had lived, discreetly, self-effacing in death as in life. Saccard stood trembling before her lifeless eyes, still open, which continued to watch him. Little Clotilde nursed her doll on the edge of the sheets, gently, so as not to awaken her mother.

When Madame Sidonie returned, it was all over. With a trick of the fingers of a woman used to this operation, she closed Angèle's eyes, to Saccard's intense relief. Then, after putting the little one to bed, she deftly arranged the bedroom. When she had lit two candles on the chest of drawers, and carefully drawn the sheet up to the corpse's chin, she cast a satisfied glance around her and stretched out in an armchair, where she slept till daybreak. Saccard spent the night in the next room, writing out the announcements of the death. He paused from time to time to jot down figures on scraps of paper.

On the evening of the funeral Madame Sidonie carried Saccard off to her entresol. There, great decisions were taken. The clerk decided to send little Clotilde to one of his brothers, Pascal Rougon,* a doctor who lived alone in Plassans, sunk in research, and who had offered on several occasions to take in his niece to enliven his silent scientific home. Madame Sidonie gave Aristide to understand that he must not remain in the Rue Saint-Jacques. She would take an elegant set of furnished rooms for him for a month, somewhere near the Hôtel de Ville; she would try to find some rooms in a private house, so that the furniture might seem to belong to him. As to the chattels in the Rue Saint-Jacques, they would be sold, so as to remove the last traces of the past. He could use some of the money to buy himself a wedding outfit and some decent clothes. Three days later Clotilde was handed over to an old lady who happened to be going to the south. Aristide Saccard, exultant and rosy-cheeked, fattened already in three days by the first smiles of Fortune, rented in the Marais,* Rue Payenne, in a sober and respectable house, a smart five-roomed apartment through which he moved from room to room in embroidered slippers. They were the rooms of a young priest who had left suddenly for Italy and had sent instructions to his housekeeper to let them. This woman was a friend of Madame Sidonie, who affected the cloth a little; she loved priests with the love she bestowed on women, instinctively, making perhaps a certain subtle link between cassocks and silk skirts. Saccard was now ready; he had prepared his role exquisitely; he awaited without flinching the difficulties and niceties of the situation he had accepted.

During the terrible night of Angèle's agony Madame Sidonie had faithfully related, in a few words, the case of the Béraud family. Its head, Monsieur Béraud du Châtel, a tall old man of sixty, was the last representative of an old bourgeois family whose pedigree went further back than that of certain noble houses. One of his ancestors

was a friend of Étienne Marcel.* In '93* his father had died on the
scaffold after welcoming the Republic with all the enthusiasm of a
burgher of Paris in whose veins flowed the revolutionary blood of the
city. He himself was a Republican of ancient Sparta, whose dream
was a reign of universal justice and true liberty. Grown old in the
judiciary, where he had developed a professional inflexibility and
severity, he had resigned his position in 1851, at the time of the coup
d'état, after refusing to take part in one of those mixed committees*
which at that time dishonoured French justice. Since then he had
been living alone in retirement in his house on the Île Saint-Louis,
on the tip of the island, almost opposite the Hôtel Lambert.* His wife
had died young. Some secret tragedy, whose wound remained
unhealed, added to the gloom of the judge's countenance. He was
already the father of an eight-year-old daughter, Renée, when his
wife died while giving birth to a second. The latter, who was called
Christine, was taken charge of by a sister of Monsieur Béraud du
Châtel, the wife of Aubertot the solicitor. Renée was sent to a convent. Madame Aubertot, who had no children, soon developed a
maternal fondness for Christine, whom she brought up as if she were
her own daughter. On her husband's death, she brought the little girl
back to her father and took up residence with the silent old man and
the smiling, fair-haired child. Renée was forgotten at her school.
During the holidays she filled the house with such a din that her aunt
heaved a great sigh of relief when she had at last taken her back to
the Sisters of the Visitation, where she had been a boarder since the
age of eight. She remained at the convent until she was nineteen, and
went straight to spend the summer at the home of her friend Adeline,
whose parents owned a beautiful estate in the Nivernais. When she
returned in October her Aunt Élisabeth was surprised to find her
subdued and deeply depressed. One evening she found her sobbing
into her pillow, writhing on her bed in a paroxysm of uncontrollable
grief. In the throes of her despair the girl told her a heart-rending
story: how a man of forty, rich, married—his wife, a young and
charming woman, lived there—had raped her while she was in the
country, without her daring or knowing how to defend herself. This
confession terrified Aunt Élisabeth: she blamed herself, as if she felt
that she was responsible; her preference for Christine made her very
unhappy; she thought that, had she not allowed Renée to be sent
away to convent school, this fate would not have befallen the poor

child. From that moment on, in order to drive away her remorse, which was made even worse by her kind nature, she did everything in her power to support the erring daughter. She bore the brunt of the anger of her father, to whom they both revealed the horrible truth through the very excess of their precautions. In her confusion and concern, she invented the strange project of marriage, which she thought would settle the whole affair, appease Renée's father, and restore her to the world of respectable women; she had no desire to see its shameful side or disastrous consequences.

Nobody ever knew how Madame Sidonie got wind of this good bit of business. The honour of the Bérauds had been dragged about in her basket with the protested bills of every prostitute in Paris. Once she knew the story, she almost forced her brother, whose wife lay dying, upon them. Aunt Élisabeth began to believe that she owed a great debt to this gentle, humble lady, whose devotion to the unhappy Renée was so great that she had found a husband for her in her own family. The first interview between the aunt and Saccard took place on the entresol in the Rue du Faubourg-Poissonnière. The clerk, who had arrived by the carriage entrance in the Rue Papillon, realized, when he saw Madame Aubertot coming through the shop and the little staircase, the ingenious arrangement of the two entrances. He was a model of tact and good behaviour. He treated the marriage as a business affair, but like a man of the world settling his debts. Aunt Élisabeth was far less at ease than he; she stammered, she did not have the courage to mention the hundred thousand francs she had promised him.

It was he who broached the question of money, like a solicitor discussing a client's case. He felt that a hundred thousand francs was a ridiculous sum for the husband of Mademoiselle Renée to bring into settlement. He laid some stress on the 'Mademoiselle'. Monsieur Béraud du Châtel would despise a poor son-in-law even more: he would accuse him of having seduced his daughter for the sake of her fortune; it might even occur to him to make some private enquiries. Startled and dismayed by Saccard's calm and polite phrases, Madame Aubertot lost her head, and agreed to double the amount when he declared that he would never dare to ask for Renée's hand with less than two hundred thousand francs in his pocket; he did not want to be taken for a contemptible fortune-hunter. The good lady took her leave quite confused, not knowing what to think of a man capable of so much indignation, and yet willing to accept a bargain of this kind.

This first interview was followed by an official visit which Aunt Élisabeth paid Saccard at his rooms in the Rue Payenne. This time she came in the name of Monsieur Béraud. The former judge had refused to see 'that man', as he called his daughter's seducer, as long as he was not married to Renée, to whom he had also forbidden entry to his house. Madame Aubertot had full powers of treaty. She seemed pleased with the clerk's luxurious abode; she had feared that the brother of Madame Sidonie, with her frayed skirts, might be a boorish person. He received her swathed in a splendid dressing gown. It was at the time when the adventurers of 2 December, after paying their debts, flung their worn boots and dirty coats into the sewers, shaved their week-old beards, and became respectable. Saccard was at last to join the gang; he cleaned his nails and washed with the most expensive powders and perfumes. He behaved most courteously; he changed his tactics and affected to be totally disinterested. When the old lady began to talk about the contract, he made a gesture as if to say that it did not matter to him. He had spent the previous week studying the Code,* pondering the serious question that would determine his freedom of action as a sharp business practitioner.

'Please,' he said, 'let us hear no more of this unpleasant question of money. I think Mademoiselle Renée should remain mistress of her fortune and I master of mine. The solicitor will take care of it.'

Aunt Élisabeth approved of this way of looking at things; she was afraid that this fellow, whose iron will she could vaguely sense, might wish to make a grab for her niece's dowry. She now broached the question.

'My brother's fortune', she said, 'consists mainly of houses and property. He isn't the kind of man to punish his daughter by reducing her share of the inheritance. He'll give her an estate in the Sologne valued at three hundred thousand francs, as well as a house in Paris which is worth about two hundred thousand francs.'

Saccard was most impressed; he had not expected such a large amount; he turned away so as to hide his excitement.

'That will make five hundred thousand francs,' continued the aunt, 'but I'm bound to add that the Sologne property yields only two per cent.'

He smiled and repeated his disinterested gesture, implying that that did not concern him, as he declined to interfere with his wife's property. He sat in his armchair in an attitude of supreme indifference, distracted, balancing his slipper on his foot, seeming to listen out of sheer politeness. Madame Aubertot, with her simple-minded good nature, spoke haltingly, choosing her words so as not to cause him any offence. She continued:

'And I want to give Renée something myself. I have no children, my property will one day go to my nieces, and I'm not going to ignore them now because one of them is in trouble. Their wedding presents were ready for them. Renée's is some large plots of lands in the Charonne area,* worth at least two thousand francs. But...'

At the word 'land' Saccard started slightly. In spite of his assumed indifference he was listening intently. Aunt Élisabeth became confused, apparently at a loss for the right expression, and continued, blushing:

'But I want the ownership of this land to be transferred to Renée's first child. You understand why. I don't want this child ever to be your responsibility. If the child died, Renée would become the sole owner.'

He remained impassive, but his intense expression revealed his apprehension. The mention of the land at Charonne had set his thoughts racing. Madame Aubertot was afraid that she had offended him by speaking of Renée's child, and was unsure how to continue the conversation.

'You haven't told me in which street the house worth two hundred thousand francs is,' he said, resuming his smiling, genial air.

'In the Rue de la Pépinière,' she replied. 'Near the Rue d'Astorg.'

This simple sentence produced a marked effect on him. He could no longer conceal his delight;* he drew up his chair, and with his Provençal volubility, in coaxing tones, said:

'Dear lady, have we not said enough, need we continue to talk of this confounded money? Please listen, I want to tell you everything about myself because I would be most unhappy if I failed to earn your respect. I lost my wife recently, I have two children on my hands, and I'm a sensible, practical man. By marrying your niece I am doing good all round. If you still have any reservations about me, you will lose them later on when I've dried everyone's tears and made a fortune for the whole family. Success is a golden flame that purifies everything. I want Monsieur Béraud himself to shake my hand and thank me.'

He was carried away. He talked for a long time in the same bantering tone, whose cynicism from time to time showed through his genial air. He referred to his brother the deputy, and his father the receiver of taxes in Plassans. He ended by winning over Aunt Élisabeth who, with involuntary joy, saw the tragedy she had been living through for the past month ending in the hands of this clever man, in something that was almost a comedy. It was agreed that they would see the solicitor the following day.

As soon as Madame Aubertot had gone, Saccard went to the Hôtel de Ville and spent the day leafing through certain documents he knew about. At the solicitor's he raised a problem, pointing out that as Renée's dowry consisted entirely of landed property, he feared it would cause her a great deal of trouble, and he thought it would be wise to sell the house in the Rue de la Pépinière so that she could invest the capital. Madame Aubertot proposed to refer the matter to Monsieur Béraud du Châtel, who remained cloistered in his apartment. Saccard went out again till the evening. He visited the Rue de la Pépinière and walked about Paris with the preoccupied air of a general on the eve of a decisive battle. Next day Madame Aubertot declared that Monsieur Béraud du Châtel had left the whole matter in her hands. The contract was drawn up along the lines discussed. Saccard would provide two hundred thousand francs, Renée's dowry was the Sologne property and the house in the Rue de la Pépinière, which she agreed to sell; and in the event of the death of her first child, she would be the sole owner of the land at Charonne given to her by her aunt. The contract was in keeping with the system of separate estates by which husband and wife retain full control of their respective fortunes. Aunt Élisabeth listened attentively to the solicitor and seemed content with this system, whose provisions apparently assured her niece's independence by placing her fortune beyond reach of any attempts to appropriate it. Saccard smiled as he saw the good lady nodding her approval of each clause. It was agreed that the marriage would take place as soon as possible.

When everything was settled, Saccard paid a ceremonial visit to his brother Eugène to announce his marriage to Mademoiselle Renée Béraud du Châtel. This masterstroke took the deputy by surprise. As he made no attempt to conceal this, the clerk said:

'You told me to look, and I looked until I found.'

Eugène, bewildered at first, began to see what had happened. In an affable tone he said:

'Well, you're a clever fellow. I suppose you've come to ask me to be your witness. You can rely on me. If necessary, I'll bring the whole right-wing faction of the Corps Législatif to your wedding; that would give you a good send-off.'

Then, as he had opened the door, he lowered his voice to add:

'I don't want to take too many risks just now, we've got a very tough bill to pass. The lady's not very far gone, I hope?'

Saccard gave him such a ferocious look that Eugène said to himself, as he closed the door:

'That's a joke that would cost me dear if I were not a Rougon.'

The wedding took place at the Church of Saint-Louis-en-l'Île. Saccard and Renée did not meet until the day before. The introduction took place early in the evening, in a small reception room at the Hôtel Béraud. They eyed each other curiously. Renée, since the news of the marriage arrangement, had resumed her mad, reckless style. She was a tall girl of exquisite, tempestuous beauty, who had grown up at the convent, indulging her whims without any parental control. She found Saccard short and ugly, but ugly in a lively and interesting way; moreover, he was perfect in manner and deportment. As for him, he made a little grimace at first sight of her; she struck him as being too tall, taller than he was. They exchanged a few words, without embarrassment. If her father had been there he might easily have believed that they had known each other for a long time, and that they shared a guilty past. Aunt Élisabeth, present at their meeting, was the one who blushed.

The day after the wedding, which the presence of Eugène Rougon, who had recently made a speech that had attracted a great deal of attention, turned into quite an event on the Île Saint-Louis, the newly married couple were finally admitted to the presence of Monsieur Béraud du Châtel. Renée cried on finding her father aged, graver, and sadder. Saccard, whom until then nothing had put out of countenance, was frozen by the chill and gloom of the room, by the sombre austerity of the tall old man whose piercing gaze seemed to penetrate to the depths of his conscience. The former judge kissed his daughter slowly on the forehead, as if to tell her that he forgave her, and turning to his son-in-law, said simply:

'Monsieur, we have suffered a great deal. I trust you will give us reason to forget the wrong you have done us.'

He held out his hand. But Saccard remained unsure of himself. He thought how, if Monsieur Béraud du Châtel had not been so affected by the tragic sorrow of Renée's shame, he might with a glance or a gesture have destroyed Madame Sidonie's plans. The latter, after bringing her brother and Aunt Élisabeth together, had prudently disappeared. She had not even come to the wedding. Saccard decided to be very direct with the old man, having read in his face a look of surprise at finding his daughter's seducer ugly, short, and forty years old. The newly married couple were compelled to spend their first nights at the Hôtel Béraud. Christine had been sent away two months earlier, so that this child of fourteen would know nothing of the drama that was taking place in the house, which remained as quiet as a convent. When she returned home she stood in mute horror before her sister's husband, whom she too thought old and ugly. Renée alone seemed untroubled by her husband's age or his sly look. She treated him neither with contempt nor affection, but very calmly, with an occasional glimmer of ironical disdain. Saccard strutted about, made himself at home, and really succeeded by his directness and energy in gradually winning everybody over. When they left, to install themselves in an imposing apartment in a new house in the Rue de Rivoli,* Monsieur Béraud du Châtel had lost his look of surprise and Christine had taken to playing with her brother-in-law as with a schoolfriend. Renée was now four months pregnant; her husband was on the point of sending her to the country, proposing afterwards to lie about the child's age, when, as Madame Sidonie had foretold, she had a miscarriage. She had laced herself so tightly to hide her condition, which was in any case concealed under the fullness of her skirts, that she had to keep to her bed for several weeks. He was delighted with the way things had turned out. Fortune was at last on his side; he had made a golden bargain: a splendid dowry, a wife whose beauty would be worth a decoration to him within six months, and not the least responsibility. He had received two hundred thousand francs to give his name to a foetus which its mother would not even look at. From that moment his thoughts began to turn affectionately towards the Charonne property. But for the time being he devoted all his attention to a speculative venture which was to be the basis of his fortune.

Notwithstanding the high standing of his wife's family, he did not immediately resign his post as a surveying-clerk. He talked of work that had to be finished, of an occupation that had to be sought. In fact he wished to remain till the end on the battlefield on which he was venturing his first stake. He felt at home there, he was able to cheat at his ease.

His plan for making a fortune was simple and practical. Now that he had at his disposal more money than he had ever hoped for to begin his operations, he intended to put his schemes into action on a large scale. He had the whole of Paris at his fingertips; he knew that the shower of gold beating down upon the walls would fall more heavily every day. Smart people had merely to open their pockets. He had joined the clever ones by reading the future in the offices of the Hôtel de Ville. His duties had taught him what can be stolen in the buying and selling of houses and land. He was well versed in every classical swindle: he knew how you sell for a million what has cost you a hundred thousand francs; how you acquire the right to rifle the treasury of the State, which smiles and closes its eyes; how, when throwing a boulevard across the belly of an old neighbourhood, you juggle with six-storeyed houses to the unanimous applause of your dupes. In these still uncertain days, when the disease of speculation was still in its period of incubation, what made him a formidable gambler was that he saw further than his superiors into the stone-and-plaster future reserved for Paris. He had ferreted so much, collected so many clues, that he could have prophesied how the new neighbourhoods would look in 1870. Sometimes, in the street, he would look curiously at certain houses, as if they were acquaintances whose destiny, known to him alone, deeply affected him.

Two months before Angèle's death he had taken her one Sunday to the Buttes Montmartre.* The poor woman loved dining at a restaurant; she was delighted whenever, after a long walk, he sat her down at a table in some little place on the outskirts of the city. On this particular day they dined at the top of the hill, in a restaurant whose windows looked out over Paris, over the sea of houses with blue roofs, like surging billows that filled the horizon. Their table was placed at one of the windows. The sight of the roofs of Paris filled Saccard with joy. At dessert he ordered a bottle of burgundy. He smiled into space, he was unusually pleasant. His eyes constantly returned, lovingly, to the living, seething ocean from which issued the deep voice of the crowd. It was autumn; beneath the pale sky the city lay listless in a soft and tender grey, pierced here and there by dark patches of foliage that resembled the broad leaves of water-lilies floating on a lake; the sun was setting behind a red cloud and, while the background was filled with a light haze, a shower of gold dust, of golden dew, fell on the right bank of the river, near the Madeleine* and the Tuileries. It was like an enchanted corner in a city of the 'Arabian Nights', with emerald trees, sapphire roofs, and ruby weathercocks. At one moment a ray of sunlight gliding from between two clouds was so resplendent that the houses seemed to catch fire and melt like an ingot of gold in a crucible.

'Oh! Look!' said Saccard, laughing like a child. 'It's raining twenty-franc pieces in Paris!'

Angèle began to laugh too, saying that pieces like that were not easy to pick up. But her husband had risen to his feet, and leaning on the handrail of the window, said:

'That's the Vendôme Column,* isn't it, glittering over there? And over there, to the right, you can see the Madeleine. A wonderful district, where there's much to be done. Ah! Now it's all going to flare up! Can you see? You'd think the whole neighbourhood was bubbling away in a chemist's retort.'

His voice became serious and heavy with emotion. The comparison he had hit upon seemed to excite him. He had been drinking burgundy, he was getting carried away; stretching out his arm to show Paris to Angèle, who had joined him at the window, he went on:

'Yes, yes, that's what I said, whole neighbourhoods will be melted down, and gold will stick to the fingers of those who heat and stir the mortar. Poor innocent Paris! Look how enormous it is, and how easily it falls asleep! How stupid they are, those great cities! It has no idea that an army of picks will fall upon it one of these fine mornings, and some of the big houses in the Rue d'Anjou* wouldn't shine so brightly in the sunset if they knew that they've only got three or four more years to live.'

Angèle thought her husband was joking. He had a taste for gross, rather disturbing jokes. She laughed, but with a sense of fear, at the sight of this little man standing erect over the recumbent giant at his feet, and shaking his fist at it while ironically pursing his lips.

'They've started already,' he continued. 'But it's nothing much yet. Look over there, near the Halles, they've cut Paris into four pieces.'

With his outstretched hand, open and sharp as a sabre, he indicated how the city was being divided into four parts.

'You mean the Rue de Rivoli and the new boulevard they're building?' asked his wife.

'Yes, the great transept of Paris, as they call it.* They're clearing away the buildings round the Louvre and the Hôtel de Ville. That's just child's play! But it'll get the public interested. When the first network is finished the fun will begin. The second network will cut through the city in all directions to connect the suburbs with the first network. The rest will disappear in clouds of plaster. Look, just follow my hand. From the Boulevard du Temple to the Barrière du Trône,* that's one cut; then on this side another, from the Madeleine to the Plaine Monceau; and a third cut this way, another that way, a cut there, one further on, cuts everywhere, Paris slashed with sabre cuts, its veins opened, providing a living for a hundred thousand navvies and bricklayers, traversed by splendid military roads which will bring the forts into the heart of the old neighbourhoods.'

Night was falling. His dry, feverish hand kept cutting through the air. Angèle shivered slightly as she watched this living knife, those iron fingers mercilessly slicing up the boundless mass of dark roofs. For a moment the haze of the horizon had been descending slowly from the heights, and she fancied she could hear, beneath the gloom gathering in the hollows, distant cracking sounds, as if her husband's hand had really made the cuts he spoke of, splitting up Paris from one end to the other, severing beams, crushing masonry, leaving behind it the long, hideous wounds of crumbling walls. The smallness of this hand, pitilessly attacking a gigantic prey, became quite disturbing; and as it effortlessly tore apart the entrails of the great city, it seemed to take on a steely glint in the blue twilight.

'There will be a third network,' continued Saccard after a pause, as if talking to himself, 'but that one is too far off yet, I can't see it as clearly. I've heard only a little about it. It will be sheer madness, an orgy of spending, Paris will be drunk and overwhelmed.'

He fell silent again, his eyes fixed on the city, over which the shadows were darkening. He must have been trying to imagine the future. Then night fell, the city became indistinct, and it could be heard breathing heavily, like the sea when the eye can only make out the pale crests of the waves. Here and there the white patch of a wall could still be made out; and the yellow flames of the gas jets pierced the darkness one by one, like stars lighting up in the blackness of a stormy sky.

Angèle shook off her feeling of uneasiness and took up the joke her husband had made at dessert.

'Well,' she said with a smile, 'there has been a fine shower of twenty-franc pieces! The people of Paris are counting them. Look at the piles they're laying out at our feet!'

She pointed to the streets that run down opposite the Buttes Montmartre, whose gaslights seemed to be heaping up their specks of gold in two rows.

'And over there,' she cried, pointing to a bright cluster of stars, 'that must be the Caisse Générale.'*

This remark made Saccard laugh. They stayed a few moments longer at the window, delighted with this torrent of 'twenty-franc pieces', which had ended by setting light to the whole of Paris. On the way home from Montmartre the surveying-clerk no doubt regretted having spoken so freely. He put it down to the burgundy, and begged his wife not to repeat the 'nonsense' he had been talking; he did not want, he said, to be irresponsible.

For a long time Saccard had been studying these three arteries of streets and boulevards, the plans for which he had described quite accurately to Angèle. When Angèle died he was not sorry to think that she took to her grave his overexcited talk during their expedition to Montmartre. There lay his fortune, in the cuts that his hand had made in the heart of Paris, and he had resolved to keep his plans to himself, knowing very well that when the spoils were divided there would be enough crows hovering over the disembowelled city. His first plan had been to acquire at a very low price some building which he knew beforehand was condemned to imminent demolition, and to make a big profit by obtaining substantial compensation. He might have gone so far as to attempt this purchase without a sou, buying the house on credit and only receiving the difference, as at the Bourse, when his second marriage, which gave him a premium of two hundred thousand francs, fuelled his ambition. Now he knew what to do: he would buy the house in the Rue de la Pépinière from his wife through an intermediary, without allowing his own name to appear, and treble his outlay, thanks to the knowledge he had picked up in the corridors of the Hôtel de Ville and to his good relations with certain people of influence. The reason why he started when

Aunt Élisabeth told him where the house was situated was because it lay at the centre of the plans for a boulevard which had not yet been discussed outside the private office of the Prefect of the Seine. This boulevard would be swallowed up completely by the Boulevard Malesherbes. It was an old scheme of Napoleon I, which they were now thinking of carrying out, 'in order', they said earnestly, 'to give a normal outlet to districts lost behind a labyrinth of narrow streets on the slopes of the hills that mark the outskirts of Paris'. This official phrase did not, of course, reveal the Empire's interest in huge speculative ventures, in organizing the prodigious excavations and building operations that gave the working classes no time to think. Saccard had ventured one day to consult, in the Prefect's room, the famous plan of Paris on which 'an august hand' had traced in red ink the principal boulevards of the second network.* The blood-red penstrokes cut even deeper gashes into Paris than did Saccard's hand. The Boulevard Malesherbes, which was pulling down some magnificent houses in the Rue d'Anjou and the Rue de la Ville-l'Évêque, and necessitated extensive excavations, was to be one of the first to be laid out. When Saccard went to look over the property in the Rue de la Pépinière, he thought of his dinner with Angèle on the Buttes Montmartre, during which, at sunset, such a heavy shower of gold coins had fallen on the Madeleine district. He smiled, imagining that the radiant cloud had burst over his own courtyard, and that he was on his way to pick up the twenty-franc pieces.

While Renée, luxuriously installed in the apartment in the Rue de Rivoli in the centre of the new Paris, one of whose queens she was destined to become, thought about the new dresses she would buy and took her first steps in the life of a woman of fashion, her husband was hatching his first great scheme. He began by buying from her the house in the Rue de la Pépinière, thanks to the mediation of a certain Larsonneau, whom he had come across ferreting like himself in the offices of the Hôtel de Ville. Larsonneau, however, had been stupid enough to let himself get caught one day when he was prying into the Prefect's private drawers. He had just set up as a broker at the end of a dark, damp courtyard at the bottom of the Rue Saint-Jacques. His pride and greed suffered torments there. He found himself in the same position as Saccard before his marriage; he too, he would say, had invented 'a five-franc piece machine'; but he lacked the necessary funds to turn his invention to advantage. A hint was enough to enable him to come to an understanding with his former colleague; and he did his part of the work so well that he acquired the house for one hundred and fifty thousand francs. Renée was already, before many months had elapsed, in great need of money. The husband made no appearance except to authorize his wife to sell. When the sale was completed she asked him to invest a hundred thousand francs for her, handing it to him with full confidence, no doubt in order to touch him and make him close his eyes to the fact that she was keeping fifty thousand francs back. He smiled knowingly; he had reckoned on her squandering her money; those fifty thousand francs, which were about to disappear in jewellery and lace, were calculated to bring him a hundred per cent profit. So well satisfied was he with his first transaction that he carried his honesty so far as really to invest Renée's hundred thousand francs and hand her the share certificates. His wife had no power to transfer them; he was sure he would be able to lay his hands on them if ever the need arose.

'My dear, this is for your dresses,' he said gallantly.

Once he had taken possession of the house, he was clever enough to sell it again, twice in one month, to men of straw, increasing the purchase price each time. The last purchaser paid no less than three hundred thousand francs for it. Meanwhile Larsonneau alone appeared as the representative of the successive landlords, and worked the tenants. He pitilessly refused to renew the leases unless they agreed to a huge increase in rent. The tenants, who had an inkling of the imminent expropriation, were in despair; they ended by agreeing to the increase, especially when Larsonneau added, with a conciliatory air, that this increase would remain a fictitious one* for the first five years. As for the tenants who resisted, they were replaced by creatures who received the apartment for nothing and signed anything they were asked to; in their case there was a double profit: the rent was increased and the compensation due to the tenant for his lease went to Saccard. Madame Sidonie helped her brother by setting up a pianoforte agency in one of the shops on the ground floor. It was then that Saccard and Larsonneau, avid for profit, went a bit further: they concocted account books, they forged documents so as to establish a trade in pianos on a vast scale. They scribbled away together for several nights. Worked in this fashion, the house trebled in value. Thanks to the last sale, to the increase in the rents, to the fictitious tenants, and to Madame Sidonie's business, it was able to be valued at five hundred thousand francs before the Compensation Authority.

The mechanisms of expropriation, of the powerful system that for fifteen years turned Paris upside-down, creating fortunes and bringing ruin, are of the simplest. As soon as a new boulevard is decided upon, the surveyors draw up the plan in separate sections and establish a valuation of the buildings. As a rule, in the case of houses let as apartments, they add up the total amount of the rents after making enquiries, and are thus able to determine the approximate value. The Compensation Authority, consisting of members of the City Council, always makes an offer lower than this sum, knowing that the interested parties will claim more and that there will be a concession on both sides. When they are unable to come to terms the case is taken before a jury, which pronounces on the City's offer and the claim of the evicted landlord or tenant.*

Saccard, who had remained at the Hôtel de Ville for the decisive period, had the impudence at one point to wish to have himself appointed when the works for the Boulevard Malesherbes were begun, and to value his own house. But he was afraid that this would neutralize his influence with the members of the Compensation Authority. He arranged for one of his colleagues to be chosen, a young man with a sweet smile, called Michelin, whose wife, an extremely pretty woman, occasionally called to apologize to her husband's employers when he was absent because of ill health. He was often ill. Saccard had noticed that the pretty Madame Michelin, who glided with such modesty through the half-closed doorways, had enormous influence; Michelin was promoted with each illness, making his career by taking to his bed. During one of his absences, when he sent his wife to the office almost every morning to say how he was, Saccard bumped into him twice on the outer boulevards, smoking a cigar with the expression of deep contentment that never left him. This filled him with sympathy for the remarkable young man, for the happy couple, so practical and ingenious. He admired all 'five-franc-piece machines' that were made to work efficiently. When he had got Michelin appointed, he called on his charming wife, expressed a wish to introduce her to Renée, and talked about his brother the deputy, the brilliant orator. Madame Michelin understood.

From that day onward her husband was particularly friendly towards his colleague. The latter, who had no desire to take the worthy young man into his confidence, contented himself with being present, as if by chance, on the day when the other proceeded to value the house in the Rue de la Pépinière. He assisted him. Michelin, who had the emptiest head imaginable, followed the instructions of his wife, who had urged him to please Monsieur Saccard in all things. He suspected nothing; he thought the surveying-clerk was in a hurry to see him finish his work so as to take him off to a café. The leases, the rent receipts, Madame Sidonie's famous books, passed before his eyes without his even having time to check the figures Saccard read out. Larsonneau was present, and treated his accomplice as a stranger.

'Come on, put down five thousand francs,' Saccard ended by saying. 'The house is worth more... Hurry up. I think there are going to be changes at the Hôtel de Ville, and I want to talk to you about it so that you can let your wife know beforehand.'

The business was thus concluded. But he still had fears. He dreaded that the sum of five hundred thousand francs would strike the Compensation Authority as rather excessive for a house that was known to be worth at most two hundred thousand. The explosion in property values had not yet taken place. An inquiry would have exposed him to serious unpleasantness. He remembered his brother's words: 'If you create a scandal, I'll destroy you', and he knew Eugène was a man of his word. It was a question of blindfolding the gentlemen of the Authority and ensuring their good will. He glanced at two influential men, of whom he had made friends through his habit of greeting them in the corridors when he met them. The thirty-six members of the City Council were hand-picked by the Emperor himself, on the recommendation of the Prefect, from among the senators, deputies, lawyers, doctors, and great men of industry who prostrated themselves before the reigning power; but among them all, the fervour of Baron Gouraud and of Monsieur Toutin-Laroche especially attracted the good will of the Tuileries.

Baron Gouraud's life story could be summarized as follows: he was made a baron by Napoleon I as a reward for supplying damaged biscuits to the Grande Armée, he was a peer successively under Louis XVIII, Charles X, and Louis-Philippe, and he was a senator under Napoleon III. He worshipped the throne, the four gilded boards covered with velvet; it mattered little to him who sat on it.

With his enormous belly, his bovine face, and his elephantine movements, he displayed a charming roguishness; he sold himself majestically and committed the greatest infamies in the name of duty and
conscience. But he was even more remarkable in his vices. There
were stories about him which could not be told above a whisper. In
spite of his seventy-eight years, he continued to lead a life of monstrous debauchery. On two occasions it had been necessary to hush
up some filthy episode, so that his embroidered senator's coat should
not be dragged through the courts.

Monsieur Toutin-Laroche, tall and thin, had invented a mixture
of tallow and stearine for the manufacture of candles, and longed to
enter the Senate. He clung to Baron Gouraud like a leech, rubbing
up against him with the vague idea that it would bring him luck.
At bottom he was exceedingly practical; and had he come across a
senator's seat for sale, he would have haggled fiercely over the price.
The Empire was to bring into prominence this greedy nonentity, this
simpleton with a talent for industrial swindles. He was the first to sell
his name to a shady company, one of those companies that sprouted
like poisonous toadstools on the dunghill of Imperial speculation.
At that time one could see on walls a poster bearing these words in
big black letters: *Société Générale of the Ports of Morocco*, on which
the name of Monsieur Toutin-Laroche, with his title as municipal
councillor, was displayed at the head of the list of members of the
board of directors, all of whom were totally unknown. This method,
which has since been abused, succeeded admirably: the shares were
snapped up, though the question of the Ports of Morocco was not
at all clear, and the worthy people who brought their money were
quite unable to explain the use to which it would be put. The poster
spoke grandiloquently of trading posts to be established along the
Mediterranean. For two years several newspapers had been celebrating this project, which they declared to be gaining in prosperity
every quarter. In the City Council Monsieur Toutin-Laroche was
considered a first-rate administrator; he was one of the leading lights
of the place, and his tyranny over his colleagues was matched only
by his self-effacement in the presence of the Prefect. He was
now engaged in the creation of a great finance company, the Crédit
Viticole, a wine-growers' loan office, to which he referred with a
reticence and an air of solemnity that kindled the covetousness of the
idiots around him.*

Saccard secured the protection of these two gentlemen by doing them favours whose importance he cleverly pretended to ignore. He introduced his sister to the Baron when the latter was involved in a terrible scandal. He took her to see him under the pretence of seeking his support for the dear woman, who had been petitioning him for a contract to supply the Tuileries with window-curtains. But when the surveyor left them together, it was Madame Sidonie who promised the Baron that she would negotiate with certain people who were clumsy enough not to have felt honoured by the interest that a senator had condescended to take in their child, a girl of ten. Saccard took Monsieur Toutin-Laroche in hand himself; he arranged to bump into him in the corridor, and raised the topic of the famous Crédit Viticole. After five minutes the great administrator, astounded at the extraordinary things he heard, grabbed the clerk by the arm and stood talking with him for a full hour. Saccard whispered in his ear about some highly ingenious financial schemes. When Monsieur Toutin-Laroche left him, he squeezed his hand meaningfully and gave him a masonic wink.

'You must join us,' he murmured. 'You really must join us.'

Saccard excelled himself throughout this business. He was most careful not to make Baron Gouraud and Monsieur Toutin-Laroche each other's accomplices. He called on them separately, dropped a word in their ear on behalf of one of his friends who was about to be bought out in the Rue de la Pépinière; he was very careful to tell each of the two confederates that he would not mention this business to any other member of the Authority, that it was all very uncertain, but that he was counting on his full support.

The surveying-clerk was right to take precautions. When the report relating to his house came before the Compensation Authority, it just happened that one of the members lived in the Rue d'Astorg and knew the house. This member objected to the figure of five hundred thousand francs, which, according to him, should be halved. Aristide had had the impudence to have seven hundred thousand francs put down in the claim. But that day Monsieur Toutin-Laroche, who was generally very unpleasant to his colleagues, was in an even more truculent mood than usual. He became angry and sprang to the defence of the landlords.

'We're all landlords, Messieurs,' he cried. 'The Emperor wants to do things on a grand scale, let us not haggle over trifles. The house must be worth five hundred thousand francs; the amount was set down by one of our people, a municipal clerk. Really, anyone would think we were living in a den of thieves; if we behave like this, we'll end up distrusting each other.'

Baron Gouraud, sitting low down in his chair, watched Monsieur Toutin-Laroche out of the corner of his eye with an air of surprise, as he ranted and raved on behalf of the landlord of the Rue de la Pépinière. He had a suspicion. But after all, as this violent outburst saved him the trouble of speaking, he began to nod slowly, as a sign of complete approval. The member from the Rue d'Astorg resisted, refusing to give in to the two tyrants of the Authority on a matter in which he was more competent than they were. At that moment Monsieur Toutin-Laroche, noticing the Baron's gestures of approval, seized the report and said curtly:

'Very well. We'll resolve your doubts... If you'll allow me, I'll look into the matter, and Baron Gouraud will help me with the inquiry.'

'Yes, yes,' said the Baron gravely, 'nothing improper must be allowed to interfere with our decisions.'

The report had already disappeared in Monsieur Toutin-Laroche's capacious pockets. The Authority had to give in. As they went out on to the Quai, the two confederates looked at each other. They felt as if they were accomplices, and this increased their self-assurance. More vulgar minds would have sought an explanation, but these two continued to argue the case for the landlords as if they could still be heard, and to lament the mood of distrust that was infiltrating everything. Just as they were about to part, the Baron said with a smile:

'Ah, I was forgetting: I'm going to the country for a while. It would be very good if you could conduct this little inquiry without me... But please don't tell anyone, our friends complain that I take too many holidays.'

'Don't worry,' replied Monsieur Toutin-Laroche. 'I'll go straight to the Rue de la Pépinière.'

He crept back to his own house, feeling a touch of admiration for the Baron, who had such a skilful way of resolving delicate situations. He kept the report in his pocket, and at the next meeting of the Authority he declared peremptorily, in the Baron's name and his own, that they should split the difference between the offer of five hundred thousand and the claim of seven hundred thousand francs, and allow six hundred thousand. There was not the slightest opposition. The member from the Rue d'Astorg, who had no doubt thought it over, said good-naturedly that he had made a mistake: he had thought they had been talking about the house next door.

In this way Aristide Saccard won his first victory. He quadrupled his outlay and gained two accomplices. One thing alone perturbed him: when he wanted to destroy Madame Sidonie's famous account books, he was unable to find them. He hurried over to see Larsonneau, who brazenly admitted that he had them and that he meant to keep them. Saccard showed no anger; he implied that he had only been concerned for his dear friend, who was far more seriously compromised than himself by the entries, which were almost entirely in his handwriting, but that he was reassured now that he knew they were in his safekeeping. At heart he would gladly have strangled his 'dear friend'; he remembered a particularly compromising document, a false inventory which he had been fool enough to draw up, and which he knew had been left in one of the ledgers. Larsonneau, handsomely rewarded, set up a broking agency in the Rue de Rivoli, where he had a suite of offices furnished as luxuriously as a courtesan's apartment. Saccard left the Hôtel de Ville and, being in command of considerable funds to work with, launched furiously into speculation, while Renée filled Paris with the clatter of her equipages, the sparkle of her diamonds, the vertigo of her riotous existence.

Sometimes the husband and wife, feverish devotees of money and pleasure, would penetrate the icy mists of the Île Saint-Louis. They felt as if they were entering a city of the dead.

The Hôtel Béraud, built at the beginning of the sixteenth century, was one of those square, black, solemn edifices, with high, narrow windows, which are so numerous in the Marais, and are let to proprietors of schools, manufacturers of carbonated water, and bonders of wines and spirits. But it was in an excellent state of repair. On the Rue Saint-Louis-en-l'Île side it had only three storeys, each fifteen to twenty feet high. The ground floor was not so lofty, and was pierced with windows protected by enormous iron bars and sunk dismally into the gloomy thickness of the walls; it had an arched gateway almost as high as it was wide, and bearing a cast-iron knocker on its doors, which were painted dark green and studded with enormous nails that formed stars and lozenges on the two folds. This characteristic entrance was flanked on either side with spur-posts sloping backwards, and strapped with broad iron bands. One could see that formerly a gutter had run under the middle of the gateway, between the weatherings of the pebble-work of the porch; but Monsieur Béraud had decided to stop up this gutter and have the entrance asphalted: this, however, was the only concession he could ever be persuaded to make to modern architecture. The windows of the upper floors were ornamented with thin handrails of wrought iron, through which could be seen their colossal casements of strong brown woodwork with little green panes. At the top the roof was interrupted by the dormers, and the gutter alone continued its course so as to discharge the rainwater into the down-pipes. The austere bareness of the façade was heightened by the complete absence of awnings or shutters, for at no season of the year did the sun shine on those pale, melancholy stones. This façade, with its venerable air and its bourgeois severity, slumbered solemnly in the silence of the street that no carriage ever disturbed.

In the interior of the mansion was a square courtyard, surrounded by colonnades, a miniature version of the Place Royale,* paved with enormous flagstones, and completing the cloistral appearance of this lifeless house. Opposite the porch a fountain, a lion's head half worn away, its gaping jaws alone distinguishable, discharged a heavy, monotonous stream of water through an iron tube into a basin green with moss, its edges polished by wear. This water was cold as ice. Weeds sprouted between the flagstones. In the summer a feeble ray of sunlight entered the courtyard, and this infrequent visit had whitened a corner of the southern façade, while the other three walls, dull and black, were streaked with moisture. There, in the depths of the courtyard, cold and silent as a well, lighted with a pale, wintry light, one would have thought oneself a thousand miles away from the new Paris, ablaze with every form of passionate enjoyment and resounding with the sound of gold.

The rooms of the house had the sad calm, the cold solemnity of the courtyard. Approached by a broad iron-railed staircase, on which the footsteps and coughs of visitors echoed as in the aisle of a church, they stretched in long strings of wide, lofty rooms, in which the heavy, old-fashioned furniture of dark wood was lost; and the pale light was peopled only by the figures on the tapestries, whose great, pale shapes could just be made out. All the luxury of the

old-fashioned Parisian bourgeoisie was there, Spartan and ageless.
Chairs whose oak seats are barely covered with a little tow, beds with
stiff sheets, linen-chests whose roughness would probably damage
delicate modern garments. Monsieur Béraud du Châtel had chosen
to live in the darkest part of the mansion, between the street and the
courtyard, on the first floor. He had found there a refuge of tranquillity, silence, and gloom. When he opened the doors and walked
through the rooms with his slow, solemn step, he might have been
taken for one of the members of the old parlements* whose portraits
were hung on the walls, returning home deep in thought after discussing and refusing to sign an edict of the king.

Yet in this lifeless house, within these cloisters, there was one
sunny spot, full of life, a nook of childhood, fresh air, and bright
light. One had to climb endless little stairways, walk along ten or
twelve corridors, go down and up again, and then at last one reached
a huge room, a sort of belvedere built on the roof, at the back of the
house, above the Quai de Béthune. It faced due south. The window
opened so wide that the sky itself, with all its sunbeams, all its ether,
all its blue, seemed to enter the room. It was perched aloft like a
dovecote, and contained long flower-boxes, an immense aviary, and
not a single piece of furniture. There was just some matting spread
over the floor. This was 'the children's room'. Throughout the house
it was known and spoken of by that name. The house was so cold,
the courtyard so damp, that Aunt Élisabeth had been afraid that
Christine and Renée would suffer harm from the chill breath that
hung about the walls; she had often scolded the children for running
about the colonnades and amusing themselves by dipping their little
arms into the icy water of the fountain. After a while she had the idea
of using this forgotten attic for them, the only corner into which,
for nearly two centuries, the sun had entered and rejoiced, in the
midst of the cobwebs. She gave them some matting, birds, and
flowers. The children were ecstatically happy. Renée lived there during the holidays, bathing in the yellow rays of the sun, which seemed
pleased with the adornment of his retreat and with the two fair-
haired creatures sent to keep him company. The room became a
paradise, resounding with birdsong and the children's babbling. It
had been given to them for their exclusive use. They spoke of 'our
room'; it was their home; they went so far as to lock themselves in, so
as to put it beyond doubt that they were the sole mistresses of the

room. What a happy nook! On the matting lay a battlefield of toys, expiring in the bright sunshine.

But the great delight of the children's room was the vast horizon. From the other windows of the house there was nothing to look at but black walls, a few feet away. But from this window one could see all that part of the Seine and of Paris that extends from the Cité to the Pont de Bercy, infinitely flat, like some quaint Dutch city. Down below, on the Quai de Béthune, were tumbledown wooden sheds, piles of beams, and crumbling roofs; the children often amused themselves by watching enormous rats run about among them, with a vague fear of seeing them climb up the high walls. But beyond all this the real rapture began. The boom, with its tiers of timber, its buttresses like those in a Gothic cathedral, and the slender Pont de Constantine,* hanging like a strip of lace beneath the pedestrians' feet, intersected at right angles and seemed to dam up and hold back the huge mass of the river. The trees of the Halle aux Vins* opposite and the shrubbery of the Jardin des Plantes, further away, stretched out their greenness to the distant horizon; while on the other bank of the river, the Quai Henri IV and the Quai de la Rapée extended their low and irregular edifices, their row of houses which, from above, resembled the tiny wood-and-cardboard houses which the little girls kept in boxes. In the background on the right the blue-slated roof of the Salpêtrière* rose above the trees. Then, in the centre, sloping down to the Seine, the wide-paved banks formed two long grey tracks, streaked here and there by a row of casks, a cart and its team, an empty wood- or coal-barge lying high and dry. But the soul of all this, the soul that filled the whole landscape, was the Seine, the living river; it came from far away, from the vaguely shimmering edge of the horizon, emerging from the distance as from a dream, to flow straight down to the children with its tranquil majesty, its powerful swell, which spread and widened out into a great sheet of water at their feet, at the tip of the island. The two bridges that crossed it, the Pont de Bercy and the Pont d'Austerlitz, looked like necessary boundaries placed there to contain it, to prevent it from rising up to the room. The little ones loved this giant, they filled their eyes with its colossal flux, with the eternal murmuring flood which rolled towards them, branched out to left and right, and disappeared into the unknown with the docility of a conquered titan. On fine days, on mornings when the sky was clear and blue, they would be enraptured with the pretty dresses of the Seine; it wore dresses of a changeable hue that altered from blue to green with a thousand tints of infinite tenderness; dresses of silk shot with white flames and trimmed with satin frills; and the barges drawn up on either bank bordered it with a black velvet ribbon. In the distance especially, the material became beautiful and precious as the enchanted gauze of a fairy's tunic; and beyond the belt of dark green satin with which the shadow of the bridges girdled the Seine, were breastplates of gold and lappets of plaited sun-coloured stuff. The immense sky formed a vault over the water, over the low rows of houses and the green of the two parks.

Sometimes Renée, a big girl already and full of sensual curiosity brought back from her boarding school, would throw a glance into the swimming school attached to Petit's floating baths, which were moored to the end of the island. She would try to catch a glimpse, through the flapping linen clothes hung up on lines to serve as a roof, of the men in bathing-drawers with their naked bellies.

CHAPTER III

MAXIME remained at school in Plassans until the holidays of 1854. He was a few months over thirteen and had just finished the second form. It was then that his father decided to let him come to Paris. Saccard felt that a son of that age would give him a certain position, would confirm his role as a wealthy widower, twice married, and serious in his views. When he informed Renée, towards whom he prided himself on his extreme courtesy, of his intention, she answered casually:

'That's fine, have the boy sent up. He'll give us something to do. It's so deadly boring in the mornings.'

The boy arrived a week later. He was already quite tall, but slight, with a girl's face, a delicate, cheeky look, and very light blond hair. And how oddly he was got up! He was cropped to the ears, his hair was cut so short that the whiteness of his cranium was barely covered with a shadow of pale down, he wore trousers too short for him, hobnailed boots, and a hideously threadbare tunic that was much too wide and made him look almost hunchbacked. In this garb, surprised at his new surroundings, he looked about him, not timidly but with the wild, cunning air of a precocious child unwilling to come out of its shell at first sight.

A servant had just fetched him from the station, and he was waiting in the big drawing room, enraptured by the gilding on the ceiling and furniture, thoroughly delighted with this luxury in which he was about to live, when Renée, returning from her dressmaker, swept in like a gust of wind. She threw off her hat and the white burnoose she had put over her shoulders to protect her from the cold. She appeared before Maxime, who was stupefied with admiration, in all the splendour of her marvellous attire.

The child thought she was in fancy dress. She wore a delightful skirt of blue faille, with deep flounces, and over that a sort of guard's coat in pale grey silk. The flaps of the coat, lined with blue satin of a deeper shade than the faille of the skirt, were boldly caught up and secured with ribbon; the cuffs of the flat sleeves and the broad lapels of the bodice stood out wide, trimmed with the same satin. As a crowning touch, as a bold stroke of eccentricity, two rows of large buttons, made to look like sapphires fastened in blue rosettes, adorned the front of the coat. It looked both ugly and entrancing.

When Renée noticed Maxime, she asked the servant, surprised to find him as tall as herself:

'It's the boy, isn't it?'

The child was devouring her with his eyes. This lady with a skin so white, whose breasts showed through a gap in her plaited shirt-front, this sudden charming apparition, with her hair done up high, with her elegant, gloved hands, and her little Wellington boots with pointed heels that dug into the carpet, delighted him, seemed to him to be the good fairy of this warm, gilded room. He began to smile, and he was just awkward enough to retain his <u>urchin</u> gracefulness.

'Well, he's quite amusing!' cried Renée. 'But what a dreadful haircut! Listen, my little friend, your father will probably not be back until dinnertime, and I'll have to make you at home. I'm your stepmother, Monsieur. Will you give me a kiss?'

'Yes, if you like,' answered Maxime boldly.

He kissed Renée on both cheeks, taking her by the shoulders, leaving the guard's coat a little rumpled. She freed herself, laughing, and said:

'Yes, indeed, how amusing he is, this little bald-head.'*

She came back to him, more serious.

'We'll be friends, won't we? I want to be a mother to you. I was thinking about it while I was waiting for my dressmaker, and I said to myself that I must be very good and bring you up properly. That will be nice!'

Maxime continued to stare at her with his cheeky, blue, <u>girl's eyes</u>, and suddenly asked:

'How old are you?'

'You should never ask that!' she cried, clasping her hands together. 'He has no idea, poor little thing! He'll have to be taught everything. Fortunately I can still admit my age. I'm twenty-one.'

'I'll soon be fourteen. <u>You could be my sister.</u>'

He did not go on, but his look indicated that he had expected to find his father's second wife much older. He was standing quite close to her, examining her neck so carefully that she almost blushed. Her head, moreover, was turning: she was never able to concentrate for long on the same subject, and she began to walk up and down and talk about her dressmaker, forgetting that she was talking to a child.

'I wanted to be here to welcome you. You know, Worms* brought me this dress this morning. I tried it on and thought it rather suited me. It's very smart, isn't it?'

She stood before a mirror. Maxime walked around behind her to examine her from every angle.

'But,' she continued, 'when I put the coat on, I noticed that there was a large fold on the left shoulder. It doesn't look right at all, it makes me look as if I had one shoulder higher than the other.'

He went up to her and pressed his finger over the fold as if to smooth it down, and his vicious schoolboy hand seemed to linger there with a certain pleasure.

'Well,' she continued, 'I couldn't wait. I had the horses put to, and I went to tell Worms what I thought of his appalling carelessness. He promised to put it right.'

She remained before the mirror, gazing at herself, lost in a sudden reverie. She ended by placing one finger on her lips, with an air of contemplative impatience. And in a half-whisper, as if talking to herself, she said:

'There's something missing. Yes, there really is something missing.'

Then, with a quick movement, she turned round, stood in front of Maxime, and asked him:

'Is it really right? Don't you think it lacks something, a trifle, a bow somewhere or other?'

The schoolboy was reassured by Renée's familiarity, and regained all his self-confidence. He stepped back, came closer, screwed up his eyes, and murmured:

'No, no, there's nothing missing, it's very pretty, very pretty indeed... If anything, I think there's too much.'

He blushed slightly, despite his audacity, came closer still, and with his fingertip traced an acute angle on Renée's breast.

'If I were you,' he continued, 'I would hollow out the lace like this, and wear a necklace with a very big cross.'

She clapped her hands, radiant with delight.

'That's it, that's it,' she exclaimed. 'I was just going to say that!'

She folded back the chemisette, left the room for two minutes, and returned with the necklace and cross. Resuming her place in front of the mirror, she murmured triumphantly:

'Oh, perfect, quite perfect... He's no fool, that little man! Did you dress the girls in the country? You and I are sure to get on well.

But you'll have to do as I tell you. To begin with, you must let your hair grow and never wear that horrid tunic again. Then you must follow my lessons in good manners. I want you to become a smart young man.'

'Of course,' said the child naively; 'since papa is rich now and you are his wife.'

She smiled, and with her customary vivacity said:

'Then let's begin by saying *tu* to each other. I've been saying *tu* and *vous*.* It's really silly... Do you think we'll get on well together?'

'Oh, extremely well,' he replied, with the effusiveness of a boy talking to his sweetheart.

Such was the first encounter between Maxime and Renée. The child did not go to school until a month later. During the first few days his stepmother played with him like a doll; she got rid of his provincial manners, and it must be added that he was very willing to help her. When he appeared, newly arrayed from head to foot by his father's tailor, she uttered a cry of joy: he looked as pretty as a picture, she said. His hair, however, took an unconscionable time to grow. Renée always used to say that one's whole face depended on one's hair. She tended her own religiously. For a long time she had been maddened by its colour, a peculiar pale yellow, which reminded one of good butter. But when yellow hair came into fashion she was delighted, and to make people think that she was not a slave to fashion, she swore she dyed it every month.

Maxime was already terribly knowing for his thirteen years. His was one of those frail, precocious natures in which the senses assert themselves early. He had vices before he knew the meaning of desire. He had twice narrowly escaped being expelled from school. Had Renée's eyes been accustomed to provincial graces, she would have noticed that, strangely got up though he was, the little man, as she called him, had a way of smiling, of turning his head, of stretching his arms, that had the feminine air of adolescent schoolgirls. He took great pains to look after his hands, which were long and slender; and though his hair was cropped short by order of the principal, an ex-colonel of engineers, he owned a little looking-glass which he took out of his pocket during classes and placed between the leaves of his book, looking at himself for hours, examining his eyes, his gums, pulling pretty faces, training himself in the art of coquetry. His schoolfriends hung round his blouse as round a petticoat, and he buckled his belt so tightly that he had the slim waist and swaying hips of a woman. In truth, however, he received as many kicks as kisses. The school at Plassans, a den of young delinquents like most provincial schools, was a hotbed of pollution that singularly developed his epicene temperament, his childhood marked by evil from some mysterious hereditary cause. Fortunately, age was about to improve him. But the sign of his boyish debauchery, this effeminization of his whole being during the time when he played at being a girl, was destined to remain in him and to strike a lasting blow to his virility.

Renée called him 'Mademoiselle', not knowing that six months earlier she would have spoken the truth. He seemed to her very docile, very affectionate, and indeed his caresses often made her feel ill at ease. He had a way of kissing that warmed her skin. But what delighted her was his roguishness; he was as entertaining as could be, and very bold, already talking of women with a smile, holding his own against Renée's friends, against dear Adeline who had just married Monsieur d'Espanet, and the fat Suzanne, wedded quite recently to Haffner, the big industrialist. When he was fourteen he fell in love with Suzanne. He confided his passion to his stepmother, who was most amused.

'I would have preferred Adeline,' she said. 'She's prettier.'

'Perhaps so,' replied the boy. 'But Suzanne is much plumper. I like beautiful women. It would be awfully nice of you if you put in a word for me.'

Renée laughed. Her doll, this tall lad with his girlish ways, seemed to her quite special now that he had fallen in love. The time came when Madame Haffner had seriously to defend herself. Meanwhile, the ladies encouraged Maxime with their stifled laughter, their teasing allusions, and the coquettish attitudes they assumed in the presence of this precocious child. There was a touch of aristocratic debauchery in all this. All three of them, in the midst of their tumultuous lives, savoured the boy's delicious depravity like a new, harmless spice that stimulated their palates. They let him touch their dresses and finger their shoulders when he followed them into the anteroom to help them on with their wraps; they passed him from hand to hand, laughing almost hysterically when he kissed their wrists on the veined side, on the spot where the skin is so soft; and

then they became motherly, instructing him in the art of being a
gentleman and pleasing the ladies. He was their plaything, a little toy
man of ingenious workmanship, that kissed and flirted and had the
sweetest vices in the world, but remained a plaything, a little card-
board man that one need not be too afraid of, but just enough to feel
a pleasant thrill at the touch of his childish hand.

After the holidays Maxime went to the Lycée Bonaparte.* It was
the most fashionable school, the one Saccard was bound to choose
for his son. The child, frivolous though he was, had by that time a
very quick intelligence; but he applied himself to other things than
his classical studies. He was nevertheless a well-behaved pupil, never
descending to the Bohemian level of the class dunces, and associat-
ing always with the proper, well-dressed young gentlemen who never
attracted attention. All that remained of his boyhood was a veritable
cult of dress. Paris opened his eyes, turned him into a smart young
man, with tight-fitting clothes of the latest fashion. He was the
Brummel* of his class. He appeared there as if it were a society
drawing room, daintily booted, correctly gloved, with amazing neck-
ties and indescribable hats. There were about twenty like him in all;
they formed a sort of aristocracy, offering one another, as they left
school, Havana cigars out of gold-clasped cigar-cases, and having
servants in livery to carry their books. Maxime had persuaded his
father to buy him a tilbury* and a little black horse, which were the
envy of his schoolfellows. He drove himself, while a footman sat with
folded arms on the back seat, holding on his knees the schoolboy's
knapsack, a real ministerial portfolio in brown grained leather. And
how lightly, how cleverly, and with what excellent form Maxime
drove in ten minutes from the Rue de Rivoli to the Rue du Havre,
drew up before the school door, threw the reins to the footman, and
said: 'Jacques, half-past four, then?' The neighbouring shopkeepers
were delighted with the favours of this fair-haired young spark,
whom they saw twice a day arriving and leaving in his trap. On
returning home he sometimes gave a lift to a friend, whom he set
down at his door. The two children smoked, looked at the women,
splashed the passers-by, as if they were returning from the races.
A remarkable little world, a foolish, foppish brood you can see any
day in the Rue du Havre, smartly dressed in their dandy jackets,
aping the ways of rich, worldly men, while the Bohemian contingent
of the school, the real schoolboys, come shouting and shoving,

stomping on the pavement with their heavy shoes, their books hung over their backs by a strap.

Renée, who took herself seriously as a mother and governess, was delighted with her pupil. She left nothing undone, in fact, to complete his education. She was at that time passing through a period of mortification and tears; a lover had jilted her openly, before the eyes of Tout Paris, to attach himself to the Duchesse de Sternich. She dreamt of Maxime as her consolation, she made herself look older, she strained to appear maternal, and became the most eccentric mentor imaginable. Often Maxime's tilbury would be left at home, and Renée would come to fetch the boy in her barouche. They hid the brown portfolio under the seat and drove to the Bois, then in all the freshness of its novelty. There she put him through a course in high society. She pointed everyone out to him in the fat and happy Paris of the Empire, still under the spell of the magic wand that had changed yesterday's beggars and swindlers into great lords and millionaires gasping and fainting under the weight of their cash-boxes. But the child questioned her above all about the women, and as she was very familiar with him, she gave him exact particulars: Madame de Guende was stupid but had a very fine figure; Comtesse Vanska, a very rich woman, had been a street-singer before marrying a Pole who beat her, so they said; as for the Marquise d'Espanet and Suzanne Haffner, they were inseparable, and though they were Renée's close friends, she added, compressing her lips as if to prevent herself from saying more, some very nasty stories were told about them; the beautiful Madame de Lauwerens also had a very dubious reputation, but she had such lovely eyes, and after all everybody knew that she herself was quite beyond reproach, though she was a little too mixed up in the intrigues of the poor little women with whom she associated, Madame Daste, Madame Tessière, and Baronne de Meinhold. Maxime obtained the portraits of these ladies, and with them filled an album that lay on the table in the drawing room. With the vicious artfulness that was the dominant note of his character, he tried to embarrass his stepmother by asking for particulars about the courtesans, pretending to take them for society ladies. Renée became serious and moral, and told him that they were dreadful creatures and that he must be careful to keep away from them; and then, forgetting herself, she spoke of them as of people whom she had known intimately. One of the youngster's great delights was to get her on to the subject of the Duchesse de Sternich. Each time her carriage passed theirs in the Bois, he never failed to mention the Duchesse's name, with a wicked sideways glance that showed that he knew about Renée's last adventure. Whereupon, in a harsh voice, she tore her rival to pieces: how quickly she was ageing! Poor woman! She plastered her face with make-up, she had lovers hidden in every cupboard, she had given herself to a chamberlain so that she might gain admission to the Imperial bed. She went on and on, while Maxime, to exasperate her, declared that he thought Madame de Sternich delightful. Such lessons as these singularly developed the boy's intelligence, the more so as his young teacher repeated them wherever they went, in the Bois, at the theatre, at parties. The pupil became very proficient.

What Maxime loved was to live among women's skirts, in the midst of their finery, in their rice-powder. He still remained more or less a girl, with his delicate hands, his beardless face, his plump white neck. Renée consulted him seriously about her gowns. He knew the best dressmakers in Paris, summed up each of them in a word, talked about the artfulness of such and such's bonnets and the design of another's dresses. At seventeen there was not a milliner he had not assessed, nor a bootmaker he had not studied. This quaint little creature, who during his English lessons read the prospectuses which his perfumer sent him every Friday, could have delivered a brilliant lecture on the fashions of Parisian high society, customers and purveyors included, at an age when country urchins are too shy to look their housemaids in the face. Often, on his way home from school, he would bring back in his tilbury a bonnet, a box of soap, or a piece of jewellery which his stepmother had ordered the day before. He always had some strip of musk-scented lace in his pockets.

But his greatest treat was to accompany Renée to the illustrious Worms, the couturier of genius to whom the great ladies of the Second Empire bowed down. The great man's showroom was huge and square, and furnished with enormous divans. Maxime entered it with religious emotion. Dresses undoubtedly have a perfume of their own; silk, satin, velvet, and lace had mingled their faint aromas with those of hair and of amber-scented shoulders; and the atmosphere in the room had the sweet-smelling warmth, the fragrance of flesh and luxury, that transformed the apartment into a chapel consecrated to some secret divinity. It was often necessary for Renée and Maxime to wait for hours; a queue of at least twenty women sat there, waiting their turn, dipping biscuits into glasses of Madeira, helping themselves from the great table in the middle, which was covered with bottles and plates of cakes. The ladies had made themselves at home, talking freely, and when they ensconced themselves around the room, it was as if a flight of doves had alighted on the sofas of a Parisian drawing room. Maxime, whom they accepted and loved for his girlish air, was the only man admitted into the circle. There he tasted delights divine: he glided along the sofas like an adder; he would be discovered under a skirt, behind a bodice, between two dresses, where he made himself quite small and kept very quiet, inhaling the warm fragrance of his neighbours like a choirboy taking the sacrament.

'That child pokes his nose everywhere,' said the Baronne de Meinhold, tapping his cheeks.

He was so slightly built that the ladies did not think him more than fourteen. They amused themselves by making him tipsy with Worms's Madeira. He said outrageous things to them, which made them laugh till they cried. It was the Marquise d'Espanet who found the right word to describe the situation. One day, when Maxime was discovered behind her back in a corner of the divan, and seeing him blushing, glowing with satisfaction at having been so close to her, she murmured:

'That boy ought to have been born a girl.'

Then, when the great Worms finally received Renée, Maxime followed her into the consulting room. He had ventured to speak on two or three occasions while the master remained lost in contemplation of his client, as the high priests of the Beautiful hold that Leonardo da Vinci did in the presence of La Gioconda.* The master had deigned to smile at the accuracy of his observations. He made Renée stand before a mirror which rose from the floor to the ceiling, and pondered with knit brows while Renée, overcome with emotion, held her breath, so as to remain quite still. After a few minutes the master, as if gripped by inspiration, sketched in broad, jerky strokes the work of art he had just conceived, exclaiming in short phrases:

'A Montespan* dress in pale-grey faille..., the skirt describing a rounded basque* in front..., large grey satin bows to bring it up on the hips..., and a puffed apron of pearl-grey tulle, the puffs separated by strips of grey satin.'

He pondered once again, seeming to plumb the depths of his genius, and, with the triumphant facial contortion of a Pythoness* on her tripod, concluded:

'We'll have in the hair, on this delightful head, Psyche's* dreamy butterfly, with iridescent blue wings.'

But at other times inspiration was slow to come. The illustrious Worms summoned it in vain, and concentrated his faculties to no purpose. He puckered his eyebrows, turned livid, took his head in his hands and shook it in despair, and, beaten, throwing himself into an armchair, would mutter in a pitiful voice: 'No, no, not today... It's impossible... You ladies expect too much. My inspiration has completely dried up.' He would show Renée out, repeating: 'I can't relate to you this morning.'

The excellent education Maxime received bore early fruit. At seventeen the young lad seduced his stepmother's maid. The worst of the affair was that the maid had a baby. They had to send her to the country with the brat, and give her a small annuity. Renée was furious. Saccard did not interfere except to make the financial arrangement; but his young wife gave her pupil a good scolding. That he, whom she wanted to turn into a gentleman, should compromise himself with a girl like that! What a ridiculous, disgraceful beginning, what a shameful escapade! He might at least have started off with a lady!

'Quite true!' he replied. 'If your dear friend Suzanne had been willing, she might have been sent to the country.'

'Oh! the little devil!' she murmured, disarmed, amused by the idea of seeing Suzanne retiring to the country with an annuity of twelve hundred francs.

Then a funnier thought occurred to her, and forgetting that she was playing the indignant mother, bursting into pearly laughter which made her put her hand to her mouth, she stammered, giving him a sidelong glance:

'Adeline would have given you a terrible time, and what a scene she would have made with Suzanne...'

She stopped. They were both laughing hysterically. Thus concluded Renée's lecture on this episode.

Meanwhile Saccard hardly troubled himself about the two children, as he called his son and his second wife. He left them in complete freedom, glad to see them such good friends. The apartment was thus filled with noise and merriment. It was an amazing apartment, this first floor in the Rue de Rivoli. There was a slamming of doors all day long; the servants talked in loud voices; its new and dazzling luxury was continually traversed by a flood of vast, floating skirts, by processions of tradespeople, by the noise of Renée's friends, Maxime's schoolfellows, and Saccard's callers. From nine to eleven Saccard received the strangest set imaginable: senators and bailiffs' clerks, duchesses and old-clothes women, all the scum that the streets of Paris hurled at his door every morning, silk gowns, dirty skirts, workmen's blouses, dress-coats, all of whom he received in the same breathless manner, with the same impatient, nervous gestures; he clinched business arrangements with a brief command, solved twenty problems at once, and gave orders on the run. One would have thought that this restless little man with the very loud voice was fighting with people in his study, and with the furniture, tumbling head over heels, knocking his head against the ceiling to make his ideas flash out, and always falling triumphantly on his feet. At eleven o'clock he would go out; he was not seen again during the day; he breakfasted out, often he even dined out. Then the house belonged to Renée and Maxime: they took possession of the father's study; they unpacked the tradesmen's parcels there, and articles of finery lay about among the business papers. Sometimes people had to wait for an hour at the study door while the schoolboy and the young married woman discussed a bow of ribbon, seated at either end of Saccard's writing-table. Renée had the horses put to ten times a day. They rarely had a meal together; two of the three would be rushing about, forgetting themselves, staying out till midnight. An apartment full of noise, business, and pleasure, through which modern life, with the sound of jingling gold and rustling skirts, swept like a whirlwind.

Aristide Saccard was in his element at last. He had shown himself to be a great speculator, capable of making millions. After the master-stroke in the Rue de la Pépinière, he threw himself boldly into the struggle which was beginning to fill Paris with shameful disasters and overnight triumphs. He began by gambling on certainties, repeating his first success, buying up houses which he knew to be threatened with demolition, and using his friends to obtain huge compensation prices. The moment came when he had five or six houses, the same houses he had looked at with such interest, as if they were acquaintances of his, in the days when he was only a poor surveying-clerk. But these were merely the first steps in his art as a speculator. No great cleverness was needed to run out leases, conspire with tenants, and rob the State and individuals; nor did he think the game worth the candle. This was why he soon used his genius for transactions of a more complicated nature.

Saccard first invented the trick of making secret purchases of house property on the City's account. A decision of the Council of State had placed the City in a difficult position. It had acquired by private contract a large number of houses, in the hope of running out the leases and turning the tenants out without compensation. But these purchases were pronounced to be genuine acts of expropriation, and the City had to pay. It was then that Saccard offered to lend his name to the City: he bought houses, ran out the leases, and for a consideration handed over the property at a fixed date. He even began to play a double game: he acted as buyer both for the City and for the Prefect. Whenever the deal was irresistibly tempting, he stuck to the house himself. The State paid. In return for his assistance he received building concessions for bits of streets, for open spaces, which he disposed of before the new boulevard was even begun. It was a tremendous gamble: the new neighbourhoods were speculated in as one speculates in stocks and shares. Certain ladies were involved, beautiful women, intimately connected with some of the prominent officials; one of them, whose white teeth are world-famous, has eaten up whole streets on more than one occasion. Saccard was insatiable, he felt his greed grow at the sight of the flood of gold that glided through his fingers. It seemed to him as if a sea of twenty-franc pieces stretched out around him, swelling from a lake to an ocean, filling the vast horizon with a strange sound of waves, a metallic music that tickled his heart; and he grew bolder, plunging deeper every day, diving and coming up again, now on his back, now on his belly, swimming through this great expanse in fair weather and foul, and relying on his strength and skill to prevent him from ever sinking to the bottom.

Paris was at that time disappearing in a cloud of plaster-dust. The time predicted by Saccard on the Buttes Montmartre had come. The city was being slashed with sabre-cuts, and he had played a part in every gash. He owned demolished houses in every neighbourhood. In the Rue de Rome he was mixed up in the amazing story of the pit which was dug by a company in order to remove five or six thousand cubic metres of soil and create a belief that great works were in progress, and which had afterwards to be filled in when the company went bankrupt, by bringing the soil back from Saint-Ouen. Saccard came out of it with an easy conscience and full pockets, thanks to the benign intervention of his brother Eugène. At Chaillot he assisted in cutting through the heights and throwing them into a hollow in order to make way for the boulevard that runs from the Arc de Triomphe to the Pont de l'Alma.* In Passy it was he who conceived the idea of scattering the rubbish from the Trocadéro over the high ground, so that to this day the good soil is buried two metres below the surface and the weeds refuse to grow through the rubbish. He was to be found in twenty places at once, at every spot where there was some insurmountable obstacle, a heap of rubbish no one knew what to do with, a hollow that could not be filled up, a great mass of soil and plaster over which the engineers in their haste had lost patience, but in which he rummaged with his nails and invariably ended by finding some profit or some speculation to his taste. On the same day he would run from the works at the Arc de Triomphe to those at the Boulevard Saint-Michel, from the clearings in the Boulevard Malesherbes to the embankments at Chaillot, dragging after him an army of workmen, lawyers, shareholders, dupes, and swindlers.

But his greatest triumph was the Crédit Viticole, which he had founded with Toutin-Laroche. The latter was the official director; Saccard only figured as a member of the board. In this connection Eugène had done his brother another good turn. Thanks to him the Government authorized the company and watched indulgently over its career. On one delicate occasion, when a hostile newspaper ventured to criticize one of the company's operations, the *Moniteur** went so far as to publish a note forbidding any discussion of so honourable an undertaking, one which the State deigned to protect. The Crédit Viticole was based on an excellent financial system: it lent the winegrowers half of the estimated value of their property, ensured the repayment of the loan by a mortgage, and received interest from the borrowers in addition to instalments of the principal. Never was there a mechanism more prudent or more worthy. Eugène had declared to his brother, with a knowing smile, that the Tuileries expected people to be honest. Monsieur Toutin-Laroche interpreted this wish by allowing the wine-growers' loan office to work quietly, and founding by its side a banking house which attracted capital and gambled feverishly, launching into every sort of adventure. Thanks to the formidable impulse it received from its director, the Crédit Viticole soon established a solid reputation for security and prosperity. At the outset, in order to offer at the Bourse in one job a mass of shares on which no dividend had yet been paid, and to give them the appearance of having been in circulation for some time, Saccard had the ingenuity to have them trodden on and beaten, a whole night long, by the bank-messengers, armed with birch-brooms. The place was like a branch of the Banque de France. The house occupied by the offices, with its courtyard full of private carriages, its austere iron railings, its broad flight of steps and monumental staircase, its suites of luxurious reception rooms, its army of clerks and liveried lackeys, seemed to be the grave, dignified temple of Mammon; and nothing filled the public with a more religious emotion than the sanctuary, the cashier's office, which was approached by a corridor of hallowed bareness and contained the safe, the god, crouching, embedded in the wall, squat and somnolent, with its triple lock, its massive flanks, its air of a brute divinity.

Saccard carried through a big job with the City. The latter was seriously in debt, dragged into this dance of gold which it had led off to please the Emperor and to line certain people's pockets, and was now reduced to borrowing covertly, not caring to confess its violent fever, its stone-and-pickaxe madness. It had begun to issue what were called delegation bonds,* really post-dated bills of exchange, so that the contractors might be paid on the day the agreements were signed, and thus enabled to obtain money by discounting the bonds. The Crédit Viticole had graciously accepted this paper at the contractors' hands. One day when the City was in need of money, Saccard went and tempted it. It received a considerable advance on an issue of delegation bonds, which Monsieur Toutin-Laroche swore he held from contracting companies, and which he dragged through every gutter of speculation. Thenceforward the Crédit Viticole was safe from attack; it held Paris by the throat. The director now talked only with a smile about the famous Société Générale of the Ports of Morocco; yet it still existed, and the newspapers continued to extol its great commercial stations. One day when Monsieur Toutin-Laroche tried to persuade Saccard to buy shares in this company, the latter laughed in his face and asked him if he thought he was such a fool as to invest in the Société Générale of *The Arabian Nights*.

Until then, Saccard had speculated successfully, with safe profits, cheating, selling himself, making money on deals, deriving some sort of profit from each of his operations. Soon, however, this form of speculation was no longer enough for him; he disdained to glean and pick up the gold which men like Toutin-Laroche and Baron Gouraud dropped behind them. He plunged his arms in the sack up to his elbows. He went into partnership with Mignon, Charrier, and Co., those famous contractors, who were then just starting and were destined to make huge fortunes. The City had already decided no longer to carry out the works itself, but to have the boulevards laid out by contract. The tendering companies agreed to deliver a complete boulevard, with its trees planted, its benches and lamp-posts fixed, in return for a specified indemnity; sometimes they even delivered the boulevard for nothing, finding themselves amply remunerated by retaining the adjacent building-ground, for which they asked a considerably inflated price. The frenzied speculation in land and the fantastic increase in property values date from this time.* Saccard obtained through his connections a concession to lay out three lots of boulevards. He was the passionate and somewhat undisciplined member of the partnership. Mignon and Charrier, his creatures at the outset, were a pair of fat, cunning cronies, master-masons who knew the value of money. They laughed up their sleeves at Saccard's horses and carriages; more often than not they kept on their blouses, always ready to shake hands with their workmen, and returned home covered in plaster. They both came from Langres. They brought into this burning and insatiable Paris their Champenois caution and their calm temperament; they were not very imaginative, nor very intelligent, but were exceedingly quick to take advantage of opportunities to line their pockets, content to enjoy themselves later on. If Saccard was the animating spirit of the business, infusing it with his vigour and greed, Mignon and Charrier, by their matter-of-fact ways, their methodical, narrow management, saved it a score of times from being capsized by the extraordinary imagination of their partner. They would not agree to have superb offices, in a house he wanted to build in order to amaze the whole of Paris. They refused, moreover, to entertain the subsidiary speculative schemes that sprouted in his head each morning: the building of concert halls and immense baths on the building-ground bordering their boulevards; of railways along the line of the new boulevards; of glass-roofed arcades which would increase the rent of the shops tenfold and allow people to walk about Paris without getting wet. The contractors, to put a stop to these alarming projects, decided that these pieces of ground should be apportioned among the three partners, and that each of them should do as he pleased with his share. They wisely continued to sell theirs. Saccard built on his. His brain teemed with extravagant ideas. He would have proposed in all seriousness to put Paris under an immense bell-glass, so as to transform it into a hothouse for forcing pineapples and sugar-cane.

Before long, turning over money by the shovelful, he had eight houses on the new boulevards. He had four that were completely finished: two in the Rue de Marignan, and two on the Boulevard Haussmann; the four others, situated on the Boulevard Malesherbes, remained in progress, and one of them, in fact, a vast enclosure of planks from which a mansion was to arise, had got no further than the flooring of the first storey. At this period his affairs became so complicated, he had his fingers in so many pies, that he slept barely three hours a night and read his correspondence in his carriage. The marvellous thing was that his coffers seemed inexhaustible. He held shares in every company, built houses with a sort of mania, turned to every trade, and threatened to inundate Paris like a rising tide; and yet he was never seen to realize a genuine clear profit, to pocket a big sum of gold shining in the sun. This flood of gold with no known source, which seemed to flow from his office in endless waves, astonished the onlookers and made him, at one moment, a prominent public figure to whom the newspapers ascribed all the witticisms that came out of the Bourse.

With such a husband Renée could hardly be said to be married at all. She would hardly see him for weeks. For the rest he was perfect; his cash-box was always open. She liked him as she would have liked an obliging banker. When she visited the Hôtel Béraud, she praised him to the skies to her father, whose cold austerity remained quite unaffected by his son-in-law's good fortune. Her contempt had disappeared: this man seemed so convinced that life is a mere business, he was so obviously born to make money with whatever fell into his hands—women, children, pavingstones, sacks of plaster, consciences—that she could no longer reproach him for their marriage-bargain. Since that bargain he regarded her rather like one of the fine houses he owned and which would, he hoped, yield a large profit. He liked to see her well-dressed, flamboyant, attracting the attention of Tout Paris. It consolidated his position, doubled the probable size of his fortune. He seemed young, handsome, in love, and scatterbrained because of his wife. She was his partner, his unconscious accomplice. A new pair of horses, a two-thousand-crown dress, the indulgence of some lover facilitated and often ensured the success of his most successful transactions. He often pretended to be tired out and sent her to a minister, to some functionary or other, to solicit an authorization or receive a reply. He would say 'Be good!' in a tone all his own, at once bantering and coaxing; and when she returned, having succeeded, he would rub his hands, repeating his famous 'I hope you were good!' Renée would laugh. He was too busy to desire a Madame Michelin. But he loved crude jokes and risqué stories. For the rest, had Renée not 'been good', he would have experienced only the disappointment of having really paid for the minister's or the functionary's indulgence. To dupe people, to give them less than their money's-worth, was his delight. He often said: 'If I were a woman, I might sell myself, but I'd never deliver the goods: that's stupid!'

Renée, who had shot one night into the Parisian firmament as the eccentric fairy of fashionable, voluptuous pleasure, was the most complex of women. Had she been brought up at home, doubtless she would, by the aid of religion or some other nervous satisfaction, have blunted the point of that desire whose stinging sometimes drove her to distraction. Her outlook was bourgeois: she was absolutely honest, loved logical systems, feared heaven and hell, and was full of prejudices; she was the daughter of her father, of that placid, prudent race which nurtures the virtues of the hearth. And in this nature sprouted her prodigious fantasies, her insatiable curiosity, her unspeakable longings. At the Ladies of the Visitation, her mind freely roaming amid the mystic voluptuousness of the chapel and the carnal attachments of her young friends, she had acquired a fantastic education, learning vice and confusing her brain to the extent of singularly embarrassing her confessor by telling him that one day at

mass she had felt an irrational desire to get up and kiss him. Then
she beat her breast, and turned pale at the thought of the Devil and
his cauldrons. The lapse that led to her marriage with Saccard, the
brutal rape she underwent with a sort of frightened expectation,
made her despise herself, and accounted in large measure for the
subsequent abandonment of her whole life. She thought that she
need no longer struggle against evil, that it was in her, that logic
authorized her to pursue the study of wickedness to its ultimate
conclusions. She had even more curiosity than appetite. Thrown
into the world of the Second Empire, abandoned to her imagination,
kept in money, encouraged in her most extravagant eccentricities,
she gave herself, then regretted it, and finally succeeded in killing off
her good principles, driven by her insatiable desire for knowledge
and new sensations.

Yet she had turned only the first page of the book of vice. She was
fond of talking in a low voice, and laughing, about the strange cases of
the close friendship of Suzanne Haffner and Adeline d'Espanet, of
the ticklish trade of Madame de Lauwerens, and of Comtesse Vanska's rationed kisses; but she still looked upon these things from afar,
with the idea of tasting similar pleasures perhaps; and the vague
longing that arose within her at evil hours increased her anxiety, her
mad quest for a unique, exquisite form of pleasure which she alone
would enjoy. Her first lovers had not spoilt her; three times she had
thought herself in the grip of a grand passion; love burst in her head
like a cracker whose sparks failed to reach her heart. She went mad
for a month, exhibiting herself with her lord and master all over
Paris; then one morning, amid the tumult of her passion, she became
aware of a great silence, an immense void. The first, the young Duc
de Rozan, was a feast of sunshine that led to nothing; Renée, who had
noticed him because of his gentleness and his excellent manners,
found him utterly dull and shallow when they were alone together.
Mr Simpson, an attaché at the American Embassy, who came next,
all but beat her, and thanks to this remained with her for more than a
year. Then she took up with the Comte de Chibray, one of the
Emperor's aides-de-camp, a handsome but extremely vain man of
whom she was beginning to tire when the Duchesse de Sternich took
it into her head to become enamoured of him and to take him away
from her; whereupon she wept for him and gave her friends to understand that her heart was broken, and that she would never fall in love

again. So she drifted towards Monsieur de Mussy, the most insignificant creature in the world, a young man who was making his way in diplomacy by leading *cotillons** with especial grace; she never knew exactly how she had come to give herself to him, and she kept him a long time, through sheer inertia, disgusted with the unknown that is explored in an hour, and deferring the upheaval of a change until she met with some extraordinary adventure. At twenty-eight she was already world-weary. Her boredom seemed to her all the more unbearable because her bourgeois virtues took advantage of the hours when she was bored to assert themselves and to trouble her. She bolted her door, she had terrible migraines. Then, when she opened the door again, a flood of silk and lace surged through it, a luxurious, joyous being without a care in the world.

Yet she had had a romance amid the fashionable pursuits of her life. One day, when she had gone out on foot to see her father, who disliked the noise of carriages at his door, she noticed, as she was walking back in the twilight along the Quai Saint-Paul, that she was being followed by a young man. It was warm; and the day was dying in amorous languor. She was never followed except on horseback in the lanes of the Bois, and thought the adventure piquant; she felt flattered by it, as by a new and somewhat crude form of flattery whose very crudity appealed to her. Instead of returning home, she turned into the Rue du Temple and walked her admirer along the boulevards. The man, however, grew bolder and became so persistent that Renée, somewhat put out, lost her head, followed the Rue du Faubourg-Poissonnière, and took refuge in her sister-in-law's shop. The man came in after her. Madame Sidonie smiled, seemed to understand, and left them alone. When Renée made as if to follow her, the stranger held her back, addressed her respectfully, and won her forgiveness. He was a clerk, his name was Georges, and she never asked him his surname. She came twice to see him; she came in through the shop, and he by the Rue Papillon. This chance love affair, picked up in the street, was one of her greatest pleasures. She always thought of it with a certain shame, but with a nostalgic smile. Madame Sidonie profited from the affair in that she at last became the accomplice of her brother's second wife, a part to which she had been aspiring since their wedding.

Poor Madame Sidonie had experienced a disappointment. While intriguing for the match with Aristide she had expected to marry

Renée a little herself, to turn her into one of her customers and make a lot of money out of her. She judged women at a glance, as experts judge horses. So she was astonished when, after allowing the couple a month to settle down, she came upon Madame de Lauwerens enthroned in the middle of the drawing room, and realized that she was already too late. Madame de Lauwerens, a handsome woman of twenty-six, made a business of launching new arrivals. She came of a very old family, and was married to a man high up in the financial world who had the bad taste to refuse to pay her couturier's and milliner's bills. The lady, a very intelligent person, made money and kept herself. She loathed men, she said, but she supplied all her friends with them; there was always a full array of customers in the apartment she occupied in the Rue de Provence over her husband's offices. You could always have a snack there and meet your friends in a casual and pleasant fashion. There was no harm in a young girl's going to see her dear Madame de Lauwerens, and if by chance there were men there who were, moreover, respectful and moved in the best circles—there was no harm in that either. The hostess was adorable in her long lace tea-gowns. Many a visitor would have chosen her in preference to her collection of blondes and brunettes. But by all accounts her conduct was beyond reproach. That was indeed her secret. She kept up her high position in society, had all the men for her friends, kept her pride as a virtuous woman, and derived secret enjoyment from bringing others down and profiting from their fall. When Madame Sidonie discovered how the new system worked, she was taken aback. The classical school, the woman in the old black dress carrying love-letters at the bottom of her basket, was brought face to face with the modern, the *grande dame* who sells her friends in her boudoir while sipping tea. The modern school triumphed. Madame de Lauwerens looked askance at the shabby attire of Madame Sidonie, in whom she scented a rival; and it was she who provided Renée with her first lover, the young Duc de Rozan, whom the fair financier had found very difficult to dispose of. The classical school did not win the day till later on, when Madame Sidonie lent her entresol to her sister-in-law so that she might satisfy her liking for the stranger from the Quai Saint-Paul. She remained her confidante.

But one of Madame Sidonie's faithful friends was Maxime. From his fifteenth year he had been in the habit of prowling around at his aunt's, sniffing the gloves he found lying on the sideboards. She, who hated clear situations and never owned up to her little favours, ended by lending him the keys to her apartment at certain times, saying that she was going to stay in the country till the next day. Maxime talked of some friends he wanted to entertain, and whom he dared not ask to his father's house. It was in the entresol in the Rue du Faubourg-Poissonnière that he spent several nights with the poor girl who had to be sent to the country. Madame Sidonie borrowed money from her nephew, and went into ecstasies before him, murmuring in her soft voice that he was 'as soft and pink as a cherub'.

In the meantime, Maxime had grown. He was now a nice-looking, slender young man who still had the rosy cheeks and blue eyes of childhood. His curly hair had completed the 'girlish look' that so enchanted the ladies. He looked like poor Angèle, with her soft expression and blonde pallor. But he was not even the equal of that lazy, shallow woman. In him the Rougons had become refined, had grown delicate and corrupt. Born of a mother who was too young, constituting a strange, jumbled, and so to speak, diffuse mixture of his father's wild appetites and his mother's passivity and weakness, he was a defective offspring in whom the parental shortcomings were combined and exacerbated. The family lived too fast; it was dying out already in this frail creature, whose sex remained uncertain, and who represented, not greed for money and pleasure like Saccard, but a mean nature devouring ready-made fortunes, a strange hermaphrodite making a timely entrance in a society that was rotting. When Maxime rode in the Bois, pinched in at the waist like a woman, bouncing lightly in the saddle, swayed by the canter of his horse, he was the god of his generation, with his swelling hips, his long, slender hands, his sickly, lascivious air, his correct elegance, and his comic-opera argot. He was twenty, and already there was nothing left to surprise or disgust him. He had certainly dreamt of the most extreme forms of debauchery. Vice with him was not an abyss, as with certain old men, but a natural, external growth. It waved over his fair hair, smiled upon his lips, dressed him in his clothes. But his special characteristic was his eyes, two clear blue apertures, coquettes' mirrors behind which one could see the emptiness of his brain. These whorish eyes were never lowered: they roamed in search of pleasure, a pleasure that comes without effort, that is summoned, then enjoyed.

The never-ending whirlwind that swept through the apartment in the Rue de Rivoli and made its doors slam backwards and forwards blew stronger as Maxime grew up, as Saccard enlarged the sphere of his operations, and Renée became more feverish in her quest for unknown delights. The three of them ended by leading an astonishingly undisciplined and demented existence. The street invaded the apartment with its rumbling carriages, jostling strangers, and permissive language. The father, the stepmother, and the stepson behaved, talked, and made themselves at home as if they led quite separate lives. Three close friends, three students sharing the same furnished room, could not have used the apartment with less restraint for the installation of their vices, their loves, and their noisy, adolescent gaiety. They accepted one another with a handshake, never seeming aware of the reasons that united them under one roof, happy to leave each other completely alone. The idea of a family was replaced for them by the notion of a sort of investment company where the profits are shared equally; each took his part of the pleasure, and it was tacitly agreed that each could do with his part whatever he wanted. They went so far as to take their pleasure in each other's presence, displaying it, describing it, without provoking in the others anything but a little envy and curiosity.

It was Maxime now who was Renée's teacher. When he went to the Bois with her, he told her stories about courtesans that amused them both tremendously. A new woman could not appear by the lake without his immediately striving to ascertain the name of her lover, the allowance he gave her, the style in which she lived. He knew these ladies' homes and all sorts of intimate details about them; he was a living catalogue in which all the courtesans in Paris were listed, with a complete description of each of them. This gazette of scandal was Renée's delight. On race-days, at Longchamps, when she drove by in her barouche, she listened eagerly while retaining the haughtiness of a woman of the real world, to how Blanche Muller deceived her attaché with a hairdresser; or how the little Baron had found the Count in his underclothes in the alcove of a skinny, red-haired celebrity nicknamed The Crayfish. Each day brought a new piece of gossip. When the story was rather too crude, Maxime lowered his voice, but told it to the end. Renée opened her eyes wide, like a child listening to an account of a practical joke, restrained her laughter, then stifled it in her embroidered handkerchief, which she pressed daintily to her lips.

Maxime also brought these ladies' photographs. He had actresses'
photographs in all his pockets, and even in his cigar-case. From time
to time he cleared them out and placed these ladies in the album that
lay about on the furniture in the drawing room, and already contained the photographs of Renée's friends. There were men's photographs there too, Monsieur de Rozan, Simpson, de Chibray, and de
Mussy, as well as actors, writers, and deputies, who had come some-
how to swell the collection. A strangely mixed society, a symbol of
the jumble of people and ideas that moved through Renée's and
Maxime's lives. Whenever it rained or they felt bored, this album
was their great subject of conversation. They always ended up looking at it. Renée opened it with a yawn, for the hundredth time
perhaps. Then her curiosity would reawaken, the young man came
and leant behind her, and there followed long discussions about The
Crayfish's hair, Madame de Meinhold's double chin, Madame de
Lauwerens' eyes, and Blanche Muller's bust;* about the Marquise's
nose, which was a little on one side, and little Sylvia's mouth, which
was renowned for the thickness of its lips. They compared the
women with each other.

'If I were a man,' said Renée, 'I'd choose Adeline.'

'That's because you don't know Sylvia,' replied Maxime. 'She's so
funny! I must say I prefer Sylvia.'

The pages were turned over; sometimes the Duc de Rozan
appeared, or Mr Simpson, or the Comte de Chibray, and he added,
laughing at her:

'Besides, your taste is perverted, everybody knows that... Can
you imagine anything more stupid than the faces of those men!
Rozan and Chibray are both like Gustave, my hairdresser.'

Renée shrugged, as if to say that she was immune to sarcasm. She
was again lost in contemplation of the pale, smiling, or impassive
faces in the album; she lingered longest over the portraits of the
courtesans, studying the exact microscopic details of the photographs, the minute wrinkles, the tiny hairs. One day she even sent for
a powerful magnifying glass, fancying she had spotted a hair on The
Crayfish's nose. In fact the glass did reveal a thin golden thread,
which had strayed from the eyebrows down to the middle of the
nose. This hair kept them amused for a long time. For a whole week
the ladies who called were made to verify for themselves the presence
of this hair. From then on the magnifying glass served to pick the

women's faces to pieces. Renée made astonishing discoveries: she
found unknown wrinkles, coarse skin, cavities imperfectly filled with
rice-powder, until Maxime finally hid the glass, declaring that it was
not right to become so disgusted with the human face. The truth was
that she scrutinized too closely the thick lips of Sylvia, for whom he
had rather a soft spot. They invented a new game. They asked the
question: 'Whom would I like to spend a night with?' and they
looked for an answer in the album. This produced some hilarious
couplings. They played this game for several evenings. Renée was in
this way married successively to the Archbishop of Paris, Baron
Gouraud, Monsieur de Chibray, which caused much laughter, and
her own husband, which distressed her greatly. As to Maxime, either
by chance or by the mischievous design of Renée, who opened the
album, he always fell to the Marquise. But they never laughed as
much as when fate coupled two men or two women together.

The familiarity between Renée and Maxime went so far that she
told him of her sorrows. He consoled and advised her. His father did
not seem to exist. Then they confided in one another about their
childhoods. It was especially during their outings in the Bois that
they felt a vague languour, a longing to tell each other things that are
difficult to say, that are never told. The delight children take in
whispering about forbidden things, the fascination that exists for a
young man and a young woman in descending together into sin, if
only in words, brought them back constantly to scabrous stories.
They revelled shamelessly in the pleasure of this story-telling, reclining lazily in the corners of the carriage like two old schoolfriends
recalling their first erotic adventures. They ended by boasting about
their immorality. Renée confessed that the little girls at the boarding
school were very smutty. Maxime went further and boldly related
some of the shameful behaviour at the school in Plassans.

'Ah! I can't tell you,' murmured Renée. Then she put her mouth
to his ear, as if the sound of her voice would have made her blush,
and confided to him one of those convent stories that are spun out in
dirty songs. He knew too many similar anecdotes to be outdone. He
hummed some very bawdy couplets in her ear; and little by little they
fell into a peculiar state of beatitude, lulled by all the visions of
carnal desire they stirred up. The carriage rolled on, and they
returned home deliciously tired, more exhausted than in the morning
after a night of lovemaking. They had sinned like two young men

who, wandering down country lanes without their mistresses, satisfy themselves with an exchange of reminiscences.

Even greater familiarity and licence existed between father and son. Saccard had realized that a great financier must love women and commit extravagances for them. He was a rough lover, and preferred money; but it became part of his programme to frequent alcoves, to scatter banknotes on certain mantelpieces, and from time to time to use a prominent courtesan as a signboard for his speculations. After Maxime had left school they used to meet in the same women's apartments and laugh about it. They were even rivals to some extent. Occasionally, when Maxime was dining at the Maison d'Or* with some noisy crowd, he heard Saccard's voice in an adjacent private room.

'I say! Papa is next door!' he cried, pulling a face like a well-known actor.

He went and knocked at the door of the private room, curious to see his father's conquest.

'Ah! It's you,' said the latter jovially. 'Come in. You're making so much noise that a man can't hear himself eat. Who are you with?'

'Well, there's Laure d'Aurigny, and Sylvia, and The Crayfish, and two more, I believe. They're wonderful: they dig their fingers into their plates and throw handfuls of salad at us. My coat's covered in oil.'

Saccard laughed, thinking this very amusing.

'Ah! Young people, young people,' he murmured. 'That's not like us, is it, my pet? We've had a nice quiet dinner, and now we're going to have a little sleep.'

He touched the woman under the chin and cooed with his Provençal snuffle, producing a strange sort of love music.

'Oh! you old rascal!' cried the woman. 'How are you, Maxime? I must be fond of you, to agree to have supper with this father of yours. I never see you these days. Come and see me the day after tomorrow, in the morning, early. I've got something to tell you.'

Saccard finished an ice cream or a piece of fruit, savouring small mouthfuls. He kissed the woman on the shoulder, saying jokingly:

'You know, my dears, if I'm in the way I'll go out. You can ring to tell me when I can come in again.'

Then he carried the lady off, or sometimes went with her and joined the noisy company in the next room. Maxime and he shared the same shoulders; their hands met round the same waists. They called to one another on the sofas, and repeated to one another out loud the confidences the women had whispered in their ears. They carried their intimacy to the point of plotting together to carry off from the company the blonde or the brunette whom one of them had chosen.

They were well known at Mabille.* They went there arm in arm, after a good dinner, strolling round the garden, nodding to the women, tossing them a remark as they went by. They laughed out loud, without unlocking their arms, and came to one another's aid if necessary whenever the conversation became too lively. The father negotiated his son's love affairs very successfully. At times they sat down and drank with a group of courtesans. Then they moved to a different table or resumed their stroll. Until midnight they were seen, arm in arm, following the petticoats along the yellow pathways, under the bright flames of the gas jets.

When they returned home they brought with them, in their coats, something of the women they had been with. Their jaunty attitudes, the tags of certain suggestive phrases and vulgar gestures, gave the apartment in the Rue de Rivoli the aura of a disreputable alcove. The carefree way in which the father shook hands with his son was enough to proclaim where they had been. It was in this atmosphere that Renée developed her sensual whims and longings. She mocked them nervously.

'Where on earth have you been?' she asked. 'You smell of musk and tobacco. I know I'll have a headache.'

The strange aroma in fact disturbed her profoundly. It was the dominant perfume of this singular household.

In the meantime Maxime became smitten with little Sylvia. He bored his stepmother with this girl for several months. Renée soon knew her from top to bottom, from the crown of her head to the sole of her feet. She had a birthmark on her hip; nothing was sweeter than her knees; her shoulders had the peculiarity that only the left one was dimpled. Maxime took malicious delight in filling their drives with accounts of his mistress's perfection. One evening, returning from the Bois, Renée's carriage and Sylvia's, caught in a traffic jam, had to draw up side by side in the Champs-Élysées. The two women eyed each other, while Maxime, amused by this confrontation, tittered to himself. When the barouche moved forward again his stepmother maintained a gloomy silence; he thought she was sulking, and expected one of those maternal scenes, one of those strange lectures with which she still occasionally filled her moments of lassitude.

'Do you know that person's jeweller?' she asked him suddenly, just as they reached the Place de la Concorde.

'Yes, alas!' he replied with a smile. 'I owe him ten thousand francs. Why do you ask?'

'No reason.'

Then, after a fresh pause:

'She had a very pretty bracelet, the one on her left wrist. I would have liked to have a closer look.'

They reached home. She said no more on the matter. But the next day, just as Maxime and his father were going out together, she took the young man aside and spoke to him in an undertone, with an air of embarrassment and a pretty, apologetic smile. He seemed surprised and went off, laughing his wicked laugh. In the evening he brought Sylvia's bracelet, which his stepmother had begged him to show her.

'Here's what you wanted,' he said. 'I've become a thief for you, stepmamma.'

'Did she see you take it?' asked Renée, who was greedily examining the bracelet.

'I don't think so. She wore it yesterday, she certainly wouldn't want to wear it again today.'

Renée went to the window. She put on the bracelet, held her wrist up a little and turned it round, enraptured, repeating:

'Oh! Very pretty, very pretty. I like everything about it, except the emeralds.'

At that moment Saccard entered, and as she was still holding up her wrist in the white light of the window, he cried in astonishment: 'What's this? Sylvia's bracelet!'

'Do you know this piece of jewellery?' she said, more embarrassed than he, not knowing what to do with her arm.

He had recovered, and wagged his finger at his son, murmuring:

'That rascal has always got some forbidden fruit in his pocket. One of these days he'll bring us the lady's arm with the bracelet on it.'

'But it wasn't me,' replied Maxime with mock cowardice. 'Renée wanted to see it.'

'Ah!' was all Saccard said.

He examined the bracelet in his turn, repeating like his wife:

'It's very pretty, very pretty.'

He took his leave without another word, and Renée scolded Maxime for giving her away like that. But he declared that his father didn't care a fig! Then she handed back the bracelet, adding:

'You must go to the jeweller and order one exactly like it for me: but it must have sapphires instead of emeralds.'

Saccard could not be near a thing or a person for long without wanting to sell it or derive some profit from it. His son was not yet twenty when he began to think about how to use him. A good-looking boy, nephew to a minister and son of a prominent financier, ought to be a good investment. He was still a trifle young, but it was always possible to find a wife and dowry for him and then put the wedding off, or arrange it quickly, according to the demands of domestic economy. Saccard was fortunate. He discovered on a board of directors of which he was a member a tall, handsome man, Monsieur de Mareuil, who was in his pocket within two days. Monsieur de Mareuil was a retired sugar-refiner from Le Havre, and his real name was Bonnet. After making a large fortune, he had married a young girl of noble birth, also very rich, who was on the lookout for a fool of imposing appearance. Bonnet obtained permission to assume his wife's name, which was a first satisfaction for his bride; but his marriage had made him madly ambitious, and his dream was to repay Hélène for the noble name she had given him by achieving a high political position. From that time onward he put money into new newspapers, bought large estates in the heart of the Nièvre, and by all the usual means made himself a candidate for the Corps Législatif. So far he had failed, but without losing any of his pomposity. He was the most empty-headed individual one could come across. He was of splendid stature, with the white, pensive face of a great statesman; and as he had a marvellous way of listening, with a profound gaze and a majestically calm expression, he gave the impression of a prodigious inner labour of comprehension and deduction. In reality he was thinking of nothing, but he succeeded in perplexing people, who no longer knew whether they were dealing with a man of distinction or a fool. Monsieur de Mareuil attached himself to Saccard as to a raft. He knew that an official candidature was about to fall vacant in the Nièvre, and he fervently hoped that the minister would nominate him: it was his last card. So he handed himself over, bound hand and foot, to the minister's brother. Saccard, who scented a good piece of business, put into his head a match between his daughter Louise and Maxime. Monsieur de Mareuil became most effusive, imagined he was the first to have thought of this marriage, and considered himself very fortunate to enter into a minister's family and to give Louise to a young man who seemed to have such fine prospects.

Louise, her father said, would have a million francs for her dowry. Deformed, ugly, and adorable, she was doomed to die young; consumption was slowly undermining her, giving her a nervous gaiety and a delicate grace. Sick little girls grow old quickly, and become women before their time. She was naively sensual, she seemed to have been born when she was fifteen, in full puberty. When her father, that healthy, stupid colossus, looked at her he could not believe that she was his daughter. Her mother during her lifetime had also been a tall, strong woman; but stories were told about her that explained the child's stuntedness, her manners like a millionaire gypsy's, her vicious and charming ugliness. It was said that Hélène de Mareuil had died in the midst of the most shameful debauchery.* Pleasure had eaten into her like an ulcer, without her husband noticing the lucid madness of his wife, whom he ought to have had locked up in a lunatic asylum. Carried in this diseased body, Louise had issued from it with impoverished blood, deformed limbs, her brain affected and her memory already filled with a dissolute life. She occasionally fancied she could remember a former existence; she saw before her, in shadowy outline, strange scenes, men and women kissing, a whole drama of carnality that engaged her childish curiosity. It was her mother speaking within her. This vice continued through her childhood. As she grew up, nothing could surprise her; she remembered everything, or rather she knew everything, and she reached out for forbidden things with a sureness of hand that made her, in life, resemble a man returning home after a long absence, and having only to stretch out his arm to make himself comfortable and enjoy the pleasures of his home. This odd little girl, whose evil instincts made Maxime seem almost angelic, had in this second life, which she lived as a virgin with all the knowledge and shame of a grown woman, an ingenuous boldness, a piquant mixture of childishness and audacity; she was bound in the end to attract

Maxime, and to seem to him even more diverting than Sylvia, a respectable stationer's daughter who had the heart of a moneylender and was terribly bourgeois by nature.

The marriage was arranged amidst laughter, and it was decided that 'the youngsters' should be allowed to grow up. The two families became very close. Monsieur de Mareuil pursued his candidature. Saccard watched his prey. It was understood that Maxime would place his nomination as an auditor to the Council of State among the wedding presents.

Meanwhile the Saccards' fortune seemed to be at its height. It blazed in the heart of Paris like a huge bonfire. This was the time when the rush for spoils filled a corner of the forest with the yelping of hounds, the cracking of whips, the flaring of torches. The appetites let loose were satisfied at last, shamelessly, amid the sound of crumbling neighbourhoods and fortunes made in six months. The city had become an orgy of gold and women. Vice, coming from on high, flowed through the gutters, spread out over the ornamental waters, shot up in the fountains of the public gardens, and fell on the roofs as fine rain. At night, when people crossed the bridges, it seemed as if the Seine drew along with it, through the sleeping city, all the refuse of the streets, crumbs fallen from tables, bows of lace left on couches, false hair forgotten in cabs, banknotes that had slipped out of bodices, everything thrown out of the window by the brutality of desire and the immediate satisfaction of appetites. Then, amid the troubled sleep of Paris, and even more clearly than during its feverish quest in broad daylight, one felt a growing sense of madness, the voluptuous nightmare of a city obsessed with gold and flesh.* The violins played until midnight; then the windows became dark and shadows descended over the city. It was like a giant alcove in which the last candle had been blown out, the last remnant of shame extinguished. There was nothing left in the darkness except a great rattle of furious and wearied lovemaking; while the Tuileries, by the riverside, stretched out its arms, as if for a huge embrace.

Saccard had just built his mansion in the Parc Monceau, on a plot of ground stolen from the City. He had reserved for himself, on the first floor, a magnificent study, in ebony and gold, with tall glass doors to the bookcases, full of files, but without a book to be seen; the safe, built into the wall, yawned like an iron alcove, large enough to accommodate the love affairs that a hundred thousand francs could

buy. Here his fortune bloomed and insolently displayed itself. Everything he touched seemed to succeed. When he left the Rue de Rivoli,
enlarging his household and doubling his expenses, he talked to his
friends of considerable gains. According to him, his partnership with
Mignon and Charrier brought him enormous profits; his speculations in real estate came off even better; while the Crédit Viticole was
an inexhaustible milch-cow. He had a way of enumerating his riches
that bewildered his listeners and prevented them from seeing the
truth. His Provençal accent grew more pronounced: with his short
phrases and nervous gestures he let off fireworks in which millions
shot up like rockets and ended by dazzling the most incredulous.
These frenetic performances were mainly responsible for his reputation as a lucky speculator. In truth, no one knew whether he had
any solid capital assets. His various partners, who were necessarily
acquainted with his position as regards themselves, explained his
colossal fortune by believing in his absolute luck in other speculations, those in which they had no share. He spent money madly; the
flow from his cash-box continued, though the sources of that stream
of gold had not yet been discovered. It was pure folly, a frenzy of
money, handfuls of louis flung out of the windows, the safe emptied
every evening to its last sou, filling up again during the night, no one
knew how, and never supplying such large sums as when Saccard
pretended to have lost the keys.

In this fortune, which roared and overflowed like a winter torrent,
Renée's dowry was tossed about, carried off, and drowned. The
young wife, who had been mistrustful in the early days of the marriage and wanted to manage her property herself, soon grew weary of
business; she felt poor beside her husband and, crushed by debt, she
was obliged to ask him for help, to borrow money from him and place
herself in his hands. With each fresh bill that he paid, with the smile
of a man indulgent towards human foibles, she surrendered a little
more, confiding dividend-warrants to him, authorizing him to sell
this or that. When they moved into the house in the Parc Monceau,
she already found herself stripped almost bare. He had taken the
place of the State, and paid her the interest on the hundred thousand
francs coming from the Rue de la Pépinière; on the other hand, he
had made her sell the Sologne property in order to sink the proceeds
in a great business project. She therefore had nothing left except the
Charonne building-plots, which she obstinately refused to part with

so as not to sadden her Aunt Élisabeth. But Saccard was preparing a stroke of genius, with the help of his old accomplice, Larsonneau. Renée remained his debtor; though he had taken her fortune, he paid her the income five or six times over. The interest on the hundred thousand francs, added to the revenue from the Sologne money, amounted to barely nine or ten thousand francs, just enough to pay her hosier and bootmaker. He gave her, or spent on her, fifteen or twenty times that sum. He would have worked for a week to rob her of a hundred francs, and he kept her like a queen. So, like everyone else, she respected her husband's monumental safe, without trying to penetrate the mystery of the stream of gold flowing under her eyes, and into which she threw herself every morning.

At the mansion in the Parc Monceau, life became sheer delirium, a dazzling triumph. The Saccards doubled the number of their carriages and horses; they had an army of servants whom they dressed in a dark-blue livery with drab breeches and black-and-yellow striped waistcoats, a rather severe colour scheme the financier had chosen in order to appear respectable, one of his most cherished dreams. They emblazoned their luxury on the walls, and drew back the curtains when they gave big dinner-parties. The whirlwind of contemporary life, which had made the doors on the first floor in the Rue de Rivoli constantly slam, had become an absolute hurricane which threatened to blow away the partitions. In the midst of these princely rooms, along the gilded balustrades, over the fine velvet carpets, in this fairy parvenu palace, there trailed the aroma of Mabille, there danced jaunty popular quadrilles, the whole period passed by with its mad, stupid laughter, its eternal hunger, and its eternal thirst. It was a disorderly house of pleasure, the brash pleasure that enlarges the windows so that the passers-by can share the secrets of the alcoves. The husband and wife lived there freely, under their servants' eyes. They divided the house into two, camping there, as if they had been dropped, at the end of a tumultuous journey, into some palatial hotel where they had simply unpacked their trunks before rushing out to taste the delights of a new city. They slept there at night, staying at home only on the days of their great dinner-parties, carried away by constant trips across Paris, returning sometimes for an hour as one returns to a room at an inn between excursions. Renée felt restless and nervous there; her silk skirts glided with snakelike hisses over the thick carpets, along the satin of the couches; she was irritated by the idiotic gilding that surrounded her, by the high, empty ceilings, where after nights of festivity there lingered nothing but the laughter of young fools and the sententious maxims of old rogues; and to fill this luxury, to live amid this splendour, she longed for a supreme form of pleasure, which she sought vainly in all corners of the house, in the little sun-coloured drawing room, and in the hothouse with its lush vegetation. As for Saccard, he was realizing his dream: he received representatives of high finance: Monsieur Toutin-Laroche and Monsieur de Lauwerens; he received great politicians, Baron Gouraud and Haffner the deputy; his brother the minister had even agreed to come two or three times and consolidate Saccard's position by his presence. Yet, like his wife, he felt restless and nervous. He became so giddy, so bewildered, that his acquaintances said: 'That Saccard! He makes too much money, it'll drive him mad!' In 1860 he had been decorated, in recognition of a mysterious favour he had done the Prefect, by lending his name to a lady for the sale of some land.

It was at about the time of their installation in the Parc Monceau that an apparition crossed Renée's life, leaving an indelible impression. Up until then the minister had resisted the entreaties of his sister-in-law, who was dying to be invited to the court balls. He gave in at last, thinking his brother's fortune had been made. Renée did not sleep for a month. The great evening came, and she sat trembling in the carriage that drove her to the Tuileries.

She wore a costume of extraordinary grace and originality, an inspired creation she had hit upon one sleepless night, and which three of Worms's assistants had come to her house to work on under her supervision. It was a simple dress of white gauze, but trimmed with a multitude of little flounces, scalloped out and edged with black velvet. The black velvet tunic was cut out square, very low over her bosom, which was framed with narrow lace, barely a finger deep. No flower, no; at her wrists, bracelets without any chasing, and on her head a simple gold diadem, which gave her a kind of halo.

When she reached the reception rooms, and her husband had left her to speak to Baron Gouraud, she had a sudden feeling of embarrassment. But the mirrors, in which she saw that she was adorable, reassured her, and she was becoming used to the hot air and the murmur of voices, to the crowd of dress-coats and white shoulders, when the Emperor appeared. He slowly crossed the room on the arm of a short, fat General, who was panting as if he suffered from indigestion. The shoulders drew up in two lines, while the dress-coats stepped back discreetly. Renée found herself pushed to the end of the line of shoulders, near the second door, the one which the Emperor was approaching with a faltering step. She saw him come towards her, from one door to the other.

He was in plain dress, with the red ribbon of the Legion of Honour. Renée, again overcome with emotion, could scarcely make out what she saw, and to her this bleeding stain seemed to splash the whole of the sovereign's breast. She found him quite small, with short legs and swaying hips; but she was utterly charmed, and he seemed handsome, with his wan face and the heavy, leaden lids that fell over his lifeless eyes. Under his moustache his mouth opened feebly; while only his nose stood out from the dissolution of his face.

Looking weary, vaguely smiling, the Emperor and the old General advanced with short steps, seeming to hold each other up. They looked at the bowing ladies, and their glances, cast to right and left, glided into the bodices. The General leant on one side, said something to his master, and squeezed his arm with the air of an old friend. The Emperor, lethargic and inscrutable, even more lifeless than usual, came closer and closer with his shuffling step.

They were in the middle of the room when Renée felt their eyes fixed upon her. The General examined her with a look of surprise, while the Emperor, half-raising his eyelids, showed a tawny glow in the hesitant greyness of his bleary eyes. Renée, becoming embarrassed, lowered her head, bowed, and stared at the carpet. But she followed their shadows, and realized that they were pausing for a few seconds before her. She thought she heard the Emperor, that enigmatic dreamer, murmur as he gazed at her, absorbed in her muslin skirt striped with velvet:

'Look, General, there's a flower worth picking, a special black and white carnation.'

The General replied, in a coarser voice:

'Sir, that carnation would look most fine in our buttonholes.'

Renée looked up. The vision had disappeared, the crowd was thronging round the doorway. After that evening she frequently returned to the Tuileries; she even had the honour of being complimented by His Majesty and of becoming a vague friend; but she always remembered the sovereign's slow, heavy walk across the room between the two rows of shoulders; and whenever she experienced any new joy amid her husband's growing prosperity, she remembered the Emperor gazing down at the bowing bosoms, coming towards her, comparing her to a carnation which the old General advised him to put in his buttonhole. It was the greatest thrill of her life.

CHAPTER IV

THE exquisite longing Renée had felt amid the disturbing perfumes of the hothouse, while Maxime and Louise sat laughing on a sofa in the little buttercup drawing room, seemed to vanish like a nightmare that leaves behind it nothing but a vague shudder. Throughout the night she had the bitterness of the tanghin tree on her lips; it seemed to her, when she felt the burning taste of the poisonous leaf, as if a red-hot mouth were being pressed to hers, breathing into her an all-consuming passion. Then this mouth disappeared, and her dream was drowned in the vast waves of shadow that rolled over her.

In the morning she slept a little. When she awoke, she fancied she was ill. She had the curtains drawn, spoke to her doctor of sickness and headache, and for two days refused to go out. Pretending that she was under siege, she received no one. Maxime knocked in vain. He did not sleep in the house, preferring to be free to do as he pleased in his rooms; and in fact he led the most nomadic life in the world, living in his father's new houses, choosing the floor he liked best, moving every month, often on a whim, sometimes to make room for tenants. He would keep company with some mistress while the paint was still wet. Accustomed to his stepmother's moods, he feigned great sympathy and, four times a day, went upstairs to ask after her with a most concerned expression, just to tease her. On the third day he found her in the little drawing room, pink and smiling, looking relaxed and rested.

'Well! Have you had a good time with Céleste?' he asked, alluding to her long tête-à-tête with her maid.

'Yes,' she replied, 'she's priceless. Her hands are always like ice; she put them on my forehead and soothed my poor head a little.'

'That girl can cure everything!' cried Maxime. If ever I have the misfortune to fall in love, you'll lend her to me, won't you? To put her hands on my heart.'

They continued their banter, and went for their usual drive in the Bois. Two weeks passed. Renée had thrown herself more madly into her life of visits and balls; her head seemed to have turned once more, she complained no longer of lassitude and disgust. One might have suspected that she had committed some sin which she kept to

herself, but which she betrayed by a more marked contempt for
herself and by a more reckless depravity. One evening she confessed
to Maxime that she was dying to go to a ball which Blanche Muller, a
popular actress, was giving to the princesses of the footlights and the
queens of the *demi-monde*. This confession surprised and embarrassed even Maxime, who, after all, had few scruples. He tried to
lecture his stepmother: really, that was no place for her; besides, she
would see nothing very entertaining there; and if she were recognized, what a scandal there would be. To these arguments she
answered with clasped hands, smiling and entreating:

'Oh please, Maxime, I want to go. I'll wear a very dark domino,*
and we'll just walk through the rooms.'

Maxime always gave in, and would have taken his stepmother to
every brothel in Paris if she asked. When he agreed to escort her to
Blanche Muller's ball, she clapped her hands like a child given an
unexpected holiday.

'You're such a darling,' she said. 'It's tomorrow, isn't it? Come and
fetch me very early. I want to see the women arrive. You must tell me
their names; we'll have a marvellous time.'

She reflected, and then added:

'No, don't come here. Wait for me in a cab on the Boulevard
Malesherbes. I'll leave through the garden.'

This mysteriousness gave added spice to her escapade: a simple
refinement of pleasure, for she could have left at midnight by the
front door without her husband's so much as putting his head out of
the window.

The next day, after telling Céleste to sit up for her, she ran shivering through the dark shadows of the Parc Monceau. Saccard had
taken advantage of his good understanding with the Hôtel de Ville to
acquire a key to a little gate in the gardens, and Renée had asked for
one as well. She almost lost her way, and only found the cab thanks
to the two yellow eyes of the lamps. At this period the Boulevard
Malesherbes, barely finished, was still totally deserted at night-time.
Renée glided into the vehicle in a state of great excitement, her heart
beating rapturously, as if she were on her way to an assignation.
Maxime smoked philosophically, half asleep in a corner of the cab.
He wanted to throw away his cigar, but she stopped him, and in
trying to hold his arm back in the darkness she put her hand full in
his face, which amused them both greatly.

'I told you I like the smell of tobacco,' she cried. 'Go on smoking... Besides, we can do anything we like this evening. I'm a man, you see.'

The gas lamps had not yet been lit along the boulevard. While the cab drove down to the Madeleine it was so dark inside that they could not see one another. Now and again, when the young man raised his cigar to his lips, a red spot pierced the darkness. This red spot interested Renée. Maxime, who was half covered by the black satin domino that filled the inside of the cab, continued smoking in silence, with a weary expression. The truth was that his stepmother's whim had prevented him from following a party of women who had decided to begin and end Blanche Muller's ball at the Café Anglais.* He was quite sullen, and she could sense him sulking in the darkness.

'Don't you feel well?' she asked.

'No, I'm cold,' he replied.

'Dear me! I'm burning. It's stifling in here. Put the end of my skirts over your knees.'

'Oh! your skirts,' he muttered ill-humouredly. 'I'm up to my eyes in your skirts.'

But this remark made him laugh, and little by little he became more animated. She told him how frightened she had felt in the Parc Monceau. Then she confessed another of her longings: she would like one night to go for a row on the little lake in the gardens in the little boat she could see from her windows, moored at the edge of a pathway. He thought she was becoming sentimental. The cab rolled on, the darkness remained impenetrable, they leant forward to hear each other amid the noise of the wheels, touching one another when they moved and even inhaling one another's warm breath when they approached too closely. At regular intervals Maxime's cigar glowed afresh, creating a red blur in the darkness and casting a pale pink flash over Renée's face. She looked adorable in this fleeting light; so much so that the young man was struck by it.

'Oh!' he said. 'We're looking very pretty this evening, stepmamma. Let's have a look.'

He brought his cigar closer, and drew a few rapid puffs. Renée in her corner was lit up with a warm, palpitating light. She had raised her hood a little. Her bare head, covered with a mass of little curls, adorned with a simple blue ribbon, looked like a boy's head over the black satin blouse that came up to her neck. She thought it great fun to be examined and admired by the light of a cigar. She threw herself back tittering, while he added with an air of comic gravity:

'My God! I'll have to keep a close eye on you if I'm to bring you back safe and sound to my father.'

The cab turned round the Madeleine and joined the flow of traffic on the boulevards. Here it was filled with light, reflected by the bright shop windows. Blanche Muller lived close by in one of the new houses built on the raised ground of the Rue Basse-du-Rempart.* There were very few carriages as yet at the door. It was only ten o'clock. Maxime wanted to drive down the boulevards and wait an hour, but Renée, whose curiosity was growing, told him that she would go up on her own if he did not accompany her. He followed her, and was glad to find more people upstairs than he expected. Renée had put on her mask. Leaning on Maxime's arm, and whispering peremptory orders to him, which he submissively obeyed, she ferreted about in all the rooms, lifting the corners of the door-hangings and examining the furniture, and would even have searched the drawers had she not been afraid of being seen.

The apartment, though richly decorated, had Bohemian corners that immediately suggested the chorus-girl. It was here especially that Renée's pink nostrils quivered, and that she made her companion walk slowly, so as to lose no particle of things or of their smell. She lingered in a dressing room left open by Blanche Muller, who, when she received her friends, gave up everything to them, even her alcove, where the bed was pushed aside to make room for card-tables. But the dressing room did not please her: she found it common, and even a little dirty, with its carpet covered with little round burns from cigarette-ends, and its blue silk hangings stained with pomade and splashed with soapsuds. Then, when she had fully inspected the rooms, and fixed the smallest details of the place in her memory so as to describe them later to her friends, she moved on to the guests. The men she knew; for the most part they were the same financiers, the same politicians, the same young men-about-town who came to her Thursdays. She almost thought she was in her own drawing room, when she came face to face with a group of smiling dress-coats who, the previous evening, had worn the same smiles in her house when talking to the Marquise d'Espanet or the blonde Madame Haffner. Nor was the illusion completely dispelled when she looked at the women. Laure d'Aurigny was in yellow like

Suzanne Haffner, and Blanche Muller, like Adeline d'Espanet, wore a white dress that left half of her back completely bare. At last Maxime begged her to take pity on him, and she agreed to join him on a sofa. They stayed there a moment, the young man yawning, Renée asking him the ladies' names, undressing them with her eyes, adding up the number of yards of lace they wore round their skirts. Seeing her absorbed in this serious study, he slipped away in response to a signal from Laure d'Aurigny. She teased him about the lady he was escorting. Then she made him swear to come and join them at the Café Anglais at one o'clock.

'Your father will be there,' she called to him, as he rejoined Renée.

The latter found herself surrounded by a group of women laughing very loudly, while Monsieur de Saffré had taken advantage of the seat left vacant by Maxime to slip down beside her and pay her crude compliments. Next, Monsieur de Saffré and the women had all begun to shout and smack their thighs, so much so that Renée, quite deafened, and beginning to yawn, rose and said to her companion:

'Let's go, they're so boring!'

As they were leaving, Monsieur de Mussy entered. He seemed delighted to meet Maxime and, paying no attention to the masked woman beside him, murmured with a lovesick air: 'she'll be the death of me. I know she's feeling better, but she still won't see me. Please tell her you saw me with tears in my eyes.'

'Don't worry, she'll get your message,' said the young man, with an odd laugh.

On the stairs he added:

'Well, stepmamma, did the poor fellow touch you?'

She shrugged without replying. Outside, on the pavement, she paused before getting into the cab, which had waited for them, and looked hesitantly towards the Madeleine and the Boulevard des Italiens. It was barely half-past eleven, and the boulevard was still very busy.

'So we're going home,' she murmured regretfully.

'Unless you want to take a drive along the boulevards,' replied Maxime.

She agreed. Her orgy of feminine curiosity was turning out badly, and she hated the idea of returning home disillusioned and with the beginnings of a headache. She had long imagined that an actresses' ball would be great fun. There seemed to be a return of spring, as happens sometimes in the last days of October; the night had a May warmth, and the occasional cool breeze added to the gaiety of the atmosphere. Renée, with her head at the window, remained silent, looking at the crowd, the cafés, and the restaurants as they scudded past. She had become very serious, lost in the vague longings that fill the reveries of women. The wide pavement, swept by the prostitutes' skirts and ringing with peculiar familiarity under the men's boots, and over whose grey asphalt it seemed to her that the cavalcade of pleasure and brief encounters was passing, awoke her slumbering desires and made her forget the idiotic ball she had left, giving her a glimpse of other and more highly flavoured pleasures. At the windows of the private rooms at Brébant's,* she saw the shadows of women on the white curtains. Maxime told her a very salacious story, of a husband who had noticed, on a curtain, the shadows of his wife and her lover in the act. She hardly listened. But he grew more excited, and ended by taking her hands and teasing her about poor Monsieur de Mussy.

They turned back, and as they passed once more in front of Brébant's she said suddenly: 'Do you know, Monsieur de Saffré asked me to supper this evening.'

'Oh! you wouldn't have eaten very well,' he replied, laughing. De Saffré hasn't got the faintest idea about food. He hasn't got past lobster salad.'

'No, no, he mentioned oysters and cold partridge. But he addressed me as *tu*, and that annoyed me.'

She stopped short, gazed again at the boulevard, and added after a pause, with an air of distress:

'The worst of it is that I'm awfully hungry.'

'What, you're hungry!' exclaimed the young man. 'That's very simple, we'll go and have supper together. Would you like that?'

He spoke quietly, but she refused at first, declaring that Céleste had put out something for her to eat at home. In the meantime Maxime, who did not want to go to the Café Anglais, had stopped the cab at the corner of the Rue Le Peletier, in front of the Café Riche;* he alighted, and as his stepmother still hesitated, he said:

'If you're afraid I might compromise you, do say so. I'll sit next to the driver and take you back to your husband.'

She smiled, and alighted from the cab like a bird afraid to wet its feet. She was radiant. The pavement she felt beneath her feet warmed her heels and sent a delicious sensation of fear and gratified caprice quivering over her skin. In the cab she had had a mad longing to jump out on to the pavement. She crossed it with short steps, stealthily, as if her pleasure were heightened by the fear that she might be seen. Her escapade was decidedly turning into an adventure. She certainly did not regret having refused Monsieur de Saffré's crude invitation. But she would have come home terribly cross if Maxime had not thought of letting her taste forbidden fruit. He ran upstairs, as if he were at home. She followed him a little out of breath. A slight aroma of fish and game hung about, and the stair-carpet, secured to the steps with brass rods, had a smell of dust that increased her excitement.

As they reached the first landing they met a dignified-looking waiter, who drew back to the wall to let them pass.

'Charles,' said Maxime, 'you'll wait on us, won't you? Give us the white room.'

Charles bowed, went up a few steps, and opened the door of a private room. The gas was lowered, it seemed to Renée as if she was penetrating into the half-light of a dubious and charming region.

A continuous rumbling could be heard through the wide-open window, and on the ceiling, in the reflection cast by the café below, the shadows of the people in the street passed swiftly by. But with a twist of his thumb the waiter turned on the gas. The shadows on the ceiling disappeared, the room was filled with a crude light that fell full on Renée's head. She had already thrown back her hood. The little curls had become slightly disarranged, but the blue ribbon was exactly as it was. She began to walk about, a little embarrassed by the way Charles looked at her; he blinked and screwed up his eyes to see her better, in a way that plainly suggested: 'Here's one I haven't seen before.'

'What would Monsieur like?' he asked aloud.

Maxime turned towards Renée.

'Monsieur de Saffré's supper perhaps?' he asked. 'Oysters, a partridge...'

Seeing the young man smile, Charles discreetly imitated him, murmuring:

'Wednesday's supper, then, if that's alright?'

'Wednesday's supper...' repeated Maxime.

Then, remembering, he said:

'Yes, I don't care, give us Wednesday's supper.'

When the waiter had gone, Renée took her eyeglass and went inquisitively round the room. It was a square room in white and gold, furnished with the coquetry of a boudoir. Besides the table and chairs, there was a sort of low slab that served as a sideboard, and a wide divan, as large as a bed, that stood between the fireplace and the window. A Louis XVI clock and candlesticks adorned the white marble mantelpiece. But the curiosity of the room was the huge, handsome mirror, which had been scrawled on by the ladies' diamonds with names, dates, doggerel verses, high-blown sentiments, and amazing declarations. Renée thought she saw something filthy, but lacked the courage to satisfy her curiosity. She looked at the divan, feeling embarrassed again, and at last, trying to appear composed, gazed at the ceiling and the copper-gilt chandelier with its five jets. But the uneasiness she felt was delicious. Looking up as if to examine the cornice, her eyeglass in her hand, she derived profound enjoyment from the suggestive furniture around her: from the limpid, cynical mirror whose pure surface, barely wrinkled by the filthy scrawls, had helped in the adjustment of so many false chignons; from the divan, whose width shocked her; from the table and even the carpet, in which she found the same smell as on the stairs, a subtle, penetrating, almost religious odour of dust.

Then, when she was forced at last to lower her eyes, she asked Maxime:

'What is Wednesday's supper?'

'Nothing,' he replied. 'A bet one of my friends lost.'

In any other place he would have told her without hesitation that he had supped on Wednesday with a lady he had met on the boulevard. But since entering the private room he had instinctively treated her as a woman one seeks to please and whose jealousy must be spared. She did not insist; she went and leant on the window-rail, where he joined her. Behind them Charles came and went, with a sound of crockery and silverware.

It was not yet midnight. On the boulevard below, Paris was still noisy, prolonging the day's activity before deciding to go to bed. The rows of trees separated the whiteness of the pavement from the darkness of the roadway, on which the carriages rumbled along with their fleeting lamps. On both edges of this dark belt the newsvendors' kiosks shed their light from spot to spot, like great Venetian lanterns,

tall and fantastically variegated, set on the ground at regular intervals for some colossal illumination. But at this late hour their usually
bright light was subdued and lost in the flare of the shop-fronts. Not
a shutter was up, the pavement stretched out without a line of
shadow, under a shower of rays that covered it with a golden dust,
with the warm, resplendent glare of daylight. Maxime showed Renée
the Café Anglais, whose windows shone out in front of them. The
lofty branches of the trees blocked their view a little when they tried
to see the houses and pavement opposite. They leant over and looked
down at the street. There was a continual coming and going; men
walked past in groups, prostitutes in pairs dragged their skirts,
which they lifted up from time to time with a languid movement,
casting weary, smiling glances around them. Right under the window, the tables of the Café Riche were spread out in the blaze of the
gas lamps, whose brilliancy extended half across the roadway; and it
was especially in the centre of this blaze that they saw the pale faces
and empty smiles of the passers-by. Around the little tables were
men and women mingled together, drinking. The girls wore showy
dresses, their hair dressed low on their necks; they lounged about on
chairs and made loud remarks, which the noise made inaudible.
Renée noticed one in particular, sitting alone at a table, wearing a
bright blue costume with white lace; leaning back in her chair, she
finished, sip by sip, a glass of beer, her hands on her stomach, a heavy
and resigned look of expectancy on her face. The women on foot
disappeared slowly in the crowd, and Renée, intrigued, watched
them go, gazing from one end of the boulevard to the other. The
endless procession, a crowd strangely mixed and always alike, passed
by with tiring regularity in the midst of the bright colours and
patches of darkness, in the fairy-like confusion of the thousand leaping flames that swept like waves from the shops, lending colour to the
windows and the kiosks, running along the pavements in fillets, in
fiery letters and designs, piercing the darkness with stars, gliding
endlessly along the roadway. The deafening noise had a roar, a prolonged monotonous rumbling, like an organ-note accompanying an
endless procession of little mechanical dolls. Renée at one moment
thought there had been an accident. There was a stream of people on
the left, just beyond the Passage de l'Opéra.* But, taking her eyeglass,
she recognized the omnibus office. A crowd had gathered on the
pavement, waiting, and rushing forward as soon as an omnibus

arrived. She heard the rough voice of the ticket collector calling out the numbers, followed by the tinkle of the bell. Her eyes lighted upon the advertisements on a kiosk, garishly coloured like Épinal prints;* on a pane of glass, in a green-and-yellow frame, was the head of a grinning devil with hair on end, a hatter's advertisement, which she could not understand. Every five minutes the Batignolles omnibus passed by, with its red lamps and yellow sides, turning the corner of the Rue Le Peletier, shaking the building as it went, and she saw the men on the upper deck look up at them with their tired faces, with the expectant look of famished people peering through a keyhole.

'Ah!' she said. 'The Parc Monceau must be fast asleep now.'

It was the only remark she made. They stayed there for nearly twenty minutes in silence, abandoning themselves to the intoxication of the noise and light. Then, the table having been laid, they sat down, and as Renée seemed embarrassed by the presence of the waiter, Maxime dismissed him.

'You can leave us. I'll ring for dessert.'

Renée's cheeks were slightly flushed and her eyes sparkled, as if she had just been running. She brought from the window a little of the din and animation of the boulevard. She would not let her companion close the window.

'It's like an orchestra!' she said, when he complained of the noise. 'Don't you think it's a funny sort of music? It'll make a very good accompaniment to our oysters and partridge.'

Her excitement made her seem younger than her thirty years. Her movements were quick and almost febrile, and this private room, this intimate supper with a young man amid the roar of the street, gave her the look of a prostitute. She attacked the oysters with gusto. Maxime was not hungry; he smiled as he watched her bolt her food.

'God!' he murmured. 'You would have made a good supper-companion.'

She stopped, annoyed with herself for eating so fast.

'Do I seem hungry? What do you expect? It's the hour we spent at that idiotic ball that exhausted me. Ah, my poor friend, I pity you for living in that sort of world!'

'You know very well,' he said, 'that I've promised to give up Sylvia and Laure d'Aurigny on the day your friends agree to come and have supper with me.'

She made a haughty gesture.

'I should think so! You must admit we're more fun than those women. If one of us bored her lover as your Sylvia and Laure d'Aurigny must bore all of you, the poor thing wouldn't keep him for a week! You'll never listen to me. Just try it, one of these days.'

Maxime, to avoid calling the waiter, rose, removed the oysters and brought over the partridge, which was on the slab. The table had the luxurious look of a first-class restaurant. A breath of debauchery passed over the damask cloth, and Renée felt little thrills of pleasure as she let her slender hands wander from her fork to her knife, from her plate to her glass. She usually drank water barely tinged with claret, but now drank white wine neat. Maxime, standing with his napkin over his arm, and waiting on her with comical obsequiousness, resumed:

'What can Monsieur de Saffré have said to make you so furious? Did he tell you you were ugly?'

'Oh,' she replied. 'He's a nasty man. I couldn't believe that a gentleman so distinguished, and so polite when he's at my house, could have used such language. But I forgive him. It was the women that irritated me. You would have thought they were selling apples. There was one who complained of a boil on her hip, and I'm sure she wouldn't have needed much encouragement to pull up her petticoat to show us.'

Maxime was splitting his sides with laughter.

'No, really,' she continued, getting worked up, 'I can't understand you men; those women are dirty and dull. And to think that when I saw you going off with Sylvia I imagined wonderful scenes, ancient banquets you see in paintings, with creatures crowned with roses, golden goblets, extraordinary voluptuousness. But all you showed me was a dirty dressing room and women swearing like troopers. That's not worth committing any sins for.'

He wanted to protest, but she silenced him, and holding between her fingertips a partridge-bone, which she was daintily nibbling, she added in a softer tone:

'Sin ought to be an exquisite thing, my dear. When I, a respectable woman, feel bored and commit the sin of dreaming of the impossible, I'm sure I think of much nicer things than all your Blanche Mullers.'

Looking very serious, she concluded with this profound and frankly cynical remark:

'It's a question of education, you see.'

She put the little bone gently on her plate. The rumbling of the carriages continued, with no clearer sound rising above it. She had had to raise her voice for him to hear her, and her flushed cheeks grew even redder. On the slab there were still some truffles, a sweet, and some asparagus, which was out of season. He brought them all over, so as not to have to get up again; and as the table was rather narrow, he placed on the floor between them a silver ice-bucket containing a bottle of champagne. Renée's appetite had rubbed off on him. They tasted all the dishes and emptied the bottle of champagne, launching into risqué theories and putting their elbows on the table like two friends pouring their hearts out while drinking. The noise on the boulevard was subsiding; but to Renée's ears it seemed to increase, and at moments all the wheels of the carriages seemed to be whirling round in her head.

When he spoke of ringing for dessert, she stood up, shook the crumbs from her long satin blouse, and said:

'That's it... You can light your cigar, if you want.'

She was a little giddy. She went to the window, attracted by a peculiar noise she could not identify. The shops were closing.

'Look,' she said, turning towards Maxime, 'the orchestra is thinning out.'

She leant out again. In the middle of the road the coloured eyes of the cabs and omnibuses, now fewer and faster, were still crossing one another. But on either side, along the pavements, great pits of darkness had appeared in front of the closed shops. The cafés alone were still ablaze, streaking the asphalt with sheets of light. From the Rue Drouot to the Rue du Helder she could see a long line of black and white squares, in which the last stragglers sprang up and disappeared in a curious fashion. The prostitutes in particular, with their long-trained dresses, by turns garishly illuminated and immersed in darkness, seemed like apparitions, ghostly puppets moving across a floodlit stage-set. She amused herself for a moment with this sight. The gas jets were being turned out; the variegated kiosks stood out in the darkness. From time to time a flood of people, issuing from some theatre, passed by. But soon there was no one except, under the window, groups of men in twos or threes whom a woman accosted. They stood talking. Some of their remarks rose audibly in the subsiding din; and then the women generally walked off on the arm of one of the men. Other girls wandered from café to café, strolled round the tables, pocketed the forgotten lumps of sugar, laughed with the waiters, and stared invitingly at the belated customers. And just after Renée had followed with her eyes the all but empty upper deck of a Batignolles omnibus, she recognized on the pavement the woman in the blue dress with the white lace, glancing about her, still in search of a customer.

When Maxime came to fetch Renée from the window, he smiled as he looked towards one of the half-opened windows of the Café Anglais; the idea of his father having supper there struck him as amusing, but that evening he was under the influence of a peculiar form of modesty that interfered with his customary love of fun. Renée was reluctant to leave the window-rail. A feeling of intoxication and languor rose from the boulevard. In the low rumbling of the carriages and the extinguishing of the bright lights there was a summons to pleasure and to sleep. The whispering of the groups clustered in shadowy corners turned the pavement into the passageway of some great inn at the time when the guests repair to their beds. The glimmering lights and the noise continued to grow fainter and fainter, the city fell asleep, and a breath of love passed over the rooftops.

When Renée turned round, the light of the little chandelier made her blink. She was a little pale now, and felt slight quivers at the corners of her mouth. Charles was putting out the dessert: he left the room, and came in again, opening and closing the door slowly, with the self-assurance of a man of the world.

'But I'm not hungry any more!' cried Renée. 'Take all those plates away, and bring the coffee.'

The waiter, accustomed to the whims of the ladies he waited upon, cleared away the dessert and poured the coffee. He filled the room with his presence.

'Do get rid of him,' said Renée, who was feeling sick.

Maxime dismissed him; but scarcely had he disappeared before he returned once again to draw the great window-curtains closely together. When he had at last withdrawn, the young man, growing impatient, stood up and, going to the door, said:

'Wait a minute. I know how to keep him out.'

He pushed the bolt.

'That's it,' she rejoined, 'we're alone at last.'

They resumed their intimate conversation. Maxime had lit a cigar.
Renée sipped her coffee and even indulged in a glass of chartreuse.
The room grew warmer and became filled with blue smoke. She
ended by leaning her elbows on the table and resting her chin
between her half-closed fists. Under this slight pressure her mouth
became smaller, her cheeks were slightly raised, and her eyes shone
more brightly. Her rumpled little face looked adorable under the rain
of golden curls that fell down over her eyebrows. Maxime looked at
her through his cigar smoke. He thought her quaint. At times he
was no longer quite sure of her sex: the line on her forehead, her
pouting lips, the look of slight uncertainty caused by her short-
sightedness, made her almost like a young man, the more so as her
long black satin blouse came up so high that one could barely see,
under her chin, a line of plump white neck. She let herself be looked
at, smiling, her head motionless, her eyes vacant, her lips still.

Then she woke up with a start; she went and looked at the mirror
towards which her dreamy eyes had been turning for the last few
moments. She raised herself on tiptoe and placed her hands on the
edge of the mantelpiece, to read the signatures, the coarse remarks
that had startled her before supper. She spelled out the syllables with
some difficulty, laughing, reading like a schoolboy turning the pages
of a Piron* in his desk.

' "Ernest and Clara," ' she said, 'and there's a heart underneath
that looks like a funnel. Ah! this is better: "I like men because I like
truffles." Signed, Laure. Tell me, Maxime, was it the d'Aurigny
woman who wrote that? And here's the coat-of-arms of one of these
ladies, I imagine: a hen smoking a big pipe. And more names, the
whole calendar of saints, male and female: Victor, Amélie, Alexandre,
Édouard, Marguerite, Paquita, Louise, Renée... So there's one
named after me.'

Maxime could see her face glowing in the glass. She raised herself
still higher, and her domino, drawn more tightly behind, outlined her
figure, the curve of her hips. The young man followed the line of
satin, which fitted her like a shirt. He stood up and threw away his
cigar. He seemed ill at ease. He was missing something he was used to.

'Ah! Here's your name, Maxime,' cried Renée. ' "I love..." '

But he had sat down on the corner of the divan, almost at Renée's
feet. He seized her hands; he turned away from the mirror, and said
in a peculiar voice:

'Please don't read that.'

She gave a nervous laugh.

'Why not? Am I not your confidante?'

But he insisted in a softer tone:

'No, not tonight.'

He still held her, and she tried to free herself with little jerks of the wrist. There was a strange light in their eyes, a touch of shame in their long, strained smile. She fell on her knees beside the divan. They continued struggling, although she no longer made any effort to return to the mirror, and had already given in. As Maxime threw his arms round her, she said with her faint, embarrassed laugh:

'Don't, let me go... You're hurting me.'

It was the only sound that rose to her lips. In the profound silence of the room, where the gas seemed to flare up higher, she felt the ground tremble and heard the clatter of the Batignolles omnibus turning the corner of the boulevard. The talking was over. When they resumed their positions, side by side on the divan, he stammered:

'Well, it was bound to happen sooner or later.'

She said nothing. She examined the carpet as if numbed.

'Had you ever dreamt this might happen?' continued Maxime, stammering even more. 'I hadn't for a moment. I ought to have mistrusted this private room.'

But in a deep voice, as if all the bourgeois respectability of the Bérauds du Châtel had been awakened by this supreme sin, she muttered, her face aged and very serious:

'This is terrible, what we have just done.'

She was suffocating. She went to the window, drew back the curtains, and leant out. The orchestra had fallen silent; her sin had been committed amid the last quiver of the basses and the distant sound of the violins, the vague, soft music of the boulevard asleep and dreaming of love. The roadway and pavement below stretched out and merged into grey solitude. All the rumbling cab-wheels seemed to have departed, carrying with them the lights and the crowd. Beneath the window the Café Riche was closed; no thread of light gleamed through the shutters. Across the road, shimmering lights lit up the front of the Café Anglais, one half-open window in particular, from which faint laughter could be heard. All along this ribbon of darkness, from the turn at the Rue Drouot to the other end, as far as her eyes could see, she saw nothing but the symmetrical blurs of the kiosks staining the night red and green, without illuminating it, like nightlights placed at regular intervals in a giant dormitory. She looked up. The branches of the trees were outlined against a clear sky, while the uneven line of the houses petered out, like a rocky coast on the shore of a faint blue sea. But this belt of sky saddened her still more, and only in the darkness of the boulevard could she find consolation. What lingered on the surface of the deserted road of the noise and vice of the evening made excuses for her. She thought she could feel the heat of the footsteps of all those men and women rising up from the pavement that was now growing cold. The shamefulness that had lingered there—momentary lust, whispered offers, prepaid nights of pleasure—was evaporating, floating in a heavy mist dissipated by the breath of morning. Leaning out into the darkness, she inhaled the quivering silence, the alcove-like fragrance, as an encouragement from below, as an assurance of shame shared and accepted by a complicitous city. When her eyes had grown used to the dark, she saw the woman in the blue dress trimmed with lace standing in the same place, alone in the shadows, waiting and offering herself to the empty night.

Turning round, Renée saw Charles, who was looking round the room. He spotted Renée's blue ribbon, lying crumpled and forgotten on a corner of the sofa. He politely handed it to her. Then she realized her own shame. Standing in front of the mirror, she clumsily tried to refasten the ribbon, but her chignon had slipped down, her little curls had flattened on her temples, and she was unable to tie the bow. Charles came to her aid, saying, as if he were offering some everyday thing, like a finger-bowl or a toothpick:

'Would Madame like the comb?'

'Oh no, don't bother,' interjected Maxime, giving the waiter an impatient look. 'Go and call a cab.'

Renée decided simply to pull down the hood of her domino. As she was about to leave, she again lightly raised herself to see the words which Maxime's embrace had prevented her from reading. Slanting upwards towards the ceiling, in big, ugly handwriting, was the declaration, signed Sylvia: 'I love Maxime.' She bit her lips and drew her hood a little lower.

In the cab they felt terribly awkward. They sat facing each other, as when they drove down from the Parc Monceau. They could think of nothing to say. The cab was extremely dark, and Maxime's cigar did not even mark it with a red dot, a glimmer of crimson charcoal. The young man, hidden again among the skirts, suffered from the gloom and the silence, from the silent woman he felt beside him, whose eyes he imagined he could see staring into the night. To seem less awkward he reached for her hand and, when he held it in his own, felt relieved. Soft, languid, the hand abandoned itself to him.

The cab crossed the Place de la Madeleine. Renée thought she was not to blame. She had not desired the incest. The more she thought about it, the more innocent she found herself, at the beginning of her escapade, at the moment of her stealthy departure from the Parc Monceau, at Blanche Muller's, on the boulevard, even in the private room at the restaurant. Then why had she fallen on her knees next to the sofa? She could not imagine. She had anticipated nothing. She would have refused to give herself. It was just for fun, that's all. As the cab rolled on, she rediscovered the deafening orchestra of the boulevard, the procession of men and women, while bars of fire scorched her weary eyes.

Maxime was also pondering things. He was angry at what had happened. He blamed the black satin domino. Whoever saw a woman rig herself out like that! You couldn't even see her neck. He had taken her for a boy and romped with her, and it was not his fault that the game had become serious. He would not have laid a finger on her if she had shown even a tiny bit of her shoulders. He would have remembered that she was his father's wife. Then, as he did not care for unpleasant thoughts, he forgave himself. Too bad! He would try not to do it again. It was all a lot of nonsense.

The cab stopped, and Maxime got down first to help Renée. But, at the little garden gate, he did not dare to kiss her. They shook hands as usual. She was already on the other side of the railing when, to say something, unwittingly confessing a preoccupation that had vaguely filled her thoughts since leaving the restaurant, she asked:

'What is that comb the waiter mentioned?'

'The comb,' repeated Maxime, embarrassed. 'I really don't know.'

Renée suddenly understood. The room had a comb that formed part of its apparatus, like the curtains, the bolt, and the sofa. Without waiting for an explanation, which was not forthcoming, she plunged into the darkness of the Parc Monceau, walking quickly and thinking she could see behind her the tortoiseshell teeth in which Laure d'Aurigny and Sylvia had left fair hair and black. She was now feeling very feverish. Céleste had to put her to bed and sit up with her till morning. Maxime stood for a moment on the pavement of the Boulevard Malesherbes, wondering whether he should join the party at the Café Anglais; then, thinking that he was punishing himself, he decided that he ought to go home to bed.

The next morning Renée woke late from a deep sleep. She had a large fire made, and said she would spend the day in her room. This was her refuge at times of difficulty. Towards midday, as her husband did not see her come down to breakfast, he asked if he could speak with her for a moment. She was about to refuse his request, with a touch of nervousness, when she thought better of it. The day before she had sent down to Saccard a bill from Worms for a hundred and thirty-six thousand francs, a rather high figure; and no doubt he wanted to pay her the courtesy of bringing her the receipt in person.

She thought of the little curls of the day before. Mechanically she looked in the mirror at her hair, which Céleste had plaited into long tresses. Then she curled up by the fire, burying herself in the lace of her dressing-gown. Saccard, whose rooms were also on the second floor, next to his wife's, entered in his slippers, a husband's privilege. He set foot barely once a month in Renée's bedroom, and always concerning some delicate question of money. That morning he had the red eyes and pale complexion of a man who has not slept. He kissed his wife's hand.

'Are you unwell, my dear?' he asked, sitting down on the other side of the fireplace. 'A headache? Forgive me for coming to bother you with my business talk, but it's rather serious.'

He drew Worms's bill from the pocket of his dressing-gown. Renée recognized the glazed paper.

'I found this bill on my desk yesterday,' he continued. 'I'm very sorry, but I'm absolutely unable to pay it at present.'

With a sidelong look he watched the effect his words had on her. She seemed surprised. He resumed with a smile:

'You know, my dear, I'm not in the habit of criticizing your purchases, though I must say that some items here surprised me somewhat. On the second page, for example: ball dress: material, seventy francs; making up, six hundred francs; money lent, five thousand francs; eau du Docteur Pierre, six francs. That seems rather expensive for a seventy-franc dress. But as you know, I understand every kind of weakness. Your bill comes to a hundred and thirty-six thousand francs, and you have been almost moderate, comparatively speaking. But, as I say, I can't pay it, I'm short of money.'

She held out her hand in a gesture of suppressed annoyance.

'Very well,' she said curtly, 'give me the bill. I'll think about it.'

'I see you don't believe me,' murmured Saccard, enjoying his wife's incredulity on the subject of his financial embarrassment as if it were a personal triumph. 'I'm not saying I'm in serious trouble, but business is very shaky at present. Let me explain; you entrusted me with your dowry, and I owe it to you to be completely frank.'

He put the bill on the mantelpiece, picked up the tongs, and began to stir the fire. His passion for raking the cinders while talking business was a system that had become a habit. Whenever he came to a bothersome figure or phrase, he created a subsidence, which he then laboriously built up, gathering the logs together, collecting and heaping up the little splinters. Sometimes he almost disappeared into the fireplace in search of a stray piece of charcoal. His voice grew faint, his listener lost patience, became more interested in his skilful constructions of glowing firewood, no longer listened to him, and as a rule went away defeated but satisfied. Even at other people's houses he despotically took possession of the tongs. In summertime he played with a pen, a paperknife, or a penknife.

'My dear,' he said, with a great blow that sent the fire flying, 'I am really sorry to have to say this. I have regularly made over to you the interest on the money you placed in my hands. I can even say, without hurting your feelings, that I've regarded that interest as your pocket money, and I have never asked you to contribute to the household expenses.'

He paused. Renée felt uneasy as she watched him making a large hole in the cinders to bury the end of a log. He was about to make a delicate confession.

'You see, I've had to make your money pay a high interest. You can rest assured, the principal is in good hands. As to the money coming from your property in the Sologne, it has been used partly to pay for this house; the rest is invested in an excellent company, the Société Générale of the Ports of Morocco. We haven't got to settle the accounts yet, have we? I wanted to show you that we poor husbands are sometimes not appreciated.'

A powerful motive must have impelled him to lie less than usual.

The truth was that Renée's dowry had been exhausted long ago; it had become a fictitious asset in Saccard's safe. Although he paid out interest on it at the rate of two or three hundred per cent or more, he could not have produced the least security or found the smallest solid particle of the original capital. As he half confessed, moreover, the five hundred thousand francs of the Sologne property had been used to pay a first instalment on the house and the furniture, which together cost nearly two million. He still owed a million to the up-holsterer and the builders.

'I don't want to make any claims on you,' Renée said at last. 'I know I'm very much in your debt.'

'Oh, my dear,' he cried, taking his wife's hand, without letting go of the tongs, 'what a dreadful thing to say! Listen, the long and the short of it is that I have had some bad luck at the Bourse, Toutin-Laroche has got himself into a mess, and Mignon and Charrier are a pair of crooks. That's why I can't pay your bill. You will forgive me, won't you?'

He seemed genuinely upset. He dug the tongs in among the logs and made the sparks fly up like fireworks. Renée remembered how restless he had been recently. But she was unable to realize the amazing truth. Saccard had reached the point of having to perform a daily miracle. He lived like a king in a house that cost two million, but there were mornings when he had not a thousand francs in his safe. He did not seem to spend any less. He lived on debt among an army of creditors who swallowed up each day the scandalous profits he made from his transactions. In the meantime companies crumbled beneath his feet, new and deeper holes yawned before him, over which he had to leap, unable to fill them up. He thus trod over a minefield, living in a constant state of crisis, settling bills of fifty thousand francs but leaving his coachman's wages unpaid, marching on with ever-more regal assurance, emptying over Paris with increasing frenzy his empty cash-box, from which the golden stream with the fabulous source never stopped flowing.

The world of speculation was going through a difficult period. Saccard was a worthy offspring of the Hôtel de Ville. He had experienced the rapid transformations, the frenzied pursuit of pleasure, the blindness to expense that had convulsed Paris. Now, like the City, he found himself faced with a huge deficit which he had secretly to make good, for he would not hear of prudence, of economy, of a peaceful and respectable existence. He preferred to keep up the useless luxury and real penury of the new boulevards, which had provided him with his colossal fortune which came into being every morning only to be swallowed up by nightfall. Moving from one adventure to the next, he now possessed only the gilded façade of missing capital. In this period of utter madness, Paris itself did not risk its future with greater rashness or hurry more directly towards every folly and every trick of finance. The settlement threatened to be disastrous.

The most promising speculative ventures turned out badly in Saccard's hands. As he said, he had just written off considerable losses at the Bourse. Toutin-Laroche had almost caused the Crédit Viticole to founder through a gamble for a rise that had suddenly turned against him;* fortunately the Government, intervening secretly, had put the famous wine-growers' mortgage loan-machine on its feet again. Saccard, badly shaken by this sudden blow, and taken to task by his brother for the danger that had threatened the delegation bonds of the City, which was involved with the Crédit Viticole, was even more unlucky in his real-estate speculations. The Mignon and Charrier pair had broken with him completely. If he accused them, it was because he was secretly furious at his mistake in having built on his share of the land while they prudently sold theirs. While they were making their fortunes, he was left with houses that he was only able to dispose of at a loss. He sold a house in the Rue de Marignan, on which he still owed three hundred and eighty thousand francs a year, for three hundred thousand francs. He had invented a trick that consisted in asking ten thousand francs a year for an apartment worth eight thousand at most. The terrified tenant only signed a lease when the landlord had consented to forgo the first two years' rent. In this way the apartment was brought down to its real value, but the lease bore the figure of ten thousand francs a year, and when Saccard found a purchaser and capitalized the income from the house, the calculation became quite fantastic.* He was not able to practise this swindle on a large scale: his houses could not be let; he had built them too early; the clearings in which they stood, lost in the mud of winter, isolated them and considerably reduced their value. The affair that had affected him most was the crude trick played by Mignon and Charrier, who bought back from him the house on the Boulevard Malesherbes, the building of which he had

had to abandon. The contractors were at last smitten with the desire to inhabit their boulevard. As they had sold their share of the land above its value, and suspected that their former partner was in financial difficulties, they offered to relieve him of the enclosure in the middle of which the house stood, completed up to the flooring of the second storey, whose iron girders were partly laid. But they referred to the solid freestone foundations as useless rubble, saying they would have preferred the land empty, to build on it as they wanted. Saccard was obliged to sell, without taking into account the hundred and odd thousand francs he had already spent, and what exasperated him even more was that the contractors refused to take the land back at two hundred and fifty francs a metre, the figure agreed at the time of the division. They beat him down by twenty-five francs a metre, like second-hand clothes-women who pay only four francs for something they have sold for five the day before. Two days later Saccard was mortified to see an army of bricklayers invade the boarded enclosure and start building on the 'useless rubble'.*

He was thus all the better able to play before his wife at being pressed for money, as his affairs were becoming more and more complicated. He was not a man to confess from sheer love of the truth.

'But, Monsieur,' said Renée, with an air of scepticism, 'if you're in such financial difficulty, why did you buy me that aigrette and necklace, which cost you, I believe, sixty-five thousand francs? I have no use for those jewels, and I shall have to ask your permission to dispose of them so as to give Worms something on account.'

'Don't do that!' he cried anxiously. 'If you weren't seen wearing those diamonds at the Ministry ball tomorrow, people would start gossiping about my position.'

He was in a genial mood that morning. He ended by smiling and murmuring with a wink:

'We speculators, my dear, are like pretty women, we have our little tricks. Keep your aigrette and necklace, please, for my sake.'

He could not tell the story, a very good one but a little risqué. After supper one night Saccard and Laure d'Aurigny had entered into an alliance. Laure was up to her ears in debt, and her one thought was to find a gullible young man who would elope with her and take her to London. Saccard, for his part, felt the ground crumbling under his feet; his beleaguered imagination sought an expedient that would display him to the public sprawling on a bed of gold and banknotes. The courtesan and the speculator had come to an understanding in the semi-intoxication of dessert. He hit on the idea of a sale of diamonds that would have all Paris agog; it was then, with great ostentation, that he bought the jewels for his wife. With the product of the sale, about four hundred thousand francs, he managed to satisfy Laure's creditors, to whom she owed nearly twice that amount. It is even presumed that he recouped part of his sixty-five thousand francs. When he was seen settling the lady's affairs, he was looked upon as her lover and believed to be paying her debts in full and committing extravagances for her. His credit revived wondrously. At the Bourse he was teased about his passion, with smiles and insinuations that delighted him. Meanwhile Laure d'Aurigny, brought into the limelight by all this fuss, though he had never spent a single night with her, pretended to deceive him with nine or ten idiots taken by the notion of stealing her from a man of such colossal wealth. Within a month she had two sets of furniture and more diamonds than she had sold. Saccard had got into the habit of going to smoke a cigar with her in the afternoon on leaving the Bourse; he often caught sight of coat-tails flying through the doorways in terror. When they were alone, they could not look at each other without laughing. He kissed her on the forehead as though she were a depraved woman whose wickedness delighted him. He did not give her a sou, and on one occasion she even lent him money to pay a gambling debt.

Renée tried to insist, and spoke of at least pawning the diamonds; but her husband gave her to understand that that was not possible, that Tout Paris expected to see her wearing them the next day. Then Renée, who was very worried about Worms's bill, sought another way out of her difficulty.

'But,' she suddenly exclaimed, 'my Charonne property is all right, isn't it? You were telling me just the other day that the profit would be superb. Perhaps Larsonneau would let me have a hundred and thirty-six thousand francs in advance?'

Saccard had forgotten for a moment the tongs between his legs. He now seized them again, leant forward, and almost disappeared in the fireplace, from where Renée heard him muttering indistinctly:

'Yes, yes, Larsonneau might perhaps...'

She was at last coming, of her own accord, to the point towards which he had been gently leading her since the beginning of the conversation. For two years he had been preparing his masterstroke in the Charonne district. His wife had never agreed to part with Aunt Élisabeth's estate; she had promised to keep it intact, so as to leave it to any child she might have. Faced with this obstinacy, the speculator's imagination had set to work, and ended by constructing a wonderful scheme. It was a work of exquisite villainy, a colossal piece of trickery, of which the City, the State, his wife, and even Larsonneau were to be the victims. He no longer spoke of selling the building-plots; but every day he deplored the folly of leaving them unproductive and contenting themselves with a return of two per cent. Renée, who was always in urgent need of money, began to entertain the idea of a speculative venture of some kind. Saccard based his calculations on the certainty of an expropriation for the cutting of the Boulevard du Prince-Eugène,* the plans for which were not yet clearly resolved. It was then that he produced as a partner his old accomplice Larsonneau, who made the following agreement with his wife: she would buy the building-plots, representing a value of five hundred thousand francs, while Larsonneau would spend an equal sum on building on this ground a music-hall with a large garden, where games of all kinds, swings, skittle-alleys, and bowling-greens would be set up. The profits were naturally to be divided, as the losses would be shared equally. In the event of one of the two partners wishing to withdraw, he could do so and claim his share, which would be determined by a valuation. Renée seemed surprised at the large figure of five hundred thousand francs, for the land was worth three hundred thousand at most. But Saccard explained to her that it was an ingenious plan for tying Larsonneau's hands later on, as his buildings would never achieve that value.

Larsonneau had become an elegant man-about-town, well-gloved, with dazzling linen and amazing cravats. To go on his errands he had a tilbury as light as a piece of clockwork, with a very high seat, and which he drove himself. He had a sumptuous suite of rooms in the Rue de Rivoli, in which there was not a single bundle of papers or business document to be seen. His clerks worked at tables of stained pear-wood, inlaid with marquetry and adorned with chased brass. He called himself an expropriation agent, a new occupation which the transformation of Paris had brought into being. His connection with the Hôtel de Ville enabled him to receive advance information about the cutting of any new boulevard. When he had succeeded in learning the plan for a boulevard from one of the surveyors, he went and offered his services to the landlords who would be affected. He turned his little plan for increasing the compensation to account by acting before the decree of public utility was issued. As soon as the landlords accepted his proposals, he took all the expenses on himself, drew up a plan of the property, wrote a memorandum, followed up the case before the court, and paid a lawyer, all for a percentage of the difference between the City's offer and the compensation awarded by the Authority. But to this almost justifiable form of business he added several others. He lent money at interest. He was not a usurer of the old school, ragged and dirty, with eyes pale and expressionless as five-franc pieces, and lips white and drawn together like purse-strings. He was jovial, had a charming way of ogling the ladies, bought his clothes at Dusautoy's,* lunched at Brébant's with his victim, whom he called 'old man', and offered him Havanas at dessert. In reality, beneath his waistcoats tightly buckled round his waist, Larsonneau was a terrible gentleman; he would have insisted on the payment of a promissory note to the point of driving the creditor to suicide, and this without losing a grain of his amiability.

Saccard would gladly have looked for another partner. But he was still worried about the false inventory, which Larsonneau jealously guarded. He preferred to involve him in the affair, hoping to take advantage of some circumstance to regain possession of the compromising document. Larsonneau built the music-hall, an edifice of planks and plaster surmounted by little tin turrets, which were painted bright red and yellow. The garden and the games proved successful in the populous district of Charonne. Within two years this speculative venture appeared prosperous, though in fact the profits were very small. Saccard had so far always spoken enthusiastically to his wife of the prospects of this fine idea.

Renée, seeing that her husband showed no sign of coming out of the fireplace, where his voice was becoming more and more inaudible, said:

'I'll go and see Larsonneau today. It's my only chance.'

Then he let go of the log with which he was struggling.

'The errand's done, my dear,' he replied, smiling. 'Don't I anticipate all your wishes? I saw Larsonneau last night.'

'Did he promise you the hundred and thirty-six thousand francs?' she asked anxiously.

He was building up between the two flaming logs a little mountain of embers, picking up daintily with the tongs the smallest fragments of burnt wood, looking pleased with the mound he was skilfully constructing.

'Oh! I don't know about that!' he murmured. 'A hundred and thirty-six thousand francs is a lot. Larsonneau is a good sort, but his means are still limited. He's quite ready to help you.'

He paused, blinked, and rebuilt a corner of the great mound which had collapsed. This pastime began to confuse Renée. In spite of herself she followed his work on the fire, with which he seemed to be having more and more difficulty. She felt tempted to advise him. Forgetting Worms, the bill, and her need of money, she finally said:

'Put that big piece at the bottom; then the others will stay up.'

Her husband did as she said, and added:

'All he can find is fifty thousand francs. At least that will be useful to begin with. But he doesn't want to mix this up with the Charonne affair. He's only a go-between, you see. The person lending the money is asking for an enormous rate of interest. He wants a promissory note for eighty thousand francs payable in six months.'

Having crowned his great construction with a pointed cinder, he crossed his hands over the tongs and stared at his wife.

'Eighty thousand francs!' she cried. 'But that's sheer robbery! Are you advising me to do such a crazy thing?'

'No,' he replied simply. 'But if you really need the money, I won't forbid it.'

He stood up as if to go. Renée, in a state of pained indecision, looked at her husband and at the bill, which he left on the mantelpiece. At last she took her poor head between her hands, murmuring:

'Oh, these business affairs! My head is splitting this morning. Well, I must sign this note for eighty thousand francs. If I don't I'll become totally ill. I know what I'm like, I'd spend the whole day in a terrible state. I prefer to do something stupid straight away. It makes me feel better.'

She spoke of ringing for a stamped bill. But he insisted on doing this for her personally. No doubt he had the bill in his pocket, for he was out of the room for barely two minutes. While she was writing at a little table he had pushed towards the fire, he looked at her with a kind of desire. The room was still full of the warmth of the bed she had just been sleeping in, and the fragrance of her first toilet. While talking she had allowed the folds of her dressing gown to slip down, and her husband's eyes, as he stood before her, glided over her bent head, through the gold of her hair, down to the whiteness of her neck and breasts. He wore a curious smile; the glowing fire, which had burnt his face, the stifling room, whose heavy atmosphere retained an odour of love, the yellow hair and white skin, which tempted him with a sort of conjugal scornfulness, set him dreaming, widened the scope of the drama in which he had just played a scene, and prompted some secret voluptuous calculation in his brutal jobber's mind.

When his wife handed him the acceptance, begging him to finish the matter for her, he took it without taking his eyes off her.

'You're bewitchingly beautiful,' he murmured.

As she bent forward to push away the table, he kissed her roughly on the neck. She gave a little cry. Then she stood up, quivering, trying to laugh, thinking in spite of herself of Maxime's kisses the night before. But Saccard seemed to regret this unmannerly kiss. He left her, squeezing her hand, and promised she would have the fifty thousand francs that evening.

Renée dozed all day before the fire. At times of crisis she had the languor of a Creole. Her turbulent nature would then become indolent, chilled, numbed. She shivered, she needed blazing fires, stifling heat that brought little drops of perspiration to her forehead and soothed her. In this burning atmosphere, in this bath of flames, she almost ceased to suffer; her pain became like a light dream, a vague oppression whose very vagueness became pleasurable. Thus she lulled till the evening the remorse of the day before, in the red glow of the firelight, in front of a terrible fire that made the furniture crack around her and at times made her quite unconscious of her existence. She was able to think of Maxime as of a flaming pleasure whose rays burnt her; she had a nightmare of strange passions amid flaring logs on white-hot beds. Céleste moved to and fro through the room, with her calm face, the face of a cold-blooded waiting-maid. She had orders to admit no one, she even sent away the inseparables, Adeline d'Espanet and Suzanne Haffner, who called after breakfasting together in a summer house they rented at Saint-Germain. However, when, towards the evening, Céleste came to tell her mistress that Madame Sidonie, Monsieur's sister, was asking to see her, she was told to show her up.

Madame Sidonie did not usually call till dusk. Her brother had nevertheless prevailed upon her to wear silk gowns. But although the silk she wore came fresh from the shop, it never looked new; it was shabby and dull, and looked like a rag. She had also agreed not to bring her basket to the Saccards. As if in retaliation, her pockets bulged with papers. She took an interest in Renée, of whom she was unable to make a reasonable client, resigned to the necessities of life. She called on her regularly, with the discreet smiles of a doctor who does not wish to frighten his patient by telling her the name of her complaint. She commiserated with her in her little worries, treating them as slight aches and pains which she could cure in a minute if Renée wished. The latter, who was in one of those moods when one feels the need to be pitied, received her only to tell her that she had a terrible headache.

'Oh! my beautiful creature,' murmured Madame Sidonie as she glided through the shadows, 'you must be suffocating in here! Still your migraine, is it? It comes from worry. You take things too much to heart.'

'Yes, I have so many worries,' replied Renée listlessly.

Night was falling. She had not allowed Céleste to light the lamp. The fire alone cast a great red glow that lighted her up fully, stretched out in her white dressing gown, whose lace was assuming pink tints. At the edge of the shadow one could just see a corner of Madame Sidonie's black dress and her two crossed hands, covered with grey cotton gloves. Her soft voice came out of the darkness.

'Money troubles again?' she asked, as if she had said troubles of the heart, in a voice full of gentleness and compassion.

Renée lowered her eyes and nodded.

'Ah! if my brothers listened to me, we would all be rich. But they just shrug when I mention that debt of three thousand million francs. I'm still hoping, nevertheless. For the last ten years I've wanted to go across to England. I'm so busy, though! But I decided to write to London, and I'm waiting for a reply.'

As the younger woman smiled, she went on:

'I know you think it's all nonsense. But you'd be very pleased if one of these days I gave you a million francs. The story is very simple: there was a Parisian banker who lent the money to the king of England, and as the banker died without direct heirs, the State is entitled to claim the debt back with compound interest. I've worked it out, it comes to over two thousand, nine hundred and forty-three million, two hundred and ten thousand francs. Don't worry, it will come, it will come.'

'In the meantime,' said Renée, with a touch of irony, 'I wish you would get someone to lend me a hundred thousand francs. Then I could pay my dressmaker, who is always pestering me.'

'A hundred thousand francs can be found,' calmly replied Madame Sidonie. 'It's just a question of what you'll give in exchange.'

The fire was glowing; Renée, even more languid, stretched out her legs, showing the tips of her slippers at the end of her dressing gown. The agent resumed, in her gentle voice:

'My poor dear, you're really not reasonable. I know a lot of women, but I've never seen one take such little care of her health as you. That little Michelin woman, for instance, see how well she manages! I can't help thinking of you whenever I see her in good health and spirits. Do you know that Monsieur de Saffré is madly in love with her and has already given her nearly ten thousand francs' worth of presents? I think her dream is to have a house in the country.'

She grew excited, and fumbled in her pocket.

'I've got a letter here from a poor young married woman. If we had some light, I'd let you read it. Her husband takes no notice of her. She had accepted some bills, and had to borrow the money from a gentleman I know. I went and rescued the bills from the bailiff's clutches. It was no easy matter. Those poor children, do you think they've done wrong? I receive them at home as if they were my son and daughter.'

'Do you know anyone who would lend me the money?' asked Renée casually.

'I know a dozen. You're too kind-hearted. Women can say anything to each other, can't they? It's not because your husband is my brother that I'd forgive him for running after other women and leaving a fine woman like you to mope by the fireside. That Laure d'Aurigny costs him a fortune. I wouldn't be surprised if he'd refused you money. He has refused, hasn't he? The wretch!'

Renée listened complacently to this mellifluous voice coming out of the shadows like an echo of her own dreams. With her eyes half closed, almost lying in her easy chair, she was no longer conscious of Madame Sidonie's presence, she thought she was dreaming evil thoughts that had crept up on her to tempt her. The businesswoman kept up her prattle like the monotonous flow of tepid water.

'Madame de Lauwerens has spoilt things for you. You wouldn't believe me. You wouldn't be crying by the fire if you'd trusted me. I'm extremely fond of you, you beautiful thing. What a delightful foot you have. You'll laugh at me, but I must tell you how silly I am: when I've gone three days without seeing you, I feel I absolutely have to come and admire you; yes, I feel I want something: I feel the need to feast my eyes on your lovely hair, your face, so white and delicate, your slender figure... Really, I've never seen such a figure.'

Renée began to smile. Even her lovers did not show such warmth, such ecstasy, in speaking to her about her beauty. Madame Sidonie noted the smile.

'So it's agreed,' she said, standing up. 'I go on and forget I'm giving you a headache. You'll come tomorrow, won't you? We'll talk about the money, we'll look for a lender... You must understand, I want you to be happy.'

Still motionless, enervated by the heat, Renée replied after a pause, as if it had cost her a great effort to understand what was being said to her:

'Yes, I'll come, and we'll talk; but not tomorrow. Worms will be satisfied with an instalment. When he bothers me again, we'll see... Don't talk about it any more. My head's bursting with all these business affairs.'

Madame Sidonie seemed rather put out. She was about to sit down again and resume her sweet-talk; but Renée's weary attitude made her decide to postpone her attack till later. She took a handful of papers from her pocket, and searched among them until she found something enclosed in a sort of pink box.

'I came to recommend a new soap,' she said, resuming her business voice. 'I take a great interest in the inventor, who's a charming young man. It's a very soft soap, very good for the skin. Try it, and tell your friends about it. I'll leave it here, on the mantelpiece.'

She had reached the door, when she returned once more, and standing erect in the crimson glow of the fire, with her waxen face, she began to sing the praises of an elastic belt, an invention intended to replace corsets.

'It gives you an absolutely round waist, a genuine wasp's waist,' she said. 'I saved the inventor from bankruptcy. When you come you can try on the samples if you like. I had to run after the solicitors for a week. I've got the documents in my pocket, and I'm going straight to my bailiff now to put a stop to a final objection. Goodbye for now, darling. I'll be expecting you: I want to dry those pretty eyes of yours.'

She glided out of sight. Renée did not even hear her close the door. She stayed there before the dying fire, still dreaming, her head full of dancing figures, hearing the distant voices of Saccard and Madame Sidonie offering her large sums of money, like an auction-eer putting up a lot of furniture. She felt her husband's rough kiss on her neck, and when she turned round she imagined the business-woman at her feet, with her black dress and her flaccid face, making passionate speeches to her, praising her perfections, and begging for an assignation like a lover on the verge of despair. This made her smile. The heat in the room became more and more stifling. Her stupor and her fantastic dreams were no more than an artificial slumber in which she kept seeing the little private room on the boulevard and the big sofa upon which she had fallen on her knees. She no longer felt the slightest distress. When she opened her eyes, the image of Maxime appeared in the crimson firelight.

The next day, at the Ministry ball, the beautiful Madame Saccard was dazzling. Worms had accepted the fifty thousand francs on account, and she emerged from her financial straits with the laughter of convalescence. As she walked through the reception rooms in her great dress of pink faille with its long Louis XIV train, edged with deep white lace, there was a murmur, men jostled each other to see her. Her friends bowed low, smiling discreetly, paying homage to those beautiful shoulders, so well known in high society, and looked upon as the pillars of the Empire. She had bared her breasts with such contempt for the gaze of others, she walked so serenely in her nakedness, that it almost ceased to be indecent. Eugène Rougon, the great politician, felt that her breasts were even more eloquent than his speeches in the Chamber, softer and more persuasive in making people appreciate the charms of the Empire. He went up to his sister-in-law to compliment her on her happy stroke of audacity in lowering her bodice yet another inch. Almost all the Corps Législatif was there, and from the way the deputies looked at Renée, the minister foresaw success the next day in the delicate matter of the loans of the City of Paris.* It was impossible to vote against a power that produced, on the compost of millions, a flower like Renée, such a strangely voluptuous flower, with silken flesh and statuesque nudity, a living joy that left in her wake the fragrance of pure pleasure. But what set the whole ballroom whispering was the necklace and aigrette. The men recognized the jewels. The women furtively drew each other's attention to them with a glance. Nothing else was talked of the whole evening. The reception rooms stretched out in the white light of the chandeliers, filled with a glittering throng like a medley of stars fallen into too confined a space.

At about one o'clock Saccard disappeared. He relished his wife's triumph as a successful piece of theatre. He had once more consolidated his credit. A business matter required his presence at Laure d'Aurigny's; he went off, and begged Maxime to take Renée home after the ball.

Maxime spent the evening dutifully with Louise de Mareuil, and both of them devoted themselves to saying shocking things about the women who passed to and fro. When they had uttered some coarser piece of nonsense than usual, they stifled their laughter in their pocket-handkerchiefs. When Renée wanted to leave she had to come and ask Maxime for his arm. In the carriage she was nervous and giggly; she still quivered with the intoxication of light, perfumes, and sounds that she had just passed through. She seemed to have forgotten their folly on the boulevard, as Maxime called it. She simply asked him, in an odd tone of voice:

'Is that little hunchback Louise a lot of fun, then?'

'Oh, yes,' replied the young man, still laughing. 'You saw the Duchesse de Sternich with a yellow bird in her hair, didn't you? Well, Louise suggested it's a clockwork bird that flaps its wings every hour and cries, "Cuckold! Cuckold!" to the poor Duke.'

Renée thought this schoolgirl pleasantry very amusing. When they reached home, as Maxime was about to say goodbye, she said:

'Aren't you coming up? I'm sure Céleste will have left something to eat.'

He came up in his usual compliant fashion. There was nothing to eat upstairs, and Céleste had gone to bed. Renée had to light the tapers in a small three-branched candlestick. Her hand trembled a little.

'That foolish creature', she said, speaking of her maid, 'must have misunderstood what I told her. I'll never be able to undress on my own.'

She went into her dressing room. Maxime followed her, to tell her a fresh joke of Louise's. He was as much at ease as if he had been loitering at a friend's and was feeling for his cigar-case. But when Renée put down the candlesticks, she turned round and fell into the young man's arms, speechless, gluing her mouth to his.

Renée's private apartment was a nest of silk and lace, a marvel of luxurious coquetry. A tiny boudoir led into the bedroom. The two rooms formed but one, or at least the boudoir was nothing more than the threshold of the bedroom, a large alcove, furnished with chaises-longues and with a pair of hangings instead of a door. The walls of both rooms were hung with the same material, a heavy pale-grey silk, figured with huge bouquets of roses, white lilac, and buttercups. The curtains and door-hangings were of Venetian lace over a silk lining of grey and pink bands. In the bedroom the white marble chimney-piece, a real jewel, displayed like a basket of flowers its incrustations of lapis lazuli and precious mosaics, repeating the roses, white lilac, and buttercups of the tapestry. A large pink-and-grey bed, whose wood-work was hidden beneath padding and upholstery, and whose head stood against the wall, filled at least half the room with its flow of drapery, its lace, and its silk figures with bouquets falling from the ceiling to the carpet. It was like a woman's dress, rounded and slashed and decked with puffs and bows and flounces; and the large curtain, swelling out like a skirt, brought to mind some tall, amorous girl, leaning over, swooning, almost falling back on the pillows. Beneath the curtains it was a sanctuary: cambric finely plaited, a snowy mass of lace, all sorts of delicate, diaphanous things immersed in semi-darkness. Compared to the bed, this monument whose devout ampleness recalled a chapel decorated for some festival, the rest of the furniture appeared insignificant: low chairs, a cheval-glass six feet high, presses with innumerable drawers. Underfoot, the carpet, blue-grey, was covered with pale, full-blown roses. On either side of the bed lay two big black bearskin rugs, edged with crimson velvet, with silver claws and with their heads turned towards the window, staring with their glass eyes at the empty sky.

Soft harmony and muffled silence reigned in Renée's bedroom. No shrill note, no metallic reflection, no bright gilding broke through the dreamy melody of pink and grey. Even the chimney ornaments, the frame of the mirror, the clock, the little candlesticks, were of old Sèvres, and the mountings of copper-gilt were scarcely visible. Marvellous ornaments, the clock especially, with its ring of chubby Cupids who climbed and leaned over the dial-plate like a troop of naked urchins mocking the quick flight of time. This subdued luxury gave the room a crepuscular light like that of an alcove with curtains drawn. The bed seemed to stretch out till the whole room became one immense bed, with its carpets, its bearskin rugs, its padded seats, its stuffed hangings, which continued the softness of the floor along the walls and up to the ceiling. As in a bed, Renée left upon all these things the imprint, the warmth and perfume of her body. When the double hangings of the boudoir were drawn aside, it seemed as if one were raising a silken counterpane and entering a huge bed, still warm and moist, where one found on the fine linen the adorable shape, the slumber, and the dreams of a thirty-year-old Parisian woman.

An adjoining closet, hung with antique chintz, was simply furnished on every side with tall rosewood wardrobes, containing an army of dresses. Céleste, always methodical, arranged the dresses according to their dates, and labelled them, introducing arithmetic into her mistress's blue and yellow caprices. She kept this closet as calm as a sacristy and as clean as a stable. There was no furniture in the room, nothing was lying about, and the wardrobe doors shone cold and clean like the varnished panels of a brougham.

But the wonder of the apartment, the room that was the talk of Paris, was the dressing room. People talked about 'beautiful Madame Saccard's dressing room' in the same way that they talked about 'the Hall of Mirrors at Versailles'. The room was situated in one of the towers, just above the little buttercup drawing room. On entering, one was reminded of a large circular tent, a magical tent, pitched in a dream by some lovelorn Amazon. In the middle of the ceiling a crown of chased silver supported the drapery of the tent, which curved upwards to the walls, whence it fell straight down to the floor. This drapery, these rich hangings, consisted of pink silk covered with very thin muslin, plaited in wide folds at regular intervals. A band of lace separated the folds, and wrought silver beading ran from the crown and down the hangings along the edges of the bands. The pink and grey of the bedroom grew brighter here, became pink and white, like naked flesh. Beneath this bower of lace, under these curtains that hid the whole ceiling except for a pale blue cavity inside the narrow circle of the crown, where Chaplin* had painted a laughing Cupid looking down and preparing his dart, one would have thought oneself at the bottom of a candy-box, or in some precious jewel-case enlarged as if to display a woman's naked body instead of the brilliancy of a diamond. The carpet, white as snow, stretched away without the least pattern or flower. There was a cupboard with plate-glass doors, whose two panels were inlaid with silver; a chaise-longue, two ottomans, some white satin stools; and a great washstand with a pink marble slab and legs hidden under flounces of muslin and lace. The glasses on the wash-stand, the bottles and the basin were of antique Bohemian crystal, streaked pink and white; and there was yet another table, inlaid with silver like the looking-glass cupboard, on which all the parapher-nalia and toilet utensils were laid out, like the contents of a fantastic surgeon's case, displaying a large number of little instruments of puzzling purpose, back-scratchers, nail-polishers, files of all shapes and sizes, scissors straight and curved, every type of tweezer and pin. Each of these items, of silver and ivory, bore Renée's monogram.

The dressing room had a delightful corner which, in particular, made it famous. In front of the window the folds of the tent parted and disclosed, in a kind of long, shallow alcove, a bath, a basin of pink marble sunk into the floor, with sides fluted like those of a large shell and rising to the level of the carpet. Marble steps led down into the bath. Above the silver taps, shaped like swans' necks, the back of the alcove was filled with a Venetian mirror, frameless, with curved edges and a ground design on the crystal. Every morning Renée took a long bath. This filled the dressing room for the whole day with moisture, with the fragrance of fresh, wet flesh. Sometimes an unstoppered scent-bottle, or a cake of soap left out of its dish, struck a more violent note in this languorous atmosphere. Renée was fond of staying there till midday, almost naked. The round tent was naked too. The pink bath, the pink slabs and basins, the muslin of the walls and ceiling, under which pink blood seemed to course, had the curves of flesh, the curves of shoulders and breasts; and, according to the time of day, one would have imagined the snowy skin of a child or the warm skin of a woman. It was redolent of nudity. When Renée emerged from it, her fair-skinned body added a little more pink to all the pink flesh of the room.

Maxime undressed Renée. He understood these things, and his quick hands divined pins and glided round her waist with instinctive ease. He undid her hair, took off her diamonds, dressed her hair for the night. He added caresses and amusing little remarks to the performance of his duties as lady's-maid and hairdresser, and Renée laughed, with a broad stifled laugh, while the silk of her bodice cracked and her petticoats were loosened one by one. When she saw herself naked, she blew out the tapers of the candlestick, caught Maxime round the waist, and all but carried him into the bedroom. The ball had completed her intoxication. In her fever she was conscious of the previous day spent in a stupor by the fire, a day of vague and pleasant dreams. She could still hear the harsh voices of Saccard and Madame Sidonie, calling out figures like bailiffs. These were the people who overwhelmed her, who drove her to crime; and even now, when she sought his lips in the depths of the vast, dark bed, she still saw his image in the firelight the day before, looking at her with burning eyes.

The young man did not leave until six in the morning. She gave him the key to the little gate in the Parc Monceau, and made him swear to come back every night. The dressing room communicated with the buttercup drawing room by a servant's staircase hidden in the wall, which connected all the rooms in the tower. From the drawing room it was easy to pass into the hothouse and the gardens.

Leaving at dawn in a thick fog, Maxime was a little bewildered by his adventure. He accepted it, however, with his epicene complacency. 'Too bad!' he thought. 'That's what she wanted. She's got a wonderful body; and she was right, she's twice as good in bed as Sylvia.'

They had drifted towards incest since the day when Maxime, in his threadbare schoolboy tunic, had hung on Renée's neck, creasing her guardsman's coat. From that time onwards there had been a slow, inexorable perversion of their relationship. The strange education the young woman gave the child; the familiarity that made them friends; later on, the laughter and audacity of their shared secrets: all this dangerous promiscuity had ended by binding them together in such a way that the pleasure of friendship approached carnal indulgence. They had given themselves to each other for years; the animal act was simply the culmination of this unconscious malady of passion. In the maddened world in which they lived, their sin had sprouted as on a dunghill oozing with strange juices; it had developed with strange refinements amid special conditions of perversion.

When the great calash carried them to the Bois and bore them gently along the pathways, their whispering of filthy remarks into each other's ears, their attempt to recall the instinctive bad behaviour of their childhood, was but a digression, and a tacit gratification of their desires. They felt vaguely guilty, as if they had slightly touched one another; and even this first sin, this languor born of smutty conversations, though it wearied them with a voluptuous fatigue, titillated them even more than plain, positive kisses. Their familiarity was thus the slow progress of two lovers, and was inevitably bound to lead them one day to the private room in the Café Riche and to Renée's great pink-and-grey bed. When they found themselves in each other's arms, they did not even feel the shock of sin. They might have been two old lovers, whose kisses were full of memories, and who had spent so many intimate hours together that, in spite of themselves, they talked of their past, which was full of their unconscious feelings for each other.

'Do you remember the day I arrived in Paris?' said Maxime. 'You were wearing such a funny dress, and I drew an angle on your chest with my finger and advised you to cut the bodice in a point. I felt your skin under your blouse, and my finger went in a little. It was very nice.'

Renée laughed, kissed him, and murmured:

'You were already quite corrupt. You made us laugh at Worms. Do you remember? We used to call you our little toy man. I always thought that that fat Suzanne would have let you do anything, if the Marquise hadn't kept such a close eye on her.'

'Yes, we had some good laughs,' murmured Maxime. 'The photograph album, and all the rest, our drives through Paris, the cakes we had on the boulevard; you remember those little strawberry tarts you were so fond of? I'll never forget the afternoon when you told me the story of Adeline at the convent, when she wrote letters to Suzanne and signed herself Arthur d'Espanet, like a man, and proposed to elope with her.'

The lovers laughed again over this story; and then Maxime continued in his childlike voice:

'When you came to fetch me from school in your carriage, we must have looked funny. I used to disappear under your skirts, I was so little.'

'Yes, yes,' she stammered, beginning to tremble, and drawing Maxime towards her, 'it was quite wonderful. We loved each other without knowing it, didn't we? I knew it before you did. The other day, driving back from the Bois, I just touched your leg, and gave a start. But you didn't notice anything, you weren't thinking of me, were you?'

'Oh yes,' he replied, somewhat embarrassed. 'But I didn't know, you see. I didn't dare.'

He was lying. The idea of making love to Renée had never occurred to him. He had touched her with all his pervertedness, without really desiring her. He was too weak to make the effort. He accepted Renée because she forced herself upon him, and he had slipped into her bed without willing or foreseeing it. Having found himself there, he had stayed because it was warm, and because he usually remained at the bottom of every pit he fell into. At the beginning he even felt quite pleased with himself. She was the first married woman he had had. He did not consider the fact that her husband was his father.

But Renée brought into her sin all the passion of a confused mind. She too had slipped down the slope. But she had not rolled to the bottom like a mass of inert flesh. Lust had been awakened in her when it was too late to resist, and the fall had become inevitable. This fall suddenly seemed to her a necessary consequence of her boredom, a rare and supreme pleasure, which alone was able to rouse her weary senses, her bruised heart. It was during that autumn drive in the twilight, when the Bois was falling asleep, that the vague idea of incest came to her like a titillation that sent a rare thrill over her skin; and in the evening, in the semi-intoxication of the dinner, provoked by jealousy, this idea became more precise, rose up before her, amid the flames of the hothouse, as she stood watching Maxime and Louise. At that moment she craved sin, the sin no one commits, the sin that was to fill her empty existence and transport her at last to that hell of which she was still afraid, as in the days when she was a little girl. Then, the next day, through a strange feeling of remorse and lassitude, her craving had left her. It seemed to her that she had already sinned, that it was not as pleasant as she had imagined, and that it would really be too disgusting. The crisis was bound to be inevitable, to come naturally, without the help of these two beings, these comrades who were destined one fine evening to unite in a sexual embrace when they imagined they were shaking hands. But after this simple fall, she returned to her dream of a nameless pleasure, and then she received Maxime back into her arms, curious about him, curious about the cruel delights of a passion she regarded as a crime. She willed the incest, demanded it, resolved to taste it to the end, even to the point of remorse, should that ever come. She was fully aware of what she was doing. She pursued her passion as a woman of fashion, with the prejudices of a woman of the bourgeoisie, with all the struggles, joys, and world-weariness of a woman drowning in self-disgust.

Maxime came back every night. He came through the garden at about one o'clock. Usually Renée would wait for him in the hothouse, which he had to go through to reach the little drawing room. They were absolutely shameless, ignoring the most elementary precautions of adultery. This corner of the house, it is true, belonged to them. Only Baptiste, Saccard's valet, had the right to enter, and he disappeared as soon as his duties were over. Maxime even claimed, with a laugh, that he withdrew to write his memoirs. One night, however, just after Maxime had arrived, Renée pointed out Baptiste walking through the drawing room with a candlestick in his hand. The tall valet, with his diplomatic figure, lit by the yellow light of the taper, wore that evening an even more correct and severe expression than usual. Leaning forward, the lovers saw him blow out his candle and go towards the stables, where the horses and grooms lay sleeping.

'He's doing his rounds,' said Maxime.

Renée shivered. Baptiste always made her uncomfortable. She said one day that he was the only respectable man in the house, with his coldness and his unblinking gaze that was never directed at women.

After that they were more careful. They closed the doors of the little drawing room and were thus able to use this room, the hothouse, and Renée's own rooms without being disturbed. It was a world in itself. There they tasted, during the first few months, the most refined delights. They made love in all the rooms, moving from the great pink-and-grey bed of the bedroom to the pink-and-white nudity of the dressing room and to the symphony in pale yellow of the little drawing room. Each room, with its particular odour, its hangings, its special life, gave them a different form of passion and made Renée a different kind of lover: she was dainty and pretty in her padded aristocratic couch, where, in the warm bedroom, love became a matter of good taste; under the flesh-coloured tent, amid the perfumes and the humid languor of the bathroom, she became a capricious, carnal courtesan, yielding as soon as she emerged from the bath: this was how Maxime preferred her; then, downstairs, in the bright sunrise of the little drawing room, in the yellow halo that gilded her hair, she became a goddess, with her fair Diana-like head, her bare arms which assumed chaste postures, her unblemished body which reclined on the couches in attitudes revealing noble outlines of antique grace. But there was one place that almost frightened Maxime, where Renée dragged him on bad days, when she needed a more acrid form of intoxication. This place was the hothouse. It was there that they tasted incest.

One night, in an hour of anguish, Renée sent her lover for one of the black bearskin rugs. Then they lay down on this inky fur, at the edge of an ornamental pond, in the large circular pathway. Outside it was freezing in the clear moonlight. Maxime had arrived shivering, his ears and fingers numb. The hothouse was heated to such a point that he fainted on the bearskin. Coming from the dry, biting cold into such intense heat, he felt a smarting sensation as if he had been whipped with a birch-rod. When he came to, he saw Renée on her knees, leaning over him, with staring eyes and an animal-like attitude that alarmed him. Her hair hanging down, her shoulders bare, she leant on her wrists, with her back arched, like a great cat with phosphorescent eyes. The young man, lying on his back, noticed over the shoulders of this adorable, passionate beast the marble sphinx, its haunches gleaming in the moonlight. Renée had the attitude and smile of the monster with a woman's head and, in her loosened petticoats, looked like the white sister of this black divinity.

Maxime remained supine. The heat was suffocating, a sultry heat that did not fall from the sky in a rain of fire, but trailed on the ground like a poisonous exhalation, its steam rising like a storm-laden cloud. A warm dampness covered the lovers with dew, with burning perspiration. For a while they were unable to move or speak, Maxime prostrate and inert, Renée quivering on her hands as on supple, nervous hams. Through the little panes of the hothouse they could catch glimpses of the Parc Monceau, clumps of trees with fine black outlines, lawns white as frozen lakes, a whole dead landscape whose exquisiteness and light, even tints were reminiscent of Japanese prints. The burning couch on which the lovers lay seethed strangely in the midst of the great, silent cold.

They spent a night of passion. Renée was the man, the ardent, active partner. Maxime remained submissive. Smooth-limbed, slim, and graceful as a Roman stripling, fair-haired and pretty, stricken in his virility since childhood, this epicene creature became a girl in Renée's arms. He seemed born and bred for perverted sensual pleasure. Renée enjoyed her domination, bending to her will this creature of indeterminate sex. For her this relationship brought continual experiments, new sensations, strange feelings of uneasiness and keen enjoyment. She was no longer certain: she felt doubts each time she returned to his delicate skin, his soft neck, his attitudes of abandonment, his fainting fits. She then experienced an hour of repletion. By revealing to her new forms of ecstasy, Maxime crowned her mad outfits, her prodigious luxury, her life of excess. He ingrained into her flesh the high-pitched note already singing in her ears. He was a lover who matched the follies and fashions of the age. This pretty young man, whose frail figure could be seen by his clothes, this effeminate creature that strolled along the boulevards, his hair parted in the middle, with little bursts of laughter and bored smiles, became in Renée's hands one of those corrupting, decadent influences that, at certain periods among rotten nations, lead to the exhaustion of the body and the unhinging of the brain.

It was in the hothouse especially that Renée assumed the masculine role. The night of passion they spent there was followed by many others. The hothouse loved and burned with them. In the heavy atmosphere, in the pale light of the moon, they saw the strange world of plants moving confusedly around them, exchanging embraces. The black bearskin stretched across the pathway. At their feet the tank steamed, full of a thick tangle of plants, while the pink petals of the water-lilies opened out on the surface, like virgin bodices, and the tornelias let their bushy tendrils hang down like the hair of swooning water-nymphs. Around them the palm trees and the tall Indian bamboos rose up towards the domed roof, where they bent over and mingled their leaves with the postures of exhausted lovers. Lower down the ferns, the pterides, and the alsophilas were like green ladies, with wide skirts trimmed with symmetrical flounces, standing mute and motionless at the edge of the pathway, waiting for some romantic encounter. By their side the twisted, red-streaked leaves of the begonias and the white, spear-headed leaves of the caladiums provided a vague series of bruises and pallors, which the lovers could not understand, though at times they discerned curves as of hips and knees, prone on the ground beneath the brutality of blood-stained kisses. The banana trees, bending under the weight of their fruit, spoke to them of the rich fecundity of the earth, while the Abyssinian euphorbias, whose prickly, deformed stems, covered with loathsome excrescences, they glimpsed in the shadows, seemed to exude sap, the overflowing flux of this fiery gestation. But by degrees, as their glances penetrated into the corners of the hothouse, the darkness became filled with a more furious debauch of leaves and stalks; they could not distinguish on the terraces between the marantas, soft as velvet, the gloxinias, purple-belled, the dracoenas, like blades of old lacquer; it was a great dance of living plants pursuing one another with unsatisfied fervour. In the corners, where curtains of creepers closed in the arbours, their carnal fancy grew madder still, and the supple shoots of the vanilla plants, of the Indian berries, the quisqualias, and bauhinias were like the strangely elongated arms of unseen lovers madly prolonging their embraces so as to collect all scattered delights. Those endless arms drooped with weariness, entwined in a spasm of love, sought each other, closed together like a crowd in rut. It was the boundless copulation of the hothouse, of this patch of virgin forest ablaze with tropical flora and foliage.

Maxime and Renée, their senses perverted, felt carried away in these mighty nuptials of the earth. The ground burnt their backs through the bearskin, and drops of heat fell upon them from the lofty palms. The sap that rose in the tree-trunks penetrated them, filling them with a mad longing for immediate growth, for gigantic procreation. They joined in the copulation of the hothouse. It was then, in the pale light, that they were stupefied by visions, by nightmares in which they watched the embraces of the ferns and palms; the foliage assumed confused and mysterious shapes, which their desires transformed into sensual images; murmurs and whispers reached them from the shrubbery, faint voices, sighs of ecstasy, stifled cries of pain, distant laughter, all that was audible in their own embraces and came back to them as an echo. At times they thought they were at the centre of an earthquake, as if the ground beneath them had burst into voluptuous sobs in a paroxysm of satisfied desire.

If they had closed their eyes, if the stifling heat and pale light had not distorted their senses, the scents would have been enough to throw them into an extraordinary state of excitement. The pond saturated them with a deep, pungent odour, through which passed the thousand perfumes of the flowers and plants. At times the vanilla plant sang with dove-like cooings; then came the rough notes of the stanhopeas, whose striped throats have the putrid breath of convalescent invalids. The orchids, in baskets suspended by wire chains, emitted their exhalations like living censers. But the dominant scent, in which all these vague breaths were intermingled, was a human scent, a scent of love, which Maxime recognized when he kissed Renée on the neck and plunged his head into her flowing hair. They lay intoxicated with this scent of an amorous woman, which trailed through the hothouse as through an alcove in which the earth itself was giving birth.

As a rule the lovers lay down under the Madagascan tanghin tree, the poisonous shrub whose leaf Renée had once bitten. Around them the white statues laughed as they gazed at the mighty copulation of foliage. The moon, as it revolved, displaced the groups and gave life to the drama with its changing light. They were a thousand miles from Paris, from the easy life of the Bois and official receptions, in a corner of an Indian forest, of some monstrous temple of which the black marble sphinx had become the deity. They felt themselves rolling towards crime, towards a cursed love, towards the caresses of wild beasts. All the natural growth that surrounded them, the teeming tank, the naked immodesty of the foliage, threw them into a deep, Dantesque inferno of passion. It was then, in the depths of this glass cage, boiling in the summer heat, lost in the keen December cold, that they relished their incest, as if it were the criminal fruit of an overheated soil, with the dull fear of this terrifying hotbed.

In the middle of the black bearskin Renée's body seemed whiter, as she crouched like a great cat, her back arched, her wrists tense like supple, nervous hams. She was swollen with desire, and the clear outline of her shoulders and hips stood out with feline clarity against the splash of ink with which the rug blackened the yellow sand of the pathway. She gloated over Maxime, this prey lying beneath her, completely under her spell. From time to time she leant forward suddenly and kissed him with her swollen mouth. Her mouth opened with the hungry, bleeding brilliancy of the Chinese hibiscus, which covered the side of the house. She became like one of the exotic plants in the hothouse. Her kisses bloomed and faded like the red flowers of the great mallow, which last scarcely a few hours and are endlessly renewed, like the bruised, insatiable lips of a giant Messalina.

CHAPTER V

SACCARD was haunted by the kiss he had planted on his wife's neck. He had long ceased to avail himself of his marital rights; this had happened naturally, neither of them caring about a connection that inconvenienced them. Saccard would never think of returning to Renée's bedroom unless some good piece of business were the ultimate aim of his conjugal devotion.

The Charonne venture was progressing well, though he was still anxious about its outcome. Larsonneau, with his dazzling shirt-front, had a way of smiling which he did not like. He was just a go-between, a man of straw, whose assistance he paid for by giving him a commission of ten per cent on his profits. But although the expropriation agent had not put a sou into the enterprise, and Saccard had not only found the money for the music-hall but had taken every precaution—a deed of retrocession, undated letters, pre-dated receipts—the latter remained apprehensive, and felt a presentiment of treachery. He suspected his accomplice of planning to blackmail him by using the false inventory he had carefully preserved, and which alone he had to thank for his share in the business.

So the two men shook hands. Larsonneau addressed Saccard as 'master'. He deeply admired this acrobat, and watched his performances on the tightrope of speculation with the eye of a connoisseur. The idea of hoodwinking Saccard appealed to him greatly. He was nursing a plan, as yet vague, for he did not know how to use the weapon he possessed, lest he should do himself damage with it. He felt too that he was at his former colleague's mercy. The land and the buildings, which the cunningly prepared inventories already estimated at nearly two million, though they were not worth a quarter of that amount, would be swallowed up in a great crash if the expropriation fairy failed to touch them with her magic wand. According to the original plans, which they had been able to consult, the new boulevard, opened to connect the artillery park at Vincennes with the Prince-Eugène Barracks,* and to bring the guns into the heart of Paris while avoiding the Faubourg Saint-Antoine,* cut off part of the land;* but there was still the risk that it would be only slightly affected and that the ingenious plan for the music-hall might fall through because of its sheer boldness. In that case Larsonneau would be left stranded. Still, despite the secondary role he was compelled to play, this did not prevent him from feeling disgusted when he thought of the paltry ten per cent he was to pocket in this huge robbery. At these moments he could not resist a furious longing to stretch out his hand and carve a slice for himself.

Saccard had not even allowed him to lend money to his wife, taking pleasure himself in this piece of theatre, which satisfied his weakness for complicated transactions.

'No, no, my dear fellow,' he said, with his Provençal accent, which he exaggerated whenever he wanted to add spice to a joke, 'we mustn't get our accounts mixed up. You're the only man in Paris I've sworn never to owe money to.'

Larsonneau contented himself with hinting that his wife was a spendthrift. He advised him not to give her another sou, so that she might make over the property to them at once. He would have preferred to do business with Saccard alone. He tested him out occasionally, and even went so far as to say to him, with his languid and indifferent man-about-town manner:

'All the same, I'll have to put my papers in order. Your wife frightens me, old man. I don't want to have seals put on some of the documents at my office.'

Saccard was not the sort of man to take kindly to insinuations of this sort, especially as he was well acquainted with the cold, meticulous orderliness of Larsonneau's office. His whole cunning little being revolted against the fear this great yellow-gloved fop sought to inspire in him. He shuddered when he thought of the possibility of a scandal; and he saw himself brutally exiled by his brother, and living in Belgium engaged in some shabby little trade. One day he grew angry and went so far as to address Larsonneau as *tu*:

'Look here,' he said, 'you're a decent chap, but it would be a good idea if you handed over that document, or we'll end up quarrelling over it.'

Larsonneau feigned surprise, pressing his 'master's' hands and assuring him of his devotion. Saccard regretted his momentary impatience. It was at this time that he began to think seriously of resuming marital relations with his wife; he might need her in any conflict with his accomplice, and he told himself that business matters are wonderfully easy to talk over in bed. That kiss on the neck tended little by little to reveal an entirely new policy.

But he was in no hurry, he husbanded his resources. He spent the whole winter hatching his plan, involved in a hundred different projects, each more complicated than the other. It was a terrible winter for him, full of surprises, a prodigious campaign during which he had to fight off bankruptcy every day. Far from cutting down his domestic expenses, he gave party after party. But if he overcame every obstacle, he was forced to neglect Renée, holding her in reserve for a triumphant stroke when the Charonne operation came to fruition.

He contented himself with preparing the dénouement by continuing to give her no money except through Larsonneau. When he had a few thousand francs to spare, and she complained of her poverty, he brought them to her, saying that Larsonneau's people required a promissory note for twice as much. This farce amused him greatly, the story of the promissory notes delighting him because of the air of romance they imparted to the affair. Even during the period of his biggest profits he had served out his wife's income in a very irregular fashion, giving her princely presents, throwing her handfuls of banknotes, and then for weeks leaving her just a paltry amount. Now that he found himself in dire straits, he spoke of the household expenses, treating her like a creditor to whom one is unwilling to confess one's ruin, gaining time by making excuses. She barely listened to him; she signed anything, sorry that she was not able to sign more.

Already, however, he held two hundred thousand francs' worth of her promissory notes, which had cost him barely one hundred and ten thousand francs. After having these notes endorsed by Larsonneau, to whom they were made out, he put them prudently into circulation, intending to use them as decisive weapons later on. He would never have been able to hold out to the end of that terrible winter, lending money to his wife like a usurer and keeping up his domestic expenses, had it not been for the sale of his building-plots on the Boulevard Malesherbes, which Mignon and Charrier bought from him in cash, deducting a huge discount.

For Renée this same winter was a time of joy. She suffered only from a lack of ready money. Maxime proved a great expense; he still treated her as his stepmother, and let her pay wherever they went.

But this secret poverty was for her one more delight. She taxed her ingenuity and racked her brains so that 'her dear child' would want for nothing; and when she had persuaded her husband to find her a few thousand francs, she ran through them with her lover in costly frivolities, like two schoolboys let out on their first escapade. When they had spent the last sou they stayed at home, revelling in the great piece of masonry built with such new and insolent luxury. The father was never there. The lovers sat by the fireside more often than before. The fact was that Renée had at last filled the emptiness of those gilded ceilings with the satisfaction of her desires. The disorderly house of worldly pleasure had become a chapel in which she secretly practised a new religion. Maxime struck in her not merely the shrill note that matched her extravagant costumes; he was a lover fashioned for this house, with its windows more like those of a department store and its flow of sculpture from the attic rooms down to the cellars; he gave life to all this plaster, from the two chubby Cupids in the courtyard, who exuded a sheet of water from their shell, to the great naked women who supported the balconies and played with apples and ears of corn amid the pediments; he gave meaning to the ornate hall, the narrow garden, the dazzling rooms which contained too many armchairs and not a single work of art. Renée, who had been bored to death in this house, began suddenly to take pleasure in it, using it as she might use something whose purpose she had not at first understood. It was not only in her own rooms, in her buttercup drawing room and in the hothouse that she pursued her love, but throughout the whole house. She even ended by taking her pleasure on the divan in the smoking room; she lingered there, saying that the room had a vague and very agreeable smell of tobacco.

She had two reception days every week now instead of one. On Thursdays anyone who wanted could call. But Mondays were reserved for bosom friends. Men were excluded. Maxime alone was admitted to these select gatherings, which took place in the little drawing room. One evening she had the startling idea of dressing him up as a woman and introducing him as her cousin. Adeline, Suzanne, the Baronne Meinhold, and the other ladies present rose and greeted him, astonished at his face, which they vaguely recognized. Then, when they realized, they burst out laughing and absolutely refused to let the young man go and undress. They kept him with them in his skirts, teasing him and indulging in risqué jokes. When he had seen these ladies out by the front door, he went through the gardens and returned through the hothouse. Renée's dear friends never had the slightest suspicion. The lovers could not be more intimate than they already were when they declared themselves the closest of companions. If a servant happened to see them pressing rather close together in the doorways, he was not surprised, being accustomed to the playfulness of Madame and the son of Monsieur.

This complete sense of freedom and impunity emboldened them still further. They bolted the door at night, but in the daytime they kissed in every room in the house. On rainy days they invented a thousand little games. But Renée's great delight was still to make an enormous fire and doze off before the grate. Her linen was marvellously luxurious that winter. She wore vastly expensive chemises and dressing gowns, whose cambric and lace insertions barely covered her with a cloud of white smoke. In the red glow of the fire she lay as though naked, with pink lace and skin, the heat penetrating through the thin stuff to her flesh. Maxime, crouched at her feet, kissed her knees without even feeling the cambric, which had the warmth and colour of her beautiful body. The daylight hardly came in, it fell like twilight into the grey silk room, while Céleste went quietly to and fro behind them. She had become their natural accomplice. One morning, when they had overslept, she discovered them together but remained utterly impassive. They then abandoned all restraint, she came in at all hours without the sound of their kisses causing her to turn her head. They relied on her to warn them in case of danger. They did not buy her silence. She was a very economical, respectable girl, and had never been known to have a lover.

However, Renée had not shut herself away. Taking Maxime with her, like a fair-haired page in dress-clothes, she threw herself into the life of high society, where she tasted even keener pleasures. The society season was a long triumph for her. Never had she imagined bolder costumes or headdresses. It was then that she had the courage to wear her famous satin dress the colour of bushes on which a complete deer-hunt was embroidered, with its accessories—powder horns, hunting horns, and broad-blade knives. It was then too that she set the fashion for wearing hair in the classical style; Maxime was sent to make sketches for her at the Musée Campana,* which had been recently opened. She seemed younger, she was at the height of her turbulent beauty. Incest lent a fiery glow to her eyes and warmed her laughter. Her eyeglass looked supremely insolent at the tip of her nose, and she glanced at the other women, at her dear friends preening themselves with the enormity of some vice or other, with the air of a boastful adolescent, with a fixed smile that said: 'I have my crime.'

Maxime considered high society utterly tedious. It was to seem 'smart' that he pretended to be so bored, for he did not really enjoy himself anywhere. At the Tuileries, at the ministers' houses, he disappeared behind Renée's skirts. But he resumed the reins as soon as there was a possibility of some escapade. Renée wanted to see the private room on the boulevard again, and the width of the sofa made her smile. Then he took her to all sorts of places, to the houses of courtesans, to the Opera ball, to the stage-boxes of burlesque theatres, to every dubious place where they could rub shoulders with pure vice and delight in their anonymity. When they stealthily returned home, worn out, they fell asleep in each other's arms, sleeping off the intoxication of obscene Paris, with snatches of ribald couplets still ringing in their ears. The next day Maxime imitated the actors, and Renée, seated at the piano in the little drawing room, tried to reproduce the raucous voice and jaunty attitudes of Blanche Muller as La Belle Hélène.* Her convent music lessons now only helped her to murder the verses of the new burlesque songs. She detested serious compositions. Maxime made fun of German music with her, and felt it his duty to go and hiss at *Tannhäuser* both by conviction and in defence of his stepmother's sprightly refrains.*

One of their great delights was skating; that winter skating was fashionable, the Emperor having been one of the first to try the ice on the lake in the Bois de Boulogne. Renée ordered a complete Polish suit from Worms, in velvet and fur; she made Maxime wear doeskin boots and a foxskin hat. They arrived at the Bois in intense cold, which stung their lips and noses as if the wind had blown fine sand into their faces. They thought it was fun to feel cold. The Bois was quite grey, snow threading the branches with narrow strips of lace. Under the pale sky, above the frozen lake, only the fir trees on the islands still displayed, on the horizon, their theatrical drapery, on which the snow had stitched broad bands of lace. They darted along through the icy air, like swallows skimming the ground. With one hand behind their backs and one on each other's shoulder, they sped along erect and smiling, turning in circles, in the wide space marked out by thick ropes. The sightseers stared at them from the roadway. From time to time they went and warmed themselves at the burning braziers by the side of the lake. Then they shot off again, describing wider circles, their eyes watering with pleasure and cold.

Then, when springtime came, Renée's feelings of melancholy returned. She made Maxime stroll with her at night in the Parc Monceau in the moonlight. They went into the grotto, and sat on the grass in front of the colonnade. But when she expressed a desire for a row on the little lake, they found that the boat they could see from the house, moored at the edge of a pathway, had no oars. These were evidently removed at night. This was a disappointment. Moreover, the great shadows in the gardens made the lovers anxious. They would have liked a Venetian carnival to be given there, with red lanterns and a band. They preferred it in the daytime, in the afternoon, and often they stood at one of the windows of the house to watch the carriages following the graceful curve of the main avenue. They enjoyed looking at this charming corner of the new Paris, this clean, pleasant bit of nature, these lawns like pieces of velvet, interspersed with flower-beds and shrubs, and bordered with magnificent white roses. Carriages passed by, as numerous as on the boulevards; the ladies on foot trailed their skirts languorously, as though they were walking across their drawing room carpets. They commented across the greenery on the different fashions, pointed to the horses, taking genuine pleasure in the soft colours of this great garden. A scrap of gilded railing flashed between two trees, a flock of ducks swam across the lake, the little Renaissance bridge stood out white and new amid the foliage, while on either side of the big avenue, mothers, sitting on yellow chairs, chatted and forgot their little boys and girls, who looked at each other coyly.

The lovers adored the new Paris. They often drove through the city, going out of their way in order to pass along certain boulevards, which they loved with a personal affection. The tall houses, with their great carved doors and heavy balconies, with inscriptions, signs, and company names in great gold letters, delighted them. As the brougham rolled on, they gazed fondly at the wide pavements, with their benches, their variegated columns, and their slim trees. This bright gap, which stretched as far as the horizon, grew narrower and opened upon a pale-blue square of space; this uninterrupted double row of big shops,* where the shopmen smiled at their fair customers, these currents of stamping, swarming crowds, filled them with absolute contentment, with a feeling of perfection in the life of the streets. They loved even the jets of the water-hoses, which passed like white vapour before their horses, spreading out and falling like fine rain under the wheels of the brougham, darkening the ground and raising a light cloud of dust. They drove on, and it seemed to them that the carriage was rolling over carpets along the straight, endless roadway, which had been made solely to save them from the dark backstreets. Every boulevard became a corridor of their house. The sun played on the new façades, lit up the window-panes, fell upon the awnings of the shops and cafés, and heated the asphalt under the busy footsteps of the crowd. When they returned home, a little confused by the dazzle and hubbub of these bazaars, they took renewed pleasure in the Parc Monceau, which was the flower-bed of this new Paris, displaying its luxury in the first warmth of spring.

When fashion absolutely forced them to leave Paris they went to the seaside,* but regretfully, still dreaming of the boulevard pavements while on the ocean shores. Their love subsided there. It was a flower of the hothouse, and needed the great grey-and-pink bed, the naked flesh of the dressing room, the gilded dawn of the little drawing room. Alone in the evenings, gazing at the sea, they no longer had anything to say to each other. Renée tried to sing her collection of songs from the Théâtre des Variétés at an old piano that was on its last legs in a corner of her room at the hotel; but the instrument, damp with the breezes from the open sea, had the melancholy sound of the water. *La Belle Hélène* sounded fantastic and lugubrious. Renée consoled herself by astonishing the people on the beach with her wonderful costumes. Her own crowd was there, yawning, waiting for winter, casting about in despair for a bathing costume that would not make them look too ugly. Renée could never get Maxime into the water. He was horribly frightened of it, turning quite pale when the tide came near to his boots, and on no account would have approached the edge of a cliff; he kept away from the sand-holes and made long detours to avoid the least bit of steep beach.

Saccard came down once or twice to see 'the children'. He had all sorts of problems to contend with, he said. It was not until October,

when they were all three in Paris, that he thought seriously of sleeping again with his wife. The Charonne affair was coming to a head.
His plan was very simple. He proposed to capture Renée by the same
trick that he would have played on a prostitute. She was beset by an
increasing need of money, and was too proud to ask her husband for
help except as a last resort. Saccard resolved to take advantage of her
first request for money to win her favours, and to resume their long-
severed relations in the delight brought about by the payment of a
large debt.

Terrible problems awaited Renée and Maxime in Paris. Several of
the promissory notes made out to Larsonneau were overdue; but as
Saccard naturally left them lying on the bailiff's desk, they did not
worry his young wife unduly. She was far more alarmed by her debt
to Worms, which now amounted to nearly two hundred thousand
francs. He insisted on a deposit, and threatened to stop her credit.
She shuddered at the thought of the scandal of a lawsuit, and especially of a quarrel with the illustrious dressmaker. Moreover, she
needed some pocket money. They would be bored to death, Maxime
and she, without a few louis to spend every day. The dear child was
quite broke since he had begun to rummage vainly in his father's
drawers. His fidelity, his exemplary behaviour during the last seven
or eight months, were largely due to the fact that his purse was
totally empty. He rarely had twenty francs with which to take a girl
out to supper, and so he philosophically used to return to the house.
Renée, on each of their escapades, handed him her purse so that he
might pay at the restaurants, balls, and boulevard theatres. She continued to treat him as a child; she even paid, with the tips of her
gloved fingers, at the pastry-cook's, where they stopped almost every
afternoon to eat little oyster patties. In the morning he often found
in his waistcoat a few louis he did not know he had, and which she
had put there, like a mother filling a schoolboy's pockets. To think
that this charming life of odd snacks, of satisfied whims and facile
pleasures, was to end! But a still greater fear took hold of them.
Sylvia's jeweller, to whom Maxime owed ten thousand francs, grew
angry and talked of prison. The costs had so accumulated on the
acceptances he had in hand and had long protested,* that the debt had
increased by some three or four thousand francs. Saccard declared
flatly that he could do nothing. A spell in Clichy* would settle
Maxime down, and when he took him out he would make a great

fuss about his paternal generosity. Renée was in despair; she imagined her dear child in prison, in a veritable dungeon, lying on damp straw. One night she seriously proposed to him not to leave her again, to live there unknown to everyone, safe from the bailiff's men. Then she swore she would find the money. She never spoke of the origin of the debt, of Sylvia who confided her affairs to the mirrors of private rooms. She wanted about fifty thousand francs, fifteen thousand for Maxime, thirty thousand for Worms, and five thousand for pocket money. Then they would have two weeks of happiness before them. She embarked on her campaign.

Her first thought was to ask her husband for the fifty thousand francs. She did not find this easy. The last time he came to her room to bring her money, he had planted fresh kisses on her neck and had taken her hands and talked of his affection. Women have a very subtle sense that enables them to guess men's feelings, and so she was prepared for a demand, for a tacit bargain clinched with a smile. Indeed, when she asked him for the fifty thousand francs, he protested, saying that Larsonneau would never lend such an amount, that he himself was still too short of ready cash. Then, changing his tone, as if seized with sudden emotion, he murmured:

'I can't refuse you anything. I'll do the rounds and achieve the impossible. I want you to be happy, my dear.'

Putting his lips to her ear, kissing her hair, his voice trembling slightly, he said:

'I'll bring it to your room tomorrow evening... without any promissory note.'

She interrupted him, saying that she was in no hurry, that she did not want to put him to so much trouble. Saccard, who had just put all his heart into the dangerous 'without any promissory note', which he had let slip and now regretted, pretended not to have received an unpleasant rebuff. He stood up, and said:

'Well, as you wish... I'll get the money for you when you want it. Larsonneau will have nothing to do with it. It's a present.'

He smiled good-naturedly. Renée remained in a state of anguish. She felt that she would lose the little peace of mind she had left if she gave herself to her husband. What remained of her pride lay in the fact that she was married to the father but was the wife of the son. Often, when Maxime seemed distant, she tried by very obvious allusions to make him realize the situation; but the young man, whom she expected to see fall at her feet after this revelation, remained utterly indifferent, thinking no doubt that she was trying to reassure him about the possibility of bumping into his father in the grey silk room.

When Saccard had left she dressed quickly and had the horses put to. In the brougham on the way to the Île Saint-Louis, she rehearsed how she would ask her father for the fifty thousand francs. She threw herself into this sudden idea without discussing it, feeling herself a great coward at heart, terrified at the thought of the step she was taking. When she arrived, the courtyard of the Hôtel Béraud froze her with its dreary, cloistral dampness, and she felt like running away as she climbed the wide stone staircase, on which her little high-heeled boots rang out ominously. She had been foolish enough in her haste to choose a costume of feuillemorte silk, with long flounces of white lace, trimmed with satin bows and cut crosswise by a plaited sash. This dress, which was finished off with a little flat toque with a large white veil, struck such an odd note in the gloom of the staircase that she became conscious of the strange figure she cut there. She trembled as she walked through the austere array of huge rooms, in which the vague figures of the tapestry seemed surprised at the sight of this flow of skirts passing through the twilight.

She found her father in a drawing room that looked out on the courtyard. He was reading a big book placed on a desk fastened to the arms of his armchair. At one of the windows sat Aunt Élisabeth, knitting with long wooden needles; and in the silence of the room the clicking of the needles was the only sound to be heard.

Renée sat down, ill at ease, unable to move without disturbing the severity of the lofty ceiling with a noise of rustling silk. Her lace looked crudely white against the dark background of tapestry and old-fashioned furniture. Monsieur Béraud du Châtel gazed at her with his hands resting on the edge of his reading desk. Aunt Élisabeth mentioned the imminent wedding of Christine, who was about to marry the son of a very well-to-do solicitor; she had gone shopping with an old family servant; and the aunt talked on all by herself, in her placid voice, her needles in perpetual motion, chatting away about her domestic affairs and casting smiling glances at Renée over her spectacles.

But Renée became more and more uneasy. The silence of the whole house weighed on her shoulders, and she would have given a lot for the lace of her dress to have been black. Her father's look made her so uncomfortable that she thought Worms really ridiculous to have thought of such wide flounces.

'How smart you look!' said Aunt Élisabeth suddenly. She had not even noticed her niece's lace yet.

She stopped knitting and adjusted her spectacles in order to see better. Monsieur Béraud du Châtel smiled faintly.

'It's rather white,' he said. 'A woman must feel very uncomfortable in that on the pavements.'

'But we don't go out on foot!' exclaimed Renée, immediately regretting this spontaneous cry.

The old man made as if to reply. Then he rose, drew himself up to his full height, and walked slowly up and down, without giving his daughter another look. Renée remained pale with emotion. Each time she told herself to be courageous, and waited for an opportunity to broach the question of money, she felt a twinge in her chest.

'We never see you now, father,' she complained.

'Oh!' replied the aunt, without giving her brother time to open his mouth, 'your father never goes out, except to go to the Jardin des Plantes. And I have to get cross with him before he'll do that! He says he gets lost in Paris, that the city is no longer fit for him. You really should give him a good talking to!'

'My husband would be very pleased to see you at our Thursdays from time to time,' continued Renée.

Monsieur Béraud du Châtel took a few steps in silence. Then he said softly:

'Please thank your husband for me. He seems to have a huge amount of energy, and I hope for your sake that he conducts his business honestly. But we see things differently, and I don't feel comfortable in that grand house of yours.'

Aunt Élisabeth seemed annoyed by his reply:

'How silly men are with their politics!' she said. 'Shall I tell you the truth? Your father is furious with both of you because you go to the Tuileries.'*

But the old man shrugged, as if to imply that his dissatisfaction had much more serious causes. He started pacing up and down again, lost in thought. Renée was silent for a moment, with the request for the fifty thousand francs on the tip of her tongue. Then she was overcome again with cowardice, kissed her father, and left.

Aunt Élisabeth went with her to the stairs. As they walked through the suite of rooms, she carried on chattering in her thin, old woman's voice:

'You're happy. I'm so pleased to see you looking well and so beautiful; if your marriage had turned out badly, you know, I would have blamed myself. Your husband loves you, you have all you want, haven't you?'

'Of course,' replied Renée, forcing herself to smile, but feeling sick at heart.

Aunt Élisabeth held her back, her hand on the balustrade.

'There's one thing that worries me, and it's that you might go mad with all this happiness. Be careful, and above all don't sell any of your property. If you had a baby one of these days, you'd have a little fortune ready for it.'

When Renée was back in her brougham, she heaved a sigh of relief. Drops of cold sweat stood out on her temples; she wiped them off, thinking of the icy damp of the Hôtel Béraud. Then, when the brougham rolled into the bright sunshine of the Quai Saint-Paul, she remembered the fifty thousand francs, and all her suffering came back, more poignant than ever. She, who was thought so daring, what a coward she had just been! Yet it was a question of Maxime, of her freedom, of their pleasure in being together! Amid the reproaches she heaped on herself, an idea suddenly occurred to her that threw her into even greater despair: she should have mentioned the fifty thousand francs to Aunt Élisabeth on the stairs. What had she been thinking of? She would perhaps have lent her the money, or at least have helped her. She was leaning forward to tell her coachman to drive back to the Rue Saint-Louis-en-l'Île, when the vision of her father walking slowly through the gloomy drawing room reappeared. She would never have the courage to go back there. What would she say to explain a second visit? At the bottom of her heart, she felt she no longer even had the courage to mention the matter to Aunt Élisabeth. She told the coachman to take her to the Rue du Faubourg-Poissonnière.

Madame Sidonie uttered a cry of delight when she saw her opening the discreetly curtained door of the shop. She was there by chance, and was just going out to run to the court where she was suing a customer. But she would let the judgement go by default, she would try again another day; she was so happy that her sister-in-law had felt

likc paying her a little visit at last. Renée, looking embarrassed, smiled
at her. Madame Sidonie refused to allow her to stay downstairs; she
took her up to her room, by way of the little staircase, after removing
the brass knob from the shop-door. She removed and replaced this
knob, which was held by a single nail, twenty times a day.

'There, my dear,' she said, making her sit down on a chaise-
longue, 'now we can have a nice chat. Just fancy, you came just in
time. I was coming to see you this evening.'

Renée, who knew the room, experienced the vague sense of unease
a traveller feels on finding that some trees have been felled in a
favourite forest walk.

'Ah,' she said at last, 'you've moved the bed, haven't you?'

'Yes,' the lace-dealer replied quietly, 'one of my customers prefers
it facing the mantelpiece. She was the one who advised me to get red
curtains.'

'That's what I was thinking, the curtains weren't red. It's a very
common colour, red.'

She held up her eyeglass and looked round the room, which had
the luxurious appearance of a big furnished hotel. On the mantelpiece she saw some long hairpins, which had certainly not come from
Madame Sidonie's meagre chignon. In the place where the bed uscd
to stand, the wallpaper was torn, discoloured, and soiled by the
mattress. The businesswoman had tried to hide this eyesore behind
two armchairs: but the chairs' backs were rather low, and Renée
stared at the worn strip of paper.

'Have you got something to tell me?' she asked.

'Yes, it's a long story,' said Madame Sidonie, folding her arms, like
a gourmand about to describe what she had had for dinner. 'Just
think, Monsieur de Saffré has fallen in love with the beautiful
Madame Saccard. Yes, with you, my dear.'

Renée did not even make a coquettish gesture.

'Really,' she said. 'You said he was so taken with Madame
Michelin.'

'Oh, that's all over, completely finished. I can prove it if you like.
IIaven't you heard that the little Michelin woman has managed to
catch Baron Gouraud? It's very strange. Everybody who knows the
Baron is amazed. And now, you know, she's busy getting the Legion
of Honour for her husband. Ah, she's a clever woman. She knows
what's what, you can't teach her anything!'

She said this with a certain regret mingled with admiration.

'But to come back to Monsieur de Saffré... He apparently met you at an actress's ball, wrapped in a domino, and he says that he asked you to supper. Is it true?'

The young woman was quite surprised.

'Perfectly true,' she murmured, 'but who could have told him?'

'And he says he recognized you later on, after you had left the room, and that he remembered seeing you leave on Maxime's arm. Since then he's been madly in love with you. He came to see me, to beg me to give you his apologies.'

'Well, tell him I forgive him,' interrupted Renée casually.

Then, all her anguish coming back, she continued:

'My dear Sidonie, I'm terribly worried. I absolutely must have fifty thousand francs by tomorrow morning. This is what I came to talk about. You said you know people who lend money.'

The businesswoman, offended at the abrupt way in which her sister-in-law had interrupted her, made her wait for an answer.

'Yes, absolutely, but I'd advise you to ask your friends first. If I were you, I know what I'd do. I'd go and see Monsieur de Saffré.'

Renée gave a forced smile.

'But', she retorted, 'that would hardly be proper, considering that he is so much in love.'

The old woman stared at her; then her flaccid face melted gently into a smile of affectionate pity.

'You poor dear,' she murmured, 'I can see you've been crying. You must be brave and take life as it comes. Now then, let me arrange this little matter for you.'

Renée stood up, twisting her fingers, making her gloves crack. She remained standing, gripped by uncertainty. She opened her mouth, to accept perhaps, when suddenly the bell rang in the next room. Madame Sidonie hurried out, leaving the door ajar, revealing a double row of pianos. Renée heard a man's step and the stifled sound of a conversation carried on in an undertone. Mechanically, she walked over to examine more closely the yellow stain the mattresses had left on the wall. The stain disturbed her, made her feel uncomfortable. Forgetting everything, Maxime, the fifty thousand francs, and Monsieur de Saffré, she returned to the side of the bed, thinking that it had looked much better where it used to be; some women really had no taste; surely, if you lay in that spot you would have the light in your eyes. Vaguely, in the depths of her memory, she saw the image of the stranger from the Quai Saint-Paul, the romance of her casual affair, indulged in where the bed used to be. The worn wallpaper was all that remained of it. Then the room filled her with uneasiness, and she became impatient with the murmur of voices from next door.

When Madame Sidonie returned, opening and closing the door very carefully, she made repeated signs with her fingers to get Renée to speak quietly. Then she whispered in her ear:

'You have no idea, this is a stroke of luck: it's Monsieur de Saffré.'

'You haven't told him, surely, that I'm here?' asked Renée nervously.

The businesswoman seemed surprised, and answered very innocently:

'I did indeed. He's waiting for me to ask him in. Of course, I didn't mention the fifty thousand francs.'

Renée, very pale, had drawn herself up as though struck with a whip. A feeling of infinite pride rose within her. The rough creaking of boots, which she could now hear more distinctly in the next room, exasperated her.

'I'm going,' she said curtly. 'Come and open the door for me.'

Madame Sidonie tried to smile.

'Don't be silly. I can't be left with this young man on my hands, now that I've told him you're here. You're compromising me, really.'

But Renée was already at the foot of the little staircase. She repeated before the closed shop-door:

'Open it, open it.'

The lace-dealer had a habit of putting the brass knob in her pocket after she had taken it off the door. She wanted to carry on arguing. At last, becoming angry, her meanness showing in her grey eyes, she cried:

'But what on earth do you want me to tell him?'

'That I'm not for sale,' replied Renée, with one foot on the pavement.

She thought she heard Madame Sidonie mutter, as she slammed the door: 'Get out then, you slut! You'll pay for this.'

'My God!' she thought, as she stepped into her brougham, 'I prefer my husband to this.'

She drove straight home. After dinner she asked Maxime not to

ne; she was unwell and needed to rest. The next day, when she
handed him the fifteen thousand francs for Sylvia's jeweller, she
was embarrassed by his surprise and his questions. Her husband,
she said, had had some good luck. But from that day onwards she
became more capricious; she often changed the time of the assigna-
tions she gave Maxime, and often even watched for him in the hothouse in order to send him away. He was not troubled much by these
changes of mood; he took pleasure in being a plaything in the hands
of women. What annoyed him more was the moral turn which their
tête-à-têtes sometimes took. She became quite gloomy; she sometimes even had great tears in her eyes. She would leave off her refrain
of 'le beau jeune homme' from *La Belle Hélène*, play the hymns she
had learnt at school, and ask her lover if he did not think that sin was
always punished sooner or later.

'There's no doubt she's growing old,' he thought. 'She won't be
any fun to be with in another year or two.'

The truth was that she was terribly unhappy. She would now have
preferred to deceive Maxime with Monsieur de Saffré. At Madame
Sidonie's she had reacted badly, she had yielded to instinctive pride,
to disgust at the crude bargain she had been offered. But afterwards,
when she endured the anguish of adultery, she despised herself so
much that she would have given herself to the first man who pushed
open the door of the room with the pianos. Until then the thought of
her husband had sometimes occurred to her, in her incest, like a
voluptuous accentuation of horror, but now the reality of the man
himself entered into it with a brutality that changed her most delicate feelings into intolerable pain. She, who found pleasure in the
refinement of her sin, and dreamt of a superhuman paradise where
the gods enjoyed their own kind, was now drifting towards vulgar
debauchery, and making herself the common property of two men.
She tried in vain to enjoy her infamy. Her lips were still warm with
Saccard's kisses when she offered them to Maxime. Her curiosity
explored the depths of these ill-fated pleasures; she went so far as to
mingle the two affections, and to seek the son in the embraces of the
father. She emerged even more disturbed, bruised from her journey
into the unknown regions of sin, from this dark world in which she
confused her two lovers, with terrors that seemed to herald the death
of all her pleasures.

She kept her tragedy to herself. Her feverish imagination

increased her anguish. She would rather have died than tell Maxime the truth. She was secretly afraid that he might suddenly leave her; above all, she had so absolute a belief in the monstrousness of her sin and the eternity of her damnation, that she would rather have crossed the Parc Monceau naked than have confessed her shame in a whisper. On the other hand, she still remained the scatterbrain who amazed Paris with her eccentricity. A nervous gaiety seized hold of her, and her mad whims were discussed in the newspapers with her name disguised by initials.

It was at this time that she seriously wanted to fight a duel, with pistols, with the Duchesse de Sternich, who had deliberately, so she said, spilt a glass of punch over her dress; her brother-in-law, the minister, had to speak firmly to her before she abandoned the idea. On another occasion she bet Madame de Lauwerens that she would run round the track at Longchamps in less than ten minutes, and it was only a question of costume that deterred her. Maxime began to be frightened by these fits of seeming madness, in which he thought he could hear, at night, on the pillow, all the din of a city obsessed with the pursuit of pleasure.

One night they went together to the Théâtre-Italien.* They had not even looked at the programme. They wanted to see a great Italian actress, La Ristori, who was at that time the toast of Paris, and who was so much in fashion that they were forced to take an interest in her. The play was *Phèdre.** He remembered his classical repertory well enough, and she knew enough Italian, to follow the performance. The tragedy even gave them a special emotion, played in this foreign language whose sonorousness seemed to them at times to be a simple orchestral accompaniment to the miming of the actors. Hippolyte was a tall, pale fellow, a very poor actor, who wept through his part.

'Clumsy oaf!' muttered Maxime

But La Ristori, with her broad shoulders shaken by sobs, with her tragic features and big arms, moved Renée profoundly. Phèdre was of Pasiphaé's blood,* and Renée asked herself of whose blood she could be, she, the incestuous one of modern times. She saw in the play nothing but this tall woman dragging across the stage her antique crime. In the first act, when Phèdre confides her criminal affection to Œnone; in the second, when, burning with passion, she declares herself to Hippolyte; and later, in the fourth act, when the return of Thésée overwhelms her, and she curses herself in a crisis of dark fury, she filled the theatre with a cry of such wild passion, with so great a yearning for superhuman voluptuousness, that Renée felt every shudder of her desire and remorse pass through her own body.

'Wait,' whispered Maxime in her ear, 'you'll hear Théramène tell his story.* What a sight!'

He muttered in a hollow voice:

> *Scarce had we issued forth from Troezen's gates,*
> *He on his chariot...*

But while the old man spoke, Renée had neither eyes nor ears. The light from the ceiling blinded her, a stifling wave of heat reached her from all the pale faces leaning towards the stage. The monologue continued, interminably. She was back in the hothouse, under the burning foliage, and she dreamt that her husband came in and surprised her in the arms of his son. She was in agony, she was losing consciousness, when the last death-rattle of Phèdre, repenting and dying a convulsive death by poison, made her open her eyes. The curtain fell. Would she have the strength to poison herself one day? How mean and shameful her tragedy was compared with the grand epic of antiquity! While Maxime was fastening her opera-cloak under her chin, she could still hear La Ristori's rough voice in her ears, and Œnone's complacent murmur replying.

In the brougham Maxime did all the talking. He thought tragedy 'most tedious' as a rule, and preferred the plays at the Bouffes.* Nevertheless *Phèdre* was pretty 'strong stuff'. He was interested because... and he squeezed Renée's hand in explanation. Then a strange idea occurred to him, and he yielded to the impulse to make a joke.

'I was wise', he murmured, 'not to go too near the sea at Trouville.'

Renée, lost in her melancholy dream, remained silent. He had to repeat himself.

'Why?' she asked, not understanding.

'Because of the monster...'

He tittered. The joke froze Renée. Everything was becoming distorted in her mind. La Ristori was now a big puppet, pulling up her tunic and sticking out her tongue at the audience like Blanche Muller in the third act of *La Belle Hélène*; Théramène was dancing a cancan, and Hippolyte was eating bread and jam and stuffing his fingers up his nose.

When a keener feeling of remorse than usual made Renée shudder, she would react powerfully. What was her crime after all, and why should she blush? Did she not tread on greater infamies every day? Did she not rub shoulders at ministers' houses, at the Tuileries, everywhere, with wretches like herself, who wore millions on their bodies and were adored on both knees? She thought of the shameful intimacy of Adeline d'Espanet and Suzanne Haffner, which drew occasional smiles at the Empress's Mondays. She recalled the shady dealings of Madame de Lauwerens, whose praises were sung by husbands for her propriety, her orderly conduct, her promptness in paying her bills. She recalled the names of Madame Daste, Madame Teissière, the Baronne de Meinhold, those creatures who let their lovers pay for their luxuries, and who were quoted in fashionable society as shares are quoted on the Bourse. Madame de Guende was so stupid and yet so beautiful, that she had three high-ranking officers as lovers at the same time, and was unable to tell one from the other, because of their uniform; which was why that devil Louise said that she first made them strip off so that she could tell which of the three she was talking to. The Comtesse Vanska, for her part, could remember courtyards in which she had sung, pavements on which she had been seen, dressed in calico, prowling along like a she-wolf. Each of these women had her shame, her open, triumphant sore. Finally, dominating them all, the Duchesse de Sternich, old, ugly, worn out, with the halo of a night spent in the Imperial bed; she typified official vice, from which she derived, as it were, a majesty of debauch and a sovereignty over this band of illustrious prostitutes.

Then the incestuous woman grew accustomed to her sin, as to a gala dress whose stiffness had at first bothered her. She followed the fashions, she dressed and undressed as others did. She ended by believing that she lived in a world above common morality, in which the senses became refined and developed, and in which one was allowed to strip naked for the benefit of all Olympus. Sin became a luxury, a flower set in her hair, a diamond fastened on her brow. She remembered, as a form of justification and redemption, the Emperor passing by on the general's arm between the two rows of bowing shoulders.

One man alone, Baptiste, her husband's valet, continued to disturb

morality

her. Since Saccard had started showing an interest in her, this tall, pale, dignified valet seemed to walk around her with the solemnity of mute disapproval. He never looked at her, his cold glances passed over her head above her chignon, with the modesty of a church beadle refusing to defile his eyes by allowing them to settle on the hair of a sinner. She imagined that he knew everything, and she would have bought his silence had she dared. Then she became very uneasy; she felt a sort of confused respect whenever she met Baptiste, and said to herself that all the respectability of her household had withdrawn and hidden under this lackey's dress-coat.

One day she asked Céleste:

'Does Baptiste make jokes in the kitchen? Have you ever heard any stories about him? Has he got a mistress?'

'What a question!' was all the maid replied.

'Has he ever made advances to you?'

'He never looks at women. We hardly ever see him. He's always either with Monsieur or in the stables. He says he's very fond of horses.'

Renée was irritated by this apparent respectability. She insisted, for she would have liked to be able to despise her servants. Although she had taken a liking to Céleste, she would have been very pleased to hear that she had lovers.

'But Céleste, don't you think that Baptiste is rather good-looking?'

'Me, Madame!' cried the maid, with the stupefied air of someone who has just been told something monstrous. 'Oh! I don't think about that sort of thing. I don't want a man. I've got my own plans, as you'll see. I'm not stupid, believe me.'

Renée could not get anything further out of her. Her troubles, moreover, increased. Her riotous life, her mad escapades, met with numerous obstacles which she had to overcome, however much she might sometimes be hurt by them. It was thus that one day Louise de Mareuil rose up between her and Maxime. She was not jealous of 'the hunchback', as she scornfully called her; she knew that the doctors had said there was no hope for her, and she could never believe that Maxime would marry such an ugly creature, even for a dowry of a million francs. In her downfall she had retained a bourgeois simplicity with regard to people she loved; though she despised herself, she believed that they possessed superior and admirable qualities. But while rejecting the possibility of a marriage, which would have seemed to her a sinister piece of debauchery and a theft, she felt pained by the familiarity and intimacy of the young couple. When she mentioned Louise to Maxime, he laughed with pleasure and repeated the child's sayings to her. He told her:

'She calls me her little man, you know, the silly thing.'

He was so relaxed about everything that she did not venture to explain to him that this silly thing was seventeen, and that their playfulness with each other, their eagerness, when they met in a drawing room, to find a discreet corner where they could make fun of everybody, grieved her and spoilt her most enjoyable evenings.

An incident occurred which changed the situation decisively. Renée often felt a need for bravado; she had sudden, mad whims. She would drag Maxime behind a curtain or a door, and kiss him at the risk of being seen. One Thursday evening, when the buttercup drawing room was full of people, she had the brilliant idea of calling the young man over to her, as he sat talking with Louise: she walked towards him from the end of the hothouse and suddenly kissed him on the mouth, between two clumps of shrubbery, thinking that no one could see her. But Louise had followed Maxime. When the lovers looked up they saw her, a few steps away, smiling strangely at them, with no blush or sign of surprise, but with the air of a companion in vice, knowing enough to understand and appreciate a kiss of that sort.

Maxime was really alarmed, while Renée displayed an almost light-hearted indifference. That put an end to it. It was impossible now for the hunchback to take her lover from her. She thought to herself:

'I should have done it on purpose. She knows now that "her little man" belongs to me.'

Maxime was reassured to find that Louise remained as high-spirited and amusing as before. He declared her to be 'very smart, a very good sort'. And that was all.

Renée had reason to be worried. Saccard had for some time been thinking of his son's marriage with Mademoiselle de Mareuil. There was a dowry of a million there, which he was determined not to let out of his sight, intending later on to appropriate the money for himself. Louise, at the beginning of winter, had stayed in bed for nearly three weeks, and Saccard was so afraid of seeing her die before the projected wedding that he resolved to have the children married forthwith. He did think them a trifle young, but then the doctors feared the month of March for the consumptive girl. Monsieur de Mareuil, for his part, was in a delicate position. At the last poll he had finally succeeded in being returned as a deputy; but the Corps Législatif had just quashed his election, which was the great scandal of the revisions.* The election was a mock-heroic affair, and kept the newspapers going for a month. Monsieur Hupel de la Noue, the Prefect of the department, had displayed such vigour that the other candidates had been prevented even from placarding their election addresses or distributing their voting papers. Acting on his advice, Monsieur de Mareuil had filled the constituency with tables at which the peasants ate and drank for a week. He promised, moreover, a railway line, a new bridge, and three churches, and on the eve of the poll he forwarded to the most influential electors portraits of the Emperor and Empress, two large engravings covered with glass and set in gilt frames. This gift was an enormous success, and the majority was overwhelming. But when the Chamber, faced with the derisive reaction of the whole of France, found itself compelled to send Monsieur de Mareuil back to his electors, the minister flew into a terrible rage with the Prefect and the unfortunate candidate, who had really shown themselves to be too 'hot'. He even spoke of choosing someone else as the official candidate. Monsieur de Mareuil was flabbergasted; he had spent three hundred thousand francs on the department, he owned large estates there, where he was bored to death, and which he would have to sell at a loss. So he came to beg his dear colleague to pacify his brother, and to promise him in his name an absolutely decorous election. It was on this occasion that Saccard again spoke of the children's marriage, and that the two parents finally settled the matter.

When Maxime was sounded out on the subject, he felt embarrassed. Louise amused him, and the dowry tempted him even more. He said yes, and agreed to all the dates that Saccard proposed, so as to avoid an argument. But he admitted to himself that, unfortunately, things would not fall into place so easily. Renée would never agree; she would cry, she would make scenes; she was capable of creating some great scandal that would astound Paris. It was very unpleasant. She frightened him now. She gave him terrible looks, she possessed him so despotically that he thought he could feel claws digging into his shoulder when she laid her white hand on it. Her unruliness turned to roughness, and there was a cracking sound beneath her laughter. He really feared that one night she would go mad in his arms. Remorse, the fear of being surprised, the cruel joys of adultery, did not manifest themselves in her as in other women, through tears and dejection, but in ever greater extravagance. Amid her growing distraction, a rattling sound could be heard, the sound of a wonderful, bewildering machine beginning to break down.

Maxime waited patiently for an opportunity to rid himself of this irksome mistress. He repeated once more that they had been foolish. Though their domestic closeness had at first lent an additional voluptuousness to their affair, it now prevented him from breaking it off, as he would have done with any other woman. He would have stayed away; that was his way of ending his affairs, so as to avoid all effort or argument. But he felt powerless, and he still even willingly forgot himself in Renée's embraces: she was motherly, she paid for him, she was ready to get him out of trouble whenever a creditor lost patience. Then the thought of Louise came back, the thought of the dowry of a million francs, and it made him reflect, even amid Renée's kisses, that 'this was all very well, but it was not serious and must come to an end some time'.

One night Maxime was so rapidly cleaned out at the house of a lady where cards were often played till dawn, that he had one of those fits of dumb anger common to the gambler whose pockets have been emptied. He would have given anything to be able to fling a few more louis on the table. He picked up his hat and, with the mechanical step of a man driven by an obsession, went to the Parc Monceau, opened the little gate, and found himself in the hothouse. It was past midnight. Renée had told him not to come that night. When she closed her door to him now, she no longer even invented an excuse, and he thought only of making the most of his time off. He did not remember Renée's injunction until he had reached the glass door of the little drawing room, which was closed. As a rule, when he was expected, Renée undid the latch beforehand.

'Damn it!' he thought, seeing a light in the dressing room window. 'I'll whistle and she'll come down. I won't disturb her, and if she has a few louis I'll leave at once.'

He whistled softly. He often used this signal to announce his arrival. But this evening he whistled several times in vain. He grew impatient, whistled more loudly, not wanting to abandon his idea of an immediate loan. At last he saw the glass door opened with infinite precaution, though he had heard no sound of footsteps. Renée appeared in the twilight of the hothouse, her hair undone, scantily clad, as if she were just going to bed. Her feet were bare. She pushed him towards one of the arbours, descending the steps and treading on the gravel of the pathways without seeming to feel the cold or the roughness of the ground.

'You shouldn't whistle so loud,' she murmured with repressed anger. 'I told you not to come. What do you want?'

'Let's go up,' said Maxime, surprised at this reception. 'I'll tell you upstairs. You'll catch cold.'

But as he stepped forward she held him back, and he noticed that she was terribly pale. She was gripped by a silent terror. Her petticoats, the lace of her underclothes, hung like tragic shreds on her trembling skin.

He looked at her with growing surprise.

'What's the matter? Are you ill?'

He looked up instinctively and glanced through the glass panes of the hothouse at the dressing room where he had seen a light.

'There's a man in your apartment!' he said suddenly.

'No there isn't,' she stammered, becoming distraught.

'Nonsense, I can see his shadow.'

Then for a minute they stood there, looking at each other, not knowing what to say. Renée's teeth chattered with terror, and it seemed to her as if buckets of ice-cold water were being emptied over her feet. Maxime felt angrier than he might have imagined; but he remained self-possessed enough to collect his thoughts, and to say to himself that he now had a good opportunity to break off the whole relationship.

'You're not going to tell me that Céleste wears a man's overcoat,' he continued. 'If the panes of the hothouse weren't so thick, I might recognize the gentleman.'

She pushed him further into the gloom of the foliage and said, with clasped hands:

'Please, Maxime...'

But the young man's mischievousness was aroused, a fierce sense of mischief that now sought vengeance. He was too puny to find relief in anger. His lips were compressed in spite; and instead of striking her, as he had at first felt inclined to do, he rejoined sharply:

'You should have told me, I wouldn't have come to disturb you. It's becoming clearer every day that we don't care for each other any more. I was getting fed up with it myself... Don't worry, I'll let you go up again; but not until you've told me the gentleman's name.'

'Never, never!' murmured Renée, forcing back her tears.

'It's not to challenge him to a duel, I just want to know. His name, tell me his name quickly, and I'll go.'

He was holding her by the wrists, and looked her in the eyes, laughing. She struggled, distraught, refusing to open her lips for fear that she would let slip the name he wanted.

'We'll make a noise soon, then you'll be in trouble. What are you afraid of? We're good friends, aren't we? I want to know who my successor is, that's fair enough surely. Let me help. It's Monsieur de Mussy—you've been touched by his distress?'

She did not reply, but bowed her head before this interrogation.

'Not Monsieur de Mussy? The Duc de Rozan, then? Not him either? The Comte de Chibray perhaps? Not even him?'

He stopped and reflected further.

'Well, damn it, I can't think of anybody else. It's not my father, after what you told me?'

Renée gave a start as if she had been scalded, and said in a flat tone:

'No, you know he doesn't come any more. I wouldn't allow it, it would be too degrading.'

'Then who is it?'

He tightened his grip on her wrists. She struggled a few moments longer.

'Oh, Maxime, if you knew! But I can't tell you.'

Then, overcome, crushed, looking up in fright at the window, she stammered:

'It's Monsieur de Saffré.'

Maxime, who had taken delight in his cruel game, became extremely pale at this admission, which he had sought so persistently. He was vexed at the unexpected pain this man's name caused him. Roughly he released Renée's wrists, drew even closer to her, and said, full in her face, between clenched teeth:

'You know what you are, you're a...!'

He said the word. He was walking away when she ran to him, sobbing, and took him in her arms murmuring words of love and appeals for forgiveness, and swore that she still adored him and would explain everything the next day. But he pushed her away, and slamming the door of the hothouse, replied:

'No, no, no! It's over. I've had quite enough.'

She was devastated. She watched him go through the garden. The trees in the hothouse seemed to be revolving round her. Then she dragged her bare feet over the gravel of the pathways, climbed the steps, her skin mottled with cold, appearing even more tragic in the disorder of her flimsy clothes. Upstairs she said, in reply to her husband's questions, that she thought she had remembered where a little notebook had got to that she had mislaid that morning. When she was in bed, she suddenly felt infinite despair when she thought that she ought to have told Maxime that his father had arrived home with her, and had followed her into her room to discuss some money matters.

The next day Saccard resolved to bring the Charonne business to a head. His wife belonged to him; he had just felt her, soft and inert in his hands, like a helpless plaything. On the other hand the precise plan for the Boulevard du Prince-Eugène was about to be settled, and it was necessary that Renée should be relieved of the land before the news broke of the imminent expropriation. Saccard put an artist's love of his work into this piece of business; he carefully watched his plan ripen, and set his traps with the subtlety of a hunter who prides himself on the skill with which he catches his prey. In his case it was simply the self-satisfaction of an expert gamester, of a man who derives peculiar pleasure from ill-gotten gains; he wanted to buy the land for a song, and was quite ready to give his wife a hundred thousand francs'-worth of jewellery in celebration of his triumph. The simplest operations became complicated as soon as he touched them, and turned into dramas: he became quite impassioned, he would have fought with his father for a five-franc piece, and afterwards he scattered his gold like a king.

Before obtaining from Renée the transfer of her share of the property, he had the foresight to go and sound out Larsonneau as to the blackmailing intentions of which he suspected him. His intuition saved him in this instance. The expropriation agent had thought that the fruit was now ripe for the picking. When Saccard walked into the office in the Rue de Rivoli, he found his associate in a state of despair.

'My friend,' murmured the latter, wringing his hands and trying to force out a sob, 'we're lost. I was just coming to see you to discuss the best way out of this terrible business.'

Saccard noticed that Larsonneau had been signing letters, and that the signatures were admirably firm. He looked at him calmly, and said:

'What's happened, then?'

Larsonneau did not reply immediately; he threw himself into his armchair in front of his writing-table, and there, with his elbows on his blotting-pad and his forehead between his hands, furiously shook his head. At last, in a strangled tone, he said:

'The ledger has been stolen.'

He proceeded to relate how one of his clerks, a rogue who should be in jail, had absconded with a large number of documents, among which was the famous ledger. The worst of it was that the thief had realized to what use he could put the ledger, and would only sell it back for a hundred thousand francs.

Saccard reflected. The story struck him as altogether too clumsy. Obviously Larsonneau did not really care whether he believed him or not. He simply wanted a pretext for giving him to understand that he wanted a hundred thousand francs out of the Charonne affair, and that on this condition he would restore the compromising papers in his possession. The bargain seemed too dear to Saccard. He would not have minded allowing his ex-colleague a share; but this ambush, this vain attempt at deception, irritated him. On the other hand he remained apprehensive; he knew Larsonneau, and he knew him to be quite capable of giving the documents to his brother the minister, who would certainly pay him to prevent any scandal.

'The bastard!' he muttered, sitting down, 'that's very unfortunate. Could I see this dreadful character?'

'I'll send for him,' said Larsonneau. 'He lives close by, in the Rue Jean-Lantier.'

Not ten minutes later a short young man with a squint, fair hair, and a freckled face slipped in, taking care that the door should not make a noise. He was dressed in a badly cut black frock coat, that was too big for him and horribly threadbare. He stood at a respectful distance, watching Saccard out of the corner of his eye. Larsonneau, addressing him as Baptistin, submitted him to a series of questions, to which he replied in monosyllables without being in the least disconcerted; and he received with complete indifference the epithets of thief, swindler, and scoundrel with which his employer thought fit to accompany each of his questions.

Saccard admired the wretch's coolness. At one moment the expropriation agent flew from his chair as if to strike him; and he simply took a step backwards, squinting with greater humility.

'That will do, leave him alone,' said the financier. 'So, Monsieur, you want a hundred thousand francs for those papers?'

'Yes, a hundred thousand francs,' replied the young man, and left.

Larsonneau seemed unable to contain himself.

'Ugh! What a reptile!', he stammered. 'Did you see his deceitful looks? Those fellows look timid enough, but they'd murder a man for twenty francs.'

Saccard interrupted him and said:

'Bah! He's nothing to be afraid of. I think we'll be able to come to terms with him. I came to see you about a much more distressing matter. You were right to mistrust my wife, my dear friend. Would you believe that she wants to sell her share in the property to Monsieur Haffner. She needs money, she says. Her friend Suzanne must have encouraged her.'

Larsonneau ceased his lamentations abruptly; he listened, rather pale, adjusting his stand-up collar which had become bent during his show of anger.

'The transfer', continued Saccard, 'would destroy our plan. If Monsieur Haffner becomes your co-partner, not only will our profits be lost, but I'm afraid we shall find ourselves in a very sticky position in relation to that very meticulous person, who will insist on examining the accounts.'

The expropriation agent began to pace up and down in an agitated way, his patent-leather boots creaking on the carpet.

'You see,' he muttered, 'the position one puts oneself in to oblige people! But, my dear fellow, in your place, I would certainly stop my wife from doing anything so foolish. I'd rather beat her.'

'Ah, my dear friend!' said the financier, with a cunning smile, 'I have no more power over my wife than you seem to have over that scoundrel Baptistin.'

Larsonneau stopped short before Saccard, who went on smiling, and gave him a piercing look. Then he started to pace up and down again, but with a slow, measured step. He went up to a mirror, adjusted his tie, and walked on again, regaining his elegant manner. Suddenly he shouted:

'Baptistin!'

The young man came back in, but through another door. He was no longer wearing a hat, but was twisting a pen between his fingers.

'Go and fetch the ledger,' said Larsonneau.

When the clerk had left, he discussed the amount they should give him.

'Do me this favour,' he ended by saying, quite bluntly.

Saccard agreed to give him thirty thousand francs out of the future profits of the Charonne enterprise. He thought he had escaped cheaply from the usurer's gloved hands. The latter had Saccard's undertaking made out in his name, keeping up the pretence to the end, saying that he would account for the thirty thousand francs to the young man. With a laugh of relief Saccard burnt the ledger in the fire, page by page. Then, this operation over, he shook Larsonneau's hand vigorously and took his leave, saying:

'You're going to Laure's tonight, aren't you? Look out for me. I will have settled everything with my wife; we'll make our final arrangements.'

Laure d'Aurigny, who often changed her address, was at that time living in a big apartment on the Boulevard Haussmann, opposite the Chapelle Expiatoire.* She had taken to having a reception day every week, like the ladies in real society. It enabled her to bring together at the same time all the men who saw her separately during the week. Aristide Saccard exulted in these Tuesday evenings: he was the official lover; and he looked the other way, with a vague laugh, whenever the mistress of the house deceived him in the doorways by granting an assignation the same night to one of these gentlemen. He stayed till all the rest had gone, lit another cigar, talked business, joked for a moment about the gentleman who was getting extremely bored in the street while waiting for him to go, and then, after calling Laure 'his dear child' and giving her a little pat on the cheek, quietly left through one door while the gentleman came in through another. The secret alliance, which had consolidated Saccard's credit and provided Laure with two sets of furniture in one month, continued to amuse them. But Laure wanted a dénouement to this comedy. This dénouement, arranged in advance, was to consist in a public breaking off, in favour of some idiot who would pay a very high price for the right to become the official lover and to be known as such to all Paris. The idiot was soon found. The Duc de Rozan, tired of wearying to no purpose the women of his own set, dreamt of acquiring the reputation of a debauchee, in order to give some colour to his insipid personality. He was an assiduous visitor at Laure's Tuesdays, and had conquered her by his absolute innocence. Unfortunately, although he was thirty-five, he was still dependent on his mother, so much so that the most he could dispose of was some ten louis at a time. On the evenings when Laure deigned to take his ten louis, complaining about her poverty, and the hundred thousand francs she needed, he sighed and promised to give it to her on the day he became independent. Thereupon she had the bright idea of making him friends with Larsonneau, who was one of her regular visitors. The two men breakfasted together at Tortoni's;* and over dessert Larsonneau, describing his love affair with a delicious Spaniard, professed to know some moneylenders; but he strongly advised Rozan never to fall into their clutches. This disclosure excited the duke, who succeeded in extracting a promise from his good friend that he would take care of 'his little affair'. He took so keen an interest in it that he was to bring the money on the very evening when Saccard had arranged to meet him at Laure's.

When Larsonneau entered Laure's great white-and-gold drawing room, only five or six women had arrived: they seized his hands and put their arms round his neck with a great display of affection. They called him 'big Lar!', an affectionate diminutive invented by Laure. He replied, in a piping voice:

'There, there, my little darlings; you'll squash my hat.'

They calmed down, and gathered round him on a couch, while he told them about a stomach-ache of Sylvia's, with whom he had supped the night before. Then, taking a bag of sweets from his coat pocket, he handed out some burnt almonds. But Laure came in from her bedroom, and as several gentlemen were arriving, she drew Larsonneau into a boudoir at one end of the drawing room, from which it was separated by a double set of hangings.

'Have you got the money?' she asked, when they were alone.

She addressed him as *tu* on important occasions. Larsonneau made no reply, but bowed in a funny way and tapped the inside pocket of his coat.

'Oh, that big Lar!' murmured the young woman, delighted.

She seized him round the waist and kissed him.

'Wait,' she said, 'I want the curl-papers straight away. Rozan is in my room, I'll go and fetch him.'

But he held her back, and kissing her on the shoulders in his turn, said:

'You remember what I asked you to do?'

'Yes, of course, you silly thing.'

She returned with Rozan. Larsonneau was dressed more smartly than the duke, with better-fitting gloves and a more artistic cravat. They shook hands casually, and talked about the races of two days before, when one of their friends had run a loser. Laure grew impatient.

'Never mind all that, my dear,' she said to Rozan, 'that big Lar has got the money, you know. We had better settle up.'

Larsonneau pretended to remember.

'Ah, yes, that's true,' he said. 'I've got the money. But you would have been well advised to listen to me, old chap! To think that those rogues asked me for fifty per cent. But I agreed, because you told me it didn't matter.'

Laure d'Aurigny had managed to find some bill-stamps during the day. But when it became a question of pen and ink, she looked at the two men in consternation, doubting whether she had such things in the house. She proposed to go and look in the kitchen, when Larsonneau took from his pocket—the same pocket that held the bag of sweets—two marvellous objects: a silver penholder that screwed out, and an inkstand in steel and ebony, finished as delicately as a trinket. As Rozan sat down, he said:

'Make the notes out to me,' he said. 'You understand, I didn't want to compromise you. We'll settle it between ourselves. Six bills of twenty-five thousand francs each, I think?'

Laure counted the 'curl-papers' at one end of the table. Rozan did not even see them. When he had signed, and looked up, they had disappeared into the woman's pocket. But she came up to him and kissed him on both cheeks, to his evident delight. Larsonneau watched them philosophically as he folded the bills, and put the inkstand and penholder back in his pocket.

Laure still had her arms round Rozan's neck when Aristide Saccard lifted a corner of the door-hangings.

'It's all right, don't mind me,' he said, laughing.

The duke blushed. But Laure went and shook hands with the financier, exchanging a knowing wink with him. She was radiant.

'It's taken care of, my dear,' she said. 'I warned you. You're not too angry with me, are you?'

Saccard shrugged good-naturedly. He pulled back the hangings, and standing aside to let Laure and the duke pass, he barked out like a gentleman-usher:

'Monsieur the duke, Madame the duchess!'

The joke was tremendously successful. The newspapers printed it the next day, giving Laure d'Aurigny's real name, and describing the two men by very transparent initials. The break between Aristide Saccard and fat Laure caused an even greater stir than their purported love-affair.

In the meantime Saccard had let the curtain fall on the burst of merriment which his joke had occasioned in the drawing room.

'What a splendid girl!' he said, turning towards Larsonneau. 'And you're the one, you old crook, who should get the most out of this. How much is it again?'

'Larsonneau protested, smiling, and he pulled down his shirt-cuffs, which were working up. At last he came and sat down near the door, on a couch to which Saccard beckoned him.

'Come over here, I don't want to hear your confession, for God's sake...!' said Saccard. 'Let's get down to some serious business. I had a long conversation with my wife this evening. It's all arranged.'

'So she has agreed to transfer her share?' asked Larsonneau.

'Yes, but it wasn't easy. Women are so stubborn! You know my wife had promised an old aunt of hers not to sell. She had the most terrible scruples. Fortunately I had a marvellous story ready.'

He rose to light a cigar with the candle Laure had left on the table, came back, and stretched out on the couch.

'I told my wife,' he continued, 'that you were completely ruined, that you had gambled on the Bourse, squandered your money on women, and got involved in stupid speculative ventures: in short, that you're on the brink of complete bankruptcy. I even gave her to understand that I didn't think you were completely honest. Then I explained that the Charonne affair would be swallowed up in your personal disasters, and that the best thing would be for her to accept your proposal to release her and buy her out for a song.'

'I don't call that clever,' muttered the expropriation agent. 'Do you think your wife will believe all that nonsense?'

Saccard smiled. He was in one of his expansive moods.

'You're so naive, my dear fellow!' he resumed. 'What has the plot of the story got to do with it? It's the details, the gesture and the accent, that matter. Call Rozan over; I bet I can persuade him it's broad daylight. My wife is no smarter than Rozan. I gave her a glimpse of the abyss. She has no suspicion of the expropriation. She said she was surprised that in the middle of a catastrophe you could think of taking on an even bigger challenge, so I told her that she no doubt stood in the way of some dirty trick you were planning to play on your creditors. In the end I advised her to agree, because it was the only way not to get mixed up in endless lawsuits and to derive some money from her property.'

Larsonneau still thought the story rather clumsy. His own method was less melodramatic: each of his transactions was put together and unravelled with the elegance of a drawing room comedy.

'Personally, I would have thought of something else,' he said. 'But everyone has his own system. So all we have to do now is pay up.'

'That', replied Saccard, 'is what I want to talk to you about. Tomorrow I'll take the deed to my wife, and she will only have to send it to you to receive the stipulated price. I prefer not to have a formal meeting.'

As a matter of fact he had never allowed Larsonneau to visit them socially. He never invited him to the house, and he went with him to see Renée whenever it was absolutely necessary for the two partners to meet; that had happened three times. He nearly always acted with a power of attorney from his wife, seeing no point in letting her know too much about his affairs.

He opened his wallet, and added:

'Here are the two hundred thousand francs' worth of bills accepted by my wife; you must give her those in payment, and add one hundred thousand francs, which I'll bring tomorrow morning. I'm ruining myself, my dear friend. This business will cost me a fortune.'

'But that', observed the expropriation agent, 'will only make three hundred thousand francs. Will the receipt be made out for that amount?'

'A receipt for three hundred thousand francs!' rejoined Saccard, laughing. 'I should think so! We'd be in a fix later on if it isn't.

According to our inventories, the property must be worth two-and-a-half million francs by now. The receipt will be for half that, of course.'

'Your wife will never sign it.'

'Yes, she will. I tell you it's all right. I told her it was your first condition. You're holding a pistol to our heads, don't you see, with your bankruptcy. That's where I pretended to doubt your honesty and accused you of wanting to cheat your creditors. Do you think my wife understands a word of all that?'

Larsonneau shook his head and murmured:

'It doesn't matter, but you ought to have thought of something simpler.'

'But my story is extremely simple!' said Saccard, most surprised. 'What's so complicated about it?'

He was quite unaware of the incredible number of threads with which he interwove the most ordinary piece of business. He derived real joy from the cock-and-bull story he had just told Renée; and what delighted him most was the impudence of the lie, the sheer number of impossibilities, the astonishing complication of the plot. He could have had the land long since had he not constructed all this drama; but he would have found less enjoyment in obtaining it easily. He set to work on creating a whole financial melodrama out of the Charonne affair.

He stood up, and taking Larsonneau by the arm, walked towards the drawing room.

'You understand, don't you? Just do as I say, and later on you'll applaud me. You know, my dear fellow, you shouldn't wear yellow gloves, they spoil the look of your hands.'

The expropriation agent just smiled and murmured:

'Oh, gloves have their advantages: you can touch anything without getting dirty.'

As they entered the drawing room, Saccard was surprised and somewhat alarmed to find Maxime on the other side of the hangings. He was sitting on a couch next to a blonde lady who was telling him, in a monotonous voice, a long story—her own life-story no doubt. He had, in fact, overheard his father's conversation with Larsonneau. The two accomplices seemed to him a pair of old rogues. Still annoyed by Renée's betrayal, he felt a cowardly pleasure in learning of the theft of which she was to be the victim. It avenged him a little. His father came and shook hands with him, looking suspicious, but Maxime whispered, motioning to the blonde lady:

'She's not bad, is she? I'm going to keep her for the night.'

Then Saccard began to posture and become flirtatious. Laure d'Aurigny joined them for a moment; she complained that Maxime barely called on her once a month. He claimed to have been very busy, which made everyone laugh. He added that in future they would see him constantly.

'I've been writing a tragedy,' he said, 'and I only hit on the fifth act yesterday. I now want to relax with all the pretty women in Paris.'

He laughed. He relished his allusions, which only he could understand. There was no one left in the drawing room now except Rozan and Larsonneau, at either side of the fireplace. The Saccards rose to go, as did the blonde lady, who lived in the same building. Then Laure went and said something to the duke in hushed tones. He seemed surprised and annoyed. Seeing that he could not make up his mind to get up from his armchair, she said in an undertone:

'No, really, not tonight. I've got a headache! Tomorrow, I promise.'

Rozan had no choice but to obey. Laure waited until he was on the landing, and then said quickly in Larsonneau's ear:

'You see, big Lar? I keep my word. Stuff him into his carriage.'

When the blonde lady took leave of the gentlemen to go up to her apartment, which was on the floor above, Saccard was surprised not to see Maxime follow her.

'Well?' he asked.

'Well, no,' replied the young man. 'I've thought better of it.'

Then he had an idea that struck him as very funny:

'You can take my place if you like. Hurry up, she hasn't shut her door yet.'

But the father shrugged, and said:

'Thanks, but I've had a better offer.'

The four men went downstairs. Outside the duke insisted on giving Larsonneau a lift; his mother lived in the Marais, and he could drop the expropriation agent at his door in the Rue de Rivoli. The latter refused, closed the coach door himself, and told the coachman to drive on. He stood talking on the pavement of the Boulevard Haussmann with the two others, showing no sign of moving on.

'Ah! Poor Rozan!' said Saccard, who suddenly understood.

Larsonneau swore that it was not so, that he had no interest in that, that he only cared about business affairs. As the two others continued to chat, and it was extremely cold, he exclaimed:

'I don't care, I'm going to ring. You're absolute busybodies, Messieurs.'

'Goodnight!' cried Maxime, as the door closed.

Taking his father by the arm, he walked up the boulevard with him. It was one of those clear, frosty nights when it is so pleasant to walk on the hard ground in the icy air. Saccard said that Larsonneau was wrong, that he should simply be Laure's friend; and he proceeded to declare that the love of those women was really a bad thing. He assumed quite a moral air, uttering maxims and precepts of remarkable propriety.

'You see,' he told his son, 'that only lasts for a while, my boy. It's not good for your health, and it doesn't give you real happiness. You know I'm not a Puritan. But I've had enough of it; I'm going to settle down.'

Maxime chuckled; he stopped his father, looked at him in the moonlight, and told him he was 'a decent sort'. But Saccard became even more serious:

'You can joke as much as you like. I tell you there's nothing like marriage to keep a man healthy and happy.'

Then he talked about Louise. He walked more slowly, to finish the business, he said, since they were on the subject. Everything was arranged. He even told him that he and Monsieur de Mareuil had fixed the date for signing the contract for the Sunday following the Thursday in mid-Lent. On that Thursday there would be a great party at the house in the Parc Monceau, and he would take the opportunity to make a public announcement of the marriage. Maxime thought all this very satisfactory. He was rid of Renée, he saw no further obstacle, he surrendered to his father as he had surrendered to his stepmother.

'Well then, that's settled,' he said. 'But don't talk about it to Renée. Her friends would tease me, and I'd prefer her to know about it at the same time as everybody else.'

Saccard promised to say nothing. Then, as they reached the top of the Boulevard Malesherbes, he again made free with his advice. He told him how he ought to behave to make his home a paradise.

'Above all, never break off with your wife. It's folly. It costs you a fortune. In the first place, you have to keep a woman, don't you? And household expenses are much greater: there are dresses, madame's private amusements, her close friends, the Devil and all his retinue.'

He was in an extremely generous mood. The success of the Charonne business had made him quite sentimental.

'As for me,' he continued, 'I was born to live in happy obscurity in some village, with my family around me. People don't know me, my boy. I give the impression of being very frivolous. Well, that's a mistake. I'd love to be near my wife, I'd willingly exchange my business for a modest income that would allow me to retire to Plassans. You're going to be rich: make a home with Louise in which you'll live like two turtle-doves. It's so pleasant! I'll come and visit you. It'll do me good.'

He ended almost with a sob. By now they had reached the front gate of the house, and stood talking on the kerbstone. A north wind was sweeping over the roofs of Paris. The pale night, white with frost, was completely silent. Maxime, surprised at his father's show of emotion, had had a question on his lips for the past minute.

'But,' he said at last, 'I thought...'

'What?'

'Well, with your wife!'

Saccard shrugged.

'Yes, just so! I was a fool. That's why I can say these things from experience. But we're together again, completely! It's almost six weeks now. I see her at night when I don't get home too late. Tonight the poor little dear will have to do without me; I've got to work until dawn. She has a marvellous figure!'

As Maxime held out his hand, he added, in a confidential whisper:

'You know Blanche Muller's figure; well, it's like that, only ten times softer. And her hips! They have such a beautiful shape, such elegance!'

He concluded by saying to the young man as he was going:

'You're like me, you have a good heart, you'll make your wife happy. Goodnight, my boy!'

When Maxime finally escaped from his father, he walked quickly around the gardens. What he had just heard surprised him so much that he felt an irresistible desire to see Renée. He wanted to beg forgiveness for his brutality, to know why she had told him that lie about Monsieur de Saffré, and to learn the story of her husband's affection. But he felt all this confusedly; his one clear wish was to smoke a cigar in her apartment and resume their friendly relations. If she was in the right mood, he would even tell her about his marriage, to make her see that their affair must remain dead and buried. When he had opened the little gate, of which he had fortunately kept the key, he managed to convince himself that his visit, after his father's revelations, was necessary and absolutely proper.

In the hothouse he whistled as he had done the evening before; but he was not kept waiting. Renée came and unfastened the glass door of the little drawing room, and led the way upstairs without a word. She had that instant come back from a ball at the Hôtel de Ville.* She still wore her dress of white puffed tulle, covered with satin bows; the skirts of the satin bodice were edged with a wide border of white bugles, which the light of the candles tinged with blue and pink. Upstairs, when Maxime looked at her, he was touched by her pallor and the profound emotion that prevented her from speaking. She had obviously not expected him, and was still quivering all over at seeing him arrive quite nonchalantly as usual. Céleste came in from the dressing room, where she had been to fetch a nightdress, and the lovers remained silent, waiting for the girl to go. As a rule they did not mind what they said in front of her; but they felt ashamed of the things that were on their lips. Renée told Céleste to help her to undress in the bedroom, where there was a big fire. The maidservant removed the pins and slowly took off each article of finery. Maxime, bored, mechanically picked up the nightdress, which was lying on a chair beside him, and warmed it before the fire, leaning forward with arms outstretched. In happier times he used to do this little service for Renée. She felt touched when she saw him daintily holding the nightdress in front of the fire. Then, as Céleste had not yet finished, he asked:

'Did you enjoy yourself at the ball?'

'Oh no, it's always the same, you know,' she replied. 'Far too many people, a great crush.'

He turned the nightdress round, for it was already warm on one side.

'What did Adeline wear?'

'Mauve, a badly thought-out dress. She's short, and yet she's obsessed with flounces.'

They talked about the other women. Maxime was now burning his fingers with the nightdress.

'You'll scorch it,' said Renée, whose voice sounded quite maternal.

Céleste took the nightdress from the young man's hands. He stood up and went over to the great pink-and-grey bed, examining one of the embroidered bouquets on the curtains so as to avert his eyes from the sight of Renée's bare breasts. He did this instinctively. Since he no longer considered himself her lover, he felt he no longer had the right to look. Then he took a cigar from his pocket and lit it. Renée had given him permission to smoke in her room. At last Céleste withdrew, leaving the young woman by the fireside, all white in her nightdress.

Maxime paced up and down for a few more moments without speaking, glancing at Renée, who seemed to be shaking again. Stationing himself before the fire, his cigar between his teeth, he asked abruptly:

'Why didn't you tell me it was my father who was with you last night?'

She looked up, her eyes wide open, with a look of supreme anguish; then she blushed violently and, overcome with shame, hid her face in her hands, stammering:

'You know? You know?'

She recovered, and tried to lie.

'It's not true. Who told you?'

Maxime shrugged.

'My father. He thinks you've got a marvellous figure and talked about your hips.'

He had allowed a certain annoyance to show through. But he began pacing about again, and continued in a scolding but friendly voice between two puffs at his cigar:

'I really can't understand you. You're a strange woman. It was your fault if I behaved like a brute yesterday. You ought to have told me it was my father, and I would have left without a fuss. What right have I got? But you go and tell me it's Monsieur de Saffré!'

She was sobbing, her hands over her face. He went up to her, knelt down, and forced her hands apart.

'Tell me why you said it was Monsieur de Saffré!'

Then, still looking away, she replied through her tears:

'I thought you'd leave me if you knew that your father...'

He stood up, picked up his cigar, which he had placed on the mantelpiece, and contented himself with muttering:

'You're a very funny woman, you really are!'

She had stopped crying. The flames in the grate and the fire in her cheeks had dried her tears. Her surprise at seeing Maxime so unperturbed by a revelation that she thought would destroy him made her forget her shame. She watched him pacing up and down, and listened to his voice as if she were dreaming. Without abandoning his cigar, he repeated that she was absurd, that it was quite natural that she should sleep with her husband, that he could hardly resent it. But to confess that she had a lover when it wasn't true! He kept returning to this point, which he could not understand and which he looked upon as positively monstrous, talking of women's 'foolish fancies'.

'You're not quite right in the head, my dear; you must be careful.'

He finally asked inquisitively:

'But why Monsieur de Saffré in particular?'

'He's always paying court to me,' said Renée.

Maxime refrained from being impertinent; he was on the point of saying that she was no doubt only anticipating things by a month when she confessed that Monsieur de Saffré was her lover. He smiled wickedly at this spiteful idea, and tossing his cigar into the fire, sat down on the opposite side of the fireplace. There he talked common sense, giving Renée to understand that they must remain good friends. Her stare embarrassed him, but he did not have the courage to tell her of his forthcoming marriage. She gazed at him, her eyes still swollen with tears. She thought him a poor creature, narrow-minded and contemptible, and yet she loved him, as she might love her lace. He looked handsome in the light of the candelabra on the mantelpiece, next to him. As he threw back his head, the light of the candles tinged his hair with gold and glided over the soft down on his cheeks, creating a charming effect.

'I really must go,' he said several times.

He was determined not to stay. Besides, Renée would not have let him. They both thought so and said so; they were now just good friends. When Maxime at last squeezed Renée's hand and was about to leave, she held him back a moment longer and spoke to him about his father, praising him to the skies.

'You see, I felt too much remorse. It's good that this has happened.

You don't know your father; I was surprised that he was so kind, so disinterested. The poor man has so much to worry about.'

Maxime examined the tips of his boots without replying, with an air of uneasiness. She persisted:

'As long as he didn't come here, I didn't care. But when I saw him here, so affectionate, bringing me money he must have scraped together all over the city, ruining himself for me, I became ill just thinking about it. If you knew how he has looked after me!'

The young man returned to the fireplace, and leant against the mantelpiece. He stood there embarrassed, his head bowed, a smile forming slowly on his lips.

'Yes,' he muttered, 'that's my father's strong point, looking after other people's interests.'

Renée was surprised at his tone. She looked at him and he, as if to defend himself, added:

'Oh, I don't know anything. I'm just saying that my father is very clever.'

'You'd be wrong to speak ill of him,' she replied. 'You're obviously too quick to judge him. If I told you all his troubles, if I repeated what he said this evening, you'd see how wrong people are when they think all he cares about is money.'

Maxime interrupted his stepmother with an ironical laugh.

'Believe me, I know him, I know him well. He must have told you some fine stories. Tell me what he said.'

This bantering tone offended her. She increased her praises, she talked of the Charonne affair, of the swindle of which she had understood nothing, as if it had been a catastrophe in which Saccard's intelligence and kind-heartedness had been revealed to her. She added that she would sign the deed of transfer the next day, and that if it was really a disaster, she accepted it as a punishment for her sins. Maxime let her go on, chuckling, looking at her furtively; then he said in an undertone:

'That's right, that's quite right.'

Laying his hand on Renée's shoulder, he said more loudly:

'Thank you, my dear, but I knew the story. How gullible you are!'

He moved away again as if to go. He was itching to tell her everything. She had exasperated him with her culogy of her husband, and he forgot that he had resolved not to say anything, so as to avoid any unpleasantness.

'Why? What do you mean?' she asked.

'Well, that my father has been taking you for a ride. I'm sorry for you, I really am; you're so naive!'

He told her what he had heard at Laure's, taking a secret delight in dwelling on these infamies. It seemed to him that he was taking his revenge for a vague insult he had received. His courtesan's temperament lingered over this denunciation, over this cruel gossip about what he had heard behind a door. He spared Renée no detail, neither the money her husband had lent her nor what he meant to steal from her with the help of a few ridiculous fairy-tales. Renée listened, very pale. Standing before the fireplace, she lowered her head a little as she gazed into the fire. Her nightdress, which Maxime had warmed for her, opened out, revealing the motionless whiteness of a statue.

'I'm telling you all this,' the young man concluded, 'so that you don't look a fool. But you mustn't hold it against my father. He means well. He has his faults, like all of us. Till tomorrow, then.'

He retreated towards the door. Renée stopped him with a sudden gesture.

'Don't go!' she cried imperiously.

Seizing hold of him, and drawing him to her, almost sitting him on her knees before the fire, she kissed him on the lips and said:

'I haven't told you that since yesterday, when you said you wanted to break things off, I've been quite beside myself. I feel half mad. At the ball this evening I could hardly see. The fact is I can't live without you. Don't laugh, I mean it.'

She gave him a look of infinite tenderness, as if she had not seen him for a long time.

'You were right, I was a fool, your father could have made me believe anything today. While he was talking to me I just heard a great buzzing, and I was so devastated by what you said that he could have made me go down on my knees, if he'd wanted to, to sign his wretched papers. I thought I felt remorse! Yes, I was stupid enough to think that!'

She burst out laughing, a mad light shone in her eyes. Holding her lover even tighter, she continued:

'Are we sinners, you and I? We're in love, and we enjoy ourselves as we see fit. That's what everybody does now, isn't it? Look at your father, he doesn't care. He likes money and he takes it when he can get it. He's quite right... To begin with, I won't sign a thing, and you must come back every evening. I was afraid you would refuse, because of what I told you. But you say you don't mind. Besides, I'll make sure he stays away now.'

She stood up and lit the nightlight. Maxime, in despair, did not know what to say. He saw what a piece of folly he had perpetrated; he was annoyed with himself for having talked too much. How could he tell her now about his marriage? It was his fault, the break had been made, there had been no need for him to go up to her rooms again, and above all no need to show Renée that her husband was swindling her. He became even angrier with himself when he discovered that he could no longer remember what had made him act as he did. He thought for a moment of being brutal a second time, but the sight of Renée taking off her slippers filled him with insurmountable cowardice. He was frightened. He stayed.

The next day, when Saccard came to see his wife to make her sign the deed of transfer, she replied calmly that she had no intention of doing so, that she had thought better of it. On the other hand, she gave him no hint whatever of why she had changed her mind; she had sworn to be discreet, not wishing to create problems for herself, eager only to enjoy the renewal of her affair. The Charonne business would sort itself out; her refusal to sign was merely an act of vengeance. Saccard was on the point of flying into a rage. His whole dream was crumbling. His other affairs were going from bad to worse. He had exhausted his resources, and it was only by a miracle that he did not lose his balance: that very morning he had been unable to pay his baker's bill. This did not prevent him from preparing a splendid entertainment for the Thursday in mid-Lent. Renée's refusal provoked in him the incandescent rage of an energetic man hindered in his work by a child's whim. If the deed were signed, he would be sure of being able to raise cash while waiting for the indemnity. When he had calmed down a little, and looked at things clearly, he was amazed at his wife's sudden change of mind; someone must have advised her. He suspected a lover. He had such a strong intuition that he ran round to his sister to ask her if she knew anything about Renée's private life. Sidonie showed her bitterness. She had not forgotten the affront her sister-in-law had given her in refusing to see Monsieur de Saffré. So when she understood from her brother's questions that he was accusing his wife of having a lover, she cried out that she was certain of it, and offered to spy on 'the turtle-doves'. She would show the minx what she was made of. As a rule Saccard did not seek out unpleasant truths; self-interest alone compelled him to open his discreetly closed eyes. He accepted his sister's offer.

'Don't worry, I'll find out everything there is to know,' she said, in a voice full of compassion. 'Ah, my poor brother, Angèle would never have betrayed you! Such a good, generous husband! Those Parisian dolls have no heart. And to think I always gave her good advice!'

Renée
poupée

CHAPTER VI

THERE was a costume ball at the Saccards' on Thursday in mid-Lent. The great event of the evening was the drama, *The Loves of Narcissus and Echo*,* in three tableaux, which was to be performed by the ladies. The author of the drama, Monsieur Hupel de la Noue, had for more than a month been travelling backwards and forwards between his Prefecture and the house in the Parc Monceau to superintend the rehearsals and advise on the costumes. At first he had thought of writing his work in verse; then he had decided in favour of *tableaux vivants*; it was more dignified, he said, and came nearer to the classical ideal.

The ladies were given no rest. Some of them had no fewer than three changes of costume. There were endless discussions, over which the Prefect presided. To begin with, the character of Narcissus was considered at length. Was it to be played by a man or a woman? At last, after Renée's entreaties, it was decided that the part should be entrusted to Maxime; but he was to be the only man, and even then Madame de Lauwerens declared that she would never have consented to this if 'little Maxime had not been so like a real girl'. Renée was to be Echo. The question of the costumes was far more complicated. Maxime was most helpful to the Prefect, who was becoming very harassed in the midst of the nine women, whose wild imaginations threatened to compromise the pure outline of his work. Had he listened to them, his Olympus would have worn powdered hair. Madame d'Espanet insisted on having a train cut on her dress to hide her feet, which were a trifle large, while Madame Haffner had visions of herself clad in some sort of animal skin. Monsieur Hupel de la Noue became quite angry; he had made up his mind; he said that the only reason why he had decided against verse was that he might compose his drama 'in cunningly contrived fabrics and the most beautiful eclectic poses'.

'The general effect, Mesdames,' he repeated at each fresh demand, 'you forget the general effect. I can't possibly spoil the whole thing for the sake of a lot of flounces.'

The discussions took place in the buttercup drawing room. Whole afternoons were spent deciding the cut of a skirt. Worms was called in several times. At last everything was arranged, the costumes decided on, the positions learnt. Monsieur Hupel de la Noue declared himself satisfied. Not even the election of Monsieur de Mareuil had given him as much trouble.

The Loves of Narcissus and Echo was to begin at eleven o'clock. At half-past ten the big drawing room was full, and as there was to be a costume ball afterwards the women had come in costume and were seated on chairs arranged in a semicircle before the improvised stage, a platform hidden by two wide curtains of red velvet with gold fringes, running on rods. The men stood at the back, or moved to and fro. At ten o'clock the upholsterers had driven in the last nail. The platform was erected at the end of the long drawing room, and occupied a whole section of it. The stage was approached from the smoking room, which had been turned into a green room for the actors. In addition, the ladies had at their disposal a number of rooms on the first floor, where an army of maidservants laid out the costumes for the different tableaux.

It was half-past eleven, and the curtains were still drawn. A buzz of voices filled the drawing room. The rows of chairs offered a bewildering display of marquises, noblewomen, milkmaids, Spanish ladies, shepherdesses, and sultanas, while the compact mass of dress-coats made a great black blotch next to the shimmering material and bare shoulders, all sparkling with jewellery. The women alone were in fancy dress. It was already getting warm. The three chandeliers lit up the gilt of the drawing room.

At last Monsieur de la Noue was seen to emerge from an opening to the left of the platform. He had been helping the ladies since eight o'clock. The left sleeve of his dress-coat bore the mark of three white fingers, a small woman's hand, which had been laid there after dabbling in a box of rice-powder. But the Prefect had other things on his mind! His eyes were dilated, his face swollen and rather pale. He seemed unable to see anyone. Advancing towards Saccard, whom he recognized among a group of grave-looking men, he said in an undertone:

'Damn it! Your wife has lost her girdle of leaves. We're in a complete mess!'

He swore, he could have hit someone. Then, without waiting for a reply, he turned on his heels, dived under the curtains, and disappeared. The ladies smiled at this strange apparition.

The group amid which Saccard was standing was clustered behind the last row of chairs. An armchair had even been pulled out of the row for Baron Gouraud, whose legs had been swelling for some time. Among the group were Monsieur Toutin-Laroche, whom the Emperor had just made a senator; Monsieur de Mareuil, whose second election the Chamber had deigned to confirm; Monsieur Michelin, recently decorated; and, a little further back, Mignon and Charrier, of whom one wore a big diamond in his necktie, while the other displayed a still bigger one on his finger. The gentlemen chatted to each other. Saccard left them for a moment to go and exchange a few whispered words with his sister, who had just come in and was sitting between Louise de Mareuil and Madame Michelin. Madame Sidonie was disguised as a sorceress; Louise was jauntily attired in a page's costume, which made her look like an urchin; little Madame Michelin, dressed as an almah,* smiled seductively through her veils embroidered with threads of gold.

'Have you discovered anything?' Saccard quietly asked his sister.

'No, not yet,' she replied. 'But I'll catch them tonight, you can be sure of that.'

'You'll let me know immediately, won't you?'

Saccard, turning to right and left, complimented Louise and Madame Michelin. He compared the latter to one of Mahomet's houris, the former to a *mignon* of Henri III.* His Provençal accent seemed to make the whole of his small, wiry body sing with delight. When he returned to the group of serious-looking men, Monsieur de Mareuil took him aside and spoke to him of their children's marriage. Nothing had changed, the contract would be signed the following Sunday.

'Quite so,' said Saccard. 'I intend, with your permission, to announce the match to our friends this evening. I'm just waiting for my brother the minister, who has promised to come.'

The new deputy was delighted. In the meantime, Monsieur Toutin-Laroche was speaking louder and louder, as if seized with a fit of indignation.

'Yes, Messieurs,' he said to Monsieur Michelin and the two contractors, who came closer. 'I was generous enough to let my name get mixed up in an affair like that.'

As Saccard and Mareuil came up to them, he said:

'I was telling these gentlemen about the terrible catastrophe of the

Société Générale of the Ports of Morocco. You know about it, don't you, Saccard?'

The latter did not flinch. The company in question had just collapsed amid a terrible scandal.* Shareholders had wanted to know what progress had been made with the establishment of the famous trading posts on the Mediterranean seaboard, and a judicial inquiry had shown that the Ports of Morocco existed only on the engineers' plans: very handsome plans hung on the walls of the company's offices. Since then Monsieur Toutin-Laroche had been clamouring even louder than the shareholders, waxing indignant, demanding that his reputation should be restored without a stain. He made such a fuss that the Government, in order to calm this useful man and rehabilitate him in the eyes of public opinion, decided to send him to the Senate. This was how he had landed his prize seat, in an affair that had nearly involved him in criminal proceedings.

'It's very good of you to show an interest in all that,' said Saccard, 'when you can point to your great work, the Crédit Viticole, which has survived every crisis.'

'Yes,' murmured de Mareuil, 'it's as safe as houses.'

In fact the Crédit Viticole had just emerged from a serious but carefully concealed embarrassment. A minister who was very well disposed towards this financial institution, which held the City by the throat, had brought on a bulling* operation, which Monsieur Tourin-Laroche had turned to wonderfully good account. Nothing flattered him more than praise for the prosperity of the Crédit Viticole. He thanked Monsieur de Mareuil with a glance, and bending over Baron Gouraud, on whose armchair he was leaning, asked him:

'Are you comfortable? You're not too warm?'

The Baron grunted.

'He's falling apart, getting worse every day,' added Monsieur Toutin-Laroche under his breath, turning towards the other gentlemen.

Monsieur Michelin smiled, looking down discreetly at his red ribbon from time to time. Mignon and Charrier, planted solidly there in their big boots, seemed much more at ease in their dress-clothes since they had taken to wearing diamonds. However, it was nearly midnight, and the company was growing impatient; they were not so ill-bred as to complain, but the ladies' fans fluttered more nervously, and the sound of conversations increased.

At last Monsieur Hupel de la Noue reappeared. He had thrust one shoulder through the narrow opening when he saw Madame d'Espanet finally stepping onto the platform; the other ladies, already posed for the first tableau, were waiting for her. The Prefect turned round, showing his back to the audience, and could be seen talking to the Marquise, who was hidden behind the curtains. He lowered his voice, and with compliments blown from his finger-tips, said:

'Congratulations, Marquise. Your costume is delightful.'

'I've got a much prettier one underneath!' she replied, laughing in his face, so funny did he seem to her, buried as he was in the curtains.

The boldness of this joke took Monsieur Hupel de la Noue aback for a moment; but he recovered his composure, and appreciating the remark more and more as he read hidden subtleties into it, murmured rapturously:

'Charming, quite charming!'

He dropped the corner of the curtain and joined the group of serious-looking men, wanting to enjoy his work. He was no longer the man running about desperately in search of Echo's girdle of leaves. He beamed, panted, and wiped his forehead. He still had the mark of the little white hand on the sleeve of his coat; and the thumb of his right-hand glove, which he had no doubt dipped into one of the ladies' make-up boxes, was stained with red. He smiled, fanned himself, and stammered:

'She's adorable, enchanting, astounding!'

'Who is?' asked Saccard.

'The Marquise. Do you know what she said just now?'

He told the story. It was considered very witty. The gentlemen repeated it to one another. Even the dignified Monsieur Haffner, who had drawn nearer, could not help applauding. Meanwhile a piano, which few of them had noticed, began to play a waltz. Then there was a great silence. The waltz had endless, capricious variations; a very soft phrase rose from the keyboard, finishing in a nightingale's trill; then deeper notes took up the theme, more slowly. It was very voluptuous. The ladies, their heads a little to one side, smiled. On the other hand the piano had put a sudden stop to Monsieur Hupel de la Noue's merriment. He looked anxiously in the direction of the red velvet curtains, thinking that he ought to have posed Madame d'Espanet himself, as he had posed the others.

The curtains opened slowly, the piano resumed the waltz, with the soft pedal down. A murmur ran through the drawing room. The ladies leant forward, the men craned their necks, while the audience's admiration was shown here and there by a word too loudly spoken, an unconscious sigh, a stifled laugh. This lasted for fully five minutes, under the glare of the three chandeliers.

Monsieur Hupel de la Noue, relieved, beamed beatifically upon his drama. He could not resist the temptation to repeat to those around him what he had been saying for the last month:

'I thought of doing it in verse. But don't you agree it's more dignified like this?'

Then, while the waltz rose and fell in an endless lullaby, he explained. Mignon and Charrier had drawn nearer and were listening attentively.

'You know the subject, don't you? The handsome Narcissus, son of the River Cephisus and the Nymph Liriope, scorns the love of the Nymph Echo. Echo was a member of Juno's retinue, and amused her with her stories while Jupiter found pleasure elsewhere. Echo, daughter of the Air and the Earth, as you know...'*

He went into transports over the poetry of mythology. Then, more confidentially, he said:

'I thought I might give full rein to my imagination. Echo leads the handsome Narcissus to Venus in a grotto on the seashore, so that the goddess might inflame him with her passion. But the goddess is powerless. The young man indicates by his attitude that he is unmoved.'

The explanation was not unhelpful, for few of the spectators in the drawing room understood the exact meaning of the groups. When the Prefect had named the characters in an undertone the admiration increased. Mignon and Charrier continued to stare with wide-open eyes. They had understood nothing.

On the platform, between the red velvet curtains, yawned a grotto. The scenery was made of silk stretched in large broken plaits, imitating the crevices of rocks, upon which were painted shells, fish, and large sea-plants. The stage, which was uneven, rose up like a mound, and was covered with the same silk, upon which the set-designer had depicted a fine sandy background, scattered with pearls and silver spangles. It was a retreat fit for a goddess. There, on the top of the mound, stood Madame de Lauwerens as Venus; rather stout, wearing her pink tights with the dignity of an Olympian duchess, she interpreted her part as the Queen of Love with large, voracious eyes. Behind her, showing only her mischievous head, her wings, and her quiver, little Madame Daste lent her smile to the amiable character of Cupid. Then on one side of the mound the three Graces, Mesdames de Guende, Teissière, and de Meinhold, all in muslin, stood smiling and intertwined as in Pradier's group;* while on the other side the Marquise d'Espanet and Madame Haffner, enveloped in the same flow of lace, their arms round each other's waists, their hair intermingled, added a risky note to the tableau, reminiscent of Lesbos, which Monsieur Hupel de la Noue explained quietly for the benefit of the men only, saying that he intended by this to show the extent of Venus' power. At the foot of the mound the Comtesse Vanska impersonated Voluptuousness: she lay outstretched, twisted by a final spasm, her eyes half closed, and languishing, as if satiated; very dark, she had unloosened her black hair, and her bodice, streaked with tawny flames, revealed portions of her glowing skin. The colour scale of the costumes, from the snowy white of Venus' veil to the dark red of Voluptuousness's bodice, was soft, generally pink, flesh-coloured. Under the electric light,* ingeniously directed at the stage from one of the garden windows, the gauze, the lace, all those light, diaphanous materials mingled so well with the shoulders and tights that the soft pinks seemed alive, and it was no longer possible to tell whether the ladies had not carried plastic truth so far as to strip themselves naked. All this was but the apotheosis: the play was enacted in the foreground. On the left Renée, as Echo, stretched her arms out towards the tall goddess, her head half turned towards Narcissus, pleadingly, as if inviting him to look at Venus, the mere sight of whom kindled irresistible passion; but Narcissus, on the right, made a gesture of refusal, hid his eyes with his hand, remained cold as ice. The costumes of these two characters in particular had cost Monsieur Hupel de la Noue's imagination infinite trouble. Narcissus, as a wandering demigod of the forests, wore an ideal huntsman's costume: green tights, a short, clinging jacket, a leafy twig of oak in his hair. Echo's costume was an allegory in itself: it suggested tall trees and lofty mountains, the resounding spots where the voices of the Earth and the Air reply to each other; it was rock in the white satin of the skirt, thicket in the leaves of the girdle, clear sky in the cloud of blue gauze of the bodice. The groups retained a statuesque immobility, the fleshly note of Olympus sang in the effulgence of the broad ray of light, while the piano continued its penetrating complaint of love, interspersed with deep sighs.

It was generally thought that Maxime embodied the part very well. In making his gesture of refusal he accentuated his left hip, which was much remarked upon. But all the praise was for Renée's expression. As Monsieur Hupel de la Noue put it, she represented 'the pain of unsatisfied desire'. She wore a bitter smile that tried to look humble, she sought her prey with the entreaties of a she-wolf who only half hides her teeth. The first tableau went off well, except for the mad Adeline, who moved, and could hardly repress her desire to laugh. At last the curtains closed, the piano fell silent.

The audience applauded discreetly, and the conversations were resumed. A great breath of love, of restrained desire, had come from the nude figures on the stage and passed through the drawing room, where the women leaned more languidly in their seats, while the men murmured in each others' ears, smiling. There was whispering as in an alcove, a well-bred hush, a barely formulated longing for voluptuousness; and in the mute looks exchanged amid this decorous rapture there was the frank boldness of pleasure offered and accepted with a glance.

Endless judgements were passed on the ladies' good points. Their costumes attracted almost as much attention as their bare shoulders. When Mignon and Charrier turned to question Monsieur Hupel de la Noue, they were quite surprised to find him no longer beside them; he had already dived behind the stage.

'As I was telling you, my pet,' said Madame Sidonie, resuming a conversation interrupted by the first tableau, 'I've had a letter from London, about that business of the three hundred million francs, you know. The person I used to make enquiries thinks he's found the banker's receipt. England must have paid... It made me ill all day.'

She was yellower than usual, in her sorceress's robe spangled with stars. As Madame Michelin was not listening, she continued in a lower voice, muttering that England could not have paid, and that she must go to London herself.

'Narcissus' dress was very pretty, wasn't it?' asked Louise of Madame Michelin.

The latter smiled. She looked at Baron Gouraud, who seemed quite cheerful again in his armchair. Madame Sidonie, observing the

direction of her glance, leant over and whispered in her ear, so that
the child could not hear:

'Has he settled up?'

'Yes,' replied the young woman languidly, playing her almah part
delightfully. 'I've chosen the house at Louveciennes, and I've
received the title deeds from his business agent. But we've broken
off, I don't see him any more.'

Louise was particularly sharp at catching what she was not
intended to hear. She looked at Baron Gouraud with a page's
boldness, and said quietly to Madame Michelin:

'Don't you think the Baron looks hideous?'

Then she added, bursting out laughing:

'I say! They should have made him play Narcissus. He would have
been wonderful in apple-green tights.'

The sight of Venus, of this voluptuous corner of Olympus, had
revived the old senator. He rolled his eyes in delight, turned half
round to compliment Saccard. Amid the buzz that filled the drawing
room, the group of serious-looking men continued to talk business
and politics. Monsieur Haffner said he had just been appointed
chairman of a committee charged with settling indemnity questions.
Then the conversation turned to the reconstruction of the city, to
the Boulevard du Prince-Eugène, which was beginning to attract
public attention. Saccard took the opportunity to talk about somebody he knew, a landlord who would no doubt be expropriated. He
looked the others in the eyes. The Baron nodded; Monsieur Toutin-
Laroche went so far as to declare that there was nothing so unpleasant as to be expropriated; Monsieur Michelin agreed, squinting
more than ever as he looked at his decoration.

'The indemnity can never be too high,' concluded Monsieur de
Mareuil, who wanted to please Saccard.

They had understood each other. But Mignon and Charrier began
to talk about their own affairs. They meant to retire soon, they said,
no doubt to Langres, keeping on a pied-à-terre in Paris. They made
the others smile when they related how, after completing the building of their magnificent mansion in the Boulevard Malesherbes, they
had thought it so handsome that they had not been able to resist the
desire to sell it. Their diamonds must have been a consolation they
had offered themselves. Saccard laughed ungraciously; his former
partners had just realized enormous profits in an affair in which he

had played the part of a dupe. As the interval wore on, admiring comments on Venus' breasts and Echo's costume broke into the conversation of the serious-looking gentlemen.

After more than half an hour Monsieur Hupel de la Noue reappeared. He was on the high road to success, and the disorder of his attire increased. As he regained his place, he came upon Monsieur de Mussy. He shook hands with him as he went by, and then turned back and asked him:

'Did you hear what the Marquise said?'

Without waiting for a reply, he told him the story. He appreciated it more and more, made comments on it, and ended by thinking it exquisitely ingenuous. 'I've got a much prettier one underneath!' It was a cry from the heart.

Monsieur de Mussy disagreed. He thought the remark indecent. He had just received a posting to the London Embassy, where the minister had told him that strict behaviour was expected. He refused to lead the *cotillon*, he behaved like a much older man, he no longer spoke of his love for Renée, to whom he bowed gravely when he saw her.

Monsieur Hupel de la Noue had come up to the group standing behind the Baron's armchair, when the piano struck up a triumphal march. A loud burst of harmony, produced by masterful strokes on the keyboard, introduced a full melody in which a metallic clang resounded at intervals. As each phrase was finished, it was repeated in a higher key that accentuated the rhythm. It was at once fierce and joyous.

'You'll see,' murmured Monsieur Hupel de la Noue, 'that I have perhaps carried poetic licence too far, but I think my boldness has worked. Echo, seeing that Venus has no power over Narcissus, takes him to Plutus, the god of wealth and precious metals. After the temptation of the flesh, the temptation of riches.'*

'That's very classical,' replied Monsieur Toutin-Laroche, with an amiable smile. 'You know your period, Monsieur le Préfet.'

The curtains parted, the piano played more loudly. The spectacle was dazzling. The electric light fell on a scene of fiery splendour in which the spectators at first saw nothing but a brazier, in which precious stones and ingots of gold seemed to be melting. A new grotto revealed itself; but this was not the cool retreat of Venus, lapped by waters eddying on fine sand bestrewn with pearls, but one situated seemingly in the centre of the earth, in a fiery nether region, a fissure of the hell of antiquity, a crevice in a mine of molten metals inhabited by Plutus. The silk simulating rock showed broad threads of metal, layers that looked like the veins of a primeval world, loaded with incalculable riches and the eternal life of the earth. On the ground, thanks to a bold anachronism of Monsieur Hupel de la Noue's, lay a great pile of twenty-franc pieces.

On top of this pile of gold sat Madame de Guende as Plutus, a female Plutus with generously displayed breasts set in the great stripes of her dress, which represented all the metals. Around the god, erect, reclining, grouped in clusters, or blooming apart, were posed the fairy-like flora of the grotto, into which the caliphs of the Arabian Nights seemed to have emptied their treasures: Madame Haffner as Gold, with a stiff, resplendent skirt like a bishop's cape; Madame d'Espanet as Silver, gleaming like moonlight; Madame de Lauwerens in bright blue, as a Sapphire, and by her side little Madame Daste, a smiling Turquoise in the softest blue; then there was an Emerald, Madame de Meinhold; a Topaz, Madame Teissière; and lower down, the Comtesse Vanska, lending her dark ardour to a Coral, recumbent, with raised arms loaded with rosy pendants, like a monstrous, seductive polyp displaying a woman's flesh amidst the yawning, pink pearliness of its shell. All of these ladies wore necklaces, bracelets, sets of jewels formed of the precious stones they impersonated. Especially noticeable were the jewels worn by Mesdames d'Espanet and Haffner, made up entirely of small gold and silver coins fresh from the mint. In the foreground the story remained unchanged: Echo was still tempting Narcissus, who continued to reject her overtures. The spectators' eyes were getting used to this yawning cavity opening onto the flaming bowels of the earth, onto this pile of gold upon which were strewn the riches of a world.

This second tableau was even more successful than the first. It seemed particularly ingenious. The audacity of the twenty-franc pieces, this stream of money from a modern safe that had fallen into a corner of Greek mythology, captured the imagination of the ladies and financiers present. The words, 'So much gold! So much money!' flitted round, with smiles, with long tremors of satisfaction; and each of these ladies and gentlemen dreamt of owning all this money themselves, coffered in their cellars.

'England has paid up; there are your millions,' Louise whispered maliciously in Madame Sidonie's ear.

Madame Michelin, her mouth slightly open with desire, threw back her almah's veil and fondled the gold with glittering eyes, while the group of serious-looking gentlemen went into transports of delight. Monsieur Toutin-Laroche, beaming, whispered a few words in the ear of the Baron, whose face was becoming covered with yellow blotches; while Mignon and Charrier, less discreet, crudely exclaimed:

'Damn it! There's enough there to demolish the whole of Paris and rebuild it.'

This remark seemed quite profound to Saccard, who was beginning to suspect that Mignon and Charrier just made fun of people under the pretence of idiocy. When the curtains fell once more, and the piano finished its triumphal march with a tumult of notes thrown pell-mell, like a last shovelful of crown pieces, there was a burst of applause, this time louder and more prolonged.

Meanwhile, in the middle of the tableau, the minister,* accompanied by his secretary, Monsieur de Saffré, had appeared at the door of the drawing room. Saccard, who was impatiently looking out for his brother, wanted to rush forward to welcome him. But the latter gestured for him to stay where he was. He slowly approached the group of serious-looking gentlemen. When the curtains had closed, and he was recognized, a long whisper travelled round the drawing room, all heads looked round: the minister counterbalanced the success of *The Loves of Narcissus and Echo*.

'You're a poet, Monsieur le Préfet,' he said, smiling, to Monsieur Hupel de la Noue. 'You once published a volume of verse, *Les Volubilis*, I believe? I see the cares of administration have not impaired your imagination.'

The Prefect detected in this compliment the sting of an epigram. The sudden appearance of his superior disconcerted him, the more so as, glancing to see if his dress was in order, he noticed on his sleeve the little white hand, which he did not dare to brush off. He bowed and stammered a reply.

'Really,' continued the minister, addressing Monsieur Toutin-Laroche, Baron Gouraud, and the other personages present, 'all that gold made a wonderful spectacle. We'd be able to achieve so much if Monsieur Hupel de la Noue coined money for us.'

This repeated, in ministerial language, the remark made by Mignon and Charrier. Then Monsieur Toutin-Laroche and the others paid their court, and rang the changes on the minister's last phrase: the Empire had done wonders already; there was no lack of gold, thanks to the experience and skill of the Government; never had France stood so tall in the councils of Europe; and the gentlemen ended by uttering such platitudes that the minister himself changed the subject.

He listened to them with his head high, the corners of his mouth slightly upturned, which gave his fat, white, clean-shaven face an expression of scepticism and smiling disdain.

Saccard looked for an opportunity to make his announcement of the marriage of Maxime and Louise. He assumed a very relaxed air, and his brother, with mock geniality, was good-natured enough to help him by pretending great affection for him. He was really the superior of the two, with his steady gaze, his obvious contempt for petty criminality, and his broad shoulders, which, with a shrug, could have floored all those present. When at last the marriage was mentioned, he became charming, and let it be understood that he had his wedding present ready; he even suggested that Maxime might be appointed auditor to the Council of State. He went so far as to repeat twice to his brother:

'Tell your son I'll be his witness.'

Monsieur de Mareuil blushed with delight. Saccard was congratulated. Monsieur Toutin-Laroche offered to be second witness. Then, suddenly, they began to talk of divorce. A member of the opposition, said Monsieur Haffner, had just had the audacity to defend this social scandal. Everyone protested. Their sense of propriety was expressed in very profound observations. Monsieur Michelin smiled feebly at the minister, while Mignon and Charrier noted with surprise that the collar of his dress-coat was worn.

Meanwhile Monsieur Hupel de la Noue remained ill at ease, leaning against the armchair of Baron Gouraud, who had contented himself with silently shaking hands with the minister. The poet dared not leave the spot. A vague feeling, a dread of appearing ridiculous, a fear of losing the favour of his superior detained him, despite his furious desire to go and pose the ladies on the stage for the last tableau. He waited for some happy remark to occur to him and restore him to favour. But he could think of nothing. He felt more and more embarrassed when he saw Monsieur de Saffré; he took his arm and clung on to him as to a life-raft. The young man had just arrived, he was a fresh victim.

'Have you heard what the Marquise said?' asked the Prefect.

But he was so agitated that he was no longer able to tell the story properly.

I said to her, 'You have a charming costume, and she replied...'

'I've got a much prettier one underneath,' quietly added Monsieur de Saffré. 'It's an old one, my dear sir, very old.'

Monsieur Hupel de la Noue looked at him in consternation. He was just about to refine his commentary on the ingenuousness of this cry from the heart!

'Old,' replied the secretary, 'as old as the hills: Madame d'Espanet has already said it twice at the Tuileries.'

This was the last straw. What did the Prefect care now for the minister, for the whole drawing room? He turned towards the stage, when the piano played a prelude, in a sad tone, with a tremulous series of notes; then the plaintive strain increased, dragged on for some time, and the curtains parted. Monsieur Hupel de la Noue, who had already half disappeared, returned to the drawing room when he heard the soft grating of the curtain-rings. He was pale, exasperated; he made a great effort to prevent himself from insulting the ladies. They had posed themselves without him! It must have been that little d'Espanet woman who had urged them to hasten the changes of costume and dispense with his help. It was all wrong, it was worth nothing at all!

He returned, mumbling inaudibly. He looked at the stage, and muttered:

'Echo is too near the edge. And Narcissus' leg, it's not dignified, not dignified at all.'

Mignon and Charrier, who had come closer in order to hear the explanation, ventured to ask him what the young man and the young girl were doing on the ground. He did not reply, refusing to explain his poem any further; and as the contractors insisted, he said:

'I'm not interested any more, now that the ladies have chosen to pose without consulting me!'

The piano sobbed softly. On the stage, a glade into which the electric light threw a shaft of sunshine revealed a vista of foliage. It was an ideal glade, with blue trees and big red and yellow flowers that rose as high as the oaks. There, on a grassy knoll, lay Venus and Plutus, side by side, surrounded by nymphs who had hurried from the neighbouring thickets to serve as their escort. There were daughters of the trees, daughters of the springs, daughters of the mountains, all the laughing, naked divinities of the forest. The god and goddess triumphed, punished the indifference of the proud one who had scorned them, while the group of nymphs looked on curiously and in pious terror at the vengeance of Olympus in the foreground. There the drama unfolded. The handsome Narcissus, lying at the edge of a pool that came down from the back of the stage, was looking at himself in the limpid mirror; and realism had been carried so far that a piece of real looking-glass had been placed at the bottom of the pool. But he had already ceased to be a free young man, the forest wanderer. Death surprised him in the midst of his rapt admiration of his own image, Death enervated him, and Venus, her finger outstretched, like a fairy in a transformation scene, cast the fatal spell. He was turning into a flower. His limbs became verdant, elongated, in his tight-fitting costume of green satin; the flexible stalk, formed by his slightly bent legs, was on the point of sinking into the ground and taking root, while his body, adorned with broad lappets of white satin, blossomed into a wondrous corolla. Maxime's fair hair completed the illusion, and his long curls set yellow pistils amid the whiteness of the petals. The great nascent flower, still human, inclined its head towards the spring, its eyes moist, its countenance smiling in voluptuous ecstasy, as if Narcissus had satisfied in death the passion he had inspired in himself. A few paces away Echo was dying of frustrated desire; she found herself caught little by little in the hard ground, she felt her burning limbs freezing and stiffening. She was no vulgar moss-stained rock, but one of white marble, through her arms and shoulders, through her long snow-white robe, from which the girdle of leaves and the blue drapery had slipped down. Sinking into the satin of her skirt, which was creased in large folds, like a block of Parian marble,* she threw herself back, retaining nothing of life in her cold sculptured body except her gleaming eyes, fixed on the water-lily reclining languidly above the mirror of the spring. It already seemed as if all the love-sounds of the forest, the long-drawn-out voices of the thickets, the mystic shivers of the leaves, the deep sighs of the tall oaks, were beating upon the marble flesh of Echo, whose heart, still bleeding within the rock, continued to throb, repeating from afar the slightest complaints of Earth and Air.

'Oh, how they've rigged out poor Maxime!' murmured Louise. 'And Madame Saccard looks like a corpse.'

'She's covered with rice-powder,' said Madame Michelin.

Other rather uncomplimentary remarks were heard. This third tableau was not an unqualified success like the two others, and yet it was this tragic ending that filled Monsieur Hupel de la Noue with enthusiasm for his own talent. He admired himself in it, as did Narcissus in his piece of looking-glass. He had put into it a host of poetic and philosophical allusions. When the curtains closed for the last time, and the spectators had applauded politely, he felt mortified at having yielded to anger and not explained the last page of his drama. He tried to give the people around him the key to the charming, grandiose, or simply mischievous ideas represented by Narcissus and Echo, and he even tried to say what Venus and Plutus were doing in the glade; but these ladies and gentlemen, whose practical minds had understood the grotto of flesh and the grotto of gold, were not interested in the Prefect's mythological explanations. Only Mignon and Charrier, who wanted to know everything, were kind enough to question him. He kept them standing for nearly two hours in a window-recess, telling them about Ovid's *Metamorphoses*.

Meanwhile the minister had left. He apologized for not being able to stay to congratulate the beautiful Madame Saccard on the perfect grace of her Echo. He had gone three or four times round the drawing room arm-in-arm with his brother, shaking hands with the men and bowing to the ladies. Never had he compromised himself so much for Saccard. He left him radiant when, on the threshold, he said loudly:

'I'll expect you tomorrow morning for breakfast.'

The ball was about to begin. The servants had arranged the ladies' chairs against the walls. The big drawing room now displayed, from the little yellow drawing room to the stage, its great expanse of carpet, whose large purple flowers opened out under the dripping light that fell from the crystal chandeliers. It grew hotter, the reflection of the red hangings burnished the gilt of the furniture and the ceiling. To open the ball, they were waiting for the ladies, Echo, Venus, Plutus, and the rest, to change their costumes.

Madame d'Espanet and Madame Haffner were the first to appear.

They had resumed the costumes they wore in the second tableau; one was Gold, the other Silver. They were surrounded and congratulated; they described how they had felt.

'I almost exploded with laughter,' said the Marquise, 'when I saw Monsieur Toutin-Laroche's big nose pointing at me in the distance!'

'I think I've got a crick in my neck,' drawled the fair-haired Suzanne. 'Really, if it had lasted a minute longer I would have put my head back in a normal position, my neck was hurting so much.'

From the recess into which he had driven Mignon and Charrier, Monsieur Hupel de la Noue kept glancing at the group that had formed round the two ladies; he was afraid they were laughing at him. The other nymphs arrived one after the other; all had resumed their costumes as precious stones: the Comtesse Vanska, as Coral, achieved a stupendous success when the ingenious details of her dress were looked at closely. Then Maxime entered, impeccable in dress-clothes, and wearing a smile; a crowd of women enveloped him, he was placed in the centre of the circle and teased about his floral character and his passion for mirrors; unembarrassed, as if delighted with his part, he continued to smile, joked back, confessed that he adored himself and that he was sufficiently cured of women to prefer himself to them. The laughter increased, the group grew larger and took up the whole of the middle of the drawing room, while the young man, lost in this army of shoulders, in this medley of dazzling costumes, retained his fragrance of depraved love, the gentleness of a pale, vicious flower.

When Renée finally came down, there was a hush. She had put on a new costume of such original grace and audacity that the ladies and the men, though used to her eccentricities, gave a sudden start of surprise. She was dressed as a Tahitian. This costume, it would seem, is by way of being very primitive: a pair of soft tinted tights that reached from her feet to her breasts, leaving her arms and shoulders bare, and over these tights a simple muslin blouse, short and trimmed with two flounces so as to hide her hips a little. A wreath of wild flowers in her hair; gold bangles on her wrists and ankles. And nothing more. She was naked. The tights had the suppleness of flesh under the muslin blouse; the pure naked outline was visible, vaguely blurred by the flounces from the armpits to the knees, but at the slightest movement reappearing between the meshes of the lace. She was an adorable savage, a barbarous and voluptuous woman, barely hidden beneath a white haze, a cloud of sea-mist, beneath which her whole body could be discerned.

Renée, rosy-cheeked, stepped forward. Céleste had managed to split the first pair of tights; fortunately Renée, foreseeing this eventuality, had taken precautions. The torn tights had delayed her. She seemed to care little for her triumph. Her hands burned, her eyes glittered with fever. She smiled, however, responding briefly to the men who stopped her to congratulate her on the chasteness of her attitudes in the *tableaux vivants*. She left in her wake a trail of dress-coats astounded at the transparency of her muslin blouse. When she reached the group of women surrounding Maxime, she occasioned short cries of admiration, and the Marquise began to eye her from head to foot, murmuring:

'She has a marvellous figure.'

Madame Michelin, whose almah dress appeared hideously ponderous beside this simple veil, pursed her lips, while Madame Sidonie, shrivelled up in her black sorceress's dress, whispered in her ear:

'It's the height of indecency: don't you think so, you beautiful thing?'

'Well!' said the pretty brunette at last, 'how angry Monsieur Michelin would be if I undressed like that.'

'Quite right too,' concluded the businesswoman.

The band of serious-looking men was not of this opinion. They drooled from a distance. Monsieur Michelin, whom his wife had so inappropriately quoted, went into ecstasies, in order to please Monsieur Toutin-Laroche and Baron Gouraud, who were enraptured by the sight of Renée. Saccard was greatly complimented on his wife's figure. He bowed, he professed to be quite moved. The evening was an auspicious one for him, and but for an occasional moment of distraction when he glanced in the direction of his sister, he appeared perfectly happy.

'I say, she has never showed us as much as that before,' said Louise playfully in Maxime's ear.

She corrected herself, and added, with a mystifying smile:

'At least, not to me.'

The young man looked at her in alarm, but she continued smiling, like a schoolboy delighted with a rather crude joke.

The ball began. The stage of *tableaux vivants* had been used to accommodate a small band, in which brass predominated; and the clear notes of the horns and cornets rang out in the ideal forest with the blue trees. First came a quadrille: 'Ah, il a des bottes, il a des bottes, Bastien!', which was at that time extremely popular in the dance-halls. The ladies danced. Polkas, waltzes, and mazurkas alternated with the quadrilles. The swirling couples moved backwards and forwards, filling the long gallery, bounding in response to the brass, swaying to the lullaby of the violins. The fancy dresses, the cavalcade of women from every country and every period, rocked to and fro in a swarming medley of bright materials. After mingling and carrying off the colours in cadenced confusion, the rhythm, at certain strokes of the bow, abruptly brought back the same pink satin tunic, the same blue velvet bodice, side by side with the same dress-coat. Then another stroke of the bows and blast of the cornets pushed the couples on, made them travel in single file round the drawing room, with the swaying motion of a rowing-boat with a snapped painter drifting in the wind. And so on, endlessly, for hours. Sometimes, between two dances, a lady went to a window, suffocating, to breathe in a little of the fresh air; couples rested on a sofa in the little buttercup drawing room, or went into the hothouse, strolling slowly round the pathways. Skirts, their edges alone visible, laughed languidly under the arbours of creepers, in the depths of the warm shadow, where the forte notes of the cornets penetrated during the quadrilles of 'Ohé les p'tits agneaux!' and 'J'ai un pied qui r'mue!'

When the servants opened the door to the dining room, transformed into a refreshment buffet, with sideboards against the walls and a long table in the middle laden with cold cuts, there was a great crush. A tall, handsome man, who had modestly kept his hat in his hand, was so violently flattened against the wall that the hat burst with a pitiful moan. This made everyone laugh. They rushed at the pastries and the truffled game, digging their elbows into one another. There was a general pillage, hands met over meat dishes, and the lackeys did not know whom to serve in this band of well-bred men, whose outstretched arms expressed their terrible fear of arriving too late and finding the dishes empty. An old gentleman grew angry because there was no claret, and champagne, he maintained, kept him awake.

'Gently, Messieurs, gently,' said Baptiste in his grave voice. 'There's enough for everyone.'

But nobody listened. The dining room was full, and anxious dress-coats stood on tiptoe at the door. Before the sideboards stood groups, eating quickly, crowding together. Many swallowed their food without drinking, not having been able to lay their hands on a glass. Others, on the contrary, drank and looked in vain for a morsel of bread.

'Listen,' said Monsieur Hupel de la Noue, whom Mignon and Charrier, sick of mythology, had dragged to the supper room, 'we shan't get a thing if we don't stick together. It's much worse at the Tuileries, and I know what I'm talking about. You look after the wine, I'll see to the food.'

The Prefect had his eye on a leg of mutton. He stretched out his arm at the right moment through a sudden gap in the mass of shoulders, and quietly carried it off after stuffing his pockets with rolls. The contractors reappeared, Mignon with one bottle of champagne, Charrier with two; but they had only been able to find two glasses; they said that it did not matter, they would drink out of the same one. They all supped from the corner of a flower-stand at the end of the room. They did not even take off their gloves, but put the slices already cut from the leg of mutton between their bread, and kept the bottles under their arms. Standing up, they talked with their mouths full, stretching out their chins so that the gravy would fall on the carpet.

Charrier, having finished his wine before his bread, asked a servant to get him a glass of champagne.

'You'll have to wait, Monsieur!' the servant angrily replied, forgetting that he was not in the kitchen. 'Three hundred bottles have been finished already.'

Meanwhile the band was playing louder and louder, in sudden bursts. They were dancing the Kisses Polka, extremely popular in public dance-halls, and whose rhythm each dancer had to mark by embracing his partner. Madame d'Espanet appeared at the door of the dining room, flushed, her hair a little disarranged, trailing her long silver dress with a charming air of lassitude. As hardly anyone moved, she was obliged to push people aside. She walked slowly round the table, looking sulky. Then she came up to Monsieur Hupel de la Noue, who had finished eating and was wiping his mouth with his handkerchief.

'It would be extremely kind of you, Monsieur,' she said with a bewitching smile, 'if you would find me a chair. I've been all round the table.'

The Prefect had a grudge against the Marquise, but his gallantry gave him no choice: he sprang into action, found a chair, installed Madame d'Espanet, and stood behind to wait on her. She would only have a few prawns, with a little butter, and half a glass of champagne. She ate daintily amid the gluttony of the men. The table and the chairs were reserved exclusively for the ladies. But an exception was always made for Baron Gouraud. There he was, sitting comfortably in front of a piece of game pie, slowly munching the crust. The Marquise won back the Prefect by telling him that she would never forget her artistic emotions in *The Loves of Narcissus and Echo*. She even explained, in a way that completely consoled him, why they had not waited for him: the ladies, on learning that the minister was there, had thought it would be impolite to prolong the interval. She ended by asking him to go and look for Madame Haffner, who was dancing with Mr Simpson, a brute of a man whom she disliked, she said. When Suzanne appeared, she completely forgot Monsieur Hupel de la Noue.

Saccard, followed by Messieurs Toutin-Laroche, de Mareuil, and Haffner, had taken possession of a sideboard. As there was no room at the table, and Monsieur de Saffré was passing by with Madame Michelin on his arm, he stopped them and insisted that the pretty brunette should join his party. She nibbled at some pastry, smiling, raising her bright eyes to the five men who surrounded her. They leant over her, touched her almah's veils embroidered with threads of gold, and forced her up against the sideboard, on which she ended by leaning, taking cakes from every hand, with the docility of a slave amid her masters. Monsieur Michelin, alone at the other end of the room, was finishing off a pot of pâté de foie gras which he had succeeded in capturing.

Meanwhile Madame Sidonie, who had been prowling about ever since the first strokes of the bow had opened the ball, entered the dining room and summoned Saccard with a glance.

'She isn't dancing,' she said softly. 'She seems restless. I think she's considering something desperate. But I don't know yet who the young man is. I must have something to eat and go back and see what I can see.'

Standing up, like a man, she ate a chicken wing, which she got

Monsieur Michelin, who had finished his pâté, to give her. She poured herself a large glass of malaga, and then, after wiping her lips with her fingers, returned to the drawing room. The train of her sorceress's dress seemed already to have collected all the dust from the carpets.

The ball was flagging, the band was showing signs of fatigue, when a murmur circulated: 'The *cotillon*! The *cotillon*!' This put fresh life into the dancers and the brass. Couples appeared from all the shrubberies in the hothouse; the big drawing room filled up as for the first quadrille. The men who were not dancing looked on benevolently from the window-recesses as a talkative group in the middle of the room continued to grow; the supper-eaters in the next room craned their necks to see, without abandoning their food.

'Monsieur de Mussy says he won't dance,' said a lady. 'He swears he never leads the *cotillon* now. Please, just once more, Monsieur de Mussy, just this. Just to please us.'

But the young attaché remained stiff and serious in his wing collar. It was really impossible, for he had sworn not to. There was general disappointment. Maxime refused too, saying that he was worn out. Monsieur Hupel de la Noue dared not offer his services; he was only interested in poetry. A lady who suggested Mr Simpson was promptly silenced; Mr Simpson was the most extraordinary *cotillon*-leader you ever saw; he had a penchant for fantastic and mischievous ideas; at one dance where they had been so imprudent as to choose him, it was said that he had made the ladies jump over the chairs, and one of his favourite figures was to make everybody go round the room on all fours.

'Has Monsieur de Saffré gone?' asked a childish voice.

He was just going, he was saying goodbye to the beautiful Madame Saccard, with whom he was on the best of terms since her refusal to have anything to do with him. The amiable sceptic admired the whims of others. He was brought back in triumph from the hall. He resisted, saying with a smile that they were embarrassing him, that this wasn't his kind of thing. Then, seeing all the white hands stretched out towards him, he said:

'Come on, take up your positions. But I warn you, I belong to the old school. I have no imagination at all.'

The couples sat down around the room, on all the chairs that could be found; young men were even sent to fetch the iron chairs from the hothouse. It was a monster *cotillon*. Monsieur de Saffré, who wore the rapt expression of a celebrant priest, chose as his partner Countess Vanska, whose Coral costume fascinated him. When everyone was in position, he cast a long look at the circle of skirts, each flanked by a dress-coat. Then he nodded to the band, whose brass resounded. Heads leaned forward along the smiling line of faces.

Renée declined to take part in the *cotillon*. She had been nervous all evening, scarcely dancing, mingling with the groups, unable to stay still. Her friends thought she seemed odd. She had talked, during the evening, of making a balloon journey with a celebrated aeronaut who was the talk of Paris.* When the *cotillon* began, she was annoyed at no longer being able to walk about freely; she stationed herself at the door leading to the hall, shaking hands with the men who were leaving, talking with her husband's closest associates. Baron Gouraud, whom a lackey was carrying off in his fur cloak, found a last word of praise for Renée's Tahitian costume.

Meanwhile, Monsieur Toutin-Laroche shook Saccard's hand.

'Maxime is counting on you,' said the latter.

'Quite so,' replied the new senator.

Turning to Renée, he said:

'Madame, I forgot to congratulate you. So the dear boy is fixed up now!'

As she smiled in surprise, Saccard said:

'My wife doesn't know yet. This evening we decided on the marriage between Mademoiselle de Mareuil and Maxime.'

She continued smiling, bowing to Monsieur Toutin-Laroche, who went off saying:

'You're signing the contract on Sunday, I gather? I'm going to Nevers on some mining business, but I'll be back in time.'

Renée remained alone for a moment in the middle of the hall. She had lost her smile; and as what she had just been told sank in, she began to tremble. She stared at the red velvet hangings, the rare plants, the majolica vases. Then she said out loud:

'I must speak to him.'

She returned to the drawing room. But she could not enter. A figure of the *cotillon* barred the way. The band was playing a soft waltz movement. The ladies, holding each other by the hand, formed a ring like one of those rings of little girls singing 'Giroflé girofla';*

and they danced round as quickly as possible, pulling at each other's arms, laughing, gliding. In the middle a gentleman—it was the mischievous Mr Simpson—held a long pink scarf; he raised it aloft, like a fisherman about to cast his net; but he was in no hurry, seeming to think it amusing to let the ladies dance round and tire themselves out. They panted and begged for mercy. Then he threw the scarf, with such skill that it wound round the shoulders of Madame d'Espanet and Madame Haffner, who were dancing side by side. It was one of the American's jokes. Next he wanted to waltz with both ladies at once, and he had already taken the two of them by the waist, one with his left arm and the other with his right, when Monsieur de Saffré said, in his stern voice as *cotillon*-king:

'You can't dance with two ladies.'

But Mr Simpson refused to let go of the two waists. Adeline and Suzanne threw themselves backwards in his arms, laughing. The point was argued, the ladies grew angry, the uproar was prolonged, and the dress-coats in the window recesses wondered how de Saffré proposed to extricate himself creditably from this dilemma. For a moment he seemed perplexed. Then he smiled, took Madame d'Espanet and Madame Haffner by the hand, whispered a question in their ears, received their reply, and then, addressing Mr Simpson, asked:

'Do you pick verbena or periwinkle?'

Mr Simpson, looking rather foolish, said that he picked verbena. Whereupon Monsieur de Saffré handed him the Marquise, saying:

'Here's your verbena.'

There was discreet applause. They thought this very skilful. Monsieur de Saffré was a *cotillon*-leader who was never at a loss, so the ladies said. Meanwhile the band, reinvigorated, had resumed the waltz air, and Mr Simpson, after dancing round the room with Madame d'Espanet, led her back to her seat.

Renée was able to come in. She had bitten her lips till the blood came at the sight of all this nonsense. She thought these men and women stupid to throw scarves about and call themselves by the names of plants. Her ears rang, a furious impatience gave her a sudden desire to throw herself headlong into the crowd and force her way through it. She crossed the drawing room quickly, bumping into the couples returning belatedly to their seats. She went straight to the hothouse. She had seen neither Louise nor Maxime among the

dancers, and thought that they must be there, in some nook of foliage, brought together by the instinct for fun and mischief that made
them seek out little corners as soon as they found themselves anywhere together. But she explored the dim hothouse in vain. She only
saw, behind an arbour, a tall young man kissing little Madame
Daste's hands, and murmuring:

'Madame de Lauwerens was right: you're an angel!'

This declaration made in her house, in her hothouse, shocked her.
Really, Madame de Lauwerens ought to have taken her business
elsewhere! Renée would have felt relieved had she been able to turn
out of her rooms all these people who were shouting so loudly.
Standing before the tank, she looked at the water, wondering where
Louise and Maxime could be. The band was still playing the same
waltz, whose slow, lilting tune made her feel sick. It was unbearable,
not to be able to think in one's own house. She became confused. She
forgot that the young people were not married yet, and she said to
herself that no doubt they had gone to bed. Then she thought of the
dining room, and quickly ran up the hothouse steps. But, at the door
of the ballroom, she was again stopped by a figure of the *cotillon*.

'This is the "Dark Spots",* Mesdames,' said Monsieur de Saffré.
'It's my own invention, and you will be the first to admire it.'

There was much laughter. The men explained the allusion to the
ladies. The Emperor had just made a speech in which he had
referred to the presence of certain dark spots on the horizon. These
dark spots, for no apparent reason, had had a great success. The
Parisian wits had appropriated the expression to such an extent that
for the past week the dark spots had been applied to everything.
Monsieur de Saffré placed the gentlemen at one end of the room,
making them turn their backs to the ladies, who were left at the other
end. Then he ordered them to pull up their coats so as to hide the
backs of their heads. This performance was gone through amid wild
merriment. Hunchbacked, their shoulders screwed up, their coat
tails falling no lower than their waists, the gentlemen looked quite
hideous.

'Don't laugh, Mesdames,' cried Monsieur de Saffré, with mock
seriousness, 'or I'll make you put your skirts over your heads.'

The gaiety increased. He made the most of his authority with
some of the gentlemen who refused to conceal the backs of their
heads.

'You are "dark spots",' he said, 'hide your heads, just show your backs, the ladies must see nothing but black. Now walk about, mingle, so that you can't be recognized.'

The hilarity was at its peak. The dark spots walked up and down, on their thin legs, swaying like headless crows. One gentleman's shirt showed, with braces. The ladies begged for mercy, they were dying with laughter, and Monsieur de Saffré graciously ordered them to go and fetch the 'dark spots'. They flew off, like a covey of partridges, with a loud rustle of skirts. Then, at the end of her run, each seized hold of the gentleman nearest to her. There was total chaos. One after the other the couples disengaged themselves and waltzed round the room to the louder strains of the band.

Renée leant against the wall. She looked on, pale, with pursed lips. An old gentleman came up to her to ask why she was not dancing. She had to smile and say something. She made her escape, and entered the supper room. It was empty. Amid the pillaged sideboards, the bottles and plates left lying about, Maxime and Louise sat quietly having supper at one end of the table, side by side, on a napkin they had spread out between them. They looked quite at home, laughing amid the disorder, the dirty plates, the greasy dishes, the still warm remnants of the gluttony of the white-gloved supper-eaters. They had simply brushed away the crumbs around them. Baptiste stalked solemnly round the table, without a glance at the room, which looked as if it had been attacked by a pack of wolves; he waited for the servants to come and restore a semblance of order to the sideboards.

Maxime had succeeded in putting a fine supper together. Louise adored *nougat aux pistaches*, a plate of which had remained intact on the top of a sideboard. In front of them were three partly emptied bottles of champagne.

'Perhaps Papa has gone,' said the girl.

'So much the better!' replied Maxime. 'I'll see you home.'

As she laughed, he added:

'You know, they've made up their minds that I'm to marry you. It's not a joke any more, it's serious. What are we going to do when we get married?'

'We'll do what everybody else does, of course!'

This joke slipped out rather quickly; she added immediately, as if to cancel it:

'We'll go to Italy. It will be good for my chest, I'm very ill... Ah, my poor Maxime, what a funny wife you'll have! I'm no fatter than a slither of butter.'

She smiled, with a touch of sadness, in her page's costume. A dry cough brought a sudden flush to her cheeks.

'It's the nougat,' she said. 'I'm not allowed to eat it at home. Pass me the plate, I'll put the rest in my pocket.'

She was emptying the plate when Renée entered. She went straight up to Maxime, making an enormous effort not to curse, and not to strike the hunchback sitting at table with her lover.

'I must talk to you,' she stammered in a husky voice.

He hesitated, alarmed, afraid to be alone with her.

'Alone, and straight away,' repeated Renée.

'Why don't you go, Maxime?' said Louise, with her inscrutable look. 'And at the same time you might try to find out what's become of my father. I lose him at every party we go to.'

He stood up, and then tried to stop Renée in the middle of the supper room, asking her what she needed to discuss so urgently. But she rejoined between her teeth:

'Follow me, or I'll speak out in front of everybody!'

He turned very pale, and followed her with the docility of a beaten animal. She thought Baptiste was staring at her; but at this moment she no longer cared. At the door the *cotillon* detained her a third time.

'Wait,' she muttered. 'These idiots will never finish.'

She took him by the hand, lest he should try to escape.

Monsieur de Saffré was positioning the Duc de Rozan against the wall, in a corner of the room next to the door to the dining room. He put a lady in front of him, then a gentleman back to back with the lady, then another lady facing the gentleman, and so on in a line, couple by couple, like a long snake. As the ladies dawdled and talked, he cried:

'Come along, Mesdames! Take your places for the "Columns".'

The 'columns' were formed. The indecency of finding themselves caught like this, squeezed in between two men, leaning against the back of one and feeling the chest of the other in front, made the ladies giggle. Their breasts pressed against the lapels of the dress-coats, the gentlemen's legs disappeared in the ladies' skirts, and when a sudden outburst of merriment made a head lean forward, the moustachios in front were obliged to draw back so as to avoid kissing. At one point a prankster must have given a slight push, for the line closed up, the men plunged deeper into the skirts; there were little cries and endless laughs. Baroness de Meinhold was heard to say: 'Monsieur, you're smothering me; don't squeeze so hard!', and this seemed so amusing, and provoked such a fit of hilarity in the whole row, that the columns tottered, staggered, collided, and leant against each other to avoid falling. Monsieur de Saffré waited with raised hands, ready to clap. Then he clapped. At this signal, suddenly, they all turned round. The couples who found themselves face to face clasped waists, and the column dispersed its chaplet of dancers into the room. None remained but the poor Duc de Rozan, who, as he turned round, found himself stuck with his nose against the wall. They all laughed.

'Come on,' Renée said to Maxime.

The band was still playing the waltz. This soft music, whose monotonous rhythm was becoming rather tiresome, increased Renée's exasperation. She reached the little drawing room, holding Maxime by the hand; and pushing him up the staircase that led to the dressing room, she ordered:

'Go up.'

She followed. At this moment Madame Sidonie, who had been prowling after her sister-in-law all evening, surprised at her continual wanderings through the rooms, reached the hothouse steps. She saw a man's legs disappearing into the darkness of the little staircase. A pale smile lit up her waxen face, and lifting her sorceress's dress so as to go quicker, she hunted for her brother, bumping into a figure of the *cotillon* and questioning the servants she met on her way. At last she found Saccard with Monsieur de Mareuil in a room next to the dining room, which had been fitted up as a temporary smoking room. The two fathers were discussing the contract. But when his sister came up and whispered in his ear, Saccard rose, apologized, and disappeared.

Upstairs, the dressing room was in complete disorder. On the chairs trailed Echo's costume, the torn tights, odds and ends of crumpled lace, underclothing thrown aside in a heap, everything a woman in a hurry leaves behind her. The little ivory and silver accessories lay everywhere: there were brushes and nail-files that had fallen on the carpet; and the towels, still damp, the cakes of soap forgotten on the marble slab, the scent bottles left unstoppered gave a pungent odour to the flesh-coloured tent. Renée, to remove the white from her arms and shoulders, had used the pink marble bath, after the *tableaux vivants*. Iridescent soap stains floated on the surface of the cold water.

Maxime stepped on a corset, almost fell, and tried to laugh. But he shuddered at the sight of Renée's grim face. She came up to him, pushed him, and said in a low voice:

'So you're going to marry the hunchback?'

'No,' he murmured. 'Who told you that?'

'Oh, don't tell lies. There's no point.'

He suddenly became defiant. She alarmed him, he wanted to have done with her.

'Well, yes, I am going to marry her. So what? Can't I do what I want?'

She came up to him, her head slightly lowered, and with a wicked laugh grabbed his wrists:

'What you want? You know better than that. I'm your master. I could break your arms if I wanted to; you're no stronger than a girl.'

As he struggled, she twisted his arms with all the nervous violence of her anger. He uttered a faint cry. Then she let go and continued:

'You see? We'd better not fight; I'd only beat you.'

He remained very pale, with the shame of the pain he felt in his wrists. He watched her pacing up and down in the dressing room. She pushed back the furniture, thinking, fixing on the plan she had been turning over in her mind since her husband had told her of the marriage.

'I'll lock you in here,' she said at last, 'and as soon as it's daylight we'll leave for Le Havre.'

He became even paler with alarm and disbelief:

'This is madness!' he cried. 'We can't run away. You're off your head.'

'Very likely. In any case it's you and your father who have driven me mad. I want you, and I mean to have you. Too bad for those fools!'

A red glow appeared in her eyes. She continued, approaching Maxime once more, scorching his face with her breath:

'What do you think would happen to me if you married the hunchback? You would both laugh at me, perhaps I would have to take back that fool de Mussy, who leaves me utterly cold. When people have done what you and I have done, they stick to each other. Besides, it's quite obvious. I'm bored without you, and since I'm going away, I'll take you with me. You can tell Céleste what you want her to fetch from your place.'

Maxime held out his hands, beseeching her:

'Please, Renée, don't be silly. Pull yourself together. Just think of the scandal.'

'I don't care about the scandal! If you refuse, I'll go down to the drawing room and shout out that I've slept with you and that you're cowardly enough now to marry this hunchback.'

He lowered his head, listened to her, already giving in, accepting this will that thrust itself so rudely upon him.

'We'll go to Le Havre,' she resumed in a quieter voice, 'and from there we'll go across to England. Nobody will bother us again. If that's not far enough away, we'll go to America. I'm always so cold, I'd be better off there. I've often envied the Creoles.'

But hearing her elaborating her plan, Maxime was again seized with terror. To leave Paris, to go so far away with a woman who was undoubtedly mad, to leave behind a scandal that would exile him forever! It was as if he were being suffocated by a hideous nightmare. He sought desperately for a means of escape from this dressing room, from this pink retreat where the passing bell at Charenton* seemed to be tolling. He thought he had hit on something.

'But I have no money,' he said gently, so as not to exasperate her. 'If you lock me in, I can't get any.'

'I have,' she replied triumphantly. 'I've got a hundred thousand francs. It's all working out extremely well.'

She took from the looking-glass wardrobe the deed of transfer, which her husband had left with her in the vague hope that she might lose her senses. She placed it on the dressing table, ordered Maxime to give her a pen and ink from the bedroom, and pushing back the soap-dishes, said as she signed the deed:

'There, I've done it. If I've been robbed, it's because I've chosen to be. We'll call on Larsonneau on the way to the station. Now, my little Maxime, I'm going to lock you in, and we'll escape through the garden when I've turned all these people out of the house. We don't even need to take any luggage.'

Her high spirits had returned. Her mad plan delighted her. It was a piece of supreme eccentricity, a dramatic finale, which, in her feverish state, seemed to her quite inspired. It far surpassed her desire to travel in a balloon. She took Maxime in her arms, murmuring:

'My poor darling, did I hurt you just now? You see, you refused. But you'll see how nice it will be. Could your hunchback ever love you as I do? She's not a woman, that creature...'

She laughed, drew him to her, and kissed him on the lips, when a sound made them both turn round. Saccard was standing in the doorway.

There was a terrible silence. Slowly, Renée removed her arms from Maxime's neck; she did not lower her head, but stared at her husband with wide, unblinking eyes like those of a corpse; the young man, dumbfounded and terrified, staggered forward now that he was no longer held in her embrace. Stunned by this final blow, which at last made the husband and father cry out in him, Saccard stood where he was, livid, his eyes burning into them from a distance. In the moist, fragrant atmosphere of the room, the three candles flared very high, their flames straight, with the immobility of fiery tears. The only thing that broke the terrible silence was a breath of music that floated up the narrow staircase: the waltz, with its serpentine modulations, glided, coiled, died away on the snow-white carpet, among the split tights and the skirts that had fallen on the floor.

Then the husband stepped forward. His face was red with rage, he clenched his fists to strike the guilty pair. His anger burst forth like gunfire. He gave a strangled laugh, and coming closer, said:

'You were announcing your marriage to her, I suppose?'

Maxime retreated, leaning against the wall.

'Listen,' he stammered, 'it was her...'

He was about to accuse her like a coward, to lay the blame on her, to say that she wanted to carry him off, to defend himself with the meekness and trepidation of a child caught in the act. But he was too weak, the words died in his throat. Renée remained as stiff as a statue, retaining her mute air of defiance. Then Saccard, no doubt hoping to find a weapon, glanced round the room. On the corner of the dressing table, among the combs and nail-brushes, he caught sight of the deed of transfer, whose stamped yellow paper stood out on the white marble. He looked at the deed, then at the guilty pair. Leaning forward, he saw that the deed was signed. His eyes went from the open inkstand to the pen, still wet, lying next to the candlestick. He stood gazing at the signature.

The silence seemed to increase, the flames of the candles grew longer, the waltz passed even more liltingly along the hangings. Saccard gave an imperceptible shrug. He threw another piercing look at his wife and son, as if to wring from their faces an explanation he was unable to supply. Then he slowly folded the deed and put it in the pocket of his dress-coat. His cheeks had become quite pale.

'You did well to sign, my dear,' he said quietly to his wife. 'A hundred thousand francs in cash. I'll give it to you this evening.'

He almost smiled, but his hands still trembled. He took one or two steps forward, and added:

'It's stifling in here. What an idea to come and hatch one of your jokes in this steam-bath!'

Turning to Maxime, who had raised his head, surprised at his father's conciliatory tone, he said:

'Come downstairs, you! I saw you come up. I came to fetch you to say goodnight to Monsieur de Mareuil and his daughter.'

The two men went downstairs, talking. Renée stood alone in the middle of the dressing room, staring at the gaping well of the staircase, down which she had just watched the father and son disappear. She could not take her eyes away from the well. They had gone off quietly, amicably! These two men had not set upon each other. She strained her ears to hear whether they were not rolling down the stairs, locked together in some terrible struggle. But she could hear nothing, in the darkness, but the sound of dancing, a long lullaby. She thought she could hear in the distance the Marquise's laugh and Monsieur de Saffré's voice. So the drama was ended! Her crime, the kisses on the great grey-and-pink bed, the wild nights in the hothouse, the forbidden love that had consumed her for months, had culminated in this cheap, banal ending. Her husband knew everything and did not even strike her. The silence around her, the silence through which trailed the never-ending waltz, frightened her more than the sound of a murder. She felt afraid of this tranquillity, afraid of this delicate, discreet dressing room, filled with the fragrance of love.

She saw herself in the high wardrobe mirror. She moved closer, surprised at her own image, forgetting her husband, forgetting Maxime, quite taken up with the strange woman she saw before her.

Madness rose to her brain. Her yellow hair, caught at the temples and on her neck, seemed to her a naked obscenity. The line in her forehead deepened to such a degree that it formed a dark bar above her eyes, the thin blue scar of a lash from a whip. Who had marked her like that? Her husband had not so much as raised his hand. Her lips surprised her with their pallor, her short-sighted eyes seemed dead. How old she looked! She looked down, and when she saw herself in her tights, and in her light gauze blouse, she gazed at herself with lowered eyes and sudden blushes. Who had stripped her naked? What was she doing there, bare-breasted, like a prostitute displaying herself almost to the waist? She no longer knew. She looked at her thighs, rounded out by the tights; at her hips, whose supple outlines she could see under the gauze; at her breasts, barely covered. She was ashamed of herself, and contempt for her body filled her with mute anger at those who had left her like this, with mere bangles of gold at her wrists and ankles to cover her skin.

Then, trying to remember what she was doing there, quite naked, before the mirror, her thoughts flashed back to her childhood, and she saw herself again at the age of seven in the solemn gloom of the Hôtel Béraud. She recalled a day when Aunt Élisabeth had dressed them, Christine and her, in frocks of grey homespun with little red checks. It was Christmas. How pleased they had been with these two dresses, just alike! Their aunt spoiled them, and she went so far as to give them each a coral bracelet and necklace. The sleeves were long, the bodices came up to their chins, and the trinkets showed up on the stuff, and they thought it very pretty. Renée remembered too that her father was there, that he smiled in his sad way. That day she and her sister had walked up and down the children's room like grown-ups, without playing, so as not to get dirty. Then, at the Sisters of the Visitation, her schoolfriends had laughed at her about 'her clown's dress', which came down to her fingertips and up over her ears. She had begun to cry during lesson-time. At playtime, to stop them making fun of her, she had turned up the sleeves and tucked in the neckband of the bodice. The bracelet and necklace seemed to her to look prettier on her bare neck and arm. Was that when she had first begun to strip naked?

Her life unfurled before her. She recalled her growing alarm, the cacophony of gold and flesh rising within her, at first coming up to her knees, then to her belly, then to her lips; and now she felt it submerging her, pounding on her skull. It was like a poisonous sap: it had weakened her limbs, grafted growths of shameful affection on her heart, made sickly, bestial caprices sprout in her brain. This sap had soaked into her feet on the rug of her barouche, on other carpets too, on all the silk and velvet on which she had been walking since her marriage. The footsteps of others must have left behind those poisonous seeds, which were now germinating in her blood and circulating in her veins. She clearly remembered her childhood. When she was little, she had been extremely inquisitive. Even later, after the rape, which had plunged her into wickedness, she had not wished for all that shame. She would certainly have become better if she had stayed knitting by Aunt Élizabeth's side. She heard the regular clicking of her aunt's needles, while she stood staring into the mirror to read the peaceful future that had eluded her. But she saw only her pink thighs, her pink hips, that strange, pink silk woman standing before her, whose skin of fine, closely woven silk seemed made for lovers' of dolls and puppets. She had come to that, to being a big doll from whose broken chest escaped a thin trickle of sawdust. Then, at the thought of the enormities of her life, the blood of her father, the bourgeois blood that had always tormented her at critical moments, cried out within her. She, who had always trembled at the thought of hell, ought to have spent her life buried in the austere gloom of the Hôtel Béraud. Who, then, had stripped her naked?

In the dim blue reflection of the glass she imagined she saw the figures of Saccard and Maxime rise up. Saccard, swarthy, grinning, iron-hued, with his cruel laugh and skinny legs. The strength of the man's will! For ten years she had seen him at the forge, amid the sparks of red-hot metal, his flesh scorched, breathless, pounding away, lifting hammers twenty times too heavy for his arms, at the risk of crushing himself. She understood him now; he seemed to her to have grown taller through his superhuman efforts, his stupendous roguery, his obsession with money. She remembered how he leapt over obstacles, rolling in the mud, not bothering to wipe himself down, so that he could reach his goal more quickly, not even stopping to enjoy himself on the way, chewing on his twenty-franc pieces as he ran. Then Maxime's pretty, fair-haired head appeared behind his father's shoulder: he had his prostitute's smile, his vacant, lascivious eyes, which were never lowered, his centre parting, which showed the whiteness of his skull. He laughed at Saccard, upon whom he looked down for taking so much trouble to make the money which he, Maxime, spent with such adorable ease. He was like a kept woman. His soft, slender hands bore witness to his vices. His smooth body had the languid attitude of satiated desire. In all his soft, feeble person, through which vice coursed gently like warm water, there shone not even a gleam of the curiosity of sin. He was a passive agent. Renée, as she looked at these two apparitions emerging from the faint shadows of the mirror, stepped back, saw that Saccard had used her like a stake, like an investment, and that Maxime had happened to be there to pick up the louis fallen from the gambler's pocket. She was an asset in her husband's portfolio; he urged her to buy gowns for an evening, to take lovers for a season; he wrought her in the flames of his forge, using her as a precious metal with which to gild the iron of his hands. So, little by little, the father had driven her to such a pitch of madness and abandonment as to desire the kisses of the son. If Maxime was the impoverished blood of Saccard, she felt that she was the product, the maggot-eaten fruit of the two men, the pit of infamy they had dug between them, and into which they now both rolled.

She knew now. It was they who had stripped her naked. Saccard had unhooked her bodice, and Maxime had pulled down her skirt. Then, between them, they had torn off her shift. Now she stood there without a rag, with gold bracelets, like a slave. They had looked upon her only a moment ago, and they had not said: 'You are naked.' The son had trembled like a coward, shuddering at the thought of pursuing his crime to its conclusion, refusing to follow her in her passion. The father, instead of killing her, had robbed her; this man punished people by rifling their pockets: a signature had fallen like a ray of sunshine into the depths of his anger, and by way of vengeance he had carried off the signature. Then she had seen them walk down the stairs and disappear into the darkness. No blood on the carpet, not a cry, not a moan. They were cowards. They had stripped her naked.

She recalled how, on one single occasion, she had read the future, on the day when, close to the murmuring shadows of the Parc Monceau, the thought that her husband would corrupt her and one day drive her mad had come to her and disturbed her growing desires. How her poor head hurt! She realized now the folly of the illusion that had made her believe that she lived with impunity in a blissful world of divine pleasure! She had lived in the land of shame, and she was punished by the desertion of her whole body, by the annihilation of her whole being, now in its death-throes. She wept at not having listened to the voices of the trees.

Her nudity irritated her. She turned her head and looked around. The dressing room still had its heavy odour of musk, its warm silence, broken by the phrases of the waltz, like the last ripples on a pool of water. The faint laughter of distant voluptuousness passed over her with unbearable irony. She held her hands over her ears so as not to hear it. Then she saw clearly the luxury of the room. She looked up at the pink tent, the silver crown that showed a plump Cupid preparing his dart; she gazed at the furniture, at the marble slab of the dressing table, heaped high with pots and implements that now meant nothing to her; she went up to the bath still full of stagnant water; she kicked away the things that trailed down from the white satin of the easy chairs, Echo's costume, petticoats, stray towels. From all these things feelings of shame arose: Echo's dress reminded her of the dumb-show she had acquiesced in for the eccentricity of offering herself to Maxime in public; the bath exhaled the scent of her body, the water in which she had soaked filling the room with the feverishness of a sick woman; the table with its soap dishes and cosmetics, the furniture with its bed-like fullness bore the crude insignia of her body, of her affairs, of all the filth she longed to forget. She moved back to the middle of the room, her face crimson, not knowing how she could flee from this alcove perfume, this pink display of luxury, flaunting itself with the shamelessness of a prostitute. The room was as naked as she was: the pink bath, the pink skin of the hangings, the pink marble of the two tables took on a life of their own, coiled up, surrounding her with such an orgy of lust that she closed her eyes and bowed her head, crushed and overwhelmed beneath the lace of the walls and the ceiling.

But in the darkness she again saw the flesh-coloured stain of the dressing room, and she perceived too the soft grey of the bedroom, the soft gold of the little drawing room, and the hard green of the hothouse, all this complicitous luxury. It was there that her feet had been impregnated with the poisonous sap. She would never have slept with Maxime in a garret. It would have been too cheap. Silk had given her crime a coquettish quality. She imagined tearing down the lace, spitting on the silk, kicking her great bed to pieces, dragging her luxury into some gutter from where it would emerge worn out and dirty like herself.

When she opened her eyes again, she approached the mirror and examined herself closely. It was all over. She saw herself dead. Every feature told her that the destruction of her brain was nearly complete. Maxime, the last perversion of her senses, had finished his work, exhausted her body, unhinged her mind. No joys remained for her to taste, no hope of reawakening. This thought enraged her. In a final access of desire, she dreamt of recapturing her prey, of swooning in Maxime's arms and carrying him off with her. Louise could never marry him; Louise well knew that he did not belong to her, since she had seen them kissing each other on the lips. Then she threw a fur pelisse over her shoulders, so as not to walk naked through the ball. She went downstairs.

In the little drawing room she came face to face with Madame Sidonie. The latter, in order to enjoy the drama, had again stationed herself on the hothouse steps. She did not know what to make of Saccard's reappearance with Maxime, nor of his curt replies to her whispered questions. Then she guessed the truth. Her sallow face turned pale, she thought this was really too much. She went and glued her ear to the door of the staircase, hoping to hear Renée crying upstairs. When Renée opened the door, it almost struck her sister-in-law in the face.

'You're spying on me!' said Renée angrily.

Madame Sidonie replied with fine disdain:

'Do you think I care about your filthy affairs?'

Catching up her sorceress's dress, retreating with a majestic look, she said:

'It's not my fault, my dear, if things go wrong. I bear you no ill will, you know. You could have had and could still have a second mother in me. I'd be glad to see you whenever you wish.'

Renée did not listen. She entered the big drawing room and walked through a very complicated figure of the *cotillon* without even noticing the surprise occasioned by her fur pelisse. In the middle of the room were groups of ladies and their partners mingling together, waving streamers, and Monsieur de Saffré's fluty voice was calling out:

'Now, Mesdames, it's time for the "Mexican War".* The ladies who play the bushes must spread out their skirts and stay crouched.

The gentlemen must dance round the bushes. When I clap my hands each of them must waltz with his bush.'

He clapped his hands. The brass resounded, the waltz sent the couples spinning once more round the room. The figure was not very successful. Two ladies had been left behind on the carpet, entangled in their dresses. Madame Daste declared that the only thing she liked in the 'Mexican War' was making a 'cheese'* with her dress, as at school.

Renée, reaching the hall, bumped into Louise and her father, whom Saccard and Maxime were seeing off. Baron Gouraud had left. Madame Sidonie went with Mignon and Charrier, while Monsieur Hupel de la Noue escorted Madame Michelin, followed discreetly by her husband. The Prefect had spent the latter part of the evening paying court to the pretty brunette. He had just suc-ceeded in persuading her to spend one of the summer months in his departmental town, 'where she would see some really fascinating antiquities'.

Louise, who was covertly munching the nougat she had put in her pocket, was seized with a coughing fit just as she was leaving.

'Wrap yourself up,' said her father.

Maxime quickly tightened the strings of the hood of her opera cloak. She lifted her chin and let herself be muffled up. When Madame Saccard appeared, Monsieur de Mareuil turned back to say goodbye. They all stayed talking for a moment. Renée, to explain her pallor and her shivering, said she had felt cold and had gone up to her room to put the fur over her shoulders. She was waiting for the moment when she could talk to Louise, who was looking at her calmly. When the gentlemen shook hands once more, she leant forward and murmured:

'Tell me, you're not going to marry him? It's not possible. You know quite well...'

The child interrupted her, rising on tiptoe to speak in her ear:

'Oh! Don't worry. I'll take him away. It won't make any difference, since we're going to Italy.'

She smiled her vague, vicious, sphinx-like smile. Renée was speechless. She did not understand, she had the impression that the hunchback was making fun of her. Then, when the de Mareuils had gone, after repeating several times 'See you on Sunday!', she looked at her husband and at Maxime with frightened eyes. Seeing their complacent, self-satisfied attitudes, she hid her face in her hands and fled, seeking refuge in the depths of the hothouse.

The pathways were deserted. The great clumps of foliage were asleep, and on the heavy surface of the tank two budding water-lilies were slowly opening. Renée would gladly have sought relief in tears; but this moist heat, this pungent odour, which she recognized, stuck in her throat and strangled her despair. She looked down at the spot in the yellow sand at her feet, on the edge of the tank, where the previous winter she used to spread out the bearskin rug. When she looked up, she saw yet another figure of the *cotillon* in the distance, through the two open doors.

The noise was deafening, there was a confused mêlée in which at first she could make out nothing but flying skirts and prancing black legs. Monsieur de Saffré's voice cried, 'Change your partners! Change your partners!' The couples passed by amid a fine yellow dust; each gentleman, after three or four turns in the waltz, threw his partner into the arms of his neighbour, who in turn threw him his. Baroness de Meinhold, in her costume as the Emerald, fell from the hands of the Comte de Chibray into the hands of Mr Simpson; he caught her as best he could by the shoulder, while the tips of his gloves glided under her bodice. The Comtesse Vanska, flushed, jingling her coral pendants, went with a bound from the chest of Monsieur de Saffré to the chest of the Duc de Rozan, whom she entwined in her arms and compelled to hop round for five turns, when she hung onto the hips of Mr Simpson, who had just flung the Emerald to the leader of the *cotillon*. Madame Teissière, Madame Daste, and Madame de Lauwerens shone like large, live jewels, with the blond pallor of the Topaz, the blue of the Turquoise, and the bright blue of the Sapphire; they had moments of abandonment, curved under a waltzer's outstretched wrist, then set off again, fell backwards or forwards into a fresh embrace, found themselves successively in the arms of every man in the room. However, Madame d'Espanet, standing in front of the band, had succeeded in catching hold of Madame Haffner as she sped by, and now waltzed with her, refusing to let her go. Gold and Silver danced lovingly together.

Renée suddenly understood this whirling of skirts, this prancing of legs. Standing lower down, she could see the frenzied movement of the feet, the blur of glazed shoes and white ankles. At intervals it seemed to her as if a gust of wind was about to blow away the dresses.

The bare shoulders, the bare arms, the bare heads that reeled past, caught up, thrown off, and caught up again at the end of the gallery, where the music of the band grew madder and the red hangings swooned amid the final fever of the ball, seemed to her a tumultuous symbol of her life, of her self-exposure, of her wild self-indulgence. At the thought that Maxime, in order to take the hunchback in his arms, had abandoned her there, in the very spot where they had made love, she felt a pang of pain so intense that she thought of plucking a stalk of the tanghin tree that grazed her cheek, and of chewing it dry. But she was afraid, and she remained standing before the shrub, shivering under the fur, which she drew tightly around her in a gesture of terror and shame.

CHAPTER VII

THREE months later, on one of those dismal spring mornings, which in Paris recall the greyness and damp of winter, Aristide Saccard got out of a cab in the Place du Château d'Eau* and turned with four other gentlemen into the large demolition site that was to become the Boulevard du Prince-Eugène. They formed a committee of inspection sent by the Compensation Authority to value certain houses on the spot, their owners not having been able to come to an agreement with the City.

Saccard was repeating the stroke of luck of the Rue de la Pépinière. To keep his wife's name out of it, he began with a spurious sale of the building plots and the music-hall. Larsonneau handed over the lot to an imaginary creditor. The deed of sale bore the colossal figure of three million francs. This figure was so outrageous that, when the expropriation agent, in the name of the non-existent landlord, claimed the amount of the purchase money as an indemnity, the committee at the Hôtel de Ville flatly refused to allow more than two million and a half, despite the machinations of Monsieur Michelin and the appeals of Monsieur Toutin-Laroche and Baron Gouraud. Saccard had foreseen this setback; he refused the offer, let the case go before the Commission, of which he happened to be a member together with Monsieur de Mareuil, whose membership was a coincidence to which Saccard had no doubt contributed. It was thus that, with four of his colleagues, he found himself appointed to conduct an inquiry into his own site.

Monsieur de Mareuil accompanied him. The other three consisted of a doctor, who smoked a cigar without caring the least in the world for the heaps of rubbish he stepped over, and two businessmen, of whom one, a manufacturer of surgical instruments, used to be an itinerant knife-grinder.

The path these gentlemen followed was dreadful. It had been raining all night. The sodden earth was turning into a river of mud, running between the demolished houses over a track cutting across the soft ground, in which the dobbin-carts sank up to their axles. On either side, great pieces of wall, burst open by pickaxes, remained standing; tall, gutted buildings, displaying their pale insides, opened to the skies their wells stripped of stairs, their gaping rooms suspended in mid-air like the broken drawers of a big, ugly piece of furniture. Nothing could be more forlorn than the wallpaper of these rooms, blue or yellow squares hanging in tatters, marking the positions, five or six storeys high, right up to the roofs, of wretched little garrets, cramped holes that had once contained, perhaps, a whole human existence. On the bare walls, ribbons of flues rose side by side, lugubriously black and with sharp bends. A forgotten weathercock grated at the edge of a roof, while loose gutters hung down like rags. The gap yawned still wider in the midst of these ruins, like a breach opened by cannon; the roadway, as yet hardly set out, filled with rubbish, mounds of earth, and deep puddles, stretched out under the leaden sky, amid the sinister pallor of the falling plaster dust, edged with the black strips of chimneys as with mourning border.

The gentlemen, with their polished boots, their frock coats, and top hats, struck a strange note in this muddy, dirty yellow landscape, traversed only by sallow workmen, horses splashed to their backs, carts whose sides were hidden beneath a coating of dust. They went in single file, hopping from stone to stone, avoiding the pools of liquid mire, sometimes sinking in up to their ankles and then cursing as they shook their feet. Saccard had suggested taking the Rue de Charonne, which would have spared them this tramp over rough ground; but unfortunately they had several plots to visit on the long line of the boulevard; they had decided, out of curiosity, to go through the middle of the roadworks. From time to time they stopped, balancing on a piece of plaster that had fallen into a rut, calling to one another to point out some yawning flooring, a flue stuck straight up in the air, a joist that had fallen onto a neighbouring roof. This demolition area at the end of the Rue du Temple fascinated them.

'It's extraordinary,' said Monsieur de Mareuil. 'Saccard, look at that kitchen up there; there's an old frying pan still hanging over the stove. I can see it quite clearly.'

The doctor, his cigar between his teeth, had planted himself before a demolished house of which only the ground-floor rooms remained, filled with the debris of the other storeys. A solitary piece of wall rose from the heap of bricks and rubbish; and in order to pull it down in one go they had tied a rope round it at which some thirty workmen were tugging.

'They won't do it,' muttered the doctor. 'They're pulling too much to the left.'

The four others retraced their steps to see the wall come down. All five of them, with wide eyes and bated breath, waited for the fall with a thrill of pleasure. The workmen, relaxing and then suddenly stiffening, cried, 'Heave ho!'

'They won't do it,' repeated the doctor.

Then, after a few seconds, one of the businessmen said joyously:

'It's moving, it's moving.'

When the wall at last gave way and came down with a thunderous crash, raising a cloud of plaster, the gentlemen smiled at one another. They were delighted. Their frock coats were covered with a fine dust, which whitened their arms and shoulders.

They talked about the workmen as they resumed their cautious progress through the puddles. There were not many good ones among them. They were all lazy, spendthrift, and obstinate into the bargain, dreaming only of their employer's ruin. Monsieur de Mareuil, who for the last minute had been nervously watching two poor devils perched on the corner of a roof hacking at a wall with their pickaxes, expressed the view that they were very courageous all the same. The others stopped again and looked up at the labourers balancing themselves, leaning over, striking with all their might; they shoved the stones down with their feet and calmly watched them break into pieces beneath them: if their pickaxes had gone wide of the mark, the mere momentum of their arms would have hurled them to the ground.

'Oh, they're used to it,' said the doctor, putting his cigar back in his mouth. 'They're absolute brutes.'

They reached one of the houses they had to inspect. They hurried through their task in a quarter of an hour, and resumed their walk. They gradually lost their disgust of the mud; they walked straight through the puddles, giving up all hope of keeping their boots clean. When they passed the Rue Ménilmontant, one of the businessmen, the ex-knife-grinder, became agitated. He gazed at the ruins around him, failing to recognize the neighbourhood. He said he had lived in this area more than thirty years ago, when he had arrived in Paris, and that he would really like to find his old place again. He was still looking when the sight of a house which the labourers' picks had already cut in two made him stop short in the middle of the roadway.

He studied the door and the windows. Then, pointing to a corner of the demolished building high above them, he cried:

'There it is! That's it!'

'What?' asked the doctor.

'My room! That's it!'

It was on the fifth floor, a little room that previously must have looked out onto a courtyard. A breach in the wall showed it quite bare, already cut into on one side, with wallpaper with a pattern of big yellow flowers, a broad torn strip of which fluttered in the wind. On the left they could still see a cupboard recess, lined with blue paper, and next to it the aperture for a stovepipe, with a bit of piping left in it.

The ex-workman was overcome with emotion.

'I spent five years there,' he murmured. 'It was hard in those days; but no matter, I was young... You see the cupboard; that's where I put by three hundred francs, sou by sou. And the hole for the stovepipe, I can still remember the day I made it. There was no fireplace, it was bitterly cold, all the more so because I was often on my own.'

'Come, come,' interrupted the doctor, joking, 'there's no need to tell us your secrets. You sowed your wild oats like the rest of us.'

'That's true,' ingenuously resumed the ex-knife-grinder. 'I still remember an ironing girl who lived opposite. The bed was on the right, near the window. Ah, my poor room, look what they've done to it!'

He was really very upset.

'Come on,' said Saccard. 'There's nothing wrong with pulling these old hovels down. We're going to build fine freestone houses in their place. Would you still live in a dump like that? There's nothing to stop you taking up residence on the new boulevard.'

'True enough,' replied the manufacturer, who seemed consoled.

The committee of inspection halted again two houses further on. The doctor stayed outside, smoking, looking at the sky. When they reached the Rue des Amandiers, the houses became more scattered; they now passed through large enclosures, pieces of waste ground scattered with tumbledown shacks. Saccard seemed very pleased by this walk through the demolitions. He had just remembered the dinner he had had with his first wife on the Buttes Montmartre, and he clearly recalled how he had pointed out to her, with his hand, the cutting that went from the Place du Château d'Eau to the Barrière du Trône. The realization of his prophecy delighted him. He followed the cutting with the secret joy of authorship, as though he himself had struck the first blows of the pickaxe with his iron fingers. He skipped over the puddles, reflecting that three million francs were waiting for him beneath a heap of rubble, at the end of this stream of mire.

Meanwhile the gentlemen began to fancy themselves in the country. The road passed through gardens, whose separating walls had been pulled down. There were large clumps of budding lilac. The foliage was a very delicate, pale green. Each of these gardens, looking like a hideaway hung with the greenery of the shrubs, was hollowed out with a small pond, a miniature waterfall, bits of wall on which were painted *trompe-l'oeil* in the form of foreshortened groves and blue landscapes. The buildings, far apart and discreetly hidden, were like Italian villas and Greek temples: moss was eating away the bottoms of the plaster columns, while lichens had already loosened the mortar of the pediments.

'Those are "follies",' said the doctor with a wink.

Seeing that the others did not understand him, he explained that under Louis XV the Court nobility kept up houses for their licentious parties. It was the fashion. He added:

'Those places were called their "follies". The neighbourhood is full of them... There were some fine goings on here, I can tell you.'

The committee of inquiry had become very attentive. The two businessmen's eyes glittered, they smiled and looked with great interest at these gardens, these villas which they had barely graced with a glance before hearing their colleague's comments. They stood for a long time before a grotto. But when the doctor, seeing a house already attacked by pickaxes, said that he recognized the Comte de Savigny's 'folly', well known for that nobleman's orgies, the whole committee left the boulevard to go and inspect the ruins. They climbed onto the rubbish heaps, entered the ground-floor rooms by the windows, and as the workmen were having their lunch, they were able to linger there quite at their ease. They stayed a good half-hour, examining the ceiling roses, the frescos over the door, the tortuous mouldings of the plaster yellowed with age. The doctor reconstructed the house.

'Look here', he said, 'this room must be the banquet hall. There,

in that recess, must have stood a huge divan. And I'm positive there
was a mirror over the divan; there are the mirror's feet... Those
devils certainly knew how to enjoy life!'

They would never have left these ruins, which tickled their curiosity, had not Saccard, becoming impatient, said to them with a laugh:

'You can look as long as you like, but the ladies are gone. Let's get
on with our business.'

Before moving on, the doctor climbed onto a mantelpiece in order
to detach, with a delicate blow of the pickaxe, a little painted Cupid's
head, which he put into the pocket of his frock coat.

They arrived at last at the end of their journey. The land that was
formerly Madame Aubertot's was very extensive; the music-hall and
the garden took up barely half of it, the rest had here and there a few
nondescript houses. The new boulevard cut diagonally across this
huge parallelogram, and this had allayed one of Saccard's fears: he
had long imagined that only a corner of the music-hall would be cut
off. Accordingly Larsonneau had been instructed to talk very big, as
the bordering plots ought to increase at least fivefold in value. He
was already threatening the City with a recent decree that authorized
the landowners to provide no more than the land absolutely necessary
for the public works.

The expropriation agent received them in person. He walked
them through the garden, made them go over the music-hall, showed
them a huge bundle of papers. The two businessmen had gone down
again, accompanied by the doctor, whom they were still asking about
the Comte de Savigny's folly, which had captured their imaginations.
They listened to him open-mouthed, all three standing beside one of
the amusement games. He told them about Madame de Pompadour
and the affairs of Louis XV, while Monsieur de Mareuil and Saccard
continued the inquiry alone.

'We've finished,' said the latter, returning to the garden. 'If you
will allow me, Messieurs, I'll draw up the report.'

The manufacturer of surgical instruments did not even hear. He
was deep in the Regency.*

'What strange times, all the same!' he murmured. Then they
found a cab in the Rue de Charonne, and drove off, splashed up to
their knees, but as satisfied with their walk as if they had had a day
in the country. In the cab the conversation changed, they talked
politics, they said that the Emperor was doing great things. No one

had ever seen the like of what they had just seen. That great, long, straight street would be splendid when the houses were built.

Saccard drew up the report, and the Authority granted three million francs. The speculator was in dire straits, he could not have waited another month. This money saved him from ruin and even from the dock. He paid five hundred thousand francs towards the million he owed his upholsterer and his builder for the house in the Parc Monceau. He stopped up other holes, launched new companies, deafened Paris with the sound of the real crown pieces he shovelled out onto the shelves of his iron safe. The golden stream had a source at last. But it was not yet a solid, established fortune, flowing with an even, continuous current. Saccard, saved from a crisis, thought himself a beggar with the crumbs from his three million, and said frankly that he was still too poor, that he could not stop; and soon the ground appeared once more to be giving way under his feet.

Larsonneau had conducted himself so admirably in the Charonne affair that Saccard, after a brief hesitation, had the honesty to give him his ten per cent and his bonus of thirty thousand francs. The expropriation agent immediately set up a banking house. When his accomplice peevishly accused him of being richer than himself, the yellow-gloved dandy replied with a laugh:

'You see, master, you're very clever at making the five-franc pieces rain down, but you don't know how to pick them up.'

Madame Sidonie took advantage of her brother's stroke of luck to borrow ten thousand francs from him, and used them to spend two months in London. She returned without a sou. It was never known where the ten thousand francs had gone.

'Good gracious!' she replied, when they asked her about it, 'it all costs money. I ransacked all the libraries. I had three secretaries helping me.'

When she was asked if she had at last some positive information about the three thousand million, she smiled mysteriously, and muttered:

'You're a lot of unbelievers... I've discovered nothing, but it makes no difference. You'll see one of these days.'

She had not wasted all her time, however, while she was in England. Her brother the minister took advantage of her journey to entrust her with a delicate errand. When she returned she obtained a huge volume of orders from the Ministry. It was a fresh incarnation.

She made contracts with the Government, she undertook every imaginable kind of supply. She sold it provisions and arms for the troops, furniture for the prefectures and public departments, firewood for the museums and government offices. The money she made did not induce her to change her eternal black dresses, or her dismal, sallow face. Saccard reflected that it was indeed she whom he had seen long ago furtively leaving his brother Eugène's house. She must have kept secretly in touch with him all the time, for reasons unknown to all.

Amid these interests, these insatiable appetites, Renée suffered agonies. Aunt Élisabeth was dead; her sister had married and left the Hôtel Béraud, where her father alone remained in the gloomy shadows of the big rooms. In one season she exhausted her aunt's inheritance. She had taken to gambling. She had found a house where ladies sat at the card table until three o'clock in the morning, losing hundreds of thousands of francs a night. She made an attempt to drink; but she could not, overcome with disgust. Since she had found herself alone again, she let herself go more than ever, not knowing how to kill time. She tried everything. But nothing appealed to her amid the infinite boredom that engulfed her. She seemed older, she had blue rings round her eyes, her nose became thinner, her lips pouted with sudden, inexplicable laughter. She was breaking down.

When Maxime had married Louise, and the young couple left for Italy, she no longer troubled herself about her lover, and even seemed to have forgotten him. When, six months later, Maxime returned alone, having buried 'the hunchback' in the cemetery of a small town in Lombardy, her feeling towards him was one of hatred. She remembered *Phèdre*, she doubtless recalled the poisonous love to which she had heard La Ristori lend her sobs. Then, to avoid having the young man in her house in future, to dig an abyss of shame between the father and the son, she forced her husband to acknowledge the incest, telling him that on the day when he had surprised her with Maxime, the latter, who had been running after her for a long time, was trying to rape her. Saccard was terribly annoyed by her persistent desire to open his eyes. He was compelled to break with his son, to stop seeing him. The young widower, rich with his wife's dowry, took a small house in the Avenue de l'Impératrice, where he lived alone. He gave up the Council of State, he trained racehorses. Renée thus experienced one of her last pleasures. She took her revenge, throwing back in their faces the infamy these two men had set in her; she said to herself that now she would never again see them laughing at her, arm-in-arm, like friends.

As Renée's affections crumbled there came a time when she had only her maid left to love. She had gradually developed a maternal fondness for Céleste. Perhaps this girl, who was all that remained to remind her of Maxime's love, recalled the hours of pleasure forever dead. Perhaps she simply felt touched by the fidelity of this honest soul whose devotion nothing seemed to shake. From the depths of her remorse she thanked her for having witnessed her shame without leaving her in disgust; she pictured self-denials, a whole life of renunciation, before becoming able to understand the calmness of the maidservant in the presence of incest, her icy hands, her respectful and serene attentions; and she was all the happier in the girl's devotion as she knew her to be virtuous and thrifty, with no lovers and no vices.

Sometimes, in her sadness, she would say to her:

'Ah, my girl, it will be your duty to close my eyes.'

Céleste did not reply, and smiled curiously. One morning she quietly told Renée that she was leaving, that she was going back to the country. Renée stood trembling, as if some great misfortune had overtaken her. She plied her with questions. Why was she deserting her when they got on so well together? She offered to double her wages.

But the maidservant replied no with a gesture, placidly and obstinately.

'Listen, Madame,' she said finally, 'you could offer me all the gold in Peru, I wouldn't stay a week longer. You really don't know me. I've been with you for eight years, haven't I? Well, from the first day, I said to myself, "As soon as I've saved five thousand francs, I'll go back home; I'll buy Lagache's house, and I'll live very happily." It's something I promised myself, you see. I reached my target yesterday, when you gave me my wages.'

Renée felt a sudden chill. She saw Céleste moving behind her and Maxime while they kissed, and she now saw her indifference, her complete detachment, thinking of her five thousand francs. She made one more attempt to keep her, afraid of the void that threatened her existence, hoping, in spite of everything, to keep by her side this obstinate creature whom she had looked upon as utterly devoted and whom she now discovered to be merely selfish. The girl smiled, still shaking her head, muttering:

'No, no, I can't do it. I would refuse even if my mother asked me. I'll buy two cows. I may start a little haberdasher's shop. It's very nice in our part of the country. You'd be welcome to come and see me. It's near Caen. I'll leave the address.'

Renée stopped insisting. She wept when she was alone. The next day she decided to take Céleste to the Gare de l'Ouest* in her own brougham. She gave her one of her travelling rugs, and some cash, fussed around her like a mother whose daughter is about to set off on a long journey. In the brougham she looked at her with tears in her eyes. Céleste chatted, saying how pleased she was to be leaving. Then, growing bolder, she spoke out and gave her mistress some advice.

'I would never have behaved as you did, Madame. I often said to myself, when I found you with Monsieur Maxime: "How is it possible to be so foolish about men!" It always ends badly. I've always mistrusted them!'

She laughed, throwing herself back in the corner of the brougham.

'My money would have disappeared!' she continued. 'And at this moment I might have been crying my eyes out. That's why, whenever I saw a man, I picked up a broomstick. I never dared tell you all this. Besides, it wasn't my business. You were free to do as you pleased, and I only had to earn my money and behave properly.'

At the railway station Renée said she would pay her fare, and bought her a first-class ticket. As they had arrived early, she kept her talking, took her hands in hers, and repeated:

'Take care, and look after yourself, my dear.'

Céleste stood looking happy, with a fresh, smiling face, as her mistress gazed at her with tears in her eyes. Renée again spoke of the past, and suddenly Céleste exclaimed:

'I was forgetting: I never told you about Baptiste... I suppose they didn't want to tell you...'

Renée admitted that she did not know to what she was referring.

'Well, you remember his grand, dignified air and his haughty look; you remarked on them yourself. All that was play-acting. He didn't like women, he never came down to the pantry when we were there;

and, I can tell you now, he even said it was disgusting in the drawing room because of the low-necked dresses. I'm quite sure he didn't like women!'

She leant forward and whispered something in Renée's ears, making her blush.

'When the new stable lad', she continued, 'told Monsieur everything, Monsieur preferred to dismiss Baptiste rather than have him prosecuted. It seems that filthy sort of thing had been going on in the stables for years. And to think that great beanpole pretended to be fond of horses! It was the grooms he was after.'

The bell interrupted her. She hurriedly caught up the nine or ten packages from which she had refused to be parted. She allowed herself to be kissed. Then she went off, without looking back.

Renée remained in the station until the engine whistled. When the train had gone she did not know what to do in her despair; her days seemed to stretch before her as empty as the great hall where she had been left alone. She stepped back into her brougham and told the coachman to drive her home. But on the way she changed her mind; she was afraid of her room, of the boredom awaiting her there; she did not even have the energy to go in and change her dress for her customary drive round the lake. She felt a need for sunlight, for a crowd.

She ordered the coachman to drive to the Bois.

It was four o'clock. The Bois was awakening from the drowsiness of the warm afternoon. Clouds of dust flew along the Avenue de l'Impératrice, and one could see in the distance the green expanse between the slopes of Saint-Cloud and Suresnes,* crowned by the grey mast of Mont Valérien.* The sun, high on the horizon, swept down, filling the hollows of the foliage with a golden dust, lighting up the tall branches, changing the sea of leaves into a sea of light. But past the fortifications, in the avenue leading to the lake, the roads had been watered, the carriages rolled over the brown surface as over a carpet, amid a freshness, a rising fragrance of moist earth. On either side the trees of the copses reared their crowd of young trunks amid the low bushes, disappearing in the greenish twilight, which streaks of light pierced here and there with yellow clearings; and as the lake came closer, the chairs on the side paths became more numerous, families sat with quiet, silent faces, watching the endless procession of wheels. Then, on reaching the open space in front of the lake,

there was an effulgence; the slanting sun transformed the round
sheet of water into a great mirror of polished silver. Eyes blinked,
one could only distinguish on the left, near the bank, the dark patch
of the pleasure boat. The sunshades in the carriages leaned with a
gentle, uniform movement towards this splendour, and were not
raised until they reached the avenue skirting the water, which, from
above the bank, now assumed a metallic darkness streaked with burnished gold. On the right, the clumps of fir trees stretched forth
their colonnades of straight, slender stems, whose soft violet tint was
reddened by the fiery sky; on the left, the lawns, bathed in light,
spread out like fields of emeralds to the distant lacework of the Porte
de la Muette. On approaching the waterfall, while the dimness of the
copses was renewed on one side, the islands at the far end of the lake
rose up against the blue sky, with their sunlit banks, the bold
shadows of their pine trees, and the Châlet at their feet, which
looked like a child's toy lost in a virgin forest. The whole park
laughed and quivered in the sun.

Renée felt ashamed, on this splendid day, of her brougham, of her
dress of puce-coloured silk. She settled further back in the vehicle,
and through the open windows looked out at the flood of light covering the water and the greenery. At the bends of the avenues she
caught sight of the line of wheels revolving like golden stars in a long
streak of blinding lights. The varnished panels, the gleam of brass
and steel, the bright hues of the dresses passed by, to the even trot of
the horses, and set against the background of the Bois a wide moving
bar, a ray fallen from the sky, stretching out and following the bends
of the roadway. In this ray Renée, blinking, saw at intervals a woman's
blond chignon, a footman's dark back, the white mane of a horse.
The rounded sunshades of watered silk shimmered like metallic
moons.

Then, in the presence of this broad daylight, of these sheets of
sunshine, she thought of the fine dust of twilight she had seen falling
one evening upon the yellow leaves. Maxime was with her. It was at
the time when her lust for that child was awakening within her. She
saw again the lawns soaked by the evening air, the darkened copses,
the deserted pathways. The line of carriages drove then with a
mournful sound past the empty chairs, while today the rumble of the
wheels, the trot of the horses, sounded with the joyousness of a
fanfare of trumpets. Then all her drives in the Bois came back to her.

She had lived there, Maxime had grown up there, by her side, on the cushion in her carriage. It was their garden. Rain had surprised them there, sunshine brought them back, night had not always driven them away. They drove there in every kind of weather, they tasted there the disappointments and delights of their life. In the void of her existence, amid the melancholy caused by Céleste's departure, these memories gave her a bitter joy. Her heart said, 'Never again! Never again!' She remained frozen when she evoked the image of that winter landscape, that congealed and dimmed lake on which they had skated; the sky was the colour of soot, the snow had stitched white bands of lace on the trees, the wind blew fine sand into their faces.

Meanwhile, on the left, on the track reserved for riders, she had recognized the Duc de Rozan, Monsieur de Mussy, and Monsieur de Saffré. Larsonneau had killed the duke's mother by presenting to her, as they fell due, the hundred and fifty thousand francs'-worth of bills accepted by her son, and the duke was running through his second half-million with Blanche Muller after leaving the first five hundred thousand francs in the hands of Laure d'Aurigny. Monsieur de Mussy, who had left the Embassy in London for the Embassy in Rome, had become once more a dashing man of the world; he led the *cotillon* with renewed grace. As for Monsieur de Saffré, he remained the most amiable sceptic in the world. Renée saw him urging his horse towards the carriage door of the Comtesse Vanska, with whom he was said to have been infatuated ever since the day when he had seen her as Coral at the Saccards'.

All the ladies were there: the Duchesse de Sternich in her eternal chariot, Madame de Lauwerens in a landau, with Baroness de Meinhold and little Madame Daste in front of her; Madame Teissière and Madame de Guende in a victoria. Among these ladies, Sylvia and Laure d'Aurigny were stretched out on the cushions of a magnificent barouche. Even Madame Michelin passed by, ensconced in a brougham; the pretty brunette had been on a visit to Monsieur Hupel de la Nouc's departmental town, and on her return she had appeared in the Bois in this brougham, to which she hoped soon to add an open carriage. Renée also saw the Marquise d'Espanet and Madame Haffner, the inseparables, hidden beneath their sunshades, stretched out side by side, laughing lovingly into each other's eyes.

Then the gentlemen drove by. Monsieur de Chibray in a drag;

Mr Simpson in a dog cart; Mignon and Charrier, keener than ever on their work despite their dream of retirement, in a brougham which they left at the corner of the avenues in order to go some of the way on foot; Monsieur de Mareuil, still in mourning for his daughter, looking out for gestures of acknowledgment of his first intervention, the day before, at the Corps Législatif, airing his political importance in the carriage of Monsieur Toutin-Laroche, who had once more saved the Crédit Viticole after bringing it to the verge of ruin, and who was being made still thinner and still more imposing by his work at the Senate.

To close the procession, as a last display of majesty, came Baron Gouraud, lolling in the sun on two pillows. Renée was surprised and disgusted to recognize Baptiste seated by the coachman's side, with his pale face and solemn air. The tall lackey had taken service with the Baron.

The copses sped past, the water of the lake became iridescent under the slanting rays of the sun, the line of carriages stretched out with its dancing lights. Renée, caught up and carried away amid all this splendour, was vaguely conscious of these appetites rolling along in the sunlight. She felt no anger towards these devourers of the quarry. But she hated them because of their joyous exultation in the golden dust that fell from the sky. They were gorgeous and smiling; the women were white and plump; the men had the quick glances, the contented air of successful lovers. She, with her empty heart, felt nothing but lassitude and repressed envy. Was she better than others, that she should break down under the weight of pleasure? Or was it the others who were to be praised for being stronger than her? She did not know, she longed for new desires with which to begin life afresh, when, looking round, she noticed beside her, on the side-path at the edge of the coppice, a sight that dealt her a supreme blow.

Saccard and Maxime were sauntering along, arm-in-arm. The father must have been to see the son, and together they had come down from the Avenue de l'Impératrice to the lake, chatting as they went.

'Listen,' said Saccard, 'you're stupid. A man like you, with money, doesn't let it lie idle in a drawer. There's a hundred per cent to be made in the business I'm telling you about. It's a safe investment. You know very well I wouldn't let you be taken for a ride.'

But the young man seemed wearied by this persistence. He smiled in his pretty way, and looked at the carriages.

'Look at that little woman over there, the woman in violet,' he said suddenly. 'That's a washer-girl that ass Mussy has brought out.'

They looked at the woman in violet. Then Saccard took a cigar from his pocket, and turning to Maxime, who was smoking, said:

'Give me a light.'

Then they stopped for a moment, facing each other. When the cigar was alight the father continued, once more taking his son's arm, pressing it tightly under his own:

'You'd be a fool if you didn't take my advice. So, do you agree? Will you bring me the hundred thousand francs tomorrow?'

'You know I don't come to your house any more,' replied Maxime, compressing his lips.

'Bah! Rubbish! It's time that nonsense stopped!'

As they took a few steps in silence, at the moment when Renée, feeling about to faint, pressed her head back against the padding of the brougham so as not to be seen, a rumour spread along the line of carriages. The pedestrians on the side-paths halted, turned round open-mouthed. There was a quicker sound of wheels, carriages drew aside respectfully, and two outriders appeared, clad in green, with round caps on which danced golden tassels with their cords outspread; they trotted on, leaning slightly forward on their large bay horses. Behind them they left an empty space. Then, in this empty space, the Emperor appeared.*

He sat alone on the back seat of a landau. Dressed in black, with his frock coat buttoned up to his chin, he wore, a little to one side, a very tall hat, whose silk glistened in the sunlight. In front of him, on the other seat, sat two gentlemen, dressed with that correct elegance which was in favour at the Tuileries, serious, their hands on their knees, with the silent air of two wedding guests taken for a drive amid the curiosity of the crowd.

Renée thought the Emperor had aged. His mouth opened more feebly under his thick waxed moustache. His eyelids fell more heavily, to the point of half covering his lifeless eyes, whose yellow greyness was yet more bleared. His nose alone retained its look of a dry fishbone set in the vagueness of his face.

In the meantime, while the ladies in the carriages smiled discreetly, the people on foot pointed the sovereign out to one another. A fat man asserted that the Emperor was the gentleman with his back to the coachman on the left. A few hands were raised in salute.

But Saccard, who had taken off his hat even before the outriders had passed, waited until the Imperial carriage was directly in front of him, and then shouted in his thick Provençal accent:

'Long live the Emperor!'

The Emperor, surprised, turned round, seemed to recognize the enthusiast, and returned the greeting with a smile. Everything disappeared in the sunlight, the carriages closed up, Renée could only see, above the manes of the horses, between the lackeys, the outriders' green caps dancing with their golden tassels.

She remained for a moment with wide-open eyes, full of this vision, which reminded her of another moment in her life. It seemed to her as if the Emperor, by mingling with the line of carriages, had just set in it the last necessary ray, and given a clear meaning to this triumphal procession. Now it was a glorification. All these wheels, all these men with decorations, all these women languidly reclining, vanished into the flash and the rumble of the Imperial landau. This sensation became so acute and so painful that Renée felt a compelling need to escape from this triumph, from Saccard's cry, still ringing in her ears, from the sight of the father and son sauntering along arm-in-arm. She looked round, her hands folded on her breast, as if burnt with an internal fire; and it was with sudden hope of relief, of healing coolness, that she leant forward and said to the coachman:

'The Hôtel Béraud.'

The courtyard retained its cloistral coldness; Renée went round the colonnades, happy in the damp that fell on her shoulders. She approached the tank, green with moss, its edges polished by wear; she looked at the lion's head half worn away, with gaping jaws, discharging a stream of water through an iron pipe. How often had she and Christine taken this head in their tiny arms to lean forward and reach the stream of water, which they loved to feel flowing cold as ice over their hands. Then she climbed the great silent staircase, and saw her father at the end of the succession of wide rooms; he drew up his tall figure, and seemed to merge deeper into the shadows of the old house, of the proud solitude in which he had shut himself away since his sister's death; she thought of the men in the Bois, of that other old man, Baron Gouraud, lolling in the sun, on pillows. She climbed higher, went through the passages, climbed the servants' stairs, made the journey towards the children's room. When she reached the very top, she found the key on its usual nail, a big, rusty key, on which spiders had spun their web. The lock gave a plaintive cry. How sad the children's room was! She felt a pang on finding it so deserted, so silent. She closed the open door of the aviary, with the vague idea that it must have been through that door that the joys of her childhood had flown away. She stopped before the window-boxes, still full of soil hardened and cracked like dray mud, and broke off with her fingers a rhododendron stalk; this skeleton of a plant, shrivelled and white with dust, was all that remained of their vibrant clusters of greenery. The matting, discoloured and rat-gnawed, had the melancholy of a shroud that for years has been awaiting the promised corpse. In a corner she found one of her old dolls; all the bran had flowed out through a hole, and the porcelain head continued to smile with its enamelled lips, above the wasted body which seemed as if exhausted by puppet follies.

Renée felt that she was suffocating amid this tainted atmosphere of her childhood. She opened the window and looked out at the boundless landscape. There nothing was soiled. She felt again the eternal joys, the eternal youth of the open air. The sun must be sinking behind her; she saw its rays gilding with infinite softness the part of the city she knew so well. It was a last song of daylight. Below, ruddy flames lit up the boom, while the lacework of the iron chains of the Pont de Constantine stood out against the whiteness of its supports. To the right, the dark foliage of the Halle aux Vins and the Jardin des Plantes seemed like a great pool of stagnant, moss-covered water, whose green surface blended in the distance with the mist of the sky. On the left, the Quai Henri IV and the Quai de la Rapée displayed the same row of houses that the little girls used to gaze at twenty years before, with the same brown patches of sheds, the same red factory chimneys. Above the trees, the slated roof of the Salpêtrière, made blue by the setting sun, seemed suddenly like an old friend. But what calmed her was the long grey banks, and above all the Seine itself, the giant, which she watched coming from the horizon straight down to her, as in the happy days when they had been afraid that it might swell and surge up to their window. She remembered their fondness for the river, their love of its colossal flux, the ripples of the water, spread out like a sheet at their feet, opening out around them, behind them, into two arms which they could not see, though they could still feel its great, pure caress. They were already very concerned about their appearance, and they used to say, on fine days, that the Seine had put on its pretty dress of green silk shot with white flames; and the eddies where the water rippled trimmed the dress with frills of satin, while in the distance, beyond the belt of the bridges, splashes of light spread out lappets of sun-coloured stuff.

Renée, raising her eyes, gazed at the vast arch of pale blue sky, fading slowly in the twilight. She thought of the complicitous city, of the flaring lights of the boulevards, of the sultry afternoons in the Bois, of the crude, pallid days in the great, new mansions. Then, when she lowered her head and glanced again at the peaceful horizon of her childhood, this corner of a bourgeois and workmen's city, where she had dreamt of a life of peace and tranquillity, a final bitter taste rose to her lips. With clasped hands, she sobbed as darkness came.

Next winter, when Renée died of acute meningitis, her father paid her debts. Worms's bill came to two hundred and fifty-seven thousand francs.

EXPLANATORY NOTES

5 *barouche*: a four-wheeled horse-drawn carriage with a high driver's seat at the front and a folding top over the rear seats.

lake: the following pages describe Parisian high society returning from a ride in the Bois de Boulogne, a favourite place for excursions and meetings following its redevelopment in 1855–8.

October sky: Zola's preparatory notes for his novel indicate that the narrative begins in the autumn of 1862. The finished text, however, does not give a precise date for the beginning of the action, thus avoiding the containment of the whole narrative in an implausibly short period (between the two visits to the Bois de Boulogne that open and close the novel, there are two winters). The novel's chronological framework is deliberately vague, and Zola takes considerable liberties with the explicit and implied dating of actual historical events. Since these inaccuracies are of no consequence in terms of the novel's meaning, I have not systematically noted them. The acceleration of history entailed by the concentration into two years of events (signifying expansion, crisis, and decline) scattered throughout Louis-Napoleon's nineteen-year reign as Emperor express the mad freneticism, the 'life of excess', of a society that 'lived too quickly'.

Laure d'Aurigny: this name deliberately echoes that of Blanche d'Antigny, a celebrated courtesan-actress of the period, and one of the models for Zola's Nana (see *Nana*, the ninth novel of the Rougon-Macquart cycle, available in Oxford World's Classics).

brougham: a light, closed, four-wheeled horse-drawn carriage in which the driver sits high up at the front.

polonaise: a short-sleeved elaborate dress with a fitted waist and loops of material drawn up at the sides and back to reveal a decorative underskirt.

6 *chariot*: a light four-wheeled carriage.

victoria: a low four-wheeled carriage for two with a folding hood.

hired cab: in this paragraph Zola is echoing, with name changes, articles in the society pages of contemporary newspapers (e.g. *Le Figaro*).

7 *aigrette*: a spray of gems worn on a hat or in the hair.

8 *a politician*: the character of Haffner is based on Eugène Schneider, a steel magnate who became a leading politician—a perfect example of the union of politics and business during the Second Empire.

9 *a hundred thousand francs*: one franc during the Second Empire was worth about 2.5 euros (*c.* £1.75) today.

10 *Tuileries*: this palace was the official residence of the Emperor. It was destroyed by fire in 1870.

11 *lateen sail*: a triangular sail hung from a long spar set at an angle on a low mast.

divine incests: an allusion to the mythical gods of antiquity, for whom the incest taboo did not exist (Jupiter and Juno were brother and sister, and also married).

14 *Avenue de l'Impératrice*: now the Avenue Foch; opened at the time of the development of the Bois de Boulogne into a public park.

Avenue de la Reine-Hortense: now the Avenue Hoche; runs from the Place de l'Étoile to the Parc Monceau.

Boulevard Malesherbes: in the 17th *arrondissement*; inaugurated by the Emperor on 13 August 1861.

15 *Lassouche*: Baron Louis Ange Bouquin de Lassouche was a comic actor, born in Paris in 1828.

16 *Parc Monceau*: this private eighteenth-century park, situated in the 17th *arrondissement*, was redeveloped by Robert Alphand in the 1850s and converted into a public park to coincide with the opening of the Boulevard Malesherbes and the Boulevard Monceau.

firework display: Saccard's mansion is typical of the ornate, eclectic architectural style (famously embodied in Charles Garnier's grandiose new Opéra) of the Second Empire.

hothouse: hothouses were a novelty at this time in France. Among the most famous examples of this new luxury were those of Princess Mathilde (the Emperor's sister), and La Païva (a legendary courtesan of the period). In his preparations for his descriptions of the hothouse in *The Kill*, Zola visited the hothouses in the Jardin des Plantes.

17 *the new Louvre*: the new Louvre, including the two palaces to the north and south of the Place du Carrousel, was completed in 1857.

department store: big department stores like the Bon Marché, the Louvre, the Printemps, and La Samaritaine were created during the Second Empire. The tenth volume of the Rougon-Macquart cycle, *The Ladies' Paradise* (available in Oxford World's Classics), recounts their spectacular development.

19 *battledore*: a game from which badminton was developed, played with a shuttlecock and rackets between two or four players.

21 *his wife*: in January 1870 Blanche d'Antigny was prosecuted by her jeweller for having refused to pay the whole of a bill for some diamonds worth 13,000 francs.

24 *removes*: dishes served between soup and the first course.

Toutin-Laroche: Toutin-Laroche is modelled on Louis Frémy, governor of the Crédit Foncier, a Deputy, and a close associate of Haussmann and the Pereire brothers.

Crédit Viticole: modelled on the Crédit Foncier, which was created in 1852 to meet the need of property-owners for mortgage loans. The company in fact used its funds to finance ambitious property developments.

Société Générale of the Ports of Morocco: the Société Générale of the Ports of Morocco, described by Zola later on as 'Société Générale of The Arabian Nights', evoke certain of the bolder ventures launched by the Pereire brothers (like the Crédit Mobilier and the Société des Chemins de fer du Nord de l'Espagne), or by a speculator like Mirès (for example, the Société Générale des Ports de Marseille).

Council of State: the Council of State, whose members were appointed by the Emperor, was responsible for the preparation and implementation of government legislation.

25 *His Excellency*: Saccard's brother, Eugène Rougon, the minister. The model for Zola's fictional Eugène Rougon was Eugène Rouher, who became leader of the government in the Chamber of Deputies on 18 October 1863. Eugène Rougon is the protagonist of the sixth novel of the Rougon-Macquart cycle, *His Excellency Eugène Rougon*, which describes the political system of the Second Empire.

City Council: the members of the City Council (judges, financiers, businessmen, property-owners) were appointed by the Emperor for five years.

the age: Haussmann raised several large public loans—in 1852 (50 million francs), 1855 (60 million francs), 1860 (120 million francs), 1865 (250 million francs), and 1869 (400 million francs). See Introduction.

26 *Luxembourg*: a reference to the development of the Île de la Cité and the opening of the Boulevard Saint-Michel.

productive: this conversation reflects the arguments promoted by Haussmann in the Corps Législatif, the press, and official speeches.

28 *La Fontaine's bear*: an allusion to the fable 'The Bear and the Amateur Gardener', by Jean de La Fontaine (1621–95), on the harm that may sometimes be caused unwittingly by the most well-intentioned friend.

Dindonnette: a character in *L'Oeil crevé*, a comic opera by Hervé.

elections: a reference to the legislative elections of 1863.

30 *decorations*: that is, those who had been awarded the Legion of Honour.

34 *Diana*: the goddess of hunting in Greek mythology.

38 *Messalina*: the third wife of the Roman Emperor Claudius; famous for her extravagantly dissolute life, she was executed on the orders of her husband.

41 *2 December*: On 2 December 1851 Louis-Napoleon, President of the Second Republic since December 1848, mounted a coup d'état and dissolved the National Assembly. The republican riots that followed resulted in 27,000 arrests and 10,000 deportations to Algeria. On 2 December 1852 the Second Empire was proclaimed, and Louis-Napoleon Bonaparte adopted the title of Emperor Napoleon III. The

significance of the date was that it was the anniversary of the coronation of Napoleon I in 1804 and of his famous military victory over the Russians and Austrians at the Battle of Austerlitz in 1805.

41 *Plassans*: Plassans, the origin of the Rougon-Macquart family, is Zola's fictional name for Aix-en-Provence, where he lived from 1843 until he was 18.

the fray: an allusion to the events recounted in the first novel of the Rougon-Macquart cycle, *The Fortune of the Rougons*.

Rue Saint-Jacques: in 1859, on his arrival in Paris, Zola lived with his mother in conditions of great poverty at 241 Rue Saint-Jacques.

43 *uprising in the south*: parts of rural Provence had resisted Louis-Napoleon's new regime until the insurgents were massacred by the army on 10 December 1851. These events are described in *The Fortune of the Rougons*.

46 *Corps Législatif*: the name of the National Assembly under the Second Empire.

48 *famous journey*: in September and October of 1852 Louis-Napoleon made a triumphal tour of the provinces, basically campaigning for the restoration of the Empire.

silent: the new regime imposed a strict system of censorship on the press.

49 *blood of December*: an allusion to the shooting of 300 protesters against the coup d'état on 4 December 1851 on the Boulevard Montmartre. These events are evoked in the third novel of the Rougon-Macquart series, *The Belly of Paris*.

51 *stamped bills*: documents bearing an official government stamp. Used to draw up deeds and legal titles.

protests: a 'protest' was a sworn declaration that a note or bill had been duly presented and that payment had been refused.

54 *Crimea*: in need of allies and prestige in Europe, Napoleon III joined with England in declaring war on Russia on 26 March 1854, ostensibly in defence of the Ottoman Empire. There were more casualties in the Crimean War than in any other war fought by the European powers between 1815 and 1914; but France emerged with increased prestige, reflected in her role as host for the Congress of Paris (1856), which brought the war to an end.

gold: the minting of money increased during the Second Empire. The new coins bore the image of the Emperor.

59 *Pascal Rougon*: *Doctor Pascal*, the final volume of the Rougon-Macquart cycle, is set in Plassans. Pascal Rougon is in some respects Zola's alter ego, and the novel that bears his name evokes Zola's own intellectual evolution, especially in respect to his views on science, while the relationship that develops between the elderly Pascal and the young Clotilde resembles Zola's relationship with his much younger mistress, Jeanne

Rozerot. Not long after Clotilde becomes Pascal's mistress, Pascal dies, leaving her two months pregnant. Their newborn child represents Zola's hope in the future.

the Marais: a very old area of Paris in the 4th *arrondissement*.

60 *Étienne Marcel*: a prosperous clothier and provost of the merchants of Paris, Étienne Marcel came to prominence in 1358 as the leader of a reformist movement against the royal house.

'93: 1793 was the year of 'The Terror'—a response to the situation in France when the survival of the French Revolution seemed at stake: foreign armies were invading France, there was civil war in the Vendée, and an economic crisis. Large numbers of counter-revolutionary suspects were arrested and guillotined. The Committee of Public Safety established a dictatorship in December 1793 and proceeded to eliminate all its real or imagined enemies.

mixed committees: these committees, organized in the aftermath of the coup d'état in December 1851, were 'mixed' in the sense that they included representatives of the judiciary, the army, and the Prefectorate. They decided without trial on the fate of those who had resisted Louis-Napoleon's seizure of absolute power.

Hôtel Lambert: built in the mid-seventeenth century and restored in 1860, this *hôtel* (private mansion) is to be found at 2 Rue Saint-Louis en l'Île. It was used by Zola as a model for the Hôtel Béraud.

62 *Code*: the new Civil Code established under Napoleon I, based on principles of reason rather than on the prejudices and special interests of the past. The Code dealt with the law of persons, goods, and contracts. The operation of the law was separated from political or ecclesiastical considerations, and central to it was the principle of equal rights and equal treatment for all citizens.

63 *Charonne area*: the Charonne district is in the eastern part of Paris, in the present 20th *arrondissement*. Extensive property development occurred in this area in the 1860s, and the land increased enormously in value.

delight: the construction of the Boulevard Malesherbes and the creation of the Place Saint-Augustin entailed the demolition of buildings at the intersection of the Rue d'Astorg and the Rue de la Pépinière.

66 *Rue de Rivoli*: the section of the Rue de Rivoli between the Louvre and the Hôtel de Ville was completed between 1853 and 1855. The Société des Immeubles Rivoli, created by the Pereire brothers, developed sumptuous properties along it.

67 *Buttes Montmartre*: the Buttes Montmartre was still outside Paris in the 1850s, and became the 18th *arrondissement* in 1860.

68 *Madeleine*: a church built like an ancient temple, at the end of the Rue Royale, in the 18th *arrondissement*.

Vendôme Column: a column erected on the Place Vendôme during the reign of Napoleon I. Coated in bronze, it depicts—in spiral fashion, like the Trajan Column in Rome—the feats of arms at the Battle of Austerlitz.

68 *Rue d'Anjou*: the Rue d'Anjou connected the Rue du Foubourg Saint-Honoré and the Rue de la Pépinière. The construction of the Boulevard Malesherbes and the Boulevard Haussmann entailed the demolition of numerous private mansions.

69 *call it*: the new urban 'transept' linked east and west, from the Étoile to the Bastille, by means of the Champs-Élysées and the Rue de Rivoli, and north and south, from the Gare du Nord to the Latin Quarter, by means of the Boulevards de Strasbourg, Sébastopol, and Saint-Michel. The 'new boulevard' is the Boulevard du Centre (later called the Boulevard de Sébastopol as a tribute to the allied victory in the Crimean War in 1855). The two 'cuts' indicated by Saccard anticipate the construction of the Boulevard du Prince-Eugène (later renamed the Boulevard Voltaire) and the Boulevard Malesherbes.

Barrière du Trône: now the Place de la Nation.

70 *Caisse Générale*: the Caisse Générale des Chemins de fer was founded by Mirès.

71 *second network*: the 'august hand' is that of the Emperor himself. According to Haussmann's *Memoirs*, Napoleon III had traced on a map of Paris, in different colours, the new boulevards he envisaged. Napoleon III's personal preoccupation with the transformation of Paris was reflected in the large map of the city which he had on the wall of his study in the Tuileries Palace.

72 *a fictitious one*: a fictitious rent increase artificially inflated the value of buildings destined for demolition, which meant that higher compensation prices would be obtained for them.

73 *tenant*: a law of expropriation, permitting compulsory purchase of private property by the government, was passed in 1841. The Compensation Authority was formed in 1856.

75 *around him*: Saccard's business ventures are modelled on those of the Pereire brothers and Mirès.

79 *Place Royale*: now the Place des Vosges, built during the reign of Henri IV (1589–1610).

80 *old parlements*: before the Revolution of 1789 these bodies had certain political powers and acted as a counterbalance to the power of the king.

81 *Pont de Constantine*: the Pont de Constantine was a footbridge linking the Île Saint-Louis to the left bank of the Seine. Built in 1837, it was replaced by the Pont Sully (built 1874–6).

Halle aux Vins: a wine market situated on the site of the present university of Paris at Jussieu, near the Seine in the 5th *arrondissement*.

Salpêtrière: a former women's prison, in the 13th *arrondissement*. It was converted into a home for the aged in 1823, and is now a hospital.

84 *little bald-head*: a nickname of the young Napoleon I.

85 *Worms*: the 1850s saw the emergence of *haute couture*, which was domin-
ated by an Englishman, Charles Frederick Worth (1826–95). After moving to Paris and working as an assistant for Gagelin and Opigez, the
leading fashion fabric retailers of the day, he went into business as a
couturier, and set about revolutionizing the fashion business. He brought
a new level of tailoring to women's fashion, turned visits to his salons into
special social events, and introduced the now celebrated live mannequin
to the Paris fashion world. Dictator of style, Worth attained a social
standing unheard of by any tailor before him. He became internationally
famous after being taken up by the Empress Eugénie, who was
considered the epitome of fashion in her day.

86 *tu and vous*: in French (and other languages) the second-person singular pronoun (*tu*) is used to address a friend, a relative, a child, God, or an
animal; the second-person plural pronoun (*vous*) denotes more formal
relationships.

88 *Lycée Bonaparte*: a *lycée* frequented by the sons of the aristocracy and
upper bourgeoisie. Now the Lycée Condorcet.

Brummel: George ('Beau') Brummel (1778–1830) was a celebrated
English dandy who was said to have dictated the main lines of male
fashion to the whole of Europe for a hundred years.

tilbury: a light, two-wheeled, horse-drawn carriage, named after the
nineteenth-century English coach-builder who invented it.

91 *La Gioconda*: popularly known as the *Mona Lisa*, this is the most famous
painting of Leonardo da Vinci (1452–1519).

Montespan: this type of dress (ample in design in order to conceal the fact
of pregnancy) was named after Madame de Montespan, a favourite of
Louis XIV.

basque: a close-fitting bodice, sometimes having an extension that covers
the hips.

92 *Pythoness*: a woman believed to be possessed by a soothsaying spirit, like
the priestess of Apollo at Delphi.

Psyche: the personification of the human soul, Psyche married Cupid
(Eros), the god of love, and was made immortal by Zeus.

95 *Pont de l'Alma*: this boulevard was the Avenue Joséphine, opened in 1866.
It is the present Avenue Marceau.

Moniteur: *Le Moniteur universel* was the quasi-official organ of the
Imperial regime.

96 *bonds*: see Introduction, p. xv.

97 *this time*: that is to say, from 1858 onwards.

101 *cotillons*: the *cotillon* (cotillion) ended a ball, and was a formalized dance
for a large number of people, in which a head couple leads the other
dancers through elaborate figures.

105 *Blanche Muller's bust*: Blanche Muller seems to be based on the celebrated actress, Offenbach's star, Hortense Schneider. See David Baguley, *Napoleon III and His Regime: An Extravaganza* (Baton Rouge: Louisiana State University Press, 2000), 306–7, 324–5, 376.

107 *Maison d'Or*: the Maison-Dorée, also known as the Maison d'Or, was a high-class restaurant on the Boulevard des Italiens, and was a favourite haunt of the wealthy and dissolute society depicted in *The Kill*.

108 *Mabille*: the Bal Mabille was an open-air dance-hall near the Champs-Élysées.

111 *debauchery*: an allusion to syphilis.

112 *gold and flesh*: see Zola's Preface to the first edition of the novel (p. 3).

119 *domino*: a long, loose, hooded cloak worn with a mask as a masquerade costume.

120 *Café Anglais*: a restaurant on the Boulevard des Italiens, near the Opéra-Comique.

121 *Rue Basse-du-Rempart*: an old street running alongside the Boulevard des Capucines.

123 *Brébant's*: a restaurant on the Boulevard Poissonnière.

Café Riche: a large restaurant opposite the Café Anglais.

126 *Passage de l'Opéra*: the *passages* were covered shopping arcades, built in Paris during the Restoration (1814–30) and the reign of Louis-Philippe (1830–48). The German cultural critic Walter Benjamin used the image of the arcades as the focus for his work on the 'phantasmagoria' of urban experience and modern consumer culture: see the Introduction to *The Ladies' Paradise* (Oxford World's Classics). The Passage de l'Opéra was on the Boulevard des Italiens, between the Rue Drouot and the Rue Le Peletier. It disappeared when the Carrefour Richelieu-Drouot was built in 1924, and was celebrated in Louis Aragon's novel *Paris Peasant* (*Le Paysan de Paris*).

127 *Épinal prints*: very popular, brightly coloured prints produced at Épinal.

131 *Piron*: Alexis Piron (1688–1773) was a poet and dramatist who also wrote bawdy songs.

138 *against him*: in 1866–7 there was a Stock Exchange crisis. The Pereire brothers, to save their company, the Crédit Mobilier, attempted to engineer a rise in share values by buying new securities (or stock); but the continued crisis led to the collapse of the Crédit Mobilier in 1867. These events figure prominently in the eighteenth volume of the Rougon-Macquart cycle, *Money*, which deals with the world of high finance, with Saccard appearing once again as the protagonist.

fantastic: this recalls the title of Jules Ferry's famous pamphlet *The Fantastic Accounts of Haussmann*. Saccard's manoeuvres as described here are based on the techniques of the Pereire brothers. See the Introduction.

139 *'useless rubble'*: in 1866 the situation of the Compagnie Immobilière was

precarious. Its building programme in Paris was followed by a large programme in Marseilles, but they were unable to secure good rental agreements, and the company foundered under the weight of its debts to the Crédit Foncier.

141 *Boulevard du Prince-Eugène*: opened on 7 December 1862; now the Boulevard Voltaire.

142 *Dusautoy's*: a celebrated gentlemen's tailor during the Second Empire.

149 *City of Paris*: see note to p. 25.

152 *Chaplin*: Charles Joshua Chaplin (1825–91) was an English painter who worked in Paris. He was asked to decorate the ceilings of the Empress's apartment in the Tuileries Palace.

162 *Prince-Eugène Barracks*: the present Château d'eau Barracks on the Place de la République.

Faubourg Saint-Antoine: a working-class street that runs from the Place de la Bastille to the Place de la Nation.

land: an allusion to the future Boulevard du Prince-Eugène, begun in 1860.

166 *Campana*: Campana was an Italian aristocrat who sold his collection of *objets d'art* and Italian Renaissance paintings to the French state in 1862. The collection was housed in the Palais de l'Industrie, and then in the Louvre.

167 *La Belle Hélène*: an enormously successful comic opera, with music by Jacques Offenbach; it was first performed at the Théâtre des Variétés in December 1864, with Hortense Schneider (the model for Blanche Muller) in the title role. The opera tells the story of Helen, the beautiful daughter of Zeus and Leda, and wife of Menelaus; Helen's abduction by Paris was the cause of the Trojan War. Zola detested Offenbach, and especially *La Belle Hélène*.

refrains: Wagner's *Tannhäuser* was first performed at the Paris Opéra in March 1861. The performance was disrupted by the jeering and whistling of members of the Jockey Club, all wealthy or aristocratic young men.

169 *big shops*: see note to p. 17.

seaside: trips by train to the coastal resorts of Deauville and Trouville became fashionable among Parisian high society during the Second Empire.

170 *protested*: see note to p. 51.

Clichy: there was a debtors' prison at Clichy from 1826 to 1867.

173 *Tuileries*: a reference to the extravagant receptions given by the Emperor at the Tuileries Palace.

179 *Théâtre-Italien*: the productions of the Théâtre-Italien were put on in the Salle Ventadour, near the Passage Choiseul.

179 *Phèdre*: an Italian translation of Racine's classic play *Phèdre* was performed in Paris, with Adélaïde Ristori in the title role, in 1858, 1861, and
1867. In his preparatory notes for *The Kill*, Zola wrote: 'Decidedly, the
novel will be a new *Phèdre*.'

Pasiphaé's blood: in classical mythology Phaedra was the daughter of
Minos and Pasiphaë. Minos was the king of Crete; Pasiphaë was the
mother also of Ariadne, Androgeus, and the Minotaur. Phaedra's husband,
Theseus, was the father of Hippolytus and the great hero of the
Athenians.

180 *story*: Phaedra became infatuated with her stepson Hippolytus and made
advances to him, but was rejected. In despair she hanged herself, but left
a message accusing Hippolytus of having assaulted her. The outraged
Theseus, without hearing Hippolytus' side of the story, appealed to
Poseidon, god of the sea, for appropriate revenge. Poseidon sent a sea
monster which terrified Hippolytus' horses so that they bolted and
dragged their master to his death under the wheels of his own chariot.
The famous speech by Theramenes recounts his death.

Bouffes: the Bouffes-Parisiens was a well-known theatre, built in 1826. It
was rented in 1855 by Jacques Offenbach, who modernized it and used it
for his comic operas until 1865.

184 *revisions*: the process by which the Chamber of Deputies verified the
eligibility for membership of every new Deputy.

191 *Chapelle Expiatoire*: the Boulevard Haussmann, begun in 1857, was
unfinished when the Empire fell. The Chapelle Expiatoire had been
built between 1815 and 1826 to the memory of Louis XVI and
Marie-Antoinette, whose bodies remained there until 1815.

192 *Tortoni's*: a café on the corner of the Rue Taitbout and the Boulevard des
Italiens.

200 *Hôtel de Ville*: Haussmann gave large balls every winter at the Hôtel de
Ville.

207 *Narcissus and Echo*: in classical mythology Narcissus, son of Ceciphus
and Liriope, was a beautiful youth who fell in love with his own reflection
in a pool; he was so enamoured of himself that he scorned the love of the
nymph Echo and all others. Some legends say that Nemesis (others say
Artemis) punished his arrogance and pride by causing him to fall in love
with his own reflection. When he began to pine away with longing, he
was changed into the flower that bears his name. Echo, when Narcissus
did not return her love, also pined away and was changed into a stone
which still retained the power of speech.

209 *almah*: an Egyptian dancing girl.

Henri III: Henri III (1551–89) was well known for his homosexual
proclivities. His '*mignons*' were court favourites.

210 *scandal*: a reference to the scandal caused by the collapse of the Crédit
Mobilier.

bulling: a bull or bullish market is one characterized by or hopeful of rising share prices. (The opposite is 'bearish'.)

212 *as you know*: the story here is taken from Ovid's *Metamorphoses* (iii. 342 ff.), but, like Monsieur Hupel de la Noue, Zola treats the story very flexibly to make the tableaux reflect the general symbolism of the novel.

213 *Pradier's group*: Pradier (1792–1852) was a famous sculptor; a marble representation of the Three Graces was particularly successful.

electric light: an absolute novelty: two electric lamps had recently (1861) been installed on the Place du Carrousel.

216 *riches*: see Zola's Preface to the novel (p. 3).

218 *minister*: Eugène Rougon (see note to p. 25).

221 *Parian marble*: Paros, a Greek island in the south Aegean, was noted for its white marble.

229 *talk of Paris*: an allusion to Félix Nadar—photographer, writer, artist, and aeronaut—whose experiments with an air balloon ('Le Géant') were always made before a large crowd.

Giroflé girofla: a well-known popular song from Italy.

231 *'Dark Spots'*: an allusion to a phrase used by the Emperor in August 1867. The collapse of the Crédit Mobilier, together with problems abroad, made him refer to 'dark spots on the horizon'.

236 *Charenton*: Charenton was a lunatic asylum south-west of Paris. The bell was tolled at funerals.

243 *'Mexican War'*: the Mexican War, at first quite popular in France because of early military successes, lasted from 1861 to 1867. Napoleon III's attempt to establish an empire under the Austrian emperor's brother, Maximilian, ended in embarrassing failure when French troops were driven out of Mexico and Maximilian himself was executed (19 June 1867). This execution was depicted in a series of paintings and prints by Édouard Manet.

244 *'cheese'*: a dance based on a girl's game in which the girl spun round and suddenly dropped to the floor so that her skirt formed the round shape of a cheese.

247 *Place du Château d'Eau*: now the Place de la République.

252 *Regency*: a reference to the period from 1715 to 1723 during which Louis XV was still a minor. The Regent, Philippe, Duc d'Orléans, had the reputation of living a very dissolute life.

256 *Gare de l'Ouest*: now the Gare Montparnasse.

257 *Saint-Cloud and Suresnes*: suburbs to the west of Paris.

Mont Valérien: a hill with a fort.

261 *the Emperor appeared*: the chateau at Saint-Cloud was Napoleon III's Versailles, and was reached by crossing the Bois de Boulogne.

The Oxford World's Classics Website

www.worldsclassics.co.uk

- Information about new titles
- Explore the full range of Oxford World's Classics
- Links to other literary sites and the main OUP webpage
- Imaginative competitions, with bookish prizes
- Peruse the Oxford World's Classics Magazine
- Articles by editors
- Extracts from Introductions
- A forum for discussion and feedback on the series
- Special information for teachers and lecturers

www.worldsclassics.co.uk

American Literature

British and Irish Literature

Children's Literature

Classics and Ancient Literature

Colonial Literature

Eastern Literature

European Literature

History

Medieval Literature

Oxford English Drama

Poetry

Philosophy

Politics

Religion

The Oxford Shakespeare

A complete list of Oxford Paperbacks, including Oxford World's Classics, Oxford Shakespeare, Oxford Drama, and Oxford Paperback Reference, is available in the UK from the Academic Division Publicity Department, Oxford University Press, Great Clarendon Street, Oxford OX2 6DP.

In the USA, complete lists are available from the Paperbacks Marketing Manager, Oxford University Press, 198 Madison Avenue, New York, NY 10016.

Oxford Paperbacks are available from all good bookshops. In case of difficulty, customers in the UK can order direct from Oxford University Press Bookshop, Freepost, 116 High Street, Oxford OX1 4BR, enclosing full payment. Please add 10 per cent of published price for postage and packing.